The Best Bed &

England • Scotland • Wales

1992

Sigourney Welles
Jill Darbey
Joanna Mortimer

The finest Bed & Breakfast accommodation in the British Isles

from the Hebrides to Belgravia

Country Houses, Town Houses, City Apartments, Manor Houses, Village Cottages, Farmhouses, Castles.

U.K.H.M. Publishing. London, U.K.

© **U.K.H.M. Publishing Ltd. 1992**

U.K.H.M. Publishing Ltd.

P.O. Box 2070

London W12 8QW

England

This book is sold subject to the condition that it shall not, by way of trade, be lent, re-sold, hired out or otherwise disposed of without the publishers consent, in any form of binding or cover, other than that which it is published.

All rights reserved. No part of this book may be reproduced or transmitted in any form by any means, electronic or mechanical including photocopying & recording, or by an information storage & retrieval system, except as may be expressly permitted by the 1976 Copyright Act or by the Publisher. Requests for permission should be made in writting to U.K.H.M. Publishing Limited. P.O. Box 2070, London W12 8QW.

The publishers have made every reasonable effort to ensure that the accommodation mentioned in this guide are as stated, however the Publishers cannot accept liability for any inaccuracies, errors or omissions that may occur.

U.K. ISBN 0-907500-33-1

Typeset by U.K.H.M. Publishing Ltd.London.
Printed and bound in Hong Kong

Hillards. Somerset.

Pipps Ford.   Suffolk.

Contents

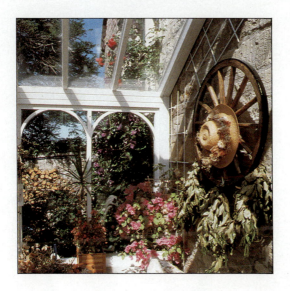

Foreword 7
How to use this Guide 8
Making a Reservation 10
The Discount Offer 11
County Map 12
Regions 13
Motorway Map 14
General Information 15
Rail Map 17
London Map 18
Tube/Subway Map 19

London Homes 21

Counties

Avon 34
Beds/Berks/Bucks/Herts. .. 50
Cambridge & Northants. 59
Cheshire & Merseyside. 68
Cornwall 73
Cumbria 92
Derby. & Staffs. 112
Devon 126
Dorset 149

Essex 162
Gloucestershire 167
Hampshire 183
Hereford & Worcester. 193
Kent 204
Lancashire 223
Leicester. & Nottingham. . 229
Lincolnshire 236
Norfolk 243
Northumbria 255
Oxfordshire 265
Shropshire 279
Somerset 287
Suffolk 302
Surrey 310
Sussex 318
Warwickshire 331
Wiltshire 346
Yorkshire 362
Scotland 380
Wales 415

Towns: Counties Index 443

Recommendations 447

Curdon Mill. Somerset.

Foreword

You may have noticed that Bed & Breakfast has suddenly become the fashionable way to travel. This is because the secret has escaped & thousands of people are discovering for themselves that it is possible to combine high quality accommodation with friendly, personal attention at very reasonable prices. The New York Times said about us that "...after an unannounced inspection of rooms booked through The Worldwide Bed & Breakfast Association it is clear that the standards of comfort & cleanliness are exemplary ...at least as good as in a five star hotel & in most cases, better, reflecting the difference between sensitive hosts taking pride in their homes & itinerant hotel staff doing as little as they can get away with..."

Discerning travellers are turning away from the impersonal hotels with the expensive little refridgerators & microwave breakfasts in each room. How much nicer to have a real English breakfast to begin the day, enough to keep you going until evening. Many of our houses will provide dinner too - often the hostess will be a Cordon Bleu cook & the price will be within your range.

We try to provide the best accommodation possible within a wide range of prices, some as little as £9.00 per person per night, whilst others will be up to £55.00 per person per night. The choice is yours, but you can be certain that each will be the best available in the area at the price.

Our inspectors are out & about visiting our homes to ensure that standards are maintained. We encourage everyone to use the recommendations & complaints page at the back of the book, to let us know your opinion of the accommodation or to inform us of any delightful homes you may have come across & would like to recommend for future inclusion.

In order to avoid the classification trap, which we feel is invidious, we encourage you to read about each home, what they offer & their respective price range, so that you find the one that best suits your expectations. Our hosts in turn offer hospitality in their own unique style, so each home naturally retains its individuality & interest. We have found this to be a very successful recipe which has often led to firm friendships with invitations being extended to visit each other again.

Bed & Breakfast really is a marvellous way to travel, meeting a delightful cross section of fellow travellers with whom to exchange information & maybe the address of ...that lovely little place which was discovered by chance and which serves the most delicious dinner or... the best route to take to a particular farmhouse but make sure you get there by 5 o'clock so that you can watch the the evening milking...

This is the fun & real pleasure that is part of Bed & Breakfasting. Once you've tried it you will be a dedicated Best Bed & Breakfaster.

How to use this Guide

To get the full benefits of staying at our Bed & Breakfast homes it is important to appreciate how they differ from hotels, so both hosts & guests know what to expect.

Arrival & Departure

These times are more important to a family than to hotel desk clerks, so your time of arrival (E.T.A.) is vital information when making a reservation either with the home directly or with one of our agencies. This becomes even more important to your reception if you intend travelling overnight & will be arriving in the early morning. So please have this information & your flight number ready when you book your rooms. Under most circumstances the usual check-in time is 6 p.m., & you will be expected to check out by 10a.m. on the morning of departure. These arrangements do vary from home to home so the secret to an enjoyable visit is to let your hosts know as much about your plans as possible & they will do their best to meet your requirements.

Other personal requests

There are a few other details that you should let your hosts know when planning your Bed & Breakfast trip that will make everyone much happier during your visit.

* Do you smoke? Would you prefer to be in a non-smoking home?

* Do you suffer from any allergies? Some families have cats, dogs, birds & other pets in the house.

* Can you make it up a flight of stairs? Would you prefer the ground floor?

* Do you have any special dietary requirements? Will you be staying for dinner?

* Do you prefer a private bathroom or are you prepared to share facilities?

* Do you prefer a shower instead of a bath?

* The ages of any children travelling

In all these cases let your host know what you need & the details can be arranged before you arrive rather than presenting a problem when you are shown to your rooms.

Prices

The prices quoted throughout the guide are the *minimum* per person per night. These prices increase during the busy seasons, so please confirm the prevailing rate when you make a reservation

Facilities

The bathroom & toilet facilities effect the prices. Sharing is the cheapest, private is a little more costly & en-suite carries a premium.

Descriptions

Rooms are described as follows: Single = 1 bed (often quite small); Double = 1 large bed (sometimes King or Queen size); Twin = 2 separate single beds; Four-poster = a King or Queen size bed with a canopy above supported by four corner posts.

Bathrooms & toilets are described as follows: Shared = these facilities are shared with some other guests or perhaps the hosts; Private = for your use only, however they may occasionally be in an adjacent room; En-suite = private facilities within your bedroom suite.

Jordans. Kent.

Making a Reservation

Once you have chosen where you want to stay, have all the following information ready & your reservation will go smoothly without having to run & find more travel documents or ask someone else what they think you should do. Here is a brief checklist of what you will probably be asked & examples to illustrate answers:

* Dates & number of days .... August 14-19 (6 days).
* Estimated time of arrival at the home ....7p.m. (evening) & flight number.
* Type & number of rooms 1 Double &2 Singles.
* Toilet & Bathroom facilities ...1 Double en-suite) & 2 singles (shared)
* Smoking or Non-smoking?
* Any allergies?
* Medical problems?
* Special dietary requests?
* Children in the party & their ages?
* Any other preferences .... Is a shower preferred to a bath?
* Maximum budget per person per night based on all the above details.

London Reservations

There is a two night minimum stay at our London Homes

These can only be made through one of the Worldwide Bed & Breakfast Agencies. A full list appears overleaf & they can be contacted by phone or fax.

All reservations must be confirmed with advance payments which are non-refundable in the event of cancellation & you simply pay the balances due after you arrive at the home. The advance payment can be made with the major credit & charge cards or by cheque. Cash is the preferred method of paying the balance & always in pounds sterling.

The advance payments confirm each day of your visit - **not just the first one**. When arriving at a later date or departing at an earlier date than those confirmed, the guest will be liable to pay only the appropriate proportion of the stated balance that is due, For example, staying three days out of four booked means paying 3/4 of the stated balance due.

Outside London

We encourage you to make use of the information in this guide & contact the homes directly. The hosts may require varying amounts of advance payments & may or may not accept credit & charge cards.

If you wish one of the agencies to make the reservations for you there will be a standard booking fee of £15 (or currency equivalent) for each location confirmed & the entire cost must be paid in advance. The scale of refunds for cancellation is shown below. This full payment can be charged to a major credit card or paid by cheque. The confirmed prices shall be those prevailing on the dates required ... as previously mentioned, *the prices shown in this guide are the minimum & increase during the busy seasons.*

Alterations

If you wish to alter or change a previously confirmed booking though one of the agencies there will be a further fee of £15 per alteration.

Cancellations

All advance payments for London are non-refundable.

All booking fees Outside London are non-refundable.

Notice of cancellation must be given as soon as possible & the following rates shall apply **outside London only**

    50 days notice - Full refund.
    30-49 days notice - 80% refund.
    10-29 days notice - 50% refund
    0-9 days notice - No refund.

The Worldwide Bed & Breakfast Agencies reserve the right to alter your accommodation should it be necessary & will inform you of any alteration as soon as possible.

The Discount Offer

This offer is made to people who have bought this book & wish to make reservations for Bed & Breakfast in London through one of our participating agencies listed below.

The offer only applies to a minimum stay of three consecutive nights at one of our London homes between the following January 1. 1992 & April 15. 1992 then from September 15 .1992 to December 1. 1992 Only one discount per booking is allowed. Call the reservation office to make your booking in the normal way & tell the clerk that you have bought the book & wish to have the discount. After a couple of questions the discount will be deducted from the advance payment required to confirm the reservation.

Participating Agencies

In the U.K. call:

Tel: 081 742 9123 (24 Hrs.)

Fax: 081 749 7084

Outside the U.K. call:

Tel: 44 81 742 9123 (24 Hrs.)

Fax: 44 81 749 7084

In the U.S call: Toll Free 800 852 2632

Look for this symbol

Regions

To assist tourists with information during their travels, counties have been grouped together under Regional Tourist Boards that co-ordinate the various efforts of each county.

The British Tourist Authority has designated these areas in consultation with the English, Scottish & Wales Tourist Boards & we have largely adopted these areas for use in this guide.

Counties are listed alphabetically throughout our guide & then have a sub heading indicating which Tourist Region they belong to.

ENGLAND
Cumbria
County of Cumbria
Northumbria.
Counties of Cleveland, Durham, Northumberland, Tyne & Wear.
North West
Counties of Cheshire, Greater Manchester, Lancashire, Merseyside, High Peaks of Derbyshire.
Yorkshire & Humberside
Counties of North Yorkshire, South Yorkshire, West Yorkshire, Humberside.
Heart of England
Counties of Gloucestershire, Herefordshire & Worcestershire, Shropshire, Staffordshire, Warwickshire, West Midlands.
East Midlands
Counties of Derbyshire, Leicestershire, Lincolnshire, Northamptonshire, Nottinghamshire.
Thames & Chilterns
Counties of Oxfordshire, Berkshire, Bedfordshire, Buckinghamshire, Hertfordshire.
East Anglia
Counties of Cambridgeshire, Essex, Norfolk, Suffolk.
West Country
Counties of Avon, Cornwall, Devon, Dorset (parts of), Somerset, Wiltshire, Isles of Scilly.
Southern
Counties of Hampshire, Dorset (East & North), Isle of Wight.
South East
Counties of East Sussex, Kent, Surrey, West Sussex.

SCOTLAND
The subdivisions of Scottish Regions in this guide differ slightly from the current Marketing Regions of the Scottish Tourist Board.

The Borders, Dumfries & Galloway
Districts & counties of Scottish Borders, Dumfries & Galloway.
Lothian & Strathclyde
City of Edinburgh, Forth Valley, East Lothian, Kirkaldy, St. Andrews & North-East Fife, Greater Glasgow, Clyde Valley, Ayrshire & Clyde Coast, Burns Country.
Argyll & The Isles
Districts & counties of Oban & Mull, Mid Argyll, Kintyre & Islay, Dunoon, Cowal, Rothesay & Isle of Bute, Isle of Arran.
Perthshire, Loch Lommond & The Trossachs.
Districts & counties of Perthshire, Loch Lomond, Stirling & Trossachs.
The Grampians
Districts & counties of Banff & Buchan, Moray, Gordon, Angus, City of Aberdeen, Kincardine & Deeside, City of Dundee.
The Highlands & Islands
Districts & counties of Shetland, Orkney, Caithness, Sutherland, Ross & Cromarty, Western Isles, South West Ross & Isle of Skye, Inverness, Loch Ness & Nairn, Aviemore & Spey Valley, Fort William & Lochaber

WALES
The regions are defined as follows:
North Wales
Counties of Clwyd & Gwynedd (northern)
Mid Wales
Counties of Gwynedd (southern), Dyfed (northern) & Powys (northern)
South Wales
Counties of Gwent, West, South & Mid Glamorgan, Dyfed (southern) & Powys (southern).

The photographs appearing in the Introductions & Gazetteers are by courtesy of the appropriate Tourist Board for each county or or W.W.B.B.A.

General Information

To help overseas visitors with planning their trip to Britain, we have compiled the next few pages explaining the basic requirements & customs you will find here.

Before you arrive

Documents you will have to obtain before you arrive;
Valid passports & visas. Citizens of Commonwealth countries or the U.S.A. don't need visas to enter the U.K.
Bring your local Driving Licence.

Medical Insurance.

This is strongly recommended although visitors will be able to receive free emergency treatment. If you have to stay in hospital here you will be asked to pay unless you are a citizen of European Community Countries.

Restrictions on arrival

Immigration procedures can be lengthy & bothersome, be prepared for questions like:
a) where are you staying in the U.K.?
b) do you have a round trip ticket?
c) how long do you intend to stay?
d) how much money are you bringing in with you?
e) do you have a credit card?
Do not bring any animals with you as they are subject to 6 months quarantine & there are severe penalties for bringing in pets without appropriate licences. Do not bring any firearms, prohibited drugs or carry these things for anyone else. If you are in doubt about items in your possession, declare them by entering the Red Channel at Customs & seek the advice of an officer.

After you have arrived

You can bring in as much currency as you like. You can change your own currency or travellers cheques at many places at varying rates.

Airports tend to be the most expensive places to change money & the 'Bureau de Change" are often closed at nights. So bring enough Sterling to last you at least 2 or 3 days. Banks often charge commission for changing money. Some Cashcard machines (or A.T.M.'s) will dispense local currency using your charge card, if they are affiliated systems, & don't charge commissions to your account.
Major credit cards/charge cards are widely accepted & you may only need to carry small amounts of cash for "pocket money".

Driving

Don't forget to drive on the Left... especially the first time you get into a car... at the airport car hire parking lot... or from the front of a railway station... or straight after breakfast... old habits are hard to shake off. If you need to know the rules, get a copy of the Highway Code. You must wear a seat belt & so must any other front seat passenger. The speed limits are clearly shown in most areas - generally 30 mph. in residential areas (48 kph) & 70 mph on motorways (113 kph.). Traffic lights are at the side of the road & not hanging overhead. Car hire is relatively expensive in the U.K. & it is often a good idea to arrange this before you arrive. Mileage charges, V.A.T. (Sales Tax) & insurance are usually charged extra & you will need to be over 21 to hire a car in the U.K. Petrol (gas) is also relatively expensive & you may find petrol stations hard to find or closed at night in rural areas... so fill up often. Driving in London is not a recommended experience for newcomers & parking is also a very complex arrangement which can become a nightmare if the car gets "clamped" (immobilised) or towed away.

General Information

Buses & Coaches
If you are not driving & only want to travel 5-10 miles there are good bus services within most towns & cities, however, rural routes have seriously declined over the last few years. There are regular & fast coach services between the major towns which are very popular - so book ahead to be sure of a seat.

Trains
There is an extensive railway system throughout the U.K. which serves the major towns on a fast & frequent basis. British Rail is a relatively expensive service & like most railway systems subject to delays.
However, if you plan to do lots of rail travel the best deal is to buy a Britrail Pass before you leave home (you can't buy these once in the U.K.)

Tubes (Subways)
London is the only city with an extensive subway system although some other towns do have "Metro" trains of linked under & overground systems.
The "tube" is a very popular means of getting around London, but it can get very crowded & unpleasant at "rush hours". It is often the preferred way to get into London from say Heathrow airport in the early morning, when there are long delays on the roads that hold up both buses & taxis with increasingly expensive rides into the city centre ... £25 is not unusual for this cab fare, compared with £3 on the "tube".
The "tube" in London is operated by London Transport which also operates the London bus service ... the famous red buses. They sell tickets which allow you to travel all over London on tubes, buses & trains at very good rates, called Travelcards... a transfer system. Ask your local travel agent about these & other travel passes throughout the U.K.

Telephones - *When calling the U.K. from abroad always drop the 0 from the area code.*
In the U.K. the only free calls are the operator - 100, enquiries - 192 (international 153), emergencies - 999.
You may use your calling card to call home which is billed to your account or call collect, ask the operator to "reverse charge" the call. The famous red telephone kiosks are slowly being replaced with new glass booths & they differ in that the old boxes only take 10 & 50 pence pieces & don't give any change, whereas the new ones take many combinations of coins & do give change. Phonecards are becoming more popular as the number of boxes that only accept these cards increases. Cards can be bought at Post Offices & many newsagents & shops.

Doctors/Chemists
All local police stations have lists of chemists & doctors should you need one, at night, for instance.

Voltage
The standard voltage throughout the country is 240v AC.50Hz. If you bring small electrical appliances with you, a converter will be required.

Tipping
Is not obligatory anywhere but a general guide if you wish to leave a tip for service is between 10%-15%.

Pubs
Open between 11 a.m. & 11 p.m. on weekdays in England & Wales. On Sundays the hours are 12 noon to 3 p.m & 5 p.m. to 11p.m. In Scotland the hours are different - 11a.m. to 2.30 p.m. & 5 p.m. to 11p.m. on weekdays & 12.30 p.m. to 2.30p.m. & 6p.m to 11 p.m. on Sundays
You must be over 18 years old to buy & drink alcohol in pubs .

All the establishments mentioned in this guide are members of the
Worldwide Bed & Breakfast Association.

If you have any comments regarding your accommodation please send them to us using the form at the back of the book.
We value your comments.

London

	minimum £ per person	children taken	evening meals	animals taken

Home No. 03 **W.W.B.B.A.** **London** **Tel: 081-742-9123(24hrs.)** **Fax: 081-749-7084** **U.S. Toll Free** **800-852-2632**	Nearest Tube: Parsons Green Located less than two minutes walk from the underground, in a quiet & leafy street in Parsons Green. A comfortable Victorian terraced house which is delightfully furnished & decorated to a high standard. The charming hosts offer two twin-bedded rooms, 1 with access to own garden, both have private bathroom, colour T.V. & hairdryer. The enjoyment of your stay is the first consideration of the hosts. Only 20 minutes from Piccadilly, Knightsbridge & Buckingham Palace.	£25.00	N	N	N
Home No. 06 **W.W.B.B.A.** **London** **Tel: 081-742-9123 (24 hrs.)** **Fax: 081-749-7084** **U.S. Toll Free** **800-852-2632**	Nearest Tube: High St. Ken. Set in a quiet street this pleasant, spacious apartment offers 1 twin & 1 single bedded room with shared bathroom. Each room has colour T.V. & a handbasin. Ideal for parties of 3. Centrally located this is an excellent base for sight seeing & shopping. Knightsbridge, The Royal Albert Hall & the Victoria & Albert Museum are only a short distance away. Good restaurants locally. Your host is pleasant & hospitable & sure to make your stay in London memorable.	£27.00	N	N	N
Home No. 08 **W.W.B.B.A.** **London** **Tel: 081-742-9123 (24 hrs.)** **Fax: 081-749-7084** **U.S. Toll Free** **800-852-2632**	Nearest Tube: Parsons Green Located in a most pleasant residential street in the fashionable Hurlingham area of Fulham, only one minute from the tube station & Thames. This charming family house offers two twin-bedded large well-decorated rooms. One with shower room en-suite; one with private bathroom & shower. Both have colour T.V. & tea/coffee making facilities. Elegant first floor drawing room, many antiques & curios. Very close to many excellent restaurants, antique shops, art galleries & parks.	£25.00 🚭	N	N	N
Home No. 09 **W.W.B.B.A.** **London** **Tel: 081-742-9123 (24hrs.)** **Fax: 081-749-7084** **U.S. Toll Free** **800-852-2632**	Nearest Tube: Queens Way A charming self-contained flat - comfortable furnished & attractively decorated with double bedroom & bathroom, kitchen, sitting/dining room. Centrally situated in Bayswater, right by Hyde Park with Knightsbridge & Piccadilly only 10 minutes away by tube. The museums, & the Royal Albert Hall are just across the beautiful park & a slow walk takes about 20 mintues.	£30.00	Y	N	Y
Home No. 10 **W.W.B.B.A.** **London** **Tel: 081-742-9123 (24hrs)** **Fax: 081-749-7084** **U.S. Toll Free** **800-852-2632**	Nearest Tube: Victoria Situated on the Embankment, a lovely modern town house on 3 floors, overlooking the River Thames. Offering 1 twin & 2 single bedded rooms both are comfortable & pleasantly decorated. Colour T.V. & tea/coffee making facilities are in each room. There is private parking for guests with cars. Only minutes from Victoria Station, Buckingham Palace & theatres.	£25.00	Y	N	N

London

	Minimum £ per person	Children taken	Evening meals	Animals taken
Home No. 11 W.W.B.B.A. London Tel: 081-742-9123 (24hrs.) Fax: 081-749-7084 U.S. Toll Free 800-852-2632	Nearest Tube: Barons Court A very pretty town house in a private square, only two minutes walk from the underground & less than 7 minutes to Harrods. The charming hostess offers a most attractive newly decorated twin & single room. Ideal for parties of 3. A comfortable lounge for guest use with antiques, china & many books. A cosy kitchen/ dining room & a pretty garden. The house is on direct underground line from Heathrow.	£25.00	N	N	N
Home No. 15 W.W.B.B.A. London Tel: 081-742-9123 (24 hrs.) Fax: 081-749-7084 U.S. Toll Free 800-852-2632	NearestTube: Parsons Green Situated in fashionable Parsons Green & located only minutes from the tube. This friendly host offers 1 twin bedded room with private shower & 1 single bedded room . Ideal for parties of three. A continental breakfast is served. An excellent base from which to go sight-seeing around London. Many & varied restaurants & interesting antique shops closeby.	£25.00	Y	N	N
Home No.16 W.W.B.B.A. London Tel: 081-742-9123 (24 hrs.) Fax: 081-749-7084 U.S. Toll Free 800-852-2632	Nearest Tube: Sloane Sq. Situated in Chelsea, in a most attractive residential area, close to the Embankment & the River Thames. The charming hosts offer accommodation in a pleasantly decorated & comfortably furnished double bedded room with private bath & shower. Close by are many exclusive shops & restaurants. This is an ideal base from which to see the sights of London. Limited street parking available.	£30.00	N	N	N
Home No. 19 W.W.B.B.A. London Tel: 081-742-9123 (24hrs.) Fax: 081-749-7084 U.S. Toll Free 800-852-2632	Nearest Tube: Parsons Green Located in the quiet Parsons Green area of Fulham. This superb house offers accommodation in 1 kingsize bedded room with private facilities & 2 double rooms with shared bathroom. Each room is beautifully decorated & comfortably furnished. This is an ideal home for visitors to London. Buckingham Palace & Knightsbridge are only 15 minutes away.	£25.00	N	N	N
Home No. 20 W.W.B.B.A. London Tel: 081-742-9123 (24hrs.) Fax: 081-749-7084 U.S. Toll Free 800-852-2632	Nearest Tube: Camden Town A Regency terraced house set in a quiet leafy street very close to Regents Park. A beautiful double or twin room with walk-in wardrobe & adjoining bathroom complete with shower. One small but attractive double room looking into a conservatory & garden. 3 mins. from underground & 15 from Knightsbridge. From here guests can easily walk to Regent Street & Piccadilly. Several excellent restaurants nearby.	£28.00	Y	N	N

London

	minimum £ per person	children taken	evening meals	animals taken

Home No. 22 W.W.B.B.A. London Tel:081-742-9123 (24hrs.) Fax: 081-749-7084 U.S. Toll Free 800-852-2632	Nearest Tube: Notting Hill Gate A delightful cottage in the heart of Bayswater offering self-catering accommodation in 2 twin-bedded rooms, which are prettily decorated to reflect the cottage atmosphere. An attractive living room, most comfortably furnished with spacious dining area. A fully fitted kitchen. Ideal for a family or two couples. Well appointed for visiting all the sights of London.	£25.00	Y	N	N
Home No. 23 W.W.B.B.A. London Tel: 081-742-9123 (24 hrs.) Fax: 081-749-7084 U.S. Toll Free 800-852-2632	Nearest Tube: Turnham Green A large Victorian house situated at the end of a quiet cul-de-sac offering a comfortable family atmosphere. There is one twin, one double & one family room, all are nicely decorated, with modern amenities & tea/coffee makers. A large comfortable living room for guests & a small garden. This is a house for non-smokers. Less than 20 minutes to Buckingham Palace & Knightsbridge. Very convenient for motorways. Children welcome.	£22.50 (no smoking)	Y	N	N
Home No. 27 W.W.B.B.A. London Tel: 081-742-9123 (24 hrs.) Fax: 081-749-7084 U.S. Toll Free 800-852-2632	Nearest Tube: Sloane Sq. This home is located in the exclusive area of Sloane Square, minutes from the tube. The warm & welcoming host offers accommodation in 1 Queen sized double bedded room with private bathroom & tea/coffee making facilities. Guests may choose either a full English or Continental breakfast. Conveniently located for Kensington Knightsbridge & the fashionable Kings Road with its many shops & restaurants.	£28.00 (no smoking)	N	N	N
Home No. 28 W.W.B.B.A. London Tel: 081-742-9123 (24 hrs.) Fax: 081-749-7084 U.S. Toll Free 800-852-2632	Nearest Tube: Earls Court Centrally located in the Earls Court area, this home is convenient for Knightsbridge, Kensington High Street & Heathrow. Beautifully decorated & furnished the accommodation offered is in 1 bright & spacious double bedded room with private bath & shower. A continental breakfast is served here. Your friendly & hospitable host will make your stay in Chelsea most enjoyable. This is a no smoking home.	£31.00 (no smoking)	N	N	Y
Home No. 30 W.W.B.B.A. London Tel: 081-742-9123 (24hrs.) Fax: 081-749-7084 U.S. Toll Free 800-852-2632	Nearest Tube: Greenwich (B.R.) Situated only 2 mins. walk from the station, this cosy house offers comfortable accommodation in one double & two twin rooms, & one single, All are spacious & pleasantly furnished. There is a large lounge where guests can relax. Only 3 miles from the Tower of London & a few mins. walk from the world famous Greenwich Observatory, Maritime Museum & the tea clipper Cutty Sark. Peaceful Greenwich is only 14 mins. from central London & theatres by train. Your host will collect you from Greenwich station. Children are very welcome.	£25.00	Y	N	N

London

	minimum £ per person	children taken	evening meals taken	animals taken

Home No. 31
W.W.B.B.A.
London
Tel: 081-742-9123 (24 hrs.)
Fax: 081-749-7084
U.S. Toll Free
800-852-2632

Nearest Tube: Holland Park
Situated in a lovely area of West London. Ideal for shopping in Kensington & Knightsbridge or for visiting London's famous museums & Parks. Pretty pictures & interesting prints can be found in this attractive home. Accommodation is in 1 spacious double bedded room with en-suite bathroom. Delicious evening meals are available on request.

£ 30.00 | N | Y | N

Home No. 32
W.W.B.B.A.
London
Tel: 081-742-9123 (24 hrs.)
Fax: 081-749-7084
U.S. Toll Free
800-852-2632

Nearest Tube: Russell Sq.
Ideally located in the Bloomsbury area of London. Only a 5 minutes walk to the British Museum. This bright & spacious apartment has a lift to its location on the 3rd floor. Accommodation is in 2 comfortable & attractively furnished rooms, 1 double en-suite with T.V. & 1 twin bedded room with shared bathroom. Convenient for the tube, this is an ideal base for theatre goers: Covent Garden, Piccadilly & Leicester Square are less than 5 minutes away.

£28.00 | N | N | N

Home No. 36
W.W.B.B.A.
London
Tel: 081-742-9123 (24 hrs.)
Fax: 081-749-7084
U.S. Toll Free
800-852-2632

Nearest Tube: Richmond
Situated in the Borough of Richmond upon Thames, this delightful home built in 1870 offers lovely accommodation in 5 well appointed rooms, 3 with private bathroom, each with tea/coffee making facilities, fridge & T.V.. One room has a four-poster bed. Public transport links it conveniently to central London. It is ideal for touring Windsor, Hampton Court, Kew & Wimbledon. Only 8 miles from Heathrow.

£25.00 | Y | Y | Y

see PHOTO over

Home No. 39
W.W.B.B.A.
London
Tel: 081-742-9123(24hrs.)
Fax: 081-749-7084
U.S. Toll Free
800-852-2632

Nearest Tube: Earls Court
A superb home, designer decorated & furnished to the highest standard with antiques throughout. 3 double & 1 twin bedded rooms. Each beautiful bedroom is large & airy with a lovely bathroom en-suite, T.V. & tea/coffee, etc. always available. A large dining room. A delightful garden where breakfast can be served if the weather is good. Only 10 mins. to Harrods. Non-smokers preferred. Children over 12 years.

£35.00 | Y | N | N

Home No. 44
W.W.B.B.A
London
Tel: 081-742-9123 (24 hrs.)
Fax: 081-749-7084
U.S. Toll Free
800-852-2632

Nearest Tube: Richmond
An Edwardian house located on the slopes of the famous Richmond Hill. Accommodation is offered in 1 single & 1 double room. Each room is attractively decorated & comfortably furnished. Delicious breakfast is served in a large country kitchen. Only a short walk from Richmond Park, the river Strawberry Hill House, Ham House & the botanical gardens at Kew. River trips from here to Hampton Court Palace. Harrods only 20 mins. Excellent for Heathrow.

£25.00 | N | N | N

Home No. 36.   London.

London

	minimum £ per person	children taken	evening meals	animals taken

Home No. 45 **W.W.B.B.A.** **London** **Tel: 081-742-9123 (24hrs)** **Fax: 081-749-7084** **U.S. Toll Free** **800-852-2632**	Nearest Tube: Barons Court A charming flat on the 4th floor of a mansion block, with a lift. Beautifully decorated with antiques & china. Offering a prettily decorated twin room & a large single room. Guests have their own bathroom. A comfortable sitting room where guests can relax. A large continental breakfast is served here. Unsuitable for small children. Situated near Earls Court Exhibition Centre. Only 10 mins. from Harrods.	£25.00	Y	N	N
Home No. 48 **W.W.B.B.A.** **London** **Tel: 081-742-9123 (24 hrs.)** **Fax: 081-749-7084** **U.S. Toll Free** **800-852-2632**	Nearest Tube: Parsons Green A beautifully decorated, very stylish early Victorian house, situated in Parsons Green & only 10 mins. from Harrods. Offering 3 twin & 1 double room, all with en-suite showers & furnished to the highest standards of comfort with tea/coffee makers in each room. Guests are welcomed with a glass of sherry. A country house breakfast is served. This is a no smoking house.	£28.00 *see PHOTO over*	N	N	N
Home No. 49 **W.W.B.B.A.** **London** **Tel: 081-742-9123 (24hrs.)** **Fax: 081-749-7084** **U.S. Toll Free** **800-852-2632**	Nearest Tube: Barons Court A beautifully restored Victorian house with walled garden situated close to Kensington High Street. Offering 3 very attractive rooms which are furnished with comfort in mind. All have tea/coffee makers & colour T.V. Antique furniture & a mini fridge. A continental breakfast only is served & brought into the rooms. The vivacious hostess will help visitors plan their itinerary. Excellent pub food available nearby.	£25.00	Y	N	N
Home No. 50 **W.W.B.B.A.** **London** **Tel: 081-742-9123 (24 hrs.)** **Fax: 081-749-7084** **U.S. Toll Free** **800-852-2632**	Nearest Tube: Wimbledon An imposing house in a quiet Wimbledon Street. Beautifully furnished & decorated with antique porcelain. A charming comfortable living room leading out onto a mature garden which guests are encouraged to relax in. A beautiful dining room with silver sparkling & a pretty breakfast room. 2 attractive bedrooms, 1 private bathroom, decorated with taste. The hostess speaks French & fluent Italian. The house is only 25 minutes from Gatwick & 30 minutes from Heathrow & Knightsbridge.	£20.00	Y	N	N
Home No. 60 **W.W.B.B.A.** **London** **Tel: 081-742-9123 (24 hrs.)** **Fax: 081-749-7084** **U.S. Toll Free** **800-852-2632**	Nearest Tube: High St. Ken. A beautifully appointed home located in a quiet cul-de-sac close to Kensington Palace. A lift will take you to the 2nd floor accommodation. A delightful, spacious double room with brass bed, T.V., tea/coffee makers & biscuits are also provided. A delicious varied breakfast is also served. Knightsbridge, Kensington & the park are all just a short walk from here.	£28.00	N	N	N

Home No. 48. London.

London

			minimum £ per person	children taken	evening meals	animals taken
Home No. 65 W.W.B.B.A. London Tel: 081-742-9123 (24 hrs.) Fax: 081-749-7084 U.S. Toll Free 800-852-2632	Nearest Tube: Pimlico This home is wonderfully convenient for Buckingham Palace, Harrods & the Kings Road etc. Accommodation is in one large, light & airy twin bedded room with plenty of cupboard space & a private bathroom. The living/dining room has a delightful balcony where breakfast is served in the summer. This home has lots of interesting paintings & antique furniture. 1 small dog.		£25.00	N	N	N
Home No. 69 W.W.B.B.A. London Tel: 081-742-9123 (24 hrs.) Fax: 081-749-7084 U.S. Toll Free 800-852-2632	Nearest Tube: Sloane Sq. Centrally located, excellent for all the attractions of London including Knightsbridge, Harrods, Chelsea, Buckingham Palace, etc. This is a beautifully decorated & comfortably furnished home offering guests a choice of one double & one single room. There is also a small garden where breakfast may be served in summer. The host is very pleasant & helpful.		£27.00	N	N	N
Home No. 72 W.W.B.B.A. London Tel: 081-742-9123 (24 hrs.) Fax: 081-749-7084 U.S. Toll Free 800-852-2632	Nearest Tube: Holland Park Situated in a conservation area, this beautiful Regency period property offers attractive accommodation in a self-contained bedroom with en-suite bathroom. Continental breakfast is provided for guests to prepare at their leisure. The private entrance offers visitors total freedom. Within easy reach of Kensington & Knightsbridge, close to all public transport. An excellent base for sightseeing & shopping.		£28.00	N	N	N
Home No. 75 W.W.B.B.A. London Tel: 081-742-9123 (24 hrs.) Fax: 081-749-7084 U.S. Toll Free 800-852-2632	Nearest Tube: South Fields This is a most charming house in Wimbledon, only five minutes walk from the All England Tennis Club. A very pretty twin room & a single which share the same bathroom suite. Quiet & luxurious. It is like being in the heart of the country with pretty gardens & trees all around. The hostess will provide dinner if ordered in advance & will collect guests from the station whenever possible.		£26.00 *see PHOTO over*	N	N	N
Home No. 76 W.W.B.B.A. London Tel: 081-742-9123 (24 hrs.) Fax: 081-749-7084 U.S. Toll Free 800-852-2632	Nearest Tube: Earls Court One very nice double or twin room with en-suite bath & shower, 1 large double with private bathroom & 1 small single for another member of the group. All rooms have colour T.V. & have been attractively decorated & furnished by this most helpful host. There's a lovely tiled patio for breakfast or tea. Very close to all the best places for shopping, sightseeing & theatres. Children over 12. Unrestricted parking.		£25.00 🚭	Y	N	N

Home No. 75 . London.

London

			minimum £ per person	children taken	evening meals	animals taken
Home No. 77 **W.W.B.B.A.** **London** **Tel: 081-742-9123 (24 hrs.)** **Fax: 081-749-7084** **U.S. Toll Free** **800-852-2632**		Nearest Tube: Clapham Jt. (B.R.) A large Edwardian house built for Earl Spencer backing onto a private park. Breakfast may be served in the dining room or large conservatory. There is 1 double en-suite room, 2 twin bedded rooms, 1 with private facilities also 1 twin & 1 single room with shared bathroom. Plenty of car parking space. There are two cats & a friendly dog. A charming & most friendly host. Smoking permitted on the ground floor.	£25.00 *see PHOTO over*	Y	Y	N
Home No. 79 **W.W.B.B.A.** **London** **Tel: 081-742-9123 (24 hrs.)** **Fax: 081-749-7084** **U.S. Toll Free** **800-852-2632**		Nearest Tube: East Putney An imposing Victorian house in large grounds offering two charming rooms, located on the 3rd floor. A large twin room with private bathroom & one large, sunny double bedroom with shower en-suite. Only 25 minutes to Windsor Castle on the train. River trips to Greenwich, Hampton Court & Kew go from Putney Bridge just 10 minutes walk away.	£23.00 🚭	Y	N	N
Home No. 80 **W.W.B.B.A** **London** **Tel: 081-742-9123 (24 hrs.)** **Fax: 081-749-7084** **U.S. Toll Free** **800-852-2632**		Nearest Tube: Knightsbridge A delightful apartment centrally located in the heart of Knightsbridge. The charming host offers excellent accommodation in 2 double bedded rooms with en-suite bath/shower & colour T.V.. Each room is tastefully & comfortably furnished. The central location offers easy access to the many exclusive shops & restaurants nearby. Harrods & the Victoria & Albert Museum are 'a stones throw away'.	£31.00	N	N	N
Home No. 82 **W.W.B.B.A.** **London** **Tel: 081-742-9123 (24 hrs.)** **Fax: 081-749-7084** **U.S. Toll Free** **800-852-2632**		Neares Tube: Shepherds Bush A very well appointed house located close to Holland Park offering attractive & comfortable accommodation in a double room with a large four-poster bed & private bathroom. This delightful home is ideally situated only 5 mins. from public transport with easy access to Kensington, Knightsbridge & the wonderful sights of London. This is a no smoking home	£27.00 🚭	N	N	N
Home No. 83 **W.W.B.B.A.** **London** **Tel: 081-742-9123 (24 hrs.)** **Fax: 081-749-7084** **U.S. Toll Free** **800-852-2632**		Nearest Tube: Shepherds Bush A charming Victorian house set in a pretty garden in a quiet street. Offering accommodation in 3 light, airy & spacious rooms. There is 1 double en-suite, a double/twin room & 1 single bedded room which share the bathroom. This delightful home has been attractively furnished by the friendly & helpful host. An ideal location close to all the amenities. Street parking available.	£23.00	Y	N	N

London

		minimum £ per person	children taken	evening meals	animals taken
Home No.84 W.W.B.B.A. London Tel: 081-742-9123 (24 hrs.) Fax: 081-749-7084 U.S. Toll Free 800-852-2632	Nearest Tube: High St. Ken. Centrally located only 5 minutes from Kensington High Street yet quietly situated in a pleasant residential area. Accommodation is in a very pretty & attractively decorated comfortable double bedded room. The warm & welcoming host really makes guests feel at home. This is an excellent base from which to see the sights of London. The Royal Albert Hall, Museums & Parks are all only a short walk away with very easy access to theatreland.	£24.00	N	N	N
Home No. 86 W.W.B.B.A. London Tel: 081-742-9123 (24 hrs.) Fax: 081-749-7084 U.S. Toll Free 800-852-2632	Nearest Tube: Earls Court Situated on the 1st. floor of a period mansion block. This very spacious & attractive apartment with elevator access, offers 1 twin with private bathroom & 2 single bedded rooms, each very comfortable & tastefully furnished. Very friendly hosts who are well travelled & speak a variety of languages. An ideal base from which to explore London. Close to all amenities.	£27.00	N	N	N
Home No. 87 W.W.B.B.A. London Tel: 081-742-9123 (24 hrs.) Fax: 081-749-7084 U.S. Toll Free 800-852-2632	Nearest Tube: Parsons Green A most comfortable home offering 1 double bedded en-suite room & 1 twin with private bathroom. Both rooms are spacious, attractive & are furnished with antiques. Conveniently located in a quiet, pleasant residential area yet only 6 mins. from the tube. This home is an ideal base from which to enjoy London. Limited street parking available. Your pleasant American host will make your stay in London memorable. This is a no smoking house.	£27.00 (no smoking)	N	N	N
Home No. 88 W.W.B.B.A. London Tel: 081-742-9123 (24 hrs.) Fax: 081-749-7084 U.S. Toll Free 800-852-2632	Nearest Tube: Knightsbridge Ideal for the single traveller: this is an excellent London stop over. Located only 5 minutes walk from the famous Harrods store in Knightsbridge. The charming host offers accommodation in 1 single & a single sofa bedded room both well furnished & attractively decorated. Museums, Parks & Palaces are all easily accessed from this centrally situated home.	£29.00 (no smoking)	N	N	N

When booking your accommodation please mention
The Best Bed & Breakfast

Home No. 77 .   London.

All the establishments mentioned in this guide are members of the
Worldwide Bed & Breakfast Association.

If you have any comments regarding your accommodation please send them to us using the form at the back of the book. We value your comments.

Avon

Avon
(West Country)

Avon emerged as a country in 1974 as a result of the rearrangement of the boundaries of Gloucestershire, Wiltshire & Somerset, but its newness is only on the surface, for the county holds a wealth of tradition & history. Getting to Avon is easy, whether by road, rail or air. The M5 runs the length of the county & rail services are fast & direct, a journey of just over an hour from Bristol to London. Bristol Airport not only serves travellers from other parts of Britain but also provides a direct link with Europe.

The country is centred on Bristol & Bath & stretches north & south of the River Avon from which it takes its name. To the west of Bristol between the Severn River & the Cotswolds, are the quiet pastoral lowlands around Thornbury, an ancient town with a castle. The great landmark of this area is the magnificent Severn Bridge forming the Southern approach to Wales.

The Cotswolds, like the Mendips to the south, are officially designated as being of outstanding natural beauty, famous for their honey-coloured limestone villages. This area is particularly rich in stately homes. A tour of Badminton House, Dodington House, Dyrham Park & Horton Court will reveal a mixture of architecture ranging from the grand Classical tradition to the small Cotswold Manor house. Chipping Sodbury is the principal town of this area & its buildings, a rich mixture of Georgian brick & Cotswold stone, reflect its position between Wold & Dale. All along the Cotswold escarpment are superb views across the valley to the Severn & the hills beyond. Tog Hill is a famous viewpoint.

Between the Avon Valley & the county's southern border is the man-made lakeland of Chew Valley & Blagdon. Here are splendid opportunities for fishing, sailing, picnicking & bird watching in the shadow of the majestic Mendip Hills.

Bath is one of the most loved historic cities in England. It owes its existence to the hot springs which bubble up five hundred thousand gallons of water a day at a temperature of some 120' F. According to legend, King Bladud appreciated the healing qualities of the waters & established his capital here, calling it Aquae Sulis. He built an elaborate healing & entertainment centre around the springs including reservoirs, baths & hypercaust rooms.

The Roman Baths, not uncovered until modern times, are on the lowest of three levels. Above them came the mediaeval city & on the top layer at modern street level is the elegant Georgian Pump Room.

Edward was crowned the first King of all England in 973, in the Saxon Abbey which stood on the site of the present fifteenth century abbey. This building, in the graceful perpendicular style with elegant fan vaulting, is sometimes called the "lantern of the West", on account of its vast clerestories & large areas of glass.

Dyrham House.

Avon

During the Middle Ages the town prospered through Royal patronage & the development of the wool industry. Bath became a city of weavers, the leading industrial town in the West of England.

The 18th century gave us the superb Georgian architecture which is the city's glory. John Wood, an ambitious young architect laid out Queen Anne's Square in the grand Palladian style, & went on to produce his masterpiece, the Royal Crescent. His scheme for the city was continued by his son & a number of other fine architects, using the beautiful Bath stone. Bath was a centre of fashion, with Beau Nash the leader of a glittering society

In 1497 John & Sebastian Cabot sailed from the Bristol quayside to the land they called Ameryke, in honour of the King's agent in Bristol, Richard Ameryke. Bristol's involvement in the colonisation of the New World & the trade in sugar, tobacco & slaves that followed, made her the second city in the kingdom in the 18th century. John Cabot is commemorated by the Cabot Tower on grassy Brandon Hill - a fine vantage point from which to view the city. On the old docks below are the Bristol Industrial Museum & the SS Great Britain, Brunel's famous iron ship. Another achievement of this master engineer, the Clifton Suspension Bridge, spans Bristol's renowned beauty spot, the Clifton Gorge. For a glimpse of Bristol's elegant past, stroll through Clifton with its stately terraces & spacious Downs.

A short walk from the busy city centre & modern shopping area, the visitor in search of history will find cobbled King Street with its merchant seamens almhouses & The Theatre Royal, the oldest theatre in continuous use in England, & also Llandoger Trow, an ancient inn associated with Treasure Island & Robinson Crusoe.

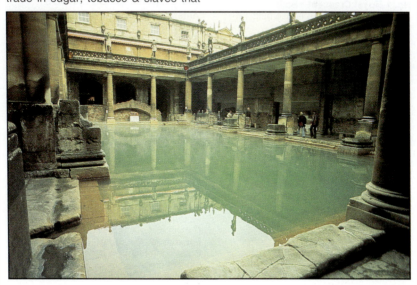

Roman Baths. Bath.

Avon

Avon Gazeteer

Areas of Outstanding Natural Beauty
The Cotswolds & the Mendip Hills

Historic Houses & Castles

Badminton House - Badminton
Built in the reign of Charles II. Huge parkland where Horse Trials are held each year. Home of the Duke of Beaufort.
Clevedon Court - Clevedon
14th century manor house, 13th century hall, 12th century tower. Lovely garden with rare trees & shrubs. This is where Thackerey wrote much of 'Vanity Fair'.
Dodington House - Chipping Sodbury
Perfect 18th century house with superb staircase. Landscape by Capability Brown.
Dyrham Park - Between Bristol & Bath
17th century house - fine panelled rooms, Dutch paintings, furniture.
Horton Court - Horton
Cotswold manor house altered & restored in 19th century.
No. 1 Royal Crescent - Bath
An unaltered Georgian house built 1767.
Red Lodge - Bristol
16th century house - period furniture & panelling.
St. Vincent's Priory - Bristol
Gothic revival house, built over caves which were sanctuary for Christians.
Blaise Castle House - Henbury Nr. Bristol
18th century house - now folk museum, extensive woodlands.
Priory Park College - Bath
18th century Georgian mansion, now Roman Catholic school.
Claverton Manor - Nr. Bath
Greek revival house - furnished with 17th, 18th, 19th century American originals.
St Catherine's Court - Nr. Bath
Small Tudor house - associations with Henry VIII & Elizabeth I.

Cathedrals & Churches

Bristol Cathedral
Mediaeval. Eastern halfnave Victorian. . Chapterhouse richly ornamented.
Bristol (St Mary Radcliffe)
Iron screen, 3 fonts" fairest parish church in all England".
Bristol (St. Stephens')
Perpendicular - monuments, magnificent tower.
Backwell (St. Andrew)
12th to 17th century, 15th century tower, repaired 17th century. 15th century tomb & chancel, 16th century screen, 18th century brass chandelier.
Bath Abbey
Perpendicular - monastic church, 15th century foundation. Nave finished 17th century, restorations in 1674.
Iron Acton (St. James the Less)
Perpendicular - 15th century memorial cross. 19th century mosaic floors, Laudian alter rails, Jacobean pulpit, effigies.
Wrington (All Souls)
15th century aisles & nave; font, stone pulpit, notable screens.
Yate (St. Mary)
Splendid perpendicular tower.

Museums & Galleries

American Museum in Britain - Claverton Nr. Bath
American decorative arts 17th to 19th century displayed in series of furnished rooms & galleries of special exhibits. Paintings, furniture, glass wood & metal work, textiles, folk sculpture, etc.
Holburne of Menstrie Museum - Bath
Old Master paintings, silver, glass, porcelain, furniture & miniatures in 18th century building. Work of 20th century craftworkers.
Victoria Art Gallery - Bath
Paintings, prints, drawings, glass, ceramics, watches, coins, etc. Bygones - permanent & temporary exhibitions. Geology collections.
Roman Museum - Bath
Material from remains of extensive Roman baths & other Roman sites.
Museum of Costume - Bath
Collection of fashion from 17th century to present day.
St. Nicholas Church & City Museum - Bristol
Mediaeval antiquities relating to local

Avon

history, Church plate & vestments. Altarpiece by Hogarth.
City of Bristol Museum - Bristol
Egyptology, archaeology, ethnography, geology. Bristol ships.
Bristol Industrial Museum - Bristol
Collections of transport items of land, sea & air. Many unique items.
City of Bristol Art Gallery - Bristol
Permanent & loan collections of paintings, English & Oriental ceramics.
Chatterton House - Bristol
Birth place of boy poet.
Historic Monuments
Kings Weston Roman Villa - Lawrence Weston
3rd & 4th centuries - mosaics of villa - some walls.
Hinton Priory - Hinton Charterhouse
13th century - ruins of Carthusian priory.

Temple Church - Bristol
14th & 15th century ruins.
Stoney Littleton Barrow - Nr. Bath
Neolithic burial chamber - restoration work 1858.
Roman Baths - Bath

Other things to see & do

Clifton Zoological Gardens - Bristol
Flourishing zoo with many exhibits - beautiful gardens.
Clifton Suspension Bridge - Bristol
Designed by Isambard Kingdom Brunel, opened in 1864. Viewpoint & picnic spot Camera Obscura.
The Pump Room - Bath
18th century neo-classical interior. Spa water can be drunk here overlooking the famous hot springs.

Clifton Suspension Bridge. Bristol.

AVON
Map reference

01 Addison	01 Kitching	01 Burridge	01 Stabbins
01 Warwick-Smith	01 Ashman	01 O'Flaherty	01 Dore
01 Besley	01 Bennetts	01 Archer	02 Baxter
01 Beckett	01 Webber	01 Stone	03 Graham
01 Tovey	01 Dodd	01 London	04 Thornely
01 James	01 West	01 Selby	05 Paz
01 Johnson	01 Willis	01 Hunt	06 Rolls
01 King			07 Shellard

Avon

		minimum £ per person	children taken	evening meals	animals taken
Margaret Addison Bailbrook Lodge Hotel 35 London Road West Bath BA1 7HZ Tel: (0225) 859090 Open: ALL YEAR Map Ref No. 01	Nearest Road: A.4 Bailbroook Lodge is a listed Georgian house located in pleasant surroundings on the ourskirts of Bath offering superb views across the Avon Valley. There is a choice of 14 en-suite bedrooms, most with colour T.V. & tea/coffee making facilities. Bailbrook offers full English. Evening meals are also available. This home is well located for touring the Bath area.	£27.00	Y	Y	N
Mr & Mrs R. Warwick-Smith Gainsborough Hotel Weston Lane Bath BA1 4AB Tel: (0225) 311380 Open: ALL YEAR Map Ref No. 01	Nearest Road: A.4 The Gainsborough is a large country house hotel, comfortably furnished & set in its own grounds near the Botanical Gardens & Victoria Park. Offering 16 attractive en-suite bedrooms with colour T.V., direct dial telephones, tea/coffee making facilities & hairdryers. The dining room & small cocktail bar overlook the lawns, where guests often relax during the summer on the sun terrace. Private parking available.	£28.00	Y	Y	N
Chrissie Besley The Old Red House 37 Newbridge Road Bath BA1 3HE Tel: (0225) 330464 Open: ALL YEAR Map Ref No. 01	Nearest Road: A.4 A warm welcome awaits at this charming guest house with attractive stained glass windows. The comfortable pretty bedrooms, some with ensuite facilities, have radio, colour T.V. & tea/coffee makers. Delicious breakfasts are served in the sunny conservatory. A residents' lounge is usually available for guests to relax in. Private parking. This is an excellent base for touring the lively interesting City of Bath & the West Country.	£15.00	Y	N	N
Derek & Maria Beckett Cedar Lodge 13 Lambridge London Road Bath BA1 6BJ Tel: (0225) 423468 Open: ALL YEAR Map Ref No. 01	Nearest Road: A.4, A.46 Conveniently located for the city centre or countryside, this beautiful detached Georgian house offers period elegance, combined with home comfort. Individually designed bedrooms, one with half-tester bed, all with h&c, colour T.V. & central heating. An English or Continental breakfast is served, using home-made preserves. Cordon Bleu dinners. Guests may relax in the lovely garden or the comfortable drawing room with open fire. Parking/excursion planning service available.	£16.00	Y	Y	N
David & Davina James Highways House 143 Wells Road Bath BA2 3AL Tel: (0225) 421258 Open: ALL YEAR (Excl. Xmas) Map Ref No. 01	Nearest Road: A.367 An elegant Victorian family run home offering superior accommodation in 7 rooms with private facilities (including 1 twin room on the ground floor) colour T.V. & tea/coffee Makers. A tastefully decorated home with a lovely guest lounge. Full English breakfast is served. Located only 10 mins. from the City centre. A perfect base from which to tour the Cotswolds, Stonehenge, Salisbury & Wells. Children over 5 please. Parking.	£24.00 *see PHOTO over*	Y	N	N

Highways House.   Bath.

Avon

		minimum £ per person	children taken	evening meals	animals taken
Mrs Elizabeth Tovey **Bathurst Guest House** **11 Walcot Parade** **London Road** **Bath BA1 5NF** Tel: (0225) 421884 Open: ALL YEAR (Excl.Xmas / New Year) Map Ref No. 01	Nearest Road: A.4 A pretty, terraced Georgian house with 6 attractively decorated guest bedrooms, one with 4 poster bed & en-suite bathroom. All with colour T.V. & tea/coffee/chocolate making facilities. There is a comfortable lounge with piano, games table, books & puzzles. Next to Hedgemead Park, the house is a stroll from the Roman Pump Rooms in the city centre & the antique shops. An excellent touring base. Exclusively for non smokers.	£16.00 see PHOTO over	Y	N	Y
Traudle Graham **Monmouth Lodge** **Norton St. Philip** **Bath BA3 6LH** Tel: (0373) 834367 Open: ALL YEAR Map Ref No. 04	Nearest Road: A.36, B.3110 Monmouth Lodge is situated in an acre of attractive gardens, looking onto the Somerset hills, surrounding this historic village. There are 3 attractively furnished en-suite bedrooms with colour T.V. & tea/coffee making facilities. Guests may relax in the comfortable sitting room or enjoy the garden with views beyond. 10 mins. drive from Bath, this is an ideal base to explore the many interesting sites nearby. Private parking. Children over 5 years.	£21.00	Y	N	N
Douglas & Lynne Johnson **Astor House** **14 Oldfield Road** **Bath BA2 3ND** Tel: (0225) 429134 Open: APR - OCT Map Ref No. 01	Nearest Road: M.4, A.367 A pleasant Victorian house tastefully decorated in the style of the period. There are hot/cold basins in all bedrooms & tea making facilities, a pretty dining room & nice gardens. Quiet situation, just 10 minutes walk from the centre of Bath. Very central for touring the Cotswolds & Wales. 3 double & 4 twin bedded rooms. Several shower bathrooms. Children over 7 years	£14.00	Y	N	N
Jenny King **Oakleigh House** **19 Upper OLdfield Park** **Bath BA2 3JX** Tel: (0225) 315698 Open: ALL YEAR Map Ref No. 01	Nearest Road: A.367 Your comfort is assured at Oakleigh House, quietly situated only 10 minutes from the city centre. Oakleigh combines Victorian elegance with todays comforts to make your stay that extra bit special. All rooms have en-suite bath/shower & w.c., hair-dryers, colour T.V., clock radios and tea/coffee making facilities. Private car park. Oakleigh is an ideal base for beautiful Bath and beyond.	£23.00	N	N	N
Geoff & Avril Kitching **Wentworth House** **106 Bloomfield Road** **Bath BA2 2AP** Tel: (0225) 339193 Open: JAN - DEC Map Ref No. 01	Nearest Road: A.367 Wentworth House is under the personal supervision of the owners Mr & Mrs Kitching who offer thoughtfully equipped rooms, well-maintained and comfortable throughout. There is a large bar, and a dining room with a conservatory overlooking the outdoor swimming pool. 20 rooms, most en-suite, have tea/coffee making facilities, colour T.V. & telephones. Large car park. Abbey & Roman Baths within walking distance.	£20.00	Y	Y	Y

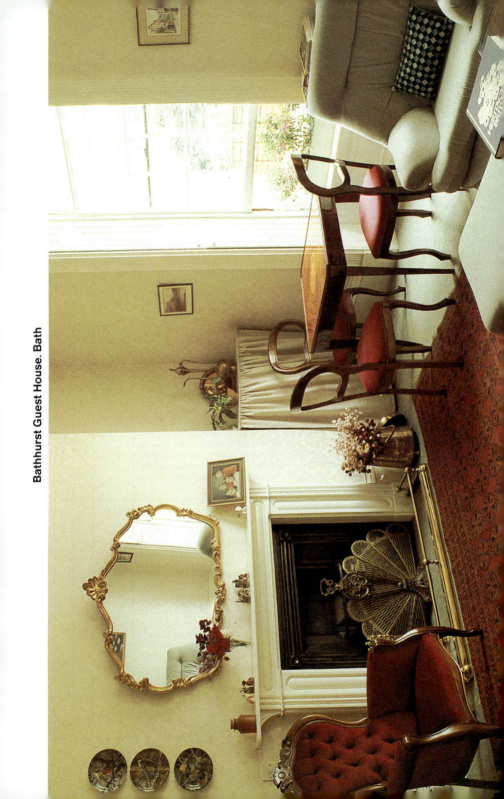

Bathhurst Guest House. Bath

Avon

		minimum £ per person	children taken	evening meals	animals taken
Mrs Magdalene Ashman **Haydon House** **9 Bloomfield Park** **Bath BA2 2OY** Tel: (0225) 427351/ 444919 Fax 0225 469020 Open: ALL YEAR Map Ref No. 01	Nearest Road: A.367 A true oasis of tranquility, this elegantly furnished Edwardian house is situated in a quiet residential area. The four tastefully decorated Laura Ashley bedrooms all have private bathroom or shower en-suite, radio alarms, colour T.V., hot drink facilities, hairdryers and direct dial telephones. Imaginative breakfasts are accompanied by gentle classical music. Secluded, yet the attractions of Georgian Bath are all close by.	£24.00	Y	N	N
Ian & Doreen Bennetts **Dorian House** **One Upper Oldfield Park** **Bath BA2 3JX** Tel: (0225) 426336 Open: ALL YEAR Map Ref No. 01	Nearest Road: A.367 A warm welcome and an aura of nostalgic luxury await every guest at this gracious Victorian house. 7 charming bedrooms, all en-suite, are fully appointed with tea/coffee trays, hairdryers, telephones and colour T.V. There is a lounge, a small licensed bar, and full English breakfast menu is served. Parking available, and only a 10 minute stroll to the city centre.	£20.00	Y	N	N
Arthur & Christine Webber **Cranleigh** **159 Newbridge Hill** **Bath BA1 3PX** Tel: (0225) 310197 Open: JAN - DEC Map Ref No. 01	Nearest Road: A.431 Delightful accommodation is found at Cranleigh, a spacious Victorian house. Thoughtfully equipped rooms (some en-suite) have colour T.V., radio alarms, hairdryers and hospitality trays. The atmosphere is comfortable, relaxed and friendly. Parking and easy access to town centre. Generous, wholesome breakfasts to set you up for the day.	£20.00	Y	N	N
Marion Dodd **Brocks** **32 Brock Street** **Bath BA1 2LN** Tel: (0225) 338374 Open: JAN - DEC Map Ref No. 01	Nearest Road: A.4 Brocks is a beautiful Georgian town house situated between the Circus and Royal Crescent. Very close to the Roman Baths, Assembly Rooms etc. This is a wonderful part of Bath. This historic house has all modern conveniences. Most rooms have private facilities. The aim here is to offer guests the highest standards and personal attention.	£18.00	Y	N	N
Anita & John West **The Plaine Guest House** **Norton St. Philip** **Bath BA3 6LE** Tel: (0373) 834723 Fax 0373 834723 Open: JAN - DEC Map Ref No. 01	Nearest Road: A.36 The Plaine is a delightful listed building dating from the 16th Century, situated in the heart of an historic conservation village. There are three beautiful en-suite rooms all with four-poster beds. Opposite is the famous George Inn - one of the oldest hostelries in England. Delicious breakfasts are prepared with local produce and free range eggs. Convenient location for Bath, Wells, Longleat and Cotwolds. Parking .	£19.50	Y	N	N

Avon

	minimum £ per person	children taken	evening meals	animals taken

Beryl & Leonard Willis **Villa Magdala Hotel** **Henrietta Road** **Bath BA2 6LX** Tel: (0225) 466329 Open: JAN - DEC Map Ref No. 01	Nearest Road: A.4 Villa Magdala is a handsome house of Italian style architecture in attractive grounds. Inside is a fine cast-iron staircase. The 17 bedrooms are all en-suite and well appointed with telephone, radio, T.V., and tea/coffee facilities. Some rooms have Four-Poster beds. Extensive English breakfast menu. Private parking. Just 5 minutes walk to the centre of Bath.	£26.00	Y	N	N
Roy & Rosalie Burridge **Grove Lodge Guest House** **11 Lambridge** **London Road** **Bath BA1 6BJ** Tel: (0225) 310860 Open: ALL YEAR Map Ref No. 01	Nearest Road: A.4, A.46 Situated in attractive gardens looking out onto the wooded hills surrounding the city; this grade II listed Georgian house offers 8 excellent rooms with modern amenities including colour T. V. in each room. Apart from Bath's own attractions, there are numerous beauty spots, walks & places of great historic interest close by. Two golf courses, fishing & tennis are well within one & a half miles.	£20.00	Y	N	N
Anthony & Nicole O'Flaherty **Oldfields Guest House** **102 Wells Road** **Bath BA2 3AL** Tel: (0225) 317984 Open: ALL YEAR(Excl. Xmas/New Year) Map Ref No. 01	Nearest Road: A.367 A Victorian house built in Bath stone overlooking the city towards Kelson Round Hill. 14 delightful rooms with T. V. & tea/coffee making facilities, 8 with bath/shower en-suite. Each room has recently been restored & completely refurbished. The character remains & the Victorian elegance has been lightened by fresh Laura Ashley wallpapers & fabrics. Anthony & Nicole provide plenty of books & newspapers &....Mozart at breakfast. Parking available.	£18.50	Y	N	N
Brian & Audrey Archer **The Tasburgh Bath** **Warminster Road** **Bathampton** **Bath BA2 6SH** Tel: (0225) 425096/ 463842 Open: ALL YEAR Map Ref No. 01	Nearest Road: A.4, A.36 Built in 1890 as a mansion for a photographer to the Royal Family. The Tasburg is set in 7 acres of lovely gardens & pasture with canal frontage & breathtaking views just 1 mile from Bath centre. Offering 13 tastefully furnished rooms (designer fabrics & Laura Ashley) with private facilities. A 4 course breakfast is served & there is ample parking. Brian & Audrey provide many extras, tourist information, maps & personal care.	£22.00 *see PHOTO over*	Y	N	N
John & Olga London **The Orchard** **80 High Street** **Bathford** **Bath BA1 7TG** Tel: (0225) 858765 Open: MAR - OCT Map Ref No. 01	Nearest Road: A.4 The Orchard is a listed grade II Georgian country house in the hillside village of Bathford just 3 miles from Bath. The 4 spacious bedrooms have private facilities & T.V. & are individually decorated & furnished to a high standard of comfort. The elegant drawing and dining rooms are filled with fine pieces of period furniture. An oasis in an acre and a half of walled gardens and orchard.	£23.50	N	N	N

The Tasburgh Bath. Bath

Avon

			minimum £ per person	children taken	evening meals	animals taken
Sonia & Rodney Stone **The Old School House** Church Street Bathford Bath BA1 7RR Tel: (0225) 859593 Open: ALL YEAR Map Ref No. 01	Nearest Road: A.4, M.4. Built in 1837 The Old School House is situated within a conservation area with beautiful views over the Avon Valley & its wooded hillsides, yet only 3 miles from the Georgian city of Bath. Offering a charming country home atmosphere with log fires on chilly evenings. 2 of the 4 double /twin rooms are on the ground floor. All have private bathrooms, 'phone, colour T.V., tea/ coffee, hairdryer & trouser press. An entirely no smoking establishment.		£26.00 *see PHOTO over*	Y	Y	N
Derek & Marjorie Dore **Arnolds Hill House** Wingfield Bath BA14 9LB Tel: (0225) 752025 Open: APR - OCT Map Ref No. 02	Nearest Road: A.366 This delightful Edwardian country house is set in 5 acres of attractive grounds & offers comfortable accommodation in gracious surroundings amid a relaxed & friendly atmosphere. Offering 3 double /twin bedrooms, 1 en-suite, each with colour T.V. & tea/coffee making facilities. Guests are free to relax in the sitting room or in the garden around the outdoor swimming pool. Ideally situated for visiting Bath, Longleat, Stonehenge, Salisbury & Wells.		£17.50	N	N	N
John & Lucile Baxter **Green Lane House** 1 Green Lane Hinton Charterhouse Bath BA3 6BL Tel: (0225) 723631 Open: FEB - NOV Map Ref No. 03	Nearest Road: A.36, A.367 Pretty, comfortably furnished 18th century stone house in a quiet location, near the centre of a conservation village, in beautiful, wooded countryside. Green Lane House tastefully combines original features including exposed beams & working fireplaces with the comforts of modern living. 4 double/twin bedrooms, 2 en-suite, tea/ coffee makers, guest lounge, dining room, parking, four-course English breakfast & friendly personal service. Convenient for Bath, Bristol, Cotswolds, Wells, Longleat, Stonehenge, etc.		£18.00	Y	N	N
Pat & Nigel Hunt **Armstrong House** 41 Crescent Gardens Upper Bristol Road Bath BA1 2NB Tel: (0225) 442211 Open: ALL YEAR Map Ref No. 01	Nearest Road: A.4 A beautifully restored, city centre, Victorian house offering 4 bedrooms all with private facilities, colour T.V. & tea/coffee making facilities. Full English breakfast is provided & the guests lounge is open at all times. Private parking is available. Only a short level walk to all Bath has to offer. It is perfect for either a short break or an extended touring holiday in this lovely area.		£20.00	Y	N	N
Mrs Nicky Stabbins **The Hollies** Hatfield Road Wellsway Bath BA2 2BD Tel: (0225) 313366 Open: JAN - DEC Map Ref No. 01	Nearest Road: A. 367 The Hollies is a lovely old Victorian, Grade II listed, Bath stone house 1 mile from the city centre. With just 3 pretty guest rooms, 2 with shower en-suite, all with colour T.V. and beverage making facilities, personal attention and hospitality is assured. English, vegetarian or Continental breakfast served. There is private parking and a secluded garden where apple blossom and wild meadow flowers bloom.		£15.00	Y	N	N

The Old School House. Bathford.

Avon

		minimum £ per person	children taken	evening meals	animals taken
David & Sue Selby **Brompton House Hotel** St. Johns Road Bathwick Bath BA2 6PT Tel: (0225) 448423 Open: ALL YEAR (Excl. Xmas & New Year) Map Ref No. 01	Nearest Road: A.4, A.36 Brompton House is a delightful Regency residence with a country house atmosphere. Set in a peaceful central position within secluded gardens close to the main attractions only 5 minutes walk to the city centre. A former Georgian rectory (1777) retaining the charm of a bygone age. Offering 12 en-suite rooms with T.V. Tea/coffee making facilities & 'phones. A choice of wholefood or full English breakfast is available. Licenced. Car park.	£27.00 *see PHOTO over*	Y	N	N
Elizabeth Rolls **Hillside** Sutton Hill Road Bishop Sutton Bristol BS18 4UN Tel: (0272) 332208 Open: ALL YEAR Map Ref No. 07	Nearest Road: A.368 Hillside is an attractive converted stone cottage located in quiet farmland with glorious views overlooking Chew Valley Lake. Accommodation is in 2 rooms with central heating & colour T.V. & a super garden to relax in. This makes an excellent base for touring & walking. It is within easy reach of Bath, Bristol, Mendip Hills, Cheddar Gorge & Wells, trout fishing & bird sanctuary are close by. Good pub food locally.	£13.00	Y	N	Y
Ruth Shellard **Overbrook** Stowey Bottom Bishop Sutton Bristol BS18 4TN Tel: (0275) 332648 Open: APR-OCT Map Ref No. 07	Nearest Road: A.368 A delightful wisteria covered family house of charm & character standing in a lovely garden with a stream. Accommodation is in 1 en-suite twin bedroom & 1 double with private shower room, each has tea/coffe maker. There is an attractive sitting room with T.V. & log fires on chilly evenings. Situated in the peaceful Chew Valley, Bath, Bristol, Wells & Cheddar Gorge are all within easy reach.	£12.50	Y	Y	N
Mrs Ann Thornely **Eastcote Cottage** Knapp Road East Crossways, Thornbury Bristol BS12 2HJ Tel: (0454) 413106 Open: ALL YEAR Map Ref No. 05	Nearest Road: M.4, M.5 Eastcote is a very pleasant 200 year-old stone house located in a lovely rural setting with splendid views across open countryside. Guests have a choice of 3 comfortable bedrooms with modern amenities. A colour T.V. lounge is available for guests use. Conveniently situated for the M.4/M.5 interchange for the Cotswolds, with Bristol, Bath, Cheltenham & the Wye Valley easily accessible.	£17.00	Y	N	N
John & Daphne Paz **Dornden Guest House** Church Lane Old Sodbury Bristol BS17 6NB Tel: (0454) 313325 Open: ALL YEAR (Excl. Xmas & New Year) Map Ref No. 06	Nearest Road: A.432 Dornden, built of local Cotswold stone, stands in a beautiful garden enjoying the peace of the countryside & magnificent views to the west. There are 9 attractive rooms, 5 en-suite, overlooking the garden and open country beyond. Delicious meals are prepared, with home-grown produce where possible and free-range eggs. There is a grass tennis court available to guests. A delightful home with a warm, friendly atmosphere.	£19.00	Y	Y	Y

Brompton House Hotel. Bath.

Beds:Berks:Bucks:Herts.

Bedfordshire
(Thames & Chilterns)

The county of Bedfordshire is an area of great natural beauty from the Dunstable Downs in the south to the great River Ouse in the north, along with many country parks & historic houses & gardens.

Two famous wildlife parks are to be found, at Woburn & Whipsnade. The Woburn Wild Animal Kingdom is Britain's largest drive-through safari park, with entrance to an exciting leisure park all included in one admission ticket.

Whipsnade Zoo came into existence in the 1930's as a country retreat for the animals of London Zoo, but is now very much a zoo in its own right & renowned for conservation work.

Woburn Abbey, home of the Dukes of Bedford for three centuries, is often described as one of England's finest showplaces. Rebuilt in the 8th century the Abbey houses an important art collection & is surrounded by a magnificent 3,000 acre deer park.

John Bunyan drew on local Bedfordshire features when writing the Pilgrims Progress, & the ruins of Houghton House, his "House Beautiful" still remain.

Buckinghamshire
(Thames & Chilterns)

Buckinghamshire can be divided into two distinct geographical regions: The high Chilterns with their majestic beechwoods & the Vale of Aylesbury chosen by many over the centuries as a beautiful & accessible place to build their historical homes.

The beechwoods of the Chilterns to the south of the county are crisscrossed with quiet lanes & footpaths., Ancient towns & villages like Amersham & Chesham lie tucked away in the

Rose gardens. St.Albans. Herts.

folds of the hills & a prehistoric track; the Ichniend Way winds on its 85 mile journey through the countryside.

The Rothschild family chose the Vale of Aylesbury to create several impressive homes, & Waddesdon House & Ascott House are both open to the public. Benjamin Disraeli lived at Hughenden Manor, & Florence Nightingale, "the Lady with the Lamp", at Claydon House. Sir Francis Dashwood, the 18th century eccentric founded the bizarre Hellfire Club, which met in the man-made caves near West Wycombe House.

Berkshire
(Thames & Chilterns)

Berkshire is a compact county but one of great variety & beauty.

In the East is Windsor where the largest inhabited castle in the world stands in its majestic hilltop setting. Nine centuries of English monarchy have lived here, & it is home to the present Queen. The surrounding parkland, enormous yards, vast interior & splendour of the State Apartments make a trip to Windsor Castle an unforgettable experience.

To the West are the gently rolling Berkshire Downs where many a champion racehorse has been trained.

Beds:Berks:Bucks:Herts.

To the north of the county, the River Thames dominates the landscape - an opportunity for a river-bank stroll & a drink at a country pub.

In the south is the Kennet & Avon Canal, a peaceful waterway with horse-drawn barges.

Historically, Berkshire has occupied an important place due to its strategic position commanding roads to & from Oxford & the north, & Bath & the west. Roundheads & Cavaliers clashed twice near Newbury during the 17th century English Civil Wars. Their battles are colourfully recreated by historic societies like the Sealed Knot.

The Tudor period brought great wealth from wool-weaving. Merchants built wonderful houses & some built churches but curiously, there is no cathedral in Berkshire.

Hertfordshire
(Thames & Chilterns)

Old & new exist side by side in Hertfordshire. This attractive county includes historic sites, like the unique Roman theatre in St. Albans, as well as new additions to the landscape such as England's first Garden City at Letchworth.

The countryside varies from the chalk hills & rolling downlands of the Chilterns to rivers, lakes, canals & pretty villages. The county remains largely rural despite many large towns & cities. The Grand Union Canal, built at the end of the 18th century to link the Midlands to London, passes through some glorious scenery, particularly at Cassiobury Park in Watford.

Verulamium was a newly-built town of the Roman Empire. It was the first name of Alban, himself a Roman, who became the first Christian to be martyred for his faith in England. The great Abbey church was built by the Normans around his original church, & it was re-established under the Rule of St. Benedict & named St. Albans some 600 years after his death.

Tussauds Exhibition. Windsor. Berks.

Beds:Berks:Bucks:Herts.

Bedfordshire
Gazeteer
Area of outstanding natural beauty. Dunstable Downs, Ivinghoe Beacon.
Historic Houses
Woburn Abbey - house & gardens, extensive art collection, deer park, antiques centre.
Luton Hoo - the Wernher collection of Old Masters, tapestries, furniture, ivories & porcelain, unique collection of Russian Faberge jewellry. Parkland landscaped by Capability Brown.

Other Things to see & do
Woburn Wildlife Park
Whipsnade Zoo-Whipsnade
Old Warden - the village houses a collection of working vintage aeroplanes with flying displays each month from April to October.

Berkshire
Gazeteer
Areas of outstanding natural beauty. North West Downs.
Historic Houses & Castles
Windsor Castle - Royal Residence at Windsor
State apartments, house, historic treasures. The Cloisters, Windsor Chapel. Mediaeval house.
Basildon Park - Nr. Pangbourne Overlooking the Thames. 18th century Bath stone building, massive portico & linked pavilions. Painted ceiling in Octagon Room, gilded pier glasses. Garden & wooded walks.
Cliveden - Nr. Taplow
Once the home of Nancy Astor.
Churches
Lambourn (St. Michael & All Saints) Norman with 15th century chapel. 16th century brasses, glass & tombs.
Padworth (St. John the Baptist) 12th century Norman with plastered exterior, remains of wall paintings, 18th century monuments.
Warfield (St. Michael & All Angels) 14th century decorated style. 15th century wood screen & loft.
Henry Reitlinger Bequest - Maidenhead Chinese, Italian, Persian & European pottery, paintings, sculpture.

Museums
Newbury Museum - Newbury
Natural History & Archaeology - Paleolithic to Saxon & Mediaeval times.
Household Cavalry Museum - Windsor

Other Things to see & do
Racing - at Newbury, Ascot & Windsor Highlight of the racing year is the Royal Meeting at Ascot each June, attended by the Queen & other members of the Royal Family.
Antiques - Hungerford is a famous centre for antiques.
Windsor Safari Park.

Buckinghamshire
Gazeteer
Area of outstanding natural beauty.
Burnham Beeches - 70 acres of unspoilt woodlands, inspiration to poet Thomas Gray.
Historic Houses
Waddesdon Manor & Ascott House - homes of the Rothschilds.
Chalfont St. Giles - cottage home of great English poet John Milton.
Old Jordans & the Meeting House - 17th century buildings associated with William Penn, the founder of Pennsylvania & with the Society of Friends, often called the Quakers.

Things to see & do
Buckinghamshire Railway Centre - at Quainton
Vintage steam train rides & largest private railway collection in Britain.
Chalfont Shire Horse Centre - home of the gentle giants of the horse world.

Beds:Berks:Bucks:Herts.

Hertfordshire
Gazeteer
Areas of outstanding natural beauty. Parts of the Chilterns.

Historic Houses & Castles
Hatfield House - Hatfield
Home of the Marquess of Salisbury. Jacobean House & Tudor Palace - childhood home of Queen Elizabeth I.
Knebworth House - Knebworth
Family home of the Lyttons. 16th century house transformed into Victorian High Gothic. Furniture, portraits. Formal gardens & unique Gertrude Jekyll herb garden.
Shaw's Corner - Ayot St. Lawrence
Home of George Bernard Shaw.

Cathedrals & Churches
St. Albans Cathedral - St. Albans
9th century foundation, murals, painted roof over choir, 15th century reredos, stone rood screen
Stanstead St. Abbots (St. James)12th century nave, 13th century chancel, 15th century tower & porch, 16th century North chapel, 18th century box pews & 3-decker pulpit.
Watford (St. Mary)
13 - 15th century. Essex chapel. Tuscan arcade. Morryson tombs

Museums
Rhodes Memorial Museum & Commonwealth Centre - at Bishop Stortford
Zoological Museum - Tring Gardens
Gardens of the Rose - Chiswell Green Nr. St Albans
Showgrounds of the Royal National Rose Society
Capel Manor - extensive grounds of horticultural college. Many fine trees, including the largest copper beech in the country.

Bledlow Village; Bucks.

BEDS/BUCKS
BERKSHIRE
HERTS

Map reference

01	Lochrie	12	Cooper
03	Walsh	13	Parish
03	Purbrick	14	Rowe
03	Smith	16	Baldwin
04	Ryder		
05	Thornely		
07	Steeds		
08	Dixon		
08	Jackson		
09	Hermon		
10	Must		

Berkshire

	minimum £ per person	children taken	evening meals	animals taken
Mrs M. Lochrie **'Lyndrick House'** **The Avenue** **Ascot SL5 7ND** **Tel: (0344) 883520** **Open: All Year** **Map Ref No. 01** Nearest Road: A. 30, M.4 'Lyndrick' is a 5 bedroom Victorian house in a quiet tree-lined avenue. All bedrooms have colour televisions & tea/coffee making facilities, most are ensuite. Breakfast is served in a pleasant conservatory. Windsor 4 miles, Ascot race course is 2 mins. & 10 mins. to Wentworth Golf Club. Waterloo 40 mins. by train. Heathrow Airport 25 mins. Easy access to M.4, M.3, M.25,& A.30	£20.00	Y	N	Y
Mrs Pamela Walsh **Speen Cottage** **Speen Lane** **Newbury RG13 1RJ** **Tel: (0635) 40859** **Open: All Year** **Map Ref No. 03** Nearest Road: M.4, A.4 A fine Georgian house built in 1790 comfortably furnished with a blend of the modern & antique. Speen Cottage is well situated mid-way between Bath, London, Oxford & Winchester. Offering 3 comfortable rooms, 2 with private facilities, radio & tea/coffee makers. There are many pretty villages in the vicinity as is the vale of the White Horse. Pamela is an excellent cook & dinner or supper are usually available.	£20.00	N	Y	N
Tim & Jennifer Purbrick **Pilgrims Rest Guest House** **Oxford Road** **Newbury RG13 1XB** **Tel: (0635) 40694/44273** **Open: All Year** **Map Ref No. 03** Nearest Road: M.4, A.34 A personal friendly service is always asssured at the Pilgrims Rest. Conveniently located just half a mile from the town centre & railway station. Offering guests a choice of 14 comfortable rooms, 2 en-suite. All have modern amenities, T.V. & tea/coffee making facilities. A guests' T.V. lounge & garden are also available. A delicious English breakfast is served & vegetarian diets can be catered for.	£18.00	Y	Y	Y
Mrs Madelaine Smith **Greenways** **Garden Close Lane** **Newbury RG14 6PP** **Tel: (0635) 40496** **Open: All Year** **Map Ref No. 03** Nearest Road: A.343, M.4 This is a comfortable country house set in pleasant secluded parkland gardens. Offering a choice of 2 bedrooms with modern amenities including tea/coffee making facilities & colour T.V. A delightful garden & guests' lounge available. This house is ideally situated for London. Close by are Crookham Common 18-hole golf course, pony trekking & canal-side walks. Donnington Castle & Littlecote House are within easy reach. Children over 5 years.	£18.00	Y	N	N
Mrs A. F. Thornely **Bridge Cottage** **Station Road** **Woolhampton** **Reading RG7 5SF** **Tel: (0734) 713138** **Open: All Year (Excl. Xmas)** **Map Ref No. 05** Nearest Road: A.4, M.4 A warm welcome awaits the visitor to this delightful 300 year-old riverside cottage. Offering 4 bedrooms, with beamed ceilings, including a twin bedded room with en-suite facilities. Breakfast is served in a lovely conservatory overlooking the River Kennet where old narrow boats pass by. It is surrounded by lovely countryside. Close by is the local pub which serves excellent home-cooked suppers. London 1 hour away. Ideal for Heathrow Airport.	£18.00	Y	N	N

Berkshire

			minimum £ per person	children taken	evening meals	animals taken
Susan Dixon Green Meadows Paradise Lane, Chapel Row Bucklebury Reading RG7 6NU Tel: (0734) 713353 Open: JAN - DEC Map Ref No. 08		Nearest Road: A.4, M.4 A substantial private country house set in two acres of delightful grounds within a rural setting. There are 3 comfortable and attractively decorated bedrooms with T.V. and tea/coffee making facilities. Guests may relax in the beautiful garden or enjoy use of the tennis court. Bucklebury is a charming village, ideally placed for touring Windsor, Oxford, Bath and London. Well located & within easy driving distance of Heathrow.	£20.00	Y	N	Y
Mrs P.J. Hermon "Inverloddon" Ferry Lane Wargrave RG10 8ET Tel: (0734) 40223 Open: ALL YEAR Map Ref No. 09		Nearest Road: A.4, M.4 Situated on the edge of an ancient Roman village, this 200 year-old house stands in a lovely garden sweeping down to the Thames. A very large and chintzy twin bedroom furnished with antiques adjoins an en-suite bathroom with views onto the garden, river and Chilton Hills. An English afternoon tea is served in the comfortable, cosy living room looking onto the beautiful garden. Children is over 10 years.	£17.50	Y	N	N
Jonathan & Diana Ryder Langley Hall Farm Beedon Newbury RG16 8SD Tel: (0635) 248222 Open: ALL YEAR Map Ref No. 04		Nearest Road: M.4, A.34 A large early Victorian Manor farmhouse situated in 600 acres of unspoilt Berkshire countryside with far-reaching glorious views. Working farm with livestock. Every comfort is offered in spacious attractive bedrooms with colour T.V. & tea/coffee making facilities. Delicious farmhouse breakfast served in large dining room. Excellent base for visiting Oxford, Bath, Stratford, London. Within easy reach of Heathrow. A warm & friendly welcome is guaranteed.	£16.00	Y	N	Y
Jane Steeds Highwoods Burghfield Common Reading RG7 3BG Tel: (0734) 832320 Fax 071 930 4261 Open: ALL YEAR (Excl. Xmas) Map Ref No. 07		Nearest Road: A.4, M.4 Highwoods is a fine Victorian country house set in 4 acres of attractive grounds with far reaching views. Offering 2 spacious and comfortable rooms, 1 ensuite, & all modern amenities including T.V.. Guests are welcome to use the garden & hard tennis court. Also a gallery specialising in English watercolours & prints. Easy access to Heathrow, Windsor, Oxford & Bath. This makes a convenient location for touring many of the historic sites in the region.	£18.00	Y	N	N
Auriol Jackson Hunts Cottage Midgham Green Reading RG7 5TT Tel: (0734) 712540 Open: ALL YEAR (Excl. Xmas & New Year) Map Ref No. 08		Nearest Road: M.4, A.4 Built around 1620, Hunts Cottage is a listed timber-framed house with masses of exposed beams & a pair of inglenook fireplaces. There are 3 guest rooms; a twin with en-suite bath, a double with a full tester oak four-poster bed & private bath & a single. All have colour T.V. & tea making equipment. Guests are welcome to use the sitting room, the outdoor heated pool & the large garden.	£22.00	N	N	N

Bedfordshire & Buckinghamshire

			minimum £ per person	children taken	evening meals	animals taken
Mrs Janet Must Church Farm 41 High Street Roxton MK44 3EB Tel: (0234) 870234 Open: ALL YEAR Map Ref No. 10	Nearest Road: A.1, A.428 Church Farm is a lovely 17th century farmhouse with Georgian frontage, set in a secluded village. Furnished with a pleasant mixture of family antiques, the comfortable guest accommodation has its own staircase & bathroom, with tea/coffee making facilities in the rooms. Breakfast is served in the beamed dining room & a guest lounge is available with open fire & colour T.V.. Whether on business or a short break a warm welcome awaits you.		£14.00	Y	N	Y

Buckinghamshire

Mrs Anita Cooper Poletrees Farm Ludgershall Road Brill Aylesbury HP18 9TZ Tel: (0844) 238276 Open: All Year (Excl. Xmas) Map Ref No. 12	Nearest Road: A.41 Guests will receive a warm welcome from a friendly helpful host at this 500 year-old farmhouse. Accommodation is in 3rooms, sharing bathroom. Tea/coffee making facilities. There is a T.V. lounge, a delightful garden and an outdoor swimming pool available for guests' use. Buckingham Golf Course is nearby. Excellent farmhouse meals are served. Poletrees Farm is conveniently located for touring Oxford, Blenheim Palace and Waddesdon Manor.		£15.00	N	Y	N
Mrs J. M. Parish The Old Farm Hog LaneAshley Green Ashley Green Chesham HP5 3PY Tel: (0442) 866430 Fax 0442 866430 Open:All Year(Excl. Xmas) Map Ref No. 13	Nearest Road: A.41, M1 Old Farm is a delightful 16th century farmhouse retaining its original Tudor features including oak beams & inglenook fireplaces. Located in beautiful countryside, but with easy access to town. 2 comfortable bedrooms, one with private facilities, T.V./radio & tea/coffee makers. Conveniently located for St. Albans, Windsor, Woburn & Waddesdon. London 1/2 hour. Heathrow & Gatwick airports are both easily accessible from here.		£17.50	Y	N	Y
Mrs Patricia Rowe The Elms Country House Radnage Stockenchurch High Wycombe HP14 4DW Tel: (0494) 482175 Open: All Year Map Ref No. 14	Nearest Road: A.40, M.40 The Elms is a delightful 17th century farmhouse standing in two acres of ground, set in an area of outstanding natural beauty. The house retains many original features including handmade roof tiles & many oak beams. There are 5 bedrooms, some with radio, T.V. & tea/coffee making facilities, 1 en-suite bedroom. A colour T.V. lounge is also available & guests may use the garden. This makes a pleasant location from which to tour the region.		£17.50	Y	Y	Y

Hertfordshire

		minimum £ per person	children taken	evening meals	animals taken
Mrs Leslie Baldwin Venus Hill Farm Venus Hill Bovingdon HP3 0PG Tel: (0442) 833396 Open: APR - Oct Map Ref No. 16	Nearest Road: A.41, M.25 An absolutely delightful listed black & white 300 year old converted farmhouse standing in 2 acres of garden & surrounded by open farmland. Guests will receive a warm welcome & very comfortable accommodation. There is a choice of 3 bedrooms with modern amenities & tea/coffee makers. T.V. available. Guests may also use the outdoor heated swimming pool. London & Heathrow easily accessable.	£16.50	N	N	N
Peter & Rosemary Jones The Cottage 71 Birchanger Lane Birchanger Bishops Stortford CM23 5QA Tel: (0279) 812349 Open: ALL YEAR Map Ref No. 17	Nearest Road: M.11, exit 8 Situated within a quiet village this charming 17th century listed house offers 8 comfortable en-suite bedrooms all with colour T.V. & tea/coffee makers. Oak panelled reception rooms with log burners & a conservatory/dining room looking onto mature gardens. A convenient base for trips to Cambridge, London, East Anglia & within easy reach of Stanstead Airport & Bishops Stortford. Private parking.	£20.00	Y	Y	Y

All the establishments mentioned in this guide are members of

The Worldwide Bed & Breakfast Association

Cambridge & Northants.

Cambridgeshire
(East Anglia)

A county very different from any other, this is flat, mysterious, low-lying Fenland crisscrossed by a network of waterways both natural & man-made.

The Fens were once waterlogged, misty marshes but today the rich black peat is drained & grows carrots, sugar beet, celery & the best asparagus in the world.

Drive north across the Fens & slowly you become aware of a great presence dominating the horizon. Ely cathedral, the "ship of the Fens", sails closer. The cathedral is a masterpiece with its graceful form & delicate tracery towers. Begun before the Domesday Book was written, it took the work of a full century before it was ready to have the timbered roof raised up. Norman stonemasons worked with great skill & the majestic nave is glorious in its simplicity. Their work was crowned by the addition of the Octagon in the 14th century. Despite the ravages of the Reformation, the lovely Lady Chapel survives as one of the finest examples of decorated architecture in Britain with its exquisitely fine stone carving.

To the south, the Fens give way to rolling chalk hills & fields of barley, wheat & rye, & Cambridge. Punts gliding through the broad river, between smooth, lawned banks, under willow trees, past college buildings as extravagant as wedding cakes. The names of the colleges resound through the ages - Peterhouse, Corpus Christi, Kings, Queens, Trinity, Emmanuel. A city of learning & progress, & a city of great tradition where cows graze in open spaces, just 500 yards from the market square.

Northamptonshire
(East Midlands)

Northamptonshire has many features to attract & interest the visitor, from the town of Brackley in the south with its charming buildings of mellow stone, to ancient Rockingham Forest in the north. There are lovely churches, splendid historic houses & peaceful waterways.

The Waterways Museum at Stoke Bruerne makes a popular outing, with boat trips available on the Grand Union Canal beside the museum. Horse-racing at Towcester & motor-racing at Silverstone draws the crowds, but there are quieter pleasures in visits to Canons Ashby, or to Sulgrave Manor, home of George Washington's ancestors.

In the pleasantly wooded Rockingham Forest area are delightful villages, one of which is Ashton with its thatched cottages, the scene of the World Conker Championships each October. Mary Queen of Scots was executed at Fotheringay, in the castle of which only the mound remains.

Rockingham Castle has a solid Norman gateway & an Elizabethan hall; Deene Park has family connections with the Earl of Cardigan who led the Charge of the Light Brigade & Kirby Hall is a dramatic Elizabethan ruin.

The county is noted for its parish churches, with fine Saxon examples at Brixworth & at Earl's Barton, as well as the round Church of the Holy Sepulchre in the county town itself.

Northampton has a fine tradition of shoemaking, so it is hardly surprising that boots & shoes & other leather-goods take pride of place in the town';s museums. The town has one of the country's biggest market squares, an historic Royal Theatre & a mighty Wurlitzer Organ to dance to at Turner's Musical Merry-go-round ! !

Cambridge & Northants.

Cambridgeshire Gazeteer

Areas of outstanding natural beauty
The Nene Valley

Historic Houses & Castles

Anglesy Abbey - Nr. Cambridge
Origins in the reign of Henry I. Was redesigned into Elizabethan Manor by Fokes family. Houses the Fairhaven collection of Art treasures - stands in 100 acres of Ground.
Hinchingbrooke House - Huntingdon
13th century nunnery converted mid-16th century into Tudor house. Later additions in 17th & 19th centuries.
King's School - Ely
12th & 14th centuries - original stonework & vaulting in the undercroft, original timbering 14th century gateway & monastic barn.
Kimbolton Castle - Kimbolton
Tudor Manor house - has associations with Katherine of Aragon. Remodelled by Vanbrugh 1700's - gatehouse by Robert Adam.
Longthorpe Tower - Nr. Peterborough
13th & 14th century fortification - rare wall paintings.
Peckover House - Wisbech
18th century domestic architecture - charming Victorian garden.

University of Cambridge Colleges
Peterhouse ------------------ 1284
Clare ------------------------ 1326
Pembroke -------------------- 1347
Gonville & Caius ------------- 1348
Trinity Hall ------------------ 1350
Corpus Christi --------------- 1352
King's ----------------------- 1441
Queen's --------------------- 1448
St. Catherine's -------------- 1473
Jesus ------------------------ 1496
Christ's --------------------- 1505
St. John's ------------------- 1511
Magadalene ------------------ 1542
Trinity- --------------------- 1546
Emmanuel-------------------- 1584
Sidney Sussex --------------- 1596
Downing---------------------- 1800

Wimpole Hall - Nr. Cambridge
18th & 19th century - beautiful staterooms - aristocratic house.

Cathedrals & Churches

Alconbury (St. Peter & St. Paul)
13th century chancel & 15th century roof. Broach spire.
Babraham (St. Peter)
13th century tower - 17th century monument.
Ely Cathedral
Rich arcading - west front incomplete. Remarkable interior with Octagon - unique in Gothic architecture.
Great Paxton (Holy Trinity)
12th century.
Harlton (Blessed Virgin Mary)
Perpendicular - decorated transition. 17th century monuments
Hildersham (Holy Trinity)
13th century - effigies, brasses & glass.
Lanwade (St. Nicholas)
15th century - mediaeval fittings
Peterborough Cathedral
Great Norman church fine example - little altered. Painted wooden roof to nave - remarkable west front - Galilee Porch & spires later additions.
Ramsey (St. Thomas of Canterbury)
12th century arcades - perpendicular nave. Late Norman chancel with Angevin vault.
St. Neots (St. Mary)
15th century
Sutton (St. Andrew)
14th century
Trumpington (St. Mary & St. Nicholas)
14th century. Framed brass of 1289 of Sir Roger de Trumpington.
Westley Waterless (St. Mary the Less)
Decorated. 14th century brass of Sir John & Lady Creke.
Wimpole (St. Andrew)
14th century rebuilt 1749 - splendid heraldic glass.
Yaxley (St. Peter)
15th century chancel screen, wall paintings, fine steeple.

Museums & Galleries

Cromwell Museum - Huntingdon
Exhibiting portraits, documents, etc. of the Cromwellian period.
Fitzwilliam Museum - Cambridge
Gallery of masters, old & modern, ceramics, applied arts, prints & drawing,

Cambridge & Northants.

mediaeval manuscripts, music & art library, antiquities.
Scott Polar Research Institute - Cambridge
Relics of expeditions & the equipment used. Current scientific work in Arctic & Antarctic.
University Archives - Cambridge
13th century manuscripts, Charters, Statutes, Royal letters & mandates. Wide variety of records of the University.
University Museum of Archaeology & Anthropology - Cambridge
Collections illustrative of Stone Age in Europe, Africa & Asia. Britain prehistoric to mediaeval times. Prehistoric America. Ethnographic material from South-east Asia, Africa & America.
University Museum of Classical Archaeology - Cambridge
Casts of Greek & Roman Sculpture - representative collection.
Whipple Museum of the History of Science - Cambridge
16th, 17th & 18th century scientific instruments - historic collection.

Other Things to see & do
Nene Valley Railway
Steam railway with locomotives & carriages from many countries.

Caius College; Cambridge.

Cambridge & Northhants

Northamptonshire
Gazeteer
Historic Houses & Castles
Althorp - Nr. Northampton
Family home of the Princess of Wales, with fine pictures & porcelain.
Boughton House - Nr. Kettering
Furniture, tapestries & pictures in late 17th century building modelled on Versailles, in beautiful parkland.
Canons Ashby House - Nr. Daventry
Small 16th century manor house with gardens & church.
Deene Park - Nr. Corby
Family home for over 4 centuries, surrounded by park, extensive gardens & lake.
Holdenby House - Nr. Northampton
Gardens include part of Elizabethan garden, with original entrance arches, terraces & ponds. Falconry centre. Rare breeds.
Kirby Hall - Nr. Corby
Large Elizabethan mansion with fine gardens.
Lamport Hall - Nr. Northampton
17th & 18th century house with paintings, furniture & china. One of the first garden rockeries in Britain. Programme of concerts & other special events.
Rockingham Castle - Rockingham, Nr. Market Harborough
Norman gateway & walls surrounding mainly Elizabethan house, with pictures & Rockingham china. Extensive gardens with 16th century yew hedge.
Rushton Triangular Lodge - Nr. Kettering
Symbolic of the Trinity, with 3 sides, 3 floors, trefoil windows.
Sulgrave Manor - Nr. Banbury
Early English Manor, home of George Washington's ancestors.

Museums
Abington Museum - Northampton
Domestic & social life collections in former manor house.
Museum of Leathercraft - Northampton
History of leather use, with Queen Victoria's saddle, & Samuel Pepys' wallet.

Waterways Museum - Stoke Bruerne Nr. Towcester
200 years of canal & waterway life, displayed beside the Grand Union Canal.

Cathedrals & Churches
Brixworth Church - Nr. Northampton
One of the finest Anglo-Saxon churches in the country, mostly 7th century.
Earls Barton Church - Nr. Northampton
Fine Anglo-Saxon tower & Norman arch & arcading.
Church of the Holy Sepulchre - Northampton
Largest & best preserved of four remaining round churches in England, dating from 1100.

Other Things to see & do
Billing Aquadrome - Nr. Northampton
Boating, fishing, swimming & amusements.
Wicksteed Park - Kettering
Large playground & variety of amusements for families.
Lilford Park - Nr. Oundle
Birds & farm animals in parkland setting where many special events are held.

Rushton Triangular Lodge.

CAMBRIDGESHIRE & NORTHAMPTONSHIRE

Map reference

- 01 Percival
- 01 Webb
- 01 Axhorn
- 01 Greening
- 02 Brash
- 03 Bailey
- 04 Morbey
- 04 Sherrin
- 05 Elbourn
- 07 Clarke
- 08 Faulkner
- 09 Parnell

Cambridge

		minimum £ per person	children taken	evening meals	animals taken
Mrs Alice Percival 136 Huntingdon Road Cambridge CB3 0HL Tel: (0223) 65285 Open: JAN - DEC Map Ref No. 01	Nearest Road: M.11 A large and attractive family house with a secluded garden and private parking, within walking distance of Magdalene College and the centre of Cambridge. The two bedrooms are en-suite, furnished to a high standard, and equipped with tea/coffee facilities, T.V. & radio. Much thought has been put into the comfort and well-being of guests.	£22.50	Y	N	Y
Mrs Alison Morbey Forge Cottage Lower Road Stuntney Ely CB7 5TN Tel: (0831) 833932 Open: JAN - DEC Map Ref No. 04	Nearest Road: A.142 This 17th century listed farmhouse is a Shire-horse and arable farm and set in the centre of a quiet village in an elevated position over the Fens to Ely Cathedral. Elegantly furnished with antiques and featuring oak beams and ingle-nook fireplaces. Two very comfortable en-suite rooms have colour T.V. and tea/coffee making facilities. Superbly situated for Ely, Cambridge and Newmarket.	£22.50	N	N	N
Julie Webb 'Redby Lodge' 15 Queen Edith's Way Cambridge CB1 4PH Tel: (0223) 242559 Open: All Year Map Ref No. 01	Nearest Road: M.11, A.10, Delightful, beautifully kept detached cottage style house with a large garden in a very select area of Cambridge. Exposed beams are a feature of this pleasant quiet house. Offering 2 comfortable & newly decorated bedrooms,1 en-suite, both have modern amenities including T.V./radio & tea/coffee makers. Excellent meals are served in the dining room overlooking the garden. Julie & Tom are very helpful hosts.	£18.00	N	Y	N
Pamela Axhorn Kirkwood House 172 Chesterton Road Cambridge CB4 1DA Tel: (0223) 313874 Open: ALL YEAR Map Ref No. 01	Nearest Road: M.11 A.10 This small, comfortable Edwardian guest house is situated close to the river only a 12 minute walk from Cambridge city centre & its historic colleges. The 5 guest bedrooms are individually & tastefully decorated, all with central heating & modern amenities including shaver points, colour T.V. and tea/coffee making facilities. A delicious full English breakfast is served. Special diets provided by arrangement. Children over 7 years.	£19.00	Y	N	N

All the establishments mentioned in this guide

are members of

The Worldwide Bed & Breakfast Association

Cambridge

			minimum £ per person	children taken	evening meals	animals taken
Jane Greening 7 Water Street Cambridge CB4 1NZ Tel: (0223) 355550 Open: All Year Map Ref No. 01	Nearest Road: M.11, A.45 A warm welcome & friendly atmoshphere await you at this lovely mediaeval coaching house overlooking the River Cam. Accommodation is in a choice of 3 charming rooms with tea/coffee making facilities & views across the delightful walled garden. A colour T.V. lounge is available for guests use. A pleasant walk along the tow path leads to the many historic sights.		£17.00	N	N	N
Mr & Mrs D. Bailey Springfields Ely Road Little Thetford Ely CB6 3HJ Tel: (0353) 663237 Open: JAN - NOV Map Ref No. 03	Nearest Road: A.10 Located in a quiet area yet only 2 miles from the historic Ely Cathedral & city centre. Springfields is a lovely home set in an acre of beautiful garden. Offering 3 delightful bedrooms, 1 en-suite. All rooms have modern amenities, tea/coffee makers & T.V. A full English breakfast is served. A warm & friendly welcome awaits you at Springfields where the accent is on hospitality.		£17.50	N	N	N
Mrs A. E. Brash Bridge House 5 Cambridge Road Great Shelford Cambridge CB2 5JE Tel: (0223) 842920 Open: ALL YEAR Map Ref No. 02	Nearest Road: M.11 An old farmhouse tastefully decorated offering 3 attractive bedrooms furnished with antiques, in an acre of beautiful gardens with a sunny terrace where meals can be taken & only 4 miles from the centre of the University town of Cambridge. Dinner can usually be provided if requested. John & Annie take much pleasure in entertaining their guests with a wide range of imaginative dishes.		£20.00	N	Y	N
Mrs S. L. Sherrin The Tinder Box 10 High Street Kimbolton Huntingdon PE18 0H Tel: (0480) 860983 Open: ALL YEAR(Excl Xmas/New Year) Map Ref No. 04	Nearest Road: A.45 Situated in the idyllic village of Kimbolton. The Tinder Box dates back to the mid 17th century. Accommodation is in 3 lovely rooms all with colour T.V.. Tea/coffee served on request. On warm days there is an intimate walled garden for guests use. Thoughtful touches & an atmosphere of calm tranquility make this an ideal base for touring or for an overnight stay.		£15.00	Y	N	N

When booking your accommodation please

mention

The Best Bed & Breakfast

Cambridge & Northamptonshire

			minimum £ per person	children taken	evening meals	animals taken
Bernice & John Elbourn Chiswick House Chiswick End Meldreth Royston SG8 6LZ Tel: (0763) 260242 Open: ALL YEAR (Excl. Xmas) Map Ref No. 05	Nearest Road: A.10 A beautiful timber-framed farmhouse dating from the 16th century. The Royal crest of King James I is found above the fireplace, suggesting this was his hunting lodge in the early 1600's. Jacobean panelling, oak beams & open fire places create a wonderful atmosphere. 6 en-suite rooms, with tea/coffee making facilities. T.V. is available. Many excellent inns nearby. An ideal base for touring Cambridge, Suffolk & Hertfordshire.		£19.00 *see PHOTO over*	Y	N	Y

Northamptonshire

Katie Parnell Hall Farm Wigsthorpe Oundle Peterborough PE8 5SE Tel: (08015) 277 Open: ALL YEAR Map Ref No. 09	Nearest Road: A.1, A.605 A homely welcome awaits you at Hall Farm, formerly the dower house to Lilford Hall. This is a working farm, mostly arable, set in gardens in a quiet village. Twin, double or family rooms, all with T. V. Evening meals by request. There ia a games room and gymnasium in the house, and many sporting activities,walks and picnic areas close by. A good base to explore historic places in Cambridgeshire and Northamptonshire.	£17.50	Y	Y	N
Audrey Clarke Dairy Farm Cranford St. Andrews Kettering NN14 4AQ Tel: (053678) 273 Open: ALL YEAR Map Ref No. 07	Nearest Road: A.604 Situated in an idyllic Northamptonshire village, Dairy Farm is a charming 17th century farmhouse, featuring oak beams & inglenook fireplaces. 3 comfortable bedrooms, 2 with private bath. Families are well catered for. There is a delightful garden containing an ancient circular dovecoat for guests to enjoy in a relaxed & friendly atmosphere. Delicious meals are served using farmhouse produce.	£18.00	Y	Y	Y
Margaret Faulkner The Maltings Aldwincle Oundle NN14 3EP Tel: (08015) 233 Fax 08015 326 Open: All Year Map Ref No. 08	Nearest Road: A.1, A.605 A personal welcome awaits the vistor to The Maltings, a 500 year-old former farmhouse with its inglenooks & beams. Furnished in antiques throughout, the accommodation is in 3 cosy comfortable rooms with well-apppointed private bathrooms, 24 hour central heating, T.V., tea/coffee at any time. The lovely traditional walled garden opened to the public twice a year is of special interest to plant lovers. Good eating places nearby. Children over 10 please.	£19.00	Y	N	N

Chiswick House, Royston

Cheshire & Merseyside

Cheshire & Merseyside (North West)

Cheshire is located between the Peak District & the mountains of North Wales & is easily accessible from three major motorways. It has much to attract long visits but is also an ideal stopping-off point for travellers to the Lake District & Scotland, or to North Wales or Ireland. There is good access eastwards to York & the east coast & to the south to Stratford-upon-Avon & to London.

Cheshire can boast seven magnificent stately homes, the most visited zoo outside London, four of Europe's largest Garden Centres & many popular venues which feature distinctive Cheshire themes such as silk, salt, cheese, antiques & country crafts.

The Cheshire plain with Chester, its fine county town, & its pretty villages, rises up to Alderley Edge in the east from where there are panoramic views, & then climbs dramatically to meet the heights of the Peaks.

To the west is the coastline of the Wirral Peninsula with miles of sandy beaches & dunes &, of course, Liverpool.

The countryside shelters very beautiful houses. Little Moreton Hall near Congleton, is one of the most perfect imaginable. It is a black & white "magpie" house & not one of its walls is perpendicular, yet it has withstood time & weather for nearly four centuries, standing on the waterside gazing at its own reflection.

Tatton Hall is large & imposing & is splendidly furnished with many fine objects on display. The park & gardens are a delight & especially renowned for the azaleas & rhododendrons. In complete contrast is the enormous radio telescope at Jodrell Bank where visitors can be introduced to planetary astronomy in the planetarium .

Chester is a joy; a walk through its streets is like walking through living history. The old city is encircled by city walls enclosing arcaded streets with handsome black & white galleried buildings that blend well with modern life. There are many excellent shops along these "Rows". Chester Cathedral is a fine building of monastic foundation, with a peaceful cloister & outstanding wood carving in the choir stalls. Boat rides can be taken along the River Dee which flows through the city.

Manchester has first rate shopping, restaurants, sporting facilities, theatres & many museums ranging from an excellent costume museum to the fascinating Museum of Science & Industry.

Little Moreton Hall.

Liverpool grew from a tiny fishing village on the northern shores of the Mersey River, receiving its charter from King John in 1207. Commercial & slave trading with the West Indies led to massive expansion in the 17th & 18th centuries. The Liverpool of today owes much to the introduction of the steam ship in the mid 1900s, which enabled thousands of Irish to emigrate when the potatoe famine was at its height in Ireland. This is a city with a reputation for patronage of art, music & sport.

Cheshire & Merseyside

Cheshire & Merseyside Gazeteer
Area of outstanding natural beauty
Part of the Peaks National Park

Houses & Castles
Addington Hall - Macclesfield
15th century Elizabethan Black & White half timbered house.
Bishop Lloyd's House - Chester
17th century half timbered house (restored). Fine carvings. Has associations with Yale University & New Haven, USA.
Chorley Old Hall - Alderley Edge
14th century hall with 16th century Elizabethan wing.
Forfold Hall - Nantwich
17th century Jacobean country house, with fine panelling.
Gawsworth Hall - Macclesfield
Fine Tudor Half timbered Manor House. Tilting ground. Pictures, furniture, sculptures, etc.
Lyme Park - Disley
Elizabethan with Palladian exterior by Leoni. Gibbons carvings. Beautiful park with herd of red deer.
Peover Hall - Over Peover, Knutsford
16th century- stables of Tudor period; has the famous magpie ceiling.
Tatton Park - Knutsford
Beautifully decorated & furnished Georgian House with a fine collection of glass, china & paintings including Van Dyke & Canaletto. Landscaping by Humphrey Repton.
Little Moreton Hall - Nr. Congleton
15th century timbered, moated house with 16th century wall-paintings.

Cathedrals & Churches
Acton (St. Mary)
13th century with stone seating around walls. 17th century effigies.
Bunbury (St. Boniface)
14th century collegiate church - alabaster effigy.
Congleton (St. Peter)
18th century - box pews, brass candelabrum, 18th century glass.
Chester Cathedral - Chester
Subjected to restoration by Victorians - 14th century choir stalls.
Malpas (St. Oswalds)
15th century - fine screens, some old stalls, two family chapels.
Mobberley (St. Wilfred)
Mediaeval - 15th century Rood Screen, wall paintings, very old glass.
Shotwick (St. Michael)
Twin nave - box pews, 14th century quatre - foil lights, 3 deck pulpit.
Winwick (St. Oswald)
14th century - splendid roof. Pugin chancel.
Wrenbury (St. Margaret)
16th century - west gallery, monuments & hatchments. Box pews.
Liverpool Cathedral - the Anglican Cathedral was completed in 1980 after 76 years of work. It is of massive proportions, the largest in the British Isles, but containing much delicate & detailed work.

Museums & Galleries
Grosvenor Museum - Chester
Art, folk history, natural history, Roman antiquities including a special display of information about the Roman army.
Chester Heritage Centre - Chester
Interesting exhibition of the architectural heritage of Chester.
Cheshire Military Museum - Chester
The three local Regiments are commemorated here.
King Charles Tower - Chester
Chester at the time of the Civil War illustrated by dioramas.
Museum & Art Gallery - Warrington
Anthropology, geology, ethnology, botany & natural history. Pottery, porcelain, glass, collection of early English watercolours.
West Park Museum & Art Gallery - Macclesfield
Egyptian collection, oil paintings, watercolours, sketches by Landseer & Tunnicliffe.
Norton Priory Museum - Runcorn
Remains of excavated mediaeval priory. Also wildlife display.
Quarry Bank Mill - Styal
The Mill is a fine example of industrial building & houses an exhibition of the

Cheshire & Merseyside

cotton industry: the various offices retain their original furnishing, & the turbine room has the transmission systems & two turbines of 1903.

Nether Alderley Mill - Nether Alderley
15th century corn mill which was still used in 1929. Now restored.

The Albert Dock & Maritime Museum - Liverpool
Housing the Liverpool Tate Gallery, the Tate of the North.

Walker Art Gallery - Liverpool

Jodrell Bank - radio telescope & planetarium.

Historic Monuments

Chester Castle - Chester
Huge square tower remaining.

Roman Amphitheatre - Chester
12th legion site - half excavated.

Beeston Castle - Beeston
Remains of a 13th century fort.

Sandbach Crosses - Sandbach
Carved stone crosses dating from 9th century.

Gardens

Arley Hall - Northwich
Walled Gardens, topiary, shrub roses, herbaceous borders, azaleas & rhododendrons.

Cholmondeley Castle Gardens - Malpas
Gardens, lake, farm with rare breeds. Ancient chapel in park.

Ness Gardens - S. Wirral
Beautiful trees & shrubs, terraces, herbaceous borders, rose collection & herb garden.

Tatton Park - Knutsford.
Framed for azaleas & rhododendrons, an Italian terraced garden, a Japanese water garden, an orangery & a fernery.

Mersey Estuary & Ferry.

CHESHIRE MERSEYSIDE & MANCHESTER

Map reference

01 Broad
02 Walsh
03 Allwood
04 Dean
05 Cohen

Cheshire & Merseyside

			minimum £ per person	children taken	evening meals	animals taken
H. A. & F. F. Broad The Folly Middlewich Road Minshull Vernon Crewe CW1 4RD Tel: (027071) 244 Open: ALL YEAR Map Ref No. 01	Nearest Road: M.6, A.530 A delightful old vicarage designed by Sir Gilbert Scott, built in 1847 on a Roman road. Accommodation is in 2 spacious double bedrooms with modern amenities sharing an attractive bathroom. A single room on the ground floor ajoins a shower room. All have tea/coffee making facilities & T.V. Appetising breakfasts are served in the guests dining room overlooking one & a half acres of garden where guests may relax, play croquet or mini golf.		£17.00	N	N	N
Mrs Charlotte Walsh Needhams Farm Uplands Road Werneth Low, Gee Cross Hyde SK14 3AQ Tel: (061) 368 4610 Open: JAN - DEC Map Ref No. 02	Nearest Road: A. 560 Needhams is a small working farm, dating back to the 16th century. Offering 6 bedrooms, 4 en-suite. All rooms have telephone, radio, colour T.V. & tea/coffee makers. Delicious meals are served with a hint of a Scottish flavour. Horse riding & a golf course are nearby. The farm is situated just outside the boundary of the Peak National Park, nestling between Werneth Low Country Park & the Etherow Valley.		£16.00	Y	Y	Y
Michael & Sandra Allwood Burland Farm Wrexham Road Nantwich CW5 8ND Tel: (027074) 210 Open: ALL YEAR (Excl. Xmas & New Year) Map Ref No. 03	Nearest Road: A.534 Burland is a charming Victorian farmhouse set in lovely gardens & furnished with antiques. Two delightful sitting rooms are available to guests throughout the day, as are the 3 luxurious en-suite, individually decorated bedrooms with colour television & hot drink facilities. We serve wonderful freshly prepared food in our dining room, traditional breakfasts & innovative dinners presented on fine china. Special diets & picnics by arrangements.		£20.00	Y	Y	Y
Barbara Ann Dean Ayrshire Guest House 31 Winnington Lane Northwich CW8 4DE Tel: (0606) 74871 Open: ALL YEAR Map Ref No. 04	Nearest Road: A.533, A.49, A charming turn of the century house, offering warmth, comfort & a friendly relaxed atmosphere. All 8 bedrooms, 4 en-suite, are tastefully decorated & have tea & coffee making facilities, a lounge with colour T.V. is available throughout the day, & a generous breakfast is served in the pleasant dining room. Conveniently situated for the many attractions of Cheshire & North West.		£15.50	Y	N	Y

Merseyside

Anna & David Cohen Anna's 65 Dudlow Lane Calderstones Liverpool L18 2EY Tel: (051) 7223708 Open:ALL YEAR Map Ref No. 05	Nearest Road: M.62 Anna's is a comfortable family home where every effort is made to ensure that visitors become one of the family. Eating well is of the utmost importance here & guests may bring their own wine if they choose. Accommodation is in 4 rooms all with modern amenities, radio & tea/coffee making facilities. A resident T.V. lounge is also available as is the garden. Anna's is right in the heart of 'Beatle land'; Penny Lane & Strawberry Fields are moments away.		£15.60	Y	N	Y

Cornwall

Cornwall
(West Country)

Cornwall is an ancient Celtic land, a narrow granite peninsula with a magnificent coastline of over 300 miles & wild stretches of moorland.

The north coast, washed by Atlantic breakers, has firm golden sands & soaring cliffs. The magnificent beaches at Bude offer excellent surfing, & a few miles to the south you can visit the picturesque harbour at Boscastle & the cliff-top castle at Tintagel with its legends of King Arthur. Newquay, with its beaches stretching for over seven miles, sheltered coves & modern hotels & shops, is the premier resort on Cornwall's Atlantic coast. St. Ives, another surfing resort, has great charm which has attracted artists for so long & is an ideal place from which to explore the Land's End peninsula.

The south coast is a complete contrast - wooded estuaries, sheltered coves, little fishing ports, & popular resorts. Penzance, with its warmth & vivid colours, is an all-the-year-round resort & has wonderful views across the bay to St. Michael's Mount. Here are excellent facilities for sailing & deep-sea fishing, as there are at Falmouth & Fowey with their superb harbours. Mevagissey, Polperro & Looe are fine examples of traditional Cornish fishing villages.

In the far west of Cornwall, you can hear about a fascinating legend: the lost land of Lyonesse - a whole country that was drowned by the sea. The legend goes that the waters cover a rich & fertile country, which had 140 parish churches. The Anglo-Saxon Chronicle records two great storms within a hundred years, which drowned many towns & innumerate people. Submerged forests are known to lie around these coasts - & in Mount's Bay beech trees have been found with the nuts still hanging on the branches, so suddenly were they swamped.

Today, St Michael's Mount & the Isles of Scilly are said to be all that remains of the vanished land. St. Michael's Mount, with its tiny fishing village & dramatic castle, can be visited on foot at low tide or by boat at high water. The Isles of Scilly, 28 miles beyond Land's End, have five inhabited islands, including Tresco with its sub-tropical gardens. Day trips to the numerous uninhabited islands are a special feature of a Scilly holiday.

Inland Cornwall also has its attractions. To the east of Bodmin, the county town, are the open uplands of Bodmin Moor, with the county's highest peaks at Rough Tor & Brown Willy. "Jamaica Inn", immortalised in the novel by Daphne du Maurier, stands on the lonely road across the moor, & "Frenchman's Creek" is on a hidden inlet of the Helford River.

There is a seemingly endless number & variety of Cornish villages in estuaries, wooded, pastoral or moorland settings, & here customs & traditions are maintained. In Helston the famous "Fleury Dance" is still performed, & at the ancient port of Padstow, May Day celebrating involves decorating the houses with green boughs & parading the Hobby Horse through the street to the tune of St. George's Song.

Helford Creek.

Cornwall

Cornwall Gazeteer

Areas of outstanding natural beauty.
Almost the entire county.

Historic Houses & Castles

Anthony House - Torpoint
18th century - beautiful & quite unspoiled Queen Anne house, excellent panelling & fine period furnishings.

Cotehele House - Calstock
15th & 16th century house, still contains the original furniture, tapestry, armour.

Ebbingford Manor - Bude
12th century Cornish manor house, with walled garden.

Godolphin House - Helston
Tudor - 17th century colonnaded front.

Lanhydrock - Bodmin
17th century - splendid plaster ceilings, picture gallery with family portraits 17th/20th centuries.

Mount Edgcumbe House - Plymouth
Tudor style mansion - restored after destruction in 1949. Hepplewhite furniture & portrait by Joshua Reynolds.

St. Michael's Mount - Penzance
Mediaeval castle & 17th century with 18th & 19th century additions.

Pencarrow House & Gardens - Bodmin
18th century Georgian Mansion - collection of paintings, china & furniture - mile long drive through fine woodlands & gardens.

Old Post Office - Tintagel
14th century manor house in miniature - large hall used as Post Office for a period, hence the name.

Trewithen - Probus Nr. Truro
Early Georgian house with lovely gardens.

Trerice - St. Newlyn East
16th century Elizabethan house, small with elaborate facade. Excellent fireplaces, plaster ceilings, miniature gallery & minstrels' gallery.

Cathedral & Churches

Altarnun (St. Nonna)
15th century, Norman font, 16th century bench ends, fine rood screen.

Bisland (St. Protus & St. Hyacinth)
15th century granite tower - carved wagon roofs, slate floor. Georgian wine - glass pulpit, fine screen.

Kilkhampton (St. James)
16th century with fine Norman doorway, arcades & wagon roofs.

Laneast (St. Michael or St. Sedwell)
13th century, 15th century enlargement, 16th century pulpit, some painted glass.

Lanteglos-by-Fowley (St. Willow)
14th century, refashioned 15th century, 13th century font, 15th century brasses & altar tomb, 16th century bench ends.

Launcells (St. Andrew)
Interior unrestored - old plaster & ancient roofs remaining, fine Norman font with 17th century cover, box pews, pulpit, reredos, 3 sided alter rails.

Probus (St. Probus & St. Gren)
16th century tower, splendid arcades, three great East windows.

St. Keverne (St. Keverne)
Fine tower & spire. Wall painting in 15th century interior.

St. Neot (St. Neot)
Decorated tower - 16th century exterior, buttressed & double-aisled. Many windows of mediaeval glass renewed in 19th century.

Museums & Galleries

Museum of Witchcraft - Boscastle
Relating to witches, implements & customs.

Military Museum - Bodmin
History of Duke of Cornwall's Light Infantry.

Public Library & Museum - Cambourne
Collections of mineralogy, archaeology, local antiquities & history.

Cornish Museum - East Looe
Collection of relics relating to witchcraft customs & superstitions. Folk life & culture of district.

Helston Borough Museum - Helston
Folk life & culture of area around Lizard.

Museum of Nautical Art - Penzance
Exhibition of salvaged gold & silver treasures from underwater wreck of 1700's.

Museum of Smuggling - Polperro
Activities of smugglers, past & present.

Penlee House Museum - Penlee, Penzance
Archaeology & local history & tin mining exhibits.

Cornwall

Barbara Hepworth Museum - St. Ives
Sculpture, letters, documents, photographs, etc., exhibited in house where Barbara Hepworth lived.
Old Mariners Church - St. Ives
St. Ives Society of Artists hold exhibitions here.
County Museum & Art Gallery - Truro
Ceramics, art local history & antiquities, Cornish mineralogy.

Historic Monuments

Cromwell's Castle - Tresco (Scilly Isles)
17th century castle.
King Charles' Fort - Tresco (Scilly Isles)
16th century fort.
Old Blockhouse - Tresco (Scilly Isles)
16th century coastal battery.
Harry's Wall - St. Mary's (Scilly Isles)
Tudor Coastal battery
Ballowall Barrow - St. Just
Prehistoric barrow.
Pendennis Castle - Falmouth
Fort from time of Henry VII.
Restormel Castle - Lostwithiel
13th century ruins.
St. Mawes Castle - St. Mawes
16th century fortified castle.
Tintagel Castle - Tintagel
Mediaeval ruin on wild coast, King Arthur's legendary castle.

Things to see & do

Camel trail - Padstow to Bodmin
12 miles of recreation path along scenic route, suitable for walkers, cyclists & horse-riders.
Tresco Abbey Gardens - Tresco
Collection of sub-tropical flora
Trethorne Leisure Farm - Launceston
Visitors are encouraged to feed & stroke the farm animals
Seal sanctuary - Gweek Nr. Helston
Seals, exhibition hall, nature walk, aquarium, seal hospital, donkey paddock.
Dobwalls Theme Park - Nr. Liskeard
2 miles of scenically dramatic miniature railway based on the American railroad.
Padstow tropical bird gardens - Padstow
Mynack Theatre - Porthcurno

Lands End.

CORNWALL
Map reference

01 Smith
02 Thompson
03 Knight
03 Crocker
04 Thomas
05 Barbour
06 Tremayne
07 Ford
08 Morton
09 Betty
10 Griffin
11 Colwill
11 Low
12 Spring
13 Norman
14 Tuckett
15 Stevenson
16 Owens
17 Gould
18 Martin
19 Hilder
19 Wood
19 Hopkins
20 Jarratt
20 J. Lee
20 Mercer
21 Compton
22 Green
23 Wooldridge
24 Richards
25 Barley
26 Studley
27 Batty
27 Mason
27 Sykes
28 Walkley
28 Rayner
29 Gartner
30 Dymond
31 Walker

Cornwall

			minimum £ per person	children taken	evening meals	animals taken
Mrs Pat Smith Treffry Farm Lanhydrock Bodmin PL30 5A Tel: (0208) 74405 Open: MAR - OCT Map Ref No. 01	Nearest Road: A.30 Historic listed Georgian farmhouse which adjoins National Trust Lanhydrock with its stately home, glorious gardens and miles of country walks. You are guaranteed a warm welcome here and delicious home-cooking in generous quantities! You can enjoy relaxing in the pretty bedrooms (one with four-poster) and in the wood panelled lounge. Search out Cornwall's rugged cliffs and sandy coves from a very central location.	🚭	£15.00	Y	Y	N
Mr & Mrs B. Thompson St. Christophers Hotel High Street Boscastle PL35 0BD Tel: (08405) 412 Open: MAR - NOV Map Ref No. 02	Nearest Road: A.39, B.3266 A superb Georgian house retaining its original character, providing excellent, comfortable accommodation in 9 charming rooms with modern facilities, 8 en-suite. Here the welcome & standards are marvellous. The lovely harbour village is unspoilt. There is a wealth of history all around with plenty of interesting places to visit. Meals are well-prepared, delicious & personally supervised.	🚭	£15.00	N	Y	Y
Mrs M. Knight Manor Farm Crackington Haven Bude EX23 0JW Tel: (08403) 304 Open: ALL YEAR Map Ref No. 03	Nearest Road: A.39 A really super 11th century manor house retaining all its former charm & elegance. Mentioned in the 1086 Domesday book, it belonged to the Earl of Mortain, half brother to William the Conqueror. Delightfully located in a beautiful & secluded position surrounded by attractive gardens & 40 acres of farmland. Guest rooms have private facilities. There is a games room for guests' use. Dining at Manor Farm is considered the highlight of the day. Only 1 mile from the beach. Non-smokers only. West Country winner of the Best Bed & Breakfast award.	🚭 see PHOTO over	£22.00	N	Y	N
Janet Crocker Trevigue Crackington Haven Bude EX23 0LQ Tel: (08403) 418 Open: MAR - OCT Map Ref No. 03	Nearest Road: A.39 A delightful 16th century house built around a cobbled courtyard, on a farm mentioned in the Domesday Book. Trevigue, now a conservation-conscious dairy and stock farm, is a comfortable and welcoming home with mullioned windows, old beams, deep sofas and log fires. 4 en-suite bedrooms, 2 with T.V., all with tea-making facilities. Hearty breakfasts and excellent evening menu. Spectacular cliffs nearby. Children over 12 welcome.		£17.00	Y	Y	N
Mrs Lucy Thomas East Cornwall Farmhouse Fullaford Road Callington PL17 8AN Tel: (0579) 50018 Open: FEB-NOV Map Ref No. 04	Nearest Road: A.390 A former Count House to a silver/lead mine, East Cornwall Farmhouse is beautifully situated with views over "Silver Valley" & is ideal for touring Devon & Cornwall. It is just 2-3 miles to Cotehele House (National Trust) & St. Mellion Golf Course. Imaginitive home cooking, using garden & local produce, to cater for most diets. T.V. lounge & tea/coffee facilities in bedrooms.		£14.00	Y	Y	Y

Manor Farm, Crackington Haven

Cornwall

		minimum £ per person	children taken	evening meals	animals taken
Mrs Judy Ford **Treviades Barton** **High Cross** **Constantine** **Falmouth** Tel: (0326) 40524 Open: ALL YEAR (Excl. Xmas & Easter) Map Ref No. 07	Nearest Road: A.394 This charming 16th century listed farmhouse stands in beautiful gardens close to the Helford River. Offering 3 comfortable double bedrooms with radio & tea/coffee makers, 2 with en-suite facilities. A T.V. lounge is also available throughout the day. Guests stay in a family atmosphere with a wide range of relaxing or energetic holiday opportunities available locally throughout the year. A good base from which to r tour the local area.	£18.00	Y	Y	Y
Mrs Buchanan Barbour **Bella's Mouse** **8 Shute Lane** **Penryn** **Falmouth TR10 8EY** Tel: (0326) 373433 Open: APR-OCT Map Ref No. 05	Nearest Road: A.39 16th century Bella's Mouse is a charming thick walled, whitewashed, traditional Cornish cottage situated in a quiet lane near the heart of the small historic port of Penryn. Lovingly restored to a very high standard, it offers guest 2 very pretty double bedrooms with luxurious private bathrooms & private cosy sitting room, book-lined study & attractive dining room. Ideally located for touring all of Cornwall.	£17.50	N	N	N
Mr & Mrs T. D. Tremayne **'The Home' Country House Hotel** **Penjerrick** **Falmouth TR11 5EE** Tel: (O326) 250427 Open: APR - OCT Map Ref No. 06	Nearest Road: A.39 A quiet & charming country house with views over Maenporth & Falmouth Bay. Accommodation is in 14 rooms, 7 with private bath/shower. All have tea/coffee making facilities. A colour T.V. lounge & bar are provided & guests may relax in the beautiful sheltered garden. Golf course & boating facilities nearby. A friendly host who prepares delicious meals using local produce. Special diets provided by arrangement.	£16.00	Y	Y	Y
Mr & Mrs John Morton **Tregonning Manor** **Laddenvean** **St. Keverne** **Helston TR12 6QE** Tel: (0326) 280222 Open: MAR-OCT Map Ref No. 08	Nearest Road: A.3083 Tregonning Manor is an old Cornish manor house, set in tranquil 10 acres with stream & mill pond, well off the beaten track on the Lizard Peninsular. Recently restored, & furnished with antiques to retain character. Only one family taken at any time in this relaxed friendly family home. One twin-bedded room with private bathroom. Also one double-bedded room available if required.	£18.00	Y	N	N
Andrea Betty **High Massetts** **Cadgwith Cove** **Ruan Minor** **Helston TR12 7LA** Tel: (0326) 290571 Open: ALL YEAR Map Ref No. 09	Nearest Road: A.3080 A warm welcome awaits visitors to High Massetts. Set in lovely gardens, the house is beautifully positioned & has splendid views over the cove. Accommodation is in 4 rooms, 1 en-suite. All have modern amenities & tea/coffee makers. Most have T.V. A guest lounge with colour T.V. is also available. The cove itself offers safe bathing, fishing, skin-diving & boating. Crab, lobster or steak suppers on request. Home grown fruit, vegetables & fresh eggs used	£14.50	Y	Y	N

Allhays Country House. Looe

Cornwall

		minimum £ per person	children taken	evening meals	animals taken
Raymond & Valerie Griffin Wheatley Farm Maxworthy Launceston PL15 8LY Tel: (056681) 232 Open: APR - SEPT Map Ref No. 10	Nearest Road: A. 39 You will be made very welcome at Wheatley, a spacious farmhouse built by the Duke of Bedford in 1871, which stands in landscaped gardens on a working farm in the peace of the Cornish countryside. 4 luxurious and charming en-suite bedrooms with colour T.V., tea/coffee making facilities. Tantalising and varied dinner menu. Log Fires. Games room (and a secret one for children!). Pony rides. Spectacular coastline nearby.	£16.00	Y	Y	N
Mrs Agnes Colwill Sutton Farm Boyton Launceston PL15 9RN Tel: (040927) 269 Open: APR - OCT Map Ref No. 11	Nearest Road: B.3254 A delightful 220 acre working farm. Accommodation is in 3 bedrooms, sharing 2 bathrooms. Lounge with colour T.V. available. Delicious full English breakfasts are served. T.V. snacks on request. Families are well catered for. There is a games room & cot/highchair. Guests are made very welcome & can relax in the beautiful garden. Sutton Farm is an ideal base for visiting the moors & many resorts.	£11.50	Y	N	Y
Alexander & Sally Low Combe Farm Widegates Looe PL13 1QN Tel: (05034) 223 Open: MAR-OCT Map Ref No. 11	Nearest Road: B.3253, A.38 A lovely country house, beautifully furnished with antiques. Set in 10 acres of lawns, meadows, woods, streams & ponds with superb views down a wooded valley to the sea. The atmosphere is delightful with open log fires, a candlelit dining room in which to enjoy delicious home cooking & an informal licenced bar. Two old barns have been converted for indoor games including snooker & table tennis. There is a croquet lawn, heated outdoor swimming pool & many birds & animals.	£16.50 see PHOTO over	Y	Y	N
Pat & Bryan Norman Fieldhead Hotel Portuan Road Looe PL13 2DR Tel: (0503) 262689 Fax 0503 264114 Open: FEB-NOV(+Xmas) Map Ref No. 13	Nearest Road: A.38 A delightful hotel with a fine reputation; guests return year after year. Set in its own grounds with panoramic views of the sea, within 200 yards of the beach. 13 most attractive & comfortable rooms with en-suite facilities. All have radio, T.V. & tea/coffee makers. An attractive residents' lounge, games room, a heated outdoor pool & lovely garden. The area is wonderful for all sports, riding, walking, fishing, sailing, golfing & the beaches are great.	£27.50	Y	Y	N
Brian & Lynda Spring Allhays Country House Talland Bay Looe PL13 2JB Tel: (0503) 72434 Fax 0503 72929 Open: ALL YEAR (Excl. Xmas.) Map Ref No. 12	Nearest Road: A.387 Overlooking the beautiful smugglers cove of Talland Bay. House guests enjoy all the warmth & comfort of a family home complete with magnificent fireplaces & log fires. All 8 bedrooms have satellite link colour T.V., telephone, tea/coffee makers. Most are en-suite including 2 ground floor rooms. Enjoy fine food & wine in the candlelit dining room or amidst the beautiful 'outdoor' surroundings of our Victorian style conservatory.	£26.00 see PHOTO over	Y	Y	Y

Coombe Farm. Widegates

Cornwall

	minimum £ per person	children taken	evening meals	animals taken
Mr & Mrs A Tuckett **Trenderway Farm** Pelynt Looe PL13 2LY Tel: (0503) 72214 Open: MAR - NOV Map Ref No. 14 — Nearest Road: A.387 Escape and unwind at Trenderway, 16th century listed farmhouse, heart of 400 acre working farm - off the beaten track yet 5 minutes from picturesque Polperro. Guests have the choice of 4 beautifully furnished, tastefully co-ordinated rooms with colour T.V.s, and tea/coffee making facilities. Four-course farmhouse breakfast (no need to interrupt the day for lunch!). Exceptional restaurants and Inns nearby for later meals.	£18.00	N	N	N
Mr M. Stevenson **Mixton House** Lerryn Lostwithiel PL22 0QE Tel: (0208) 872781 Open: ALL YEAR Map Ref No. 15 — Nearest Road: A.390 A charming Georgian country house standing in two acres of secluded gardens, overlooking the picturesque Lerryn River Valley. Mixton offer a choice of 3 spacious elegantly furnished bedrooms, stylish, comfortable reception rooms with flowers & books throughout complete the country ambience. A tennis court & a boat & mooring are also available for guests' use. This is a delightful peaceful country base from which to explore Cornwall.	£22.50	Y	N	N
Mrs D. Owens **Mevagissey House** Vicarage Hill Mevagissey PL26 6SZ Tel: (0726) 842427 Open: MAR-OCT Map Ref No. 16 — Nearest Road: A.390, B.3273 An elegant Georgian rectory standing in 4 acres of woodland, overlooking the beautiful woodland & valley to the harbour & sea beyond. Here guests can unwind & relax in pleasant comfortable surroundings. There is a choice of 6 rooms all with modern amenities, T.V. & tea/coffe making facilities. Snacks, morning coffee & cornish cream teas are available on request. Evening meals are also served. Close by are fishing, beaches & golf courses. Children over 7 years welcome.	£17.00	Y	Y	N
Mrs Sarah Gould **Lusty Glaze House** Lusty Glaze Road Newquay TR7 3AE Tel: (0637) 872668 Open: EASTER-SEPT Map Ref No. 17 — Nearest Road: A.38 A relaxed peaceful atmosphere, friendly helpful hosts & high standards of accommodation are found here. In a unique location standing in an acre of gardens & adjoining the coastal foot path, overlooking a private beach. Lusty Glaze offers 5 comfortable rooms, all with en-suite facilities, T.V. & tea/coffee makers. Home cooking is a speciality using fresh seasonal ingredients. Vegetarians are also well catered for. Min. age of children is 5 years.	£22.50	Y	Y	N
Keith & Janet Martin **Nanscawen House** Prideaux Road St. Blazey Par PL24 2SR Tel/Fax (0726) 814488 Open: ALL YEAR(Excl.Xmas) Map Ref No. 18 — Nearest Road: A.390 Nanscawen is a delightful country house set in an idyllic location. It stands in 5 acres of grounds & gardens in a nature conservation area. Guests have a choice of 3 luxury en-suite rooms with spa baths. The elegantly furnished drawing room leads into the conservatory where breakfast is enjoyed. Splendid, cordon bleu style dinners are available. An ideal base for touring all of Cornwall. Guests may like to use the heated swimming pool & whirlpool hot tub.	£19.00 🚭 *see PHOTO over*	N	Y	N

Nanscawen House. St Blazey

Cornwall

		minimum £ per person	children taken	evening meals	animals taken
Mr & Mrs R. I. Hilder Carnson House Hotel East Terrace Penzance TR18 2TD Tel: (0736) 65589 Open: ALL YEAR Map Ref No. 19	Nearest Road: A.30 Carnson offers you a Cornish welcome & a friendly atmosphere. 8 modern bedrooms with heating, colour T.V., tea/coffee makers & some en-suite. Licenced, with a pleasant lounge. Enjoying one of Penzance's most central positions close to railway & bus stations. A variety of coach & boat trips, car hire & bus tours are available all year round & can be arranged by the hotel. Add international recommendations for food & it makes a happy & memorable visit.	£14.00	Y	Y	N
Mrs F. Joan Wood Lynwood Guest House 41 Morrab Road Penzance TR18 4EX Tel: (0736) 65871 Open: ALL YEAR Map Ref No. 19	Nearest Road: A.30 A friendly relaxed atmosphere & a warm welcome await you at this Victorian house situated between promenade & town centre. Close to the sub-tropical Morrab Gardens. Offering 6 well decorated bedrooms all with modern facilities, colour T.V., tea/ coffee makers. Comfortable colour T.V. lounge & large dining room offering various menus. A varied selection of restaurants within an easy walk. Ideal for visiting Lands End, Lizard, St. Michael's Mount & Isles of Scilly. Children welcome.	£11.00	Y	N	Y
C. L. Hopkins Woodstock Guest House 29 Morrab Road Penzance TR18 4EZ Tel: (0736) 69049 Open: ALL YEAR Map Ref No. 19	Nearest Road: A.30 A warm friendly welcome awaits you at Woodstock. The sub-tropical Morrab Gardens are at the rear of the house & close to all amenities. Offering 5 charming & comfortable bedrooms, all with modern facilities including T.V. & tea/coffee makers, 1 shower en-suite. T.V. lounge. Attractive dining-room with extensive breakfast menu. An ideal base for exploring Mounts Bay & Land's End peninsula.	£10.00	Y	N	N
Mr & Mrs R. Jarratt Kenython Country Guest House Kenython Lane St. Just Penzance TR19 7PT Tel: (0736) 788607 Open: ALL YEAR Map Ref No. 20	Nearest Road: B.3306 This attractive 90 year-old modernised farmhouse stands in 3 secluded acres of ground on the Lands End Peninsula. The comfortable surroundings, friendly atmosphere & good food ensure a delightful stay. Accommodation is in 4 comfortable rooms, 2 with private facilities, all with modern amenities. Guests may also like to use the tennis court & swimming pool. The home cooking is delicious & served with guest's own wine. The house is well located for visiting Penzance, Lands End, St. Ives & St. Michael's Mount. Superb views over countryside.	£14.00	Y	Y	Y
Mr & Mrs R. J. Lee Boscean Country Hotel St Just-in-Penwith Penzance TR19 7QP Tel: (0736) 788748 Open: MAR - NOV Map Ref No. 20	Nearest Road: A.30 A warm & hospitable welcome awaits you at Boscean. A beautiful country house standing in 3 acres of walled grounds overlooking the sea & open countryside. 11 en-suite bedrooms, tea/coffee making facilities. Guest lounge & bar. Delicious meals made with fresh, local or home-grown produce. Situated in an area of natural charm & beauty, an ideal place for touring the interesting places in Lands End peninsula.	£17.00	Y	Y	Y

Ednovean House. Perranuthnoe.

Cornwall

		minimum £ per person	children taken	evening meals	animals taken
M. J. & C. J. Mercer **Roseudian** **Crippas Hill** **St. Just** **Penzance TR19 7RE** **Tel: (0736) 788556** **Open: MAR-OCT** **Map Ref No. 20**	Nearest Road: B.3306 Roseudian, a small quiet guest house, is ideally situated for enjoying all that the Lands End peninsula has to offer. It is a comfortably modernised, traditional Cornish cottage, offering 3 en-suite rooms. Lounge with colour T.V. & large garden for guests to enjoy. A warm welcome, log fire, good home-cooked meals using fresh garden produce all contribute towards a friendly & relaxing atmosphere. Children over 5 years. Dogs by r arrangement only.	£15.00	Y	Y	Y
Mr & Mrs A. Compton **Ednovean House** **Perranuthnoe** **Penzance** **TR20 9L** **Tel: (0736) 711071** **Open: ALL YEAR** **Map Ref No. 21**	Nearest Road: A.30 This really is a super place to stay; a 150 year-old house offering 9 delightful, comfortable rooms,most having ensuite facilities & panoramic sea views. Situated in 1 acre of gardens & overlooking St. Michael's Mount & the entire bay. Relax in an extremely comfortable lounge, library or informal bar. Enjoy a wide selection of fine food & wines in the candlelit dining room, where vegetarians are also catered for. Ideal for coastal walks & exploring from the Lizard to Lands End.	£16.50 *see PHOTO over*	Y	Y	Y
David & Pamela Green **Acton Vean** **Trevean Lane** **Rosudgeon** **Penzance TR20 9PF** **Tel: (0736) 762675** **Open: MAR - NOV** **Map Ref No. 22**	Nearest Road: A.394 On the edge of beyond, 6 miles from Penzance, Acton Vean is a gracious modern home of distinction on the southern coastal slope. It shares the uniquely privileged position of adjacent Acton Castle, with uninterrupted views of St. Michael's Mount & the bay, & access to the coastal footpath. Visitors welcomed as "house guests". 2 sea-facing bedrooms, barrel-ceiling sitting-room & quiet lovely gardens.	£17.00	N	N	N
Mr & Mrs K. Wooldridge **Beach Dunes Hotel** **Ramoth Way** **Perranporth TR6 0BY** **Tel: (0872) 572263** **Fax 0872 573824** **Open: MAR - OCT** **Map Ref No. 23**	Nearest Road: A.30, B.3285 A small friendly hotel pleasantly situated in almost an acre of grounds amidst the sand dunes adjoing the golf course & overlooking Perran Bay with its 3 miles of golden sands & Atlantic beach. Ten bedrooms, most en-suite, have tea/coffee, television/radio & private telephone. Excellent food is freshly prepared. Facilities include indoor pool, squash court, a cosy bar & residents' lounge. An excellent touring centre.	£20.50	Y	Y	Y
Sylvia & Derek Richards **Landaviddy Manor** **Landaviddy Lane** **Polperro** **PL13 2R** **Tel: (0503) 72210** **Open: FEB - OCT** **Map Ref No. 24**	Nearest Road: A.38 A beautiful, licenced, 18th century, small Manor House built of traditional Cornish stone. Situated in lovely grounds on a hillside above the picturesque fishing village of Polperro, commanding charming views of the bay & surrounding National Trust countryside The house retains its former character while incorporating modern comforts. All rooms are individually furnished with lovely linen,T.V. & tea/coffee makers. Many en-suite bathrooms, four-poster or Victorian beds.	£18.00	Y	Y	Y

Cornwall

			minimum £ per person	children taken	evening meals	animals taken
Mrs Marie Barley **Polmarine** **West Street** **Polruan-By Fowey** **PL23 1PL** Tel: (0726) 870459 Fax 0726 870479 Open: MAR - OCT Map Ref No. 25	Nearest Road: A.390 In an idyllic situation right on the water's edge, Polmarine is a converted early 18th Century boathouse retaining its unique character with exposed Cornish stone, oak beam fireplace and herringbone flooring. All rooms tastefully decorated and en-suite, with T.V., tea/cofee facilities. Antique Four-Poster available. Private Quay, mooring line onto the water and direct access to the beach at low tide. Children over 10 welcome.		£17.50	Y	N	N
The Studley Family **Aviary Court** **Mary's Well** **Illogan** **Redruth TR16 4QZ** Tel: (0209) 842256 Open: ALL YEAR Map Ref No. 26	Nearest Road: A.30 Aviary Court stands in two and a half acres of ground on the edge of Illogan Woods. This charming 300 year-old house offers guests a choice of 6 comfortable bedrooms, all with en-suite facilities, over looking the gardens. Each has radio, colour T.V. tea/coffee making facilities & 'phone. The comfortable lounge has a bar & in winter a log fire. The restaurant serves delicious food with a selection of wine.		£22.25	Y	Y	N
Moira & Wally Batty **The Grey Mullet** **2 Bunkers Hill** **St. Ives TR26 1LJ** Tel: (0736) 796635 Open: ALL YEAR Map Ref No. 27	Nearest Road: A.3074 The Grey Mullet, an 18th century Grade II listed building with oak beams & exposed granite walls, is situated in the old fishing & artists' quarters of St. Ives. Visitors are given a warm welcome in comfortable & homely surroundings. Some of the 7 bedrooms are en-suite & all have colour T.V. & tea/coffee making facilities. Vegetarian & low calorie diets catered for.		£15.00	Y	N	N
Diana & Derek Mason **Kandahar** **11 The Warren** **St. Ives TR26 2EA** Tel: (0736) 796183 Open: ALL YEAR (excl. Xmas & New Year) Map Ref No. 27	Nearest Road: A.3074 Kandahar has a unique water's edge location lapped by the Atlantic & overlooking the harbour. The town centre, beaches, coach & railway station are all within 150 yards. All 4 rooms have superb sea views, colour T.V., tea/coffee making facilities, & full central heating. There are 2 ensuite bedrooms & 2 with private bathrooms. English & vegetarian breakfast served. There are many restaurants close by.		£15.00	Y	N	N

When booking your accommodation please mention The Best Bed & Breakfast

Cornwall

		minimum £ per person	children taken	evening meals	animals taken
J. & I. Sykes **The Old Vicarage Hotel** Parc-an-Creet St. Ives TR26 2ET Tel: (0736) 796124 Open: APR-OCT Map Ref No. 27	Nearest Road: A.30 The Old Vicarage Hotel, set in its own wooded grounds, secluded & peaceful, on the edge of the moorlands to the west of St. Ives. Offering 8 bedrooms, 6 with private bath/shower, some with colour T.V. All rooms have tea/coffee makers. Families well catered for. A delightful large garden for guests to relax in & a safe recreation area for children. Convenient for beach & places of interest.	£15.60	Y	Y	Y
Gillian & John Walkley **Rosebud Cottage** Bossiney Tintagel PL34 0AX Tel: (0840) 770861 Open: ALL YEAR(Excl. Nov.) Map Ref No. 28	Nearest Road: A.39, B.3263 A picturesque stone Cornish cottage with secluded garden, within 10 minutes beautiful headland walk to Bossiney Cove which has a fine sandy beach & surfing. Three attractive comfortable rooms with modern facilities & tea/coffee makers. Good home cooking is the order of the day with vegetables from the garden. The evening meals are excellent value. The area has superb countryside for walking, fishing & riding & there are many ruined castles. Port Isaac, Bodwin Moor & Boscastle are a short drive away.	£13.00	Y	Y	Y
John & Christina Rayner **The Old Borough House** Bossiney Tintagel PL34 0AY Tel: (0840) 770475 Open: ALL YEAR Map Ref No. 28	Nearest Road: A.39, B.3263 A delightful 17th century Cornish stone house, formerly the home of J.B. Priestly. It is located between Tintagel & Boscastle in an area of outstanding natural beauty with National Trust property nearby. The 6 comfortable bedrooms, 3 en-suite, have modern amenities tea/coffee makers. A colour T.V. lounge & garden are also available for guests. Close by are safe bathing coves, caves & coastal walks. Delicious food & wine available. Children over 4 years.	£10.50	Y	Y	N
Mrs Jaqueline Gartner **Laniley House** St. Clement, Trispen, Truro TR4 9AU Tel: (0872) 75201 Open: ALL YEAR(Excl.Xmas/ New Year) Map Ref No. 29	Nearest Road: A.3076 Laniley House, formerly a gentleman's residence was built in 1860. It stands in 2 acres of gardens amidst beautiful unspoilt country, yet only 3 miles from the cathedral city of Truro. Offering 3 double rooms, 1 with en-suite facilities. All with T.V. & tea/coffee making facilities. A large comfortable lounge with colour T.V. & a separate breakfast/dining room is provided. A perfect location, ideal for discovering the true old Cornwall.	£15.00	N	N	N

All the establishments mentioned in this guide are members of
The Worldwide Bed & Breakfast Association

Cornwall

		minimum £ per person	children taken	evening meals	animals taken
Mr & Mrs E. Dymond Trevispian-Vean FarmHouse Trevispian-Vean St. Erme Truro TR4 9BL Tel: (0872) 79514 Open: APR - OCT Map Ref No. 30	Nearest Road: A.3076 A delightful farmhouse dating back over 300 years offering a very warm welcome & good accommodation in 12 pleasant, comfortable guest rooms, 9 en-suite. Situated only 7 miles from the coast & surrounded by beautiful countryside it is a perfect base for everyone. Families will particularly enjoy it here as children can look around the farm & there are plenty of places to visit & things to do. There's even a donkey for the children.	£13.50	Y	Y	N
Mr & Mrs M. C. Walker The Old Mill Country House Little Petherick Wadebridge PL27 7QT Tel: (0841) 540388 Open: MAR-NOV Map Ref No. 31	Nearest Road: A.39 This delightful 16th century converted corn mill, complete with water wheel stands in its own grounds at the head of Little Petherick Creek. The bedrooms are furnished with antiques, all are en-suite with tea/coffee making facilities. Licenced with a colour T.V. available for the guests' use. There is also a terraced sun garden. All meals are traditionally cooked & offer very good value. A full 5-course evening meal by arrangement.	£19.75	N	Y	Y

All the establishments mentioned in this guide are members of

The Worldwide Bed & Breakfast Association

If you have any comments regarding your accommodation please send them to us using the form at the back of the guide

All the establishments mentioned in this guide are members of the
Worldwide Bed & Breakfast Association.

If you have any comments regarding your accommodation please send them to us using the form at the back of the book.
We value your comments.

Cumbria

Cumbria

The Lake District National Park is deservedly famous for its magnificent scenery. Here, England's highest mountains & rugged fells surround shimmering lakes & green valleys. But there is more to Cumbria than the beauty of the Lake District. It also has a splendid coastline, easily accessible from the main lakeland centres, as well as a border region where the Pennines, the backbone of England, reach their highest point, towering over the Eden valley.

Formation of the dramatic Lakeland scenery began in the Caledonian period when earth movements raised & folded the already ancient rocks, submerging the whole mass underseas & covering it with limestone. During the ice age great glaciers ground out the lake beds & dales of todays landscape. There is tremendous variety, from the craggy outcrops of the Borrowdale Volcanics with Skiddaw at 3054 feet, to the gentle dales, the open moorlands & the lakes themselves. Each lake is distinctive, some with steep mountain sides sliding straight to the water's edge, others more open with sloping wooded hillsides. Ellerwater, the enchanting "lake of swans" is surrounded by reed & willows at the foot of Langdale. The charm of Ullswater inspired Wordsworth's famous poem "Daffodils". Whilst many lakes are deliberately left undisturbed for those seeking peace, there are others - notably Windermere - where a variety of water sports can be enjoyed. The changeable weather of the mountainous region can produce a sudden transformation in the character of a tranquil lake, raising choppy waves across the darkened surface to break along the shoreline. It is all part of the fascination of Lakeland.

Fell walking is the best way to appreciate the full beauty of the area. There are gentle walks along the dales, & the tops of the ridges are accessible to walkers with suitable footwear & an eye to the weather.

Ponytrekking is another popular way to explore the countryside & there are many centres catering even for inexperienced riders.

There are steamboats on lakes such as Coniston & Ullswater, where you can appreciate the scenery. On Windermere there are a variety of boats for hire, & facilities for water-skiing.

Traditional crafts & skills are on display widely. Craft centres at Keswick, Ambleside & Grasmere, & the annual exhibition of the Guild of Lakeland Craftsmen held in Windermere from mid-July to early September represent the widest variety of craft artistry.

Fairs & festivals flourish in Lakeland. The famous Appleby Horse Fair, held in June is the largest fair of its kind in the world & attracts a huge gypsy gathering. Traditional agriculture shows, sheep dog trials & local sporting events abound. The Grasmere Sports, held each August include gruelling fell races, Cumberland & Westmoreland wrestling, hound trails & pole-leaping.

The traditional custom of "Rushbearing" when the earth floors of the churches were strewn with rushes still survives as a procession in Ambleside & Grasmere & many other villages in the summer months.

The coast of Cumbria stretches from the estuaries of Grange-over-Sands & Burrow-in-Furness by way of the beautiful beaches between Bootle & Cardurnock, to the mouth of the Solway Firth. The coastal areas, especially the estuaries, are excellent for bird-watching. The sand dunes north of the Esk are famous for the colony of black-headed gulls which can be visited by arrangement, & the colony of seabirds at St. Bees Head is the largest in Britain.

Cumbria

Cumbria
Gazeteer
Area of outstanding natural beauty.
The Lake District National Park.

House & Castles
Carlisle Castle - Carlisle
12th century. Massive Norman keep - half-moon battery - ramparts, portcullis & gatehouse.
Brough Castle - Kirby Stephen
13th century - on site of Roman Station between York & Carlisle.
Dacre Castle - Penrith
14th century - massive pele tower.
Sizergh Castle - Kendal
14th century - pele tower - 15th century great hall. English & French furniture, silver & china - Jacobean relics. 18th century gardens.
Belle Island - Boweness-on-Windermere
18th century - interior by Adams Brothers, portraits by Romney.
Swarthmoor Hall - Ulverston
Elizabethan house, mullioned windows, oak staircase, panelled rooms. Home of George Fox - birthplace of Quakerism - belongs to Society of Friends.
Lorton Hall - Cockermouth
15th century pele tower, priest holes, oak panelling, Jacobean furniture.
Muncaster Castle - Ravenglass
14th century with 15th & 19th century additions - site of Roman tower.
Rusland Hall - Ulveston
Georgian mansion with period panelling, sculpture, furniture, paintings.
Levens Hall - Kendal
Elizabethan - very fine panelling & plasterwork - famous topiary garden.
Hill Top - Sawrey
17th century farmhouse home of Beatrix Potter - contains her furniture, china & some of original drawings for her children's books.
Dove Cottage - Town End, Grasmere
William Wordsworth's cottage - still contains his furnishing & his personal effects as in his lifetime.
Brantwood
The Coniston home of John Ruskin, said to be the most beautifully situated house in the Lake District. Exhibition, gardens, bookshops & tearooms

Cathedrals & Churches
Carlisle Cathedral - Carlisle
1130. 15th century choir stalls with painted backs - carved misericords, 16th century screen, painted roof.
Cartmel Priory (St. Mary Virgin)
15th century stalls, 17th century screen, large east window, curious central tower.
Lanercost Priory (St. Mary Magdalene)
12th century - Augustinian - north aisle now forms Parish church.
Greystoke (St. Andrew)
14th/15th century. 19th century misericords. Lovely glass in chancel.
Brougham (St. Wilfred)
15th century carved altarpiece.
Furness Abbey
12th century monastery beautiful setting.
Shap Abbey
12th century with 16th century tower.

Museums & Galleries
Abbot Hall - Kendal
18th century, Georgian house with period furniture, porcelain, silver, pictures, etc. Also contains modern galleries with contemporary paintings, sculptures & ceramics. Changing exhibitions on show.
Carlisle Museum & Art Gallery - Carlisle
Archaeological & natural history collections. National centre of studies of Roman Britain. Art gallery principally exhibiting paintings & porcelain.
Hawkshead Courthouse - Kendal
Exhibition of domestic & working life housed in mediaeval building.
Helena Thompson Museum - Workington
displays Victorian family life & objects of the period.
Lakeland Motor Museum - Holker Hall - Grange-over-Sands
Exhibits cars, bicycles, tricycles, motor cycles, etc., & model cars.
Millom Folk Museum - St. George's Road, Millom
Reconstructions of drift in iron ore mine, miner's cottage kitchen, blacksmith's forge & agricultural relics.
Ravenglass Railway Museum - Ravenglass
History of railways - relics, models, etc.

Cumbria

Wordsworth Museum - Town End, Grasmere
Personal effects, first editions, manuscripts, & general exhibits from the time of William Wordsworth.

Border Regiment Museum - The Castle, Carlisle.
Collection of uniforms, weapons, trophies, documents, medals from 1702, to the present time.

Whitehaven Museum - Whitehaven
History & development of area show in geology, paleontology, archaeology, natural history, etc. Interesting maritime past.

The Beatrix Potter Gallery - Hawkshead

Fitz Park Museum & Art Gallery - Keswick
Collection of manuscripts - Wordsworth, Walpole, Coleridge, Southey.

Things to see & do

Fell Walking - there is good walking throughout Cumbria, but check weather reports, clothing & footwear before tackling the heights.

Pony-trekking - opportunities for novice & experienced riders.

Watersports - Windermere is the ideal centre for sailing, waterskiing, windsurfing, scuba-diving.

Golf - championship course to the north at Silloth.

Grasmere.

CUMBRIA
Map reference

- 01 P. Hart
- 02 Williams
- 03 Wilkinson
- 04 Melling
- 05 Cervetti
- 06 Stobbart
- 07 Edwards
- 08 Sisson
- 09 Staff
- 10 Hodge
- 11 Smith
- 12 Wilkinson
- 13 Clark
- 14 Midwinter
- 15 Bell
- 16 Wightman
- 17 Appleton
- 18 Davenport
- 18 Mackerness
- 18 Graham
- 18 Davis
- 18 Tucker
- 18 Hosey
- 19 Lowe
- 20 Bryant
- 21 White
- 22 Smith
- 22 Tully
- 23 Weightman
- 24 Bewley
- 25 Whittam
- 26 F. Hart
- 27 Howard
- 28 Holmes
- 28 Greenhalgh
- 28 Holcroft
- 28 Lawless
- 28 Cox
- 28 Tyson
- 28 Fielding
- 28 Garside
- 28 Butterworth

Cumbria

		minimum £ per person	children taken	evening meals	animals taken
Peter & Anne Hart Bracken Fell Outgate Ambleside LA22 0NH Tel: (09666) 289 / (05394) 36289 Open: ALL YEAR Map Ref No. 01	Nearest Road: B.5286 Bracken Fell is situated in beautiful open countryside in the picturesque hamlet of Outgate. Located between Ambleside & Hawkshead this makes an ideal base for exploring the Lake District. Accommodation in 6 comfortable rooms all with tea/coffee making facilities & outstanding views. 4 have en-suite facilities. There is also a comfortable lounge & dining room. All major outdoor activities are catered for nearby including sailing, fishing, windsurfing & pony trekking.	£15.00	Y	N	N
Wendy, Dennis & Peter Chandler Walker Ground Manor Hawkshead Ambleside LA22 0PD Tel: (09666) 219 Open: ALL YEAR Map Ref No. 05	Nearest Road: A.591, B5286 A genuine B & B in a 16th century house enjoyed by family & visitors alike for its charm, idyllic setting & living history. Enjoy gentle walks, easy touring, spacious gardens & glorious countryside. Return to log fires, generous hospitality & restful, pretty rooms furnished with antiques. Candlelit dinner parties are held in the spacious conservatory or in the comfortable old dining room. Books, maps & music are for general use.	£25.00	N	Y	N
Mrs M. Wilkinson Long House Great Langdale Ambleside LA22 9J Tel: (09667) 222 Open: FEB-NOV Map Ref No. 03	Nearest Road: B.5343 17th century lakeland cottage enjoying a peaceful position near the foot of Langdale Pikes with superb open views. 2 acres of orchard & garden. Beamed ceilings, stained glass windows & original slate floors. Central heating throughout. Pretty bedrooms, each with a private bathroom, full of character & very individual. Enclosed parking. Ideal walking country & centrally placed for the motorist. Home cooking, with quality food a speciality.	£19.50	Y	Y	N
Tim Melling Nab Cottage Rydal Ambleside LA22 9S Tel: (09665) 311 Open: ALL YEAR Map Ref No. 04	Nearest Road: A.591 A 16th century cottage in an idyllic lakeshore setting, originally owned by De Quincey & once the home of H. Coleridge. 'Nab Cottage" offers accommodation in 7 comfortable rooms, 4 with private bath/shower. A residents' lounge & beautiful garden are available for guests. Delicious breakfasts & evening meals are served. Room service available. An ideal base for walking, fishing & touring the surrounding areas of natural beauty.	£16.50	Y	Y	Y
Mrs Evelyn Cervetti 'Lightwood Farmhouse' Cartmell Fell Bowland Bridge LA11 6NP Tel: (05395) 31454 Open: JAN - NOV Map Ref No. 06	Nearest Road: A.592 Lightwood Farmhouse was built around 1650. Possesses all the modern amenities, whilst retaining the charm of original oak beams & staircase, standing in one & a half acres of gardens with streams running through. Only 2 miles from the southern end of Lake Windermere. Guests' private lounge with T.V. & log fire. Charming dining room facing the early morning sun serving good wholesome food. Using fresh produce wherever possible.	£15.50	Y	Y	N

Cumbria

		minimum £ per person	children taken	evening meals	animals taken
Mrs Sheila Stobbart 'Hullerbank' Talkin Brampton CA8 1LB Tel: (06977) 46668 Open: ALL YEAR(Excl. Xmas./New Year) Map Ref No. 07	Nearest Road: A.69, M.6 Georgian farmhouse dated 1635-1751, standing in its own grounds near the picturesque village of Talkin 2 1/2 miles from Brampton. Superb walking country, central for visiting Hadrian's Wall, Lake District & borders. A warm, friendly, relaxed atmosphere awaits. 3 comfortable bedrooms with private facilities, central heating, electric underblankets & tea makers. A comfortable T.V. lounge & dining room with excellent home cooking including home produced lamb & fresh produce. Non smokers preferred.	£16.00	Y	Y	N
David & Dani Edwards Pickett Howe Brackenthwaite Buttermere Valley CA13 9UY Tel: (0900) 85444 Open: JAN - DEC Map Ref No. 08	Nearest Road: B.5292 A listed 17th century Lakeland longhouse offering caring, friendly and relaxing hospitality. Peacefully set in 15 acres amidst stunning mountain scenery, its slate floors, oak beams and mullioned windows are enhanced by quality furnishings and antiques. Four fully en-suite bedrooms with whirlpool baths, hot drinks trays, telephones, clock radios, Victorian brass and iron bedsteads. Renowned creative cooking, meat and vegetarian; outstanding breakfast.	£26.00	Y	Y	N
Jack & Margaret Sisson Bessiestown Farm Catlowdy, Penton Carlisle CA6 5QP Tel: (0228) 577219/ 77219 Open: ALL YEAR Map Ref No. 09	Nearest Road: B.3618 off A.7 An award-winning farm overlooking the Scottish borders where a friendly relaxing atmosphere is assured. Accommodation is in 5 en-suite rooms with radio & tea/coffee making facilities. Delicious home cooking. Residential license. Guests may also use the indoor heated pool (May-Sept). An excellent base for a holiday or touring. Restricted smoking area.	£21.00 see PHOTO over	Y	Y	N
Brian & Pauline Staff 'Holmhead' Hadrians Wall Greenhead Carlisle CA6 7HY Tel: (06977) 47402 Open: ALL YEAR (excl. Xmas, New Year) Map Ref No. 10	Nearest Road: A.69, B.6318 Standing in 300 acres of grounds with Hadrian's Wall below. Holmhead, a 150 year-old traditional farmhouse is an excellent base for visiting an area full of Roman history. 4 charming en-suite bedrooms with modern amenities. Longest breakfast menu in the world. All meals prepared with fresh produce. Birdswald, the highest remains of the Wall & the Roman Army Museum are close by. Host is a qualified tour guide & expert on Hadrian's Wall. No smoking in bedrooms, dinning or reception rooms.	£18.00 see PHOTO over	Y	'Y	N
Pauline & Bob Hodge Sundawn Carlisle Road, Bridekirk Cockermouth CA13 0PA Tel: (0900) 822384 Open: ALL YEAR Map Ref No. 11	Nearest Road: Bob & Pauline offer you a warm & friendly welcome. The emphasis here is on comfort, relaxation, personal service & imaginative home cooking. From the sunlounge view the panorama of Lakeland Fells & historic market town of Cockermouth, birthplace of William Wordsworth. Accommodation is in 4 tastefully decorated rooms, 2 en-suite, all with modern amenities & tea/coffee makers.	£12.00	Y	Y	Y

Bessiestown Farm. Catlowdy.

Riggs Cottage. Bassenthwaite Lake

Cumbria

		minimum £ per person	children taken	evening meals	animals taken

Brian & May Smith **Link House** **Bassenthwaite Lake** **Cockermouth CA13 9YD** Tel: (07687) 76291 Open: FEB - NOV Map Ref No. 12	Nearest Road: A.66 Link House is a small country house close to Bassenthwaite Lake. There are superb views over the lake, forest & fell. Accommodation is in 8 en-suite rooms with T.V. & tea/coffee makers. In the evenings relax in the lounge in front of the log fire surrounded by elegant furnishings, period pieces & antiques. Meals are always freshly prepared & you can enjoy a delicious 5 course dinner & good wine. Children over 7 years please.	£19.50	Y	Y	N
Fred & Hazel Wilkinson **Riggs Cottage** **Routenbeck** **Bassenthwaite Lake** **Cockermouth** **CA13 9YN** Tel: (07687) 76580 Open: ALL YEAR Map Ref No. 13	Nearest Road: A.66 Riggs Cottage is a super 17th century house, of great character & charm with many exposed oak beams, log burning inglenook fireplace & period furniture. The accommodation in 3 rooms, is comfortable & tastefully furnished with modern amenities. The cosy lounge is available throughout the day. In the nicely furnished dining room tasty home-cooked meals are served using only the best ingredients. Oven fresh bread & home-made preserves are a speciality. An ideal base for a Lakeland holiday.	£17.50 🚭 *see PHOTO over*	Y	Y	N
Angela & Martin Clark **Banerigg Guest House** **Lake Road** **Grasmere** **LA22 9PW** Tel: (09665) 204 Open: ALL YEAR Map Ref No. 14	Nearest Road: A.591 Delightfully situated overlooking Grasmere Lake, is this small, friendly guest house. The informal hospitality & relaxing atmosphere make this a super base for a holiday. All 6 comfortable rooms have modern amenities. There is a pleasant lounge with cosy log fire. Delicious, plentiful home-cooking is served daily. Ideally located for fell walking, sailing, canoeing & fishing. Angela & Martin ensure that guests have a memorable Lakeland holiday. Evening meals for group bookings only.	£17.00 🚭	Y	Y	Y
Mr John Williams **Ees Wyke Country House** **Nr. Sawrey** **Hawkshead LA22 0JZ** Tel: (09666) 393 Open: ALL YEAR Map Ref No. 02	Nearest Road: A.592 Beatrix Potter spent many summers at 'Ees Wyke', a charming Georgian house, standing on the shores of Esthwaite Water, surrounded by breathtaking views of lake, mountains & fells. All our 8 bedrooms have lake views, en-suite bathrooms or showers, T.V. & tea/coffee making facilities. Owners Margaret & John Williams offer a warm welcome & a guarantee of excellent food & service. Ideal for exploring Lakeland.	£28.00	Y	Y	Y
Alison & Philip Midwinter **Low Jock Scar** **Selside** **Kendal** **LA8 9LE** Tel: (053983) 259 Open: MAR - NOV Map Ref No. 15	Nearest Road: A.6 Located in a wonderfully secluded, riverside setting in 6 acres of natural garden & woodland. An idyllic spot situated between the Lakes & Yorkshire Dales - enroute to Scotland - perfect for a few days away from it all. 5 pleasant bedrooms, 3 en-suite with tea/coffee making facilities. Guests have their own comfortable lounge with T.V. Dinners by arrangement. Excellent home cooking using home produce. Vegetarians catered for. Residential licence.	£17.50 🚭 *see PHOTO over*	N	Y	N

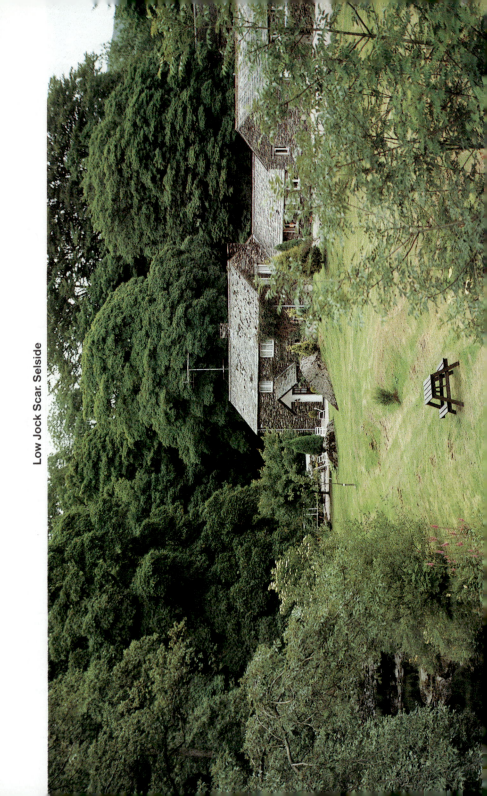

Low Jock Scar, Selside

Cumbria

			minimum £ per person	children taken	evening meals	animals taken
Mrs Ada Wightman The Glen Oxenholme Kendal LA9 7RF Tel: (0539) 726386 Open: MAR - OCT Map Ref No. 16	Nearest Road: M.6 A large detached house standing in its own grounds. Offering 3 rooms, all with private facilities & modern amenities including radio, colour T.V. & tea/coffee making facilities. A delicious full English breakfast is served & there is a lounge for guests to relax in. Situated only minutes from Oxenholme railway station 'The Glen' is an excellent base for touring the idyllic Lake District.		£16.00	N	N	N
Alan & Sheila Appleton Scales Farm Scales Threlkeld Keswick CA12 45Y Tel: (07687) 79660 Open: ALL YEAR Map Ref No. 17	Nearest Road: A66, M6ex 40 Wonderful open views & a friendly personal welcome await you at Scales Farm, a 17th century farmhouse which has been sensitively modernised. All 4 attractively decorated bedrooms have private facilities, colour T.V. & tea/coffee makers provide luxurious accommodation to highest standards. Guests have access to their rooms through a separate entrance at all times. Good pubs & restaurants close by & Keswick & all northern lakes within easy reach.		£17.00	Y	N	Y
David A. Davenport Greystones Ambleside Road Keswick CA12 4DP Tel: (07687) 73108 Open: FEB-NOV Map Ref No. 18	Nearest Road: A.66 Greystones is a comfortable traditional Lakeland house where David & Eileen aim to create a friendly atmosphere for a happy relaxed holiday. All bedrooms have private facilities, most with excellent fell views. Imaginative home-made meals are served using the best quality fresh produce available. Situated in a quiet area of Keswick on Derwentwater, Greystones is only a short distance from the town centre, fells & lakeshore.		£15.50	Y	Y	N
Hilda & Geoff Mackerness Claremont House Chestnut Hill Keswick CA12 4LT Tel: (07687) 72089 Open: ALL YEAR Map Ref No. 18	Nearest Road: A.591 Situated in a three quarter acre of woodland garden. This 150 year old lodge house offers accommodation in 1 single & 5 double bedrooms, all with en-suite facilities, 1 with spa bath, lace canopied beds, clock/radio & tea/coffee makers. A comfortable lounge, colour T.V. & bar licence. Delicious food, home-made bread. Vegetarians are especially welcome.		£24.00	Y	Y	N
Ron & Pauline Graham Thornleigh Guest House 23 Bank Street Keswick CA12 5JZ Tel: (07687) 72863 Open: ALL YEAR Map Ref No. 18	Nearest Road: A.591, A.66 A traditional Lakeland stone building situated in Keswick town, yet with magnificent views over the surrounding hills & fells. All bedrooms are en-suite with colour T.V. & tea/coffee making facilities. Thornleigh is a family run establishment with resident chef. A warm welcome is extended to all guests, old & new.		£17.00	Y	Y	Y

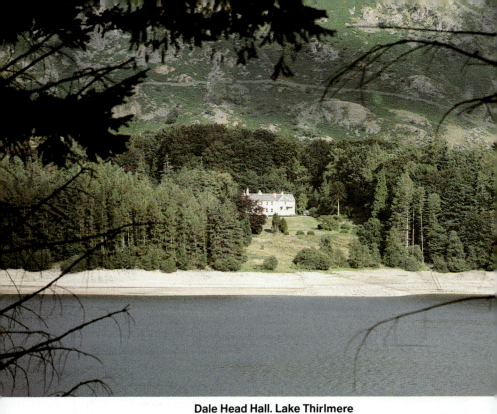

Dale Head Hall. Lake Thirlmere

Cumbria

		minimum £ per person	children taken	evening meals	animals taken
Mr & Mrs A. Lowe Dale Head Hall Lake Thirlmere Keswick CA12 4TN Tel: (07687) 72478 Open: ALL YEAR Map Ref No. 19	Nearest Road: A.591, A.66 Lose yourself in the ancient woodlands & mature gardens of an Elizabethan country manor, set serenely on the shores of Lake Thirlmere. Delicious dinners prepared by mother & daughter, using fresh prduce from the Victorian kitchen garden, served with fine wines in the oak beamed dining room. 9 individually decorated bedrooms, some with four-posters, each with bath/shower rooms. Together with the lounge & bar there are unspoilt views across lawns lakes & fells.	£35.00 *see PHOTO over*	Y	Y	Y
Mr & Mrs T. J. Tucker Rooking House Portinscale Keswick CA12 5RD Tel: (07687) 72506 Open: MAR-DEC Map Ref No. 18	Nearest Road: A.66 Rooking House is a fine Edwardian house situated in the village of Portinscale 1 mile west of Keswick. There are superb views of Lake Derwentwater & surrounding hills. Excellent cuisine & friendly atmosphere are assured. All 6 rooms have en-suite facilities, tea makers & colour T.V. There is a private spacious car park. Horse riding, sailing, rowing, sail-boarding & fishing facilities are available within 10 minutes walk. Children over 9 years.	£20.50	Y	Y	N
Mrs J. Davis The Mount Portinscale Keswick CA12 5RD Tel: (07687) 73070 Open: MAR - NOV Map Ref No. 18	Nearest Road: A.66 A large Victorian semi-detached house, tastefully decorated & maintaining original features, providing a friendly home-from-home atmosphere. Offering 4 bedrooms, 3 en-suite facilities & tea/coffee making makers. Lovely views over Lake Derwentwater & Skiddaw. Good walking around Keswick & Portinscale as well as boating, fishing, windsurfing & riding. An ideal base for touring the beautiful surrounding lakeside area.	£17.00	Y	Y	Y
Mr & Mrs R Hosey Derwentwater Marina Portinscale Keswick CA12 5RF Tel: (07687) 72912 Open: MAR - NOV Map Ref No. 18	Nearest Road: A.66 Derwentwater Marina, on the lake shore 1 mile from Keswick, offers affordable luxury in chalet type accommodation with breakfast. En-Suite rooms with patios and lake and mountain views, T.V., fridge, toaster, kettle etc. and the ingredients for you to prepare your own continental breakfast. Windsurf, sail, canoe, walk and climb, or just relax and enjoy the wonderful views - the choice is yours.	£18.00	N	N	N
Mrs Lesley White Beckfoot Country Guest House Helton Penrith CA10 2QB Tel: (09313) 241 Open: MAR - NOV Map Ref No. 21	Nearest Road: M.6, A fine old residence featuring a half-panelled hall, staircase, attractive panelled dining room. Set in 3 acres of grounds in the delightful Lake District, it is a quiet, peaceful retreat for a holiday base & is within easy reach of the many pleasure spots in the area. Offering 6 rooms, all with private shower/bathroom, & tea/coffee making facilities. A dining room, drawing & reading room. This is a delightful base for a touring holiday.	£22.50	Y	Y	Y

Cumbria

			per person minimum £	children taken	evening meals	animals taken
Ian Bryant & Jocelyn Ruffle Hipping Hall Cowan Bridge Kirkby Lonsdale LA6 2JJ Tel: (05242) 71187 Open: MAR - NOV Map Ref No. 20	Nearest Road: A.65 Hipping Hall is a 17th century country house set in 4 acres of walled gardens on the edge of the Yorkshire Dales National Park, 3 miles from pretty Kirkby Lonsdale & only half an hour from Windermere. The 5 bedrooms & 2 apartments are attractively furnished & fully equipped. Guests dine together in the beautiful Great Hall which has a Minstrel's Gallery. All dishes are freshly prepared by Jos Ruffle from home & local produce. Children over 12 years.		£34.50 see PHOTO over	Y	Y	Y
I. & D. Bewley Fair Place Wholefood Guest House Fair Place Water Millock on Ullswater Penrith CA11 0LR Tel: (07684) 86235 Open: MID FEB - MID NOV Map Ref No. 24	Nearest Road: M.6 Watermillock is a scattered hamlet on Ullswater in the English Lakes National Park. 'Fair Place', once the village school, has been modernised yet retains the original handsome rag-stone facade. 3 rooms, 1 en-suite, all with colour T.V. & tea/coffee making facilities. Delicious wholefood breakfasts are served. Lounge available throughout the day. Sailing, fishing & pony trekking nearby. Dorothy & Ian provide a caring service with every comfort & convenience.		£15.00	Y	N	N
Mrs Sheila Smith Highgate Farm Penrith CA11 0SE Tel: (07684) 83339 Open: FEB - NOV Map Ref No. 22	Nearest Road: M.6, A.66 A lovely stone built farmhouse dated 1730, set on a 400 acre mixed working farm. Offering a warm welcome & personal attention, full English breakfast served, tastefully decorated with old beams & brasses. Accommodation is in 5 bedrooms, 2 with king-sized old brass beds, all rooms have colour T.V. & tea/coffee making facilities. An ideal base for touring, Lake Ullswater is only 4 miles away. Children is over 5.		£15.00	Y	N	N
Christine Weightman Near Howe Farm Hotel Mungrisdale Penrith CA11 0SH Tel: (07687) 79678 Open: APR - OCT Map Ref No. 23	Nearest Road: A.66 A comfortable traditional Cumbrian family house where guests receive a warm friendly welcome. Standing in 300 acres of rolling moorland, it offers a choice of 7 nice bedrooms, most with private facilities, a colour T.V. lounge, games room & a smaller lounge with a well stocked bar with log fire. In the pleasant homely dining room, freshly prepared meals are served, using local produce when possible. Close by are golf, fishing, pony trekking, boating & walking.		£14.00	Y	Y	Y
Mrs Marjorie Whittam Netherdene Guest House Troutbeck Penrith CA11 0SJ Tel: (07684) 83475 Open: FEB-NOV Map Ref No. 25	Nearest Road: A.66, M.6 A traditional Lakeland house in its own quiet grounds with extensive mountain views. Offering a warm welcome & personal attention. Accommodation is in 4 very comfortable bedrooms, 1 en-suite, each with modern amenities including colour T.V. & tea/coffee making facilities. A cosy lounge with log fire & T.V. available. Delicious home cooking. An ideal base for exploring the lake District. Pony trekking, golf, fell walking & boating nearby.		£13.50	Y	Y	N

Hipping Hall. Kirkby Lonsdale

Cumbria

			minimum £ per person	children taken	evening meals	animals taken
Mrs Carole Tully **Brandelhow Guest House** **1 Portland Place** **Penrith CA11 7QN** Tel: (0768) 64470 Open: ALL YEAR Map Ref No. 22	Nearest Road: M.6, A.6, M66 Brandelhow is a very pleasant Victorian house situated in the lovely market town of Penrith. Accommodation is in 5 tastefully decorated, bright & comfortable rooms all with modern amenities, central heating, colour T.V. & tea/coffee making facilities. Penrith is an ideal base for touring the Lake District & enjoying the usual outdoor sporting activities. A warm & friendly welcome is assured.		£13.00	Y	N	N
Frank & Lesley Hart **Cross Keys Hotel** **Cautley** **Sedbergh LA10 5NE** Tel: (05396) 20284 Open: MAR-DEC Map Ref No. 26	Nearest Road: M.6 Ex 37 A tiny 400 year-old National Trust inn within the Yorkshire Dales National Park. Magnificent setting with the most impressive view of the Howgill Fells. The Cross Keys has a homely, traditional & relaxing atmosphere. Beautifully cooked food, all home-made & served with guests' own wine. Log fires & no T.V. Weekly walking holidays. Wainright's Howgill & Ourlying Fell walks with qualified mountain guide.		£22.00	Y	Y	N
Ron & Mary Howard **The Royal Oak Hotel** **5 West Street** **Wigton CM23 5QA1** Tel: (06973) 42393 Open: ALL YEAR Map Ref No. 27	Nearest Road: A.596 Nothing is too much trouble at The Royal Oak, an attractive 17th coaching inn, with original cobbled courtyard. Accommodation is in 11 pretty, comfortable bedrooms, some en-suite, all with modern amenities, h & c, colour T.V. & tea/coffee making facilities. The restaurant is unique & the dinner menu delicious. The sole aim of Ron & Mary is to make your stay happy & memorable.		£14.50	Y	Y	Y
Sheila & Trevor Holmes **Boston House** **The Terrace** **Windermere LA23 1AJ** Tel: (05394) 43654 Open: FEB - NOV Map Ref No. 28	Nearest Road: A.591 Very attractive Victorian house set on the edge of Windermere, secluded but with easy access to all facilities. Private off-street parking. Guests arriving by bus/train are met free of charge. Six spacious bedrooms, three en-suite & most with colour T.V., all with tea/coffee making facilities. Extensive a la carte breakfast. Caters exclusively for non smokers.		£12.50	Y	N	Y
Anthony & Aurea Greenhalgh **The Archway Guest House** **13 College Road** **Windermere LA23 1BY** Tel: (09662) 5613 Open: ALL YEAR Map Ref No. 28	Nearest Road: A.591 Impeccable small Victorian guest house, quietly situated a stone's throw from Windermere village centre. Yet with marvellous, open mountain views. Beautifully furnished throughout - antiques, interesting paintings & prints, good books, fresh flowers. Accommodation is in 6 individually decorated bedrooms, mostly en-suite, all with telephone, colour T.V. & tea/coffee trays, Victorian patchwork quilts. Renowned for gourmet home cooking using fresh local produce. Home baked bread. Excellent wine list. No smoking.		£19.00	Y	Y	N

Cumbria

			minimum £ per person	children taken	evening meals	animals taken
Sheila & Joe Lawless Green Gables 37 Broad Street Windermere LA23 2AB Tel: (05394) 43886 Open: ALL YEAR Map Ref No. 28	Nearest Road: A.591, A.592 Green Gables is a pleasant family-run Victorian guest house located in the centre of Windermere. The shops, restaurants, bus & railway stations close by, make it a good base for touring the area. Accommodation is in 6 cosy bedrooms, some non smoking, 2 with private facilities, all with colour T.V., tea/coffee makers & hair dryers. A comfortable T.V. lounge is also available.		£11.00	Y	Y	N
Frances & Brian Holcroft Lynwood Guest House Broad Street Windermere LA23 2AB Tel: (05394) 42550 Open: ALL YEAR Map Ref No. 28	Nearest Road: A.591 A Victorian, Lakeland stone house built in 1865; offering 9 centrally heated bedrooms, 4 with private bathrooms, all with modern amenities, including colour T.V. & tea/coffee making facilities. Guests may relax in the T.V. lounge available throughout the day. Centrally located, only 150 yards from village shops & restaurants & only 5 mins. from the bus & railway station. Host is a lakeland tour guide, & is happy to assist in planning your stay.		£10.00	Y	N	N
Mr & Mrs Cox Kirkwood Guest House Prince's Road Windermere LA23 2DD Tel: (05394) 43907/ (09662) 3907 Open: ALL YEAR Map Ref No. 28	Nearest Road: A.591 Kirkwood occupies a quiet spot between Windermere and Bowness, offering guests a warm and friendly atmosphere with individual, personal service. Rooms are large, mostly en-suite, and all have T.V. and tea/coffee facilities. Comfortable, quiet lounge. Guests can be met from train or coach, and your hosts will be pleased to help plan tours or walks, with maps provided. Drying facilities. Packed lunches available.		£14.00	Y	N	y
Barbara & Bob Tyson Hawksmoor Guest House Lake Road Windermere LA23 2EQ Tel: (05394) 42110 Open: ALL YEAR Map Ref No. 28	Nearest Road: A.591 Hawksmoor is situated halfway between the centres of Windermere & Bowness, just 10 minutes walk from the lake. Standing in lovely grounds, this creeper-clad house has 10 charming rooms all en-suite with garden views. Some with 4-poster beds, some strictly no smoking. A most comfortable residents' lounge with colour T.V. & garden for guests' enjoyment. The house has a residential licence. Boating, golf, tennis, swimming, fishing & pony trekking all nearby. Phone for availability before booking.		£18.00 see PHOTO over	Y	Y	N
Alan & Dorothy Fielding Rosemount Lake Road Windermere LA23 2EQ Tel: (05394) 43739 Open: ALL YEAR Map Ref No. 28	Nearest Road: A.591 A delightful guest house built in traditional lakeland style, ideally situated between Windermere & the lake, offering warm & comfortable accommodation. Bedrooms, including 2 singles, are attractively furnished, with private facilities, colour T.V. & tea tray. Delicious English breakfasts served (or refreshing fruit alternative). Friendly & personal attention is extended from the resident owners, Alan & Dorothy Fielding. Licenced bar. Car parking.		£18.50	Y	N	N

Hawksmoor Guest House.   Windermere.

Cumbria

		minimum £ per person	children taken	evening meals	animals taken
Iain & Jackie Garside Fayrer Holme Country House Upper Storrs Road Bowness Windermere LA23 3JP Tel / Fax: (05394) 88195 Open: FEB - DEC Map Ref No. 28	Nearest Road: A.5074 Iain & Jackie welcome you to their beautiful lakeland home peacefully set in 5 acres of landscaped gardens overlooking the lake & mountains. Delightful decor & tastefully furnished, spacious en-suite rooms with modern amenities. Some four poster rooms & jacuzzis. Convenient for golf club, sailing, restaurants etc. Free use of local leisure centre. Free colour brochure available.	£25.00	Y	N	Y
Brenda Butterworth Orrest Head House Windermere LA23 IJG Tel: (05394) 44315 Open: MAR - OCT Map Ref No. 28	Nearest Road: A.591 A traditional Lakeland style house, partly 17th century, standing in 3 acres of garden. Located above Windermere village, with distant & panoramic views towards the lake & mountains beyond. Accommodation is in 5 comfortable rooms, all with modern amenities & tea/coffee making facilities. Guests can relax in the residents' lounge with colour T.V. or in the tranquil garden with its lovely surroundings. Convenient for railway station & bus terminus. Ample parking.	£14.00 (no smoking)	Y	N	Y

All the establishments mentioned in this guide are members of
The Worldwide Bed & Breakfast Association

Derby & Staffs

Derbyshire
(East Midlands)

A county with everything but the sea, this was Lord Byron's opinion of Derbyshire, & the special beauty of the Peak District was recognised by its designation as Britain's first National Park.

Purple heather moors surround craggy limestone outcrops & green hills drop to sheltered meadows or to deep gorges & tumbling rivers.

Derbyshire's lovely dales have delightful names too - Dove Dale, Monk's Dale, Raven's Dale, Water-cum-Jolly-Dale, & they are perfect for walking. The more adventurous can take up the challenge of the Pennine Way, a 270 mile pathway from Edale to the Scottish border.

The grit rock faces offer good climbing, particularly at High Tor above the River Derwent, & underground there are extensive & spectacular caverns. There are show caves at the Heights of Abraham, which you reach by cable-car, & at Castleton, source of the rare Blue John mineral, & at Pole's Cavern in Buxton where there are remarkable stalactites & stalagmites.

Buxton's splendid Crescent reflects the town's spa heritage, & the Opera House is host to an International Festival each summer.

The waters at Matlock too were prized for their curative properties & a great Hydro was built there in the last century, to give treatment to the hundreds of people who came to "take the waters".

Bakewell is a lovely small town with a fascinating market, some fine buildings & the genuine Bakewell Pudding, (known elsewhere as Bakewell tart).

Well-dressing is a custom carried on throughout the summer in the villages & towns. It is a thanksgiving for the water, that predates the arrival of Christianity in Britain. Flower-petals, leaves, moss & bark are pressed in

Haddon Hall; Derby.

Derby & Staffs

intricate designs into frames of wet clay & erected over the wells, where they stay damp & fresh for days.

The mining of lead & the prosperity of the farms brought great wealth to the landowning families who were able to employ the finest of architects & craftsmen to design & build their great houses. Haddon Hall is a perfectly preserved 12th century manor house with with terraced gardens of roses & old-fashioned flowers. 17th century Chatsworth, the "Palace of the Peak", houses a splendid collection of paintings, drawings, furniture & books, & stands in gardens with elaborate fountains.

Staffordshire
(Heart of England)

Staffordshire is a contrast of town & county. Miles of moorland & dramatic landscapes lie to the north of the country, & to the south is the Vale of Trent & the greenery of Cannock Chase. But the name of Staffordshire invokes that of the Potteries, the area around Stoke-on-Trent where the world-renowned ceramics are made.

The factories that produce the Royal Doulton, Minton, Spode & Coalport china will arrange tours for visitors, & there is a purpose-built visitor centre at Barlaston displaying the famous Wedgwood tradition.

The Gladstone Pottery Museum is set in a huge Victorian potbank, & the award-winning City museum in Stoke-on-Trent has a remarkable ceramics collection.

There is lovely scenery to be found where the moorlands of Staffordshire meet the crags & valleys of the Peak District National Park. From the wild & windy valleys of The Roaches (from the French 'roche') you can look across the county to Cheshire & Wales. Drivers can take high moorland roads that are marked out as scenic routes.

The valleys of the Dove & Manifold are beautiful limestone dales & ideal for walking or for cycling. Sir Izzak Walton, author of 'The Compleat Angler', drew his inspiration, & his trout, from the waters here.

The valley of the River Churnet is both pretty & peaceful, being largely inaccessible to cars. The Caldon Canal, with its colourful narrowboats, follows the course of the river & there are canal-side pubs, picnic areas, boat rides & woodland trails to enjoy. The river runs through the grounds of mock-Gothic Alton Towers, now a leisure park.

The Vale of Trent is largely rural with small market towns, villages, river & canals.

Cannock Chase covers 20 square miles of heath & woodland & is the home of the largest herd of fallow deer in England. Shugborough Hall stands in the Chase. The ancestral home of Lord Lichfield, it also houses the Staffordshire County Museum & a farm for rare breeds including the famous Tamworth Pig.

Burton-on-Trent is known as the home of the British brewery industry & there are two museums in the town devoted to the history of beer.

Lichfield is a small & picturesque city with a cathedral which dates from the 12th century & has three graceful spires known as the 'Ladies of the Vale'. Dr. Samuel Johnson was born in the city & his house is now a museum dedicated to his life & work.

One of the Vale's villages retains its mediaeval tradition by performing the Abbot's Bromley Horn Dance every September.

Derby & Staffs

Derbyshire
Gazeteer
Areas of outstanding natural beauty.
Peak National Park. The Dales.

Houses & Castles
Chatsworth - Bakewell
17th century, built for 1st. Duke of Devonshire. Furniture, paintings & drawings, books, etc. Fine gardens & parklands.
Haddon Hall - Bakewell
Mediaeval manor house - complete. Terraced rose gardens.
Hardwick Hall - Nr. Chesterfield
16th century - said to be more glass than wall. Fine furniture, tapestries & furnishings. Herb garden.
Kedlestone Hall - Derby
18th century - built on site of 12th century Manor house. Work of Robert Adam - has world famous marble hall. Old Master paintings. 11th century church nearby.
Melbourne Hall - Nr. Derby
12th century origins - restored by Sir John Coke. Fine collection of pictures & works of art. Magnificent gardens & famous wrought iron pergola.
Sudbury Hall - Sudbury
Has examples of work of the greatest craftsmen of the period-Grinling Gibbons, Pierce and Laguerre.
Winster Market House   Nr. Matlock
17th century stone built market house.

Cathedrals & Churches
Chesterfield (St. Mary & All Saints)
13th & 14th centuries. 4 chapels, polygonal apse, mediaeval screens, Jacobean pulpit.
Derby (All Saints)
Perpendicular tower - classical style - 17th century plate, 18th century screen.
Melbourne (St. Michael & St. Mary)
Norman with two west towers & crossing tower. Splendid plate, 18th century screen.
Normbury (St. Mary & St. Barloke)
14th century - perpendicular tower. Wood carving & brasses.
Wirksworth (St. Mary)
13th century, restored & enlarged. Norman font & 17th century font. Brasses, mediaeval sculpture - 9th century coffin lid.

Museums & Galleries
Buxton Museum - Buxton
Local history, geology & mineralogy, including famous Blue John. Animal remains from Pleistocene period onwards.
Old House Museum - Bakewell
Early Tudor house with interior walls exposed to show wattle & daub, open-timber chamber. Kitchen implements, craftmen's tools, costumes.
Lecture Hall - Chesterfield
Exhibitions of photography, art, etc.
Museums & Art Gallery - Derby
Archeology, geology, local & natural history, model rail layout.
Industrial Museum - Derby
Rolls-Royce collection of historic aero-engines.
Regimental Museum - Derby
9th/12th Lancers.
Elvaston Castle Working Estate Museum - Nr. Derby
Life on the estate re-created as it was in 1910, with cottage, craft workshops & livestock.
Museum of Childhood - Sudbury Hall, Nr. Derby
Life of children in the past on display in the former servants' wing of Sudbury Hall.
National Tramway Museum - Crich, Nr. Matlock
Rides along a one-mile scenic tramway with a collection of tramcars from Britain & overseas.

Other things to see & do
Caudwell's Mill - Rowsley,
19th century water-powered working flour mill, with craft centre.
Blue John Cavern - Castleton
Stalagmites & stalactites, & source of the rare Blue John stone.
The Heights of Abraham - Matlock Bath
Spectacular cable car ride up to wooded landscape with two show caverns, prospect tower & visitor centre.
Poole's Cavern - Buxton
One of the finest natural limestone caverns, with stalactites & stalagmites.

Derby & Staffs

Speedwell Cavern - Castleton
Underground boat journey to show cavern.
Treak Cliff Cavern - Castleton
Richest known veins of the rare Blue John stone, stalactites & stalagmites in mainly natural cavern.
Buxton Micrarium - Buxton
Unique exhibition of the natural world under the microscope, with hundreds of specimens & living creatures to see.
Dinting Railway Centre - Glossop
Famous steam locomotives & rides.

Staffordshire
Gazeteer
Houses & Castles
Ancient High House - Stafford
16th century - largest timber-framed town house in England.
Shugborough - Nr. Stafford
Ancestral home of the Earl of Lichfield. Mansion house, paintings, silver, ceramics, furniture. County Museum. Rare Breeds Farm.
Moseley Old Hall - Nr. Wolverhampton
Elizabethan house formerly half-timbered.
Stafford Castle
Large & well-preserved Norman castle in grounds with castle trail.
Tamworth Castle
Norman motte & bailey castle with later additions. Museum.

Cathedrals & Churches
Croxden Abbey
12th century foundation Cistercian abbey. Ruins of 13th century church.
Ingestre (St. Mary the Virgin)
A rare Wren church built in 1676.
Lichfield Cathedral
Unique triple-spired 12th century cathedral.
Tamworth (St. Editha's)
Founded 963, rebuilt 14th century. Unusual double spiral staircase.
Tutbury (St. Mary's)
Norman church with impressive West front.

Museums & Galleries
City Museum & Art Gallery - Stoke-on-Trent
Modern award-winning museum. Ceramics, decorative arts, etc.
Dr. Johnson Birthplace Museum - Lichfield
Gladstone Pottery Museum - Longton
Izaak Walton Cottage & Museum - Shallowfield, Nr. Stafford
National Brewery Museum & the Bass Museum of Brewing-both in Stoke-on-Trent
Stafford Art Gallery & Craft Shop - Stafford
Major gallery for the visual arts & centre for quality craftsmanship.

Other things to see & do
Alton Towers - Alton
Former estate of the Earls of Shrewsbury, now leading leisure park. Landscape gardens, Pagoda fountain.
Dorothy Clive Garden - Willoughbridge
Rare trees, rhododendrons & azaleas.
Foxfield Steam Railway - Blythe Bridge, Nr Stoke-on-Trent
5-mile round trip through rural Staffordshire
Froghall - Caldon Canal
Canal boat trips Victorian-style.
Josiah Wedgwood Visitor Centre - Barlaston
Moorlands Farm Park - Nr. Ipstones
Rare British breeds.
Natural Sciences Centre - Newchapel
Observatory, Stoke-on-Trent
Intriguing conservation site. Observatory. Exhibitions on alternative energy.

Izaak Walton's Cottage. Staffs.

DERBYSHIRE & STAFFORDSHIRE

Map reference

01 Challinor
02 Gilbert
04 Statham
05 Moffett
06 Mackenzie
06 Harry
06 Annesley
07 Ford
08 Groom
11 Barber
12 Winterton
12 Sutcliffe
13 Martin
14 Bunce
16 Wheeler
17 Grey
18 Hodgson
17 White
19 Adams
20 Ball
21 Moreton

Derbyshire

		minimum £ per person	children taken	evening meals	animals taken
Mrs Margaret Ford Horsleygate Hall Horsleygate Lane Holmesfield S18 5WD Tel: (0742) 890333 Open: ALL YEAR Map Ref No. 07	Nearest Road: B.6051 Lying on the eastern side of the Peak Park, Horsleygate Hall is an informal country house, set amongst large, secluded grounds. The accommodation is country style, comfortable & attractive, with excellent views of the surrounding countryside from all rooms. The Hall, in the peaceful & rural Cordwell Valley, is well placed for walking, riding & exploring Derbyshire. Chatsworth House & Bakewell nearby. Stabling also available.	£16.00	Y	N	N
Mrs B. M. Challinor The Old Orchard Stoney Lane Thorpe Thorpe Ashbourne DE6 2AW Tel: (033529) 410 Open: MAR - NOV Map Ref No. 01	Nearest Road: A.515 A relaxed & friendly atmosphere is found at The Old Orchard. A modern, split-level bungalow, quietly situated in the Peak District National Park, in the heart of the Derbyshire Dales. The accommodation in 4 rooms is comfortable, 2 rooms with en-suite facilities. Lots of walks, trails, cycle hire, cycle routes & horse riding close by. An ideal centre for visiting stately homes; Chatsworth, Haddon Hall, Alton Towers, Matlock Bath, Cable Chair etc.	£16.00	Y	N	N
Capt. & Mrs D.A. Statham Rock House Alport Bakewell DE4 1LG Tel: (0629) 636736 Open: ALL YEAR Map Ref No. 04	Nearest Road: A.6 This grade II listed Georgian house, once part of the Dukes of Rutlands estate, offers 3 charming bedrooms, each with private bathroom. A hearty breakfast is cooked to order & guests choose their own selection of dishes. A private sitting room is available throughout the day. Rock House is surrounded by the Peak National Park with its stately homes, villages & many rural delights. Private car park.	£18.00	N	N	N
Mrs Sheila Gilbert Castle Cliffe Private Hotel Monsal Head Bakewell DE4 1NL Tel: (0629) 640258 Open: ALL YEAR Map Ref No. 02	Nearest Road: A.6 A Victorian stone house built on high ground with superb views from all 9 bedrooms. 2 rooms with en-suite facilities, the others with private facilities & tea/coffee makers. The cosy lounge & bar have open fires. Home-made food with an emphasis on regional British dishes. Beautiful walks straight from the hotel into Monsal Dale & over the famous viaduct. Conveniently located for visiting Derbyshire's peaks, dales, caverns & historic houses.	£18.00	Y	Y	N
Mr & Mrs J. M. Moffett Biggin Hall Biggin-by-Hartington Buxton SK17 0DH Tel: (0298) 84451 Open: ALL YEAR Map Ref No. 05	Nearest Road: A.515 Dinner, bed & breakfast only. A really delightful 17th century stone house, completely restored, keeping all the character of its origins, massive oak beams. There are 14 beautiful rooms, all charmingly furnished, 1 with 4-poster bed, all with en-suite facilities & modern amenities. Visitors have the choice of 2 sitting rooms, 1 with colour T.V. & library & a lovely garden. The house is beautifully furnished with many antiques. Price includes evening meals which are truly superb & great value.	£20.00 *see PHOTO over*	N	Y	Y

Biggin Hall.   Biggin by Hartington.

Derbyshire

	minimum £ per person	children taken	evening meals	animals taken
Mary Mackenzie **Staden Grange** **Free Post (SK1335)** **Staden** **Buxton SK17 9YB** **Tel: (0298) 24965** **Fax (0298) 72067** **Open: ALL YEAR** **Map Ref No. 06** Nearest Road: A.515 A pleasant, spacious house in 250 acres enjoying uninterrupted views over open farmland. Attractive & comfortable en-suite rooms, with colour T.V., & tea/coffee makers. A comfortable lounge with colour T.V. & a large garden for guests' use, also riding & shooting plus a sauna & spa pool, there is also a fine golf course nearby. Only 2 miles from Buxton, this is a wonderful base for touring, walking & riding in this magnificent scenic region.	£19.50	Y	Y	Y
Mrs Linda Harry **'Coningsby Guest House'** **6 Macclesfield Road** **Buxton SL17 9AH** **Tel: (0298) 26735** **Open: ALL YEAR** **Map Ref No. 06** Nearest Road: A.515, A.6, John & Linda extend a warm welcome to "non-smoking" guests. At Coningsby every comfort is catered for. Accommodation is in 3 tastefully decorated comfortable rooms, each with en-suite facilities, T.V. &fleeper tea/coffee makers. There is a separate guests' lounge & an elegant dining room where breakfast & dinner are served. Coningsby is a super place to stay & explore the Peak District's beautiful places, as well as Buxton itself.	£17.50 (no smoking)	N	Y	N
Anita & John Annesley **Buxton View** **74 Corbar Road** **Buxton** **SK17 6RJ** **Tel: (0298) 79222** **Open: MAR - NOV** **Map Ref. No. 06** Nearest Road: A.6, A.515 A warm welcome awaits you at Buxton View. A comfortable home built of local limestone, commanding a surperb view of the surrounding hills & moor. Offering 5 pleasantly decorated bedrooms each with private facilities, colour T.V. & tea/coffee makers. Delicious full English breakfasts are served. Guests can relax in the comfortable sitting room complete with maps & guide books to help plan excursions. A short walk to this elegant spa town centre.	£16.00	Y	Y	Y
Mrs R. A. Groom **The Manor Farmhouse** **Dethick** **Matlock DE4 5GG** **Tel: (0629) 534246** **Open: JAN - NOV** **Map Ref No. 08** Nearest Road: M.1 Jt 28, A.6 This part Elizabethan farmhouse stands in the peaceful unspoilt hamlet of Dethick. Accommodation is in 4 charming bedrooms, 3 en-suite, some with T.V. All comfortable & furnished with antiques. Trays of tea/coffee available on request. Delicious full English breakfasts & home cooked meals are served. Guests can relax in the lounge available throughout the day. An ideal base for touring & walking.	£15.00 (no smoking)	Y	N	N
Mary Barber **Carr Head Farm** **Church Bank** **Hathersage** **Sheffield S30 1BR** **Tel: (0433) 50383** **Open: ALL YEAR** **Map Ref No. 11** Nearest Road: A.625 High on the hillside above the village of Hathersage an unusual 17th century farmhouse of outstanding character & friendly charm, set in beautifully mature gardens with lawn tennis court. 3 fine bedrooms, 1 with 4-poster. Oak beamed dining room with wood burning stove & many interesting features. Adjoining drawing room for guests' use. Superbly decorated throughout & finished in period style. All rooms have magnificent views. Traditional & varied breakfast served. Set in the heart of the Peak District.	£13.50	Y	N	N

Pethills Bank Cottage. Bottomhouse.

Staffordshire

Address	Description	minimum £ per person	children taken	evening meals	animals taken
Yvonne Martin Pethills Bank Cottage Bottomhouse Leek ST13 7PF Tel: (0538) 304277/304555 Fax 0538 304575 Open: ALLYEAR(Excl.Xmas) Map Ref No. 13	Nearest Road: A.523 A charming 18th century former farmhouse set in 1/2 an acre of landscaped gardens amid the hilly countryside of the low Peak National Park. The picturesque beams, low ceilings, thick stone walls & fascinating nooks & crannies are complimented by charming, comfortable accommodation & detailed attention to the comfort of guests. All the rooms are fully ensuite with colour T.V. & tea/coffee Tray. The garden room has it s own sitting room & verandah.	£16.50 see PHOTO over	Y	N	N
Mrs L. Grey The Old Vicarage Leek Road Endon Stoke-on-Trent ST9 9BH Tel: (0782) 503686 Open: ALL YEAR Map Ref No. 17	Nearest Road: A.53 A friendly atmosphere is found at this delightful 70 year-old former vicarage. It is situated in a quiet spot in the village of Endon, between the Staffordshire moorlands & Stoke-on-Trent. Accommodation is in 3 rooms, all with modern amenities & tea/coffee making facilities. There is also a colour T.V. lounge. This makes a good base from which to visit the world famous potteries, wonderful countryside & museums.	£15.00	Y	N	Y
Mrs Anne Hodgson The Hollies Clay Lake Endon Stoke-on-Trent ST9 9DD Tel: (0782) 503252 Open: ALL YEAR Map Ref No. 18	Nearest Road: A.53, B.5051 A delightful Victorian family house built in 1872, quietly situated off the B.5051 at Endon. Accommodation in 5 comfortable rooms, 3 with en-suite facilities. All have tea/coffee makers. The T.V. lounge & dining room overlook a large secluded garden. Ample parking. Famous Royal Doulton, Wedgwood & interesting museums nearby, Alton Towers leisure park & lovely countryside. Sorry, no smoking.	£14.00	Y	N	Y
Barbara White Micklea Farm Micklea Lane Longsdon Stoke-on-Trent ST9 9QA Tel: (0538) 385006 Open: ALL YEAR Map Ref No. 17	Nearest Road: A.53 "Micklea Farm" is an 18th century cottage set in a lovely quiet garden. There are 2 twin & 2 single rooms, with cots available. There is a charming sitting room for guests, with an open fire & colour T.V. Evening meals are available, using home-grown garden produce & home baking. Choice of English or Continental breakfast, also packed lunches. Conveniently situated for the Potteries, Alton Towers & Peak District.	£13.00	Y	Y	N
Mrs G. Adams The Boat House 71 Newcastle Road Stone ST15 8LD Tel: (0785) 815389 Open: FEB - DEC Map Ref No. 19	Nearest Road: M.6, A.34 A friendly relaxed atmosphere awaits you at this renovated 18th century former inn, set in delightful gardens alongside the Trent & Mersey Canal. Traditionally furnished, it offers accommodation in 3 comfortable rooms, with T.V., tea/coffee making facilities. This is an ideal base for Wedgwood & the potteries, the Peak District & Alton Towers. Easy access to the M.6.	£17.00	Y	N	N

Staffordshire

		minimum £ per person	children taken	evening meals	animals taken
William & Elaine Sutcliffe Choir Cottage & House Ostlers Lane Cheddleton Leek ST13 7HS Tel: (0538) 360561 Open: ALL YEAR Map Ref No. 12	Nearest Road: A.520 This pretty 17th century small stone cottage, once the resting place for Ostlers, now offers guests a choice of 3 beautifully decorated bedrooms. All have private entrance, ensuite facilities, colour T.V., tea/cofee makers & 'phone. The pine room (a small family suite) has a king size four poster bed, the rose room has a draped four-poster, the green room with pine canopied & draped twin beds, are on the ground floor & have private patios with open countryside views. Careful attention to detail is completed by the use of the freshest fayre.	£18.00 *see PHOTO over*	Y	Y	N
Mrs D. E. Moreton Moors Farm & Country Restaurant Chillington Lane Codsall Wolverhampton WV8 1QH Tel/Fax, (09074) 2330/ (0902) 842330 Open: ALL YEAR Map Ref No. 21	Nearest Road: A.41, A.5 A farmhouse, standing on a 100 acre farm within a beautiful & picturesque valley bordering the countries of Staffordshire & Shropshire. This comfortably furnished home has oak-beamed rooms & a cosy residents' lounge. The 6 bedrooms have wonderful views of the surrounding countryside, all have colour T.V., tea/coffee making facilities & washbasins. 2 are en-suite. The food here is absolutely delicious. Mrs Moreton uses home-produced lamb, pork, beef, poultry, eggs & vegetables. All preserves, soups pies & desserts are home made. Very convenient for M.6 & M.54 Motorways.	£18.00	Y	Y	N
Elizabeth Winterton Brook House Farm Cheddleton Leek ST13 7DF Tel: (0538) 360296 Open: JAN - DEC Map Ref No. 12	Nearest Road: A.520 Brookhouse is a dairy farm in a picturesque valley 1/2 a mile from the A.520 down a private lane. Many pleasant walks locally; convenient for Peak District, Pottery Museums and Alton Towers. Comfortable rooms in farmhouse and 2 spacious family rooms with patio doors in tastefully converted cowshed. All en-suite, centrally heated, with tea/coffee facilities. Good farmhouse food served in conservatory with magnificent views. Warm welcome assured.	£13.00	Y	Y	Y
Philomena & Jack Bunce The White House Grindon Leek ST13 7TP Tel: (0538) 304250 Open: ALL YEAR(Excl. Xmas/New Year) Map Ref No. 14	Nearest Road: A.523 Some 1000ft. up in the Peak National Park, this 350 year old former village inn faces south with superb views over valleys & hills. Original stone-mullioned windows & oak beams, a haven of peace, comfort & relaxation in a friendly atmosphere. Beautifully decorated bedrooms in coordinating colours, furnished for your every comfort, each with private facilities. One half tester bed with patchwork quilt. Fresh produce served with home-made bread & preserves.	£18.00	Y	N	N

When booking your accommodation please mention
The Best Bed & Breakfast

Staffordshire

		minimum £ per person	children taken	evening meals	animals taken
Christine Ball Manor House Farm Prestwood Denstone Uttoxeter ST14 5DD Tel: (0889) 590415 Open: JAN - DEC Map Ref No. 20	Nearest Road: A.50 A beautiful grade II listed farmhouse, set amid rolling hills & rivers. 2 bedrooms, both with modern amenities. 1 room with 4-poster bed. Tastefully furnished with antiques & retaining many traditional features including oak beamed ceilings & an oak panelled breakfast room. Guests may relax in the extensive gardens with grass tennis court & Victorian summer house. Ideal base for visiting, Alton Towers, Dovedale or the Peak District.	£15.00 *see PHOTO over*	Y	N	N
Mrs Maggie Wheeler Old Furnace Farm Greendale Oakamoor Stoke on Trent ST10 3AP Tel: (0538) 702442 Open: ALL YEAR Map Ref No. 16	Nearest Road: A.52 The farm is situated in an idyllic position, overlooking the Dimmingsdale Valley. The Victorian farmhouse, which has been tastefully renovated & furnished in keeping with the period, offers quality accommodation & friendly service. It has 3 bedrooms, each with en-suite bathroom, & colour T.V. Full central heating, log fire in visitors' lounge. An ideal location for Alton Towers (2 miles), potteries (12 miles), rambling, or just simply relaxing.	£17.50	Y	N	Y

All the establishments mentioned in this guide are members of

The Worldwide Bed & Breakfast Association

Manor House Farm. Prestwood.

Devon

Devon
(West Country)

Here is a county of tremendous variety. Two glorious & contrasting coastlines with miles of sandy beaches, sheltered coves & rugged cliffs. There are friendly resorts & quiet villages of cob & thatch, two historic cities, & a host of county towns & tiny hamlets as well as the wild open spaces of two national parks.

From the grandeur of Hartland Point east to Foreland Point where Exmoor reaches the sea, the north Devon coast is incomparable. At Westward Ho!, Croyde & Woolacombe the rolling surf washes the golden beaches & out to sea stands beautiful Lundy Island, ideal for bird watching, climbing & walking. The tiny village of Clovelly with its cobbled street tumbles down the cliffside to the sea. Ilfracombe is a friendly resort town & the twin towns of Lynton & Lynmouth are joined by a cliff railway.

The south coast is a colourful mixture of soaring red sandstone cliffs dropping to sheltered sandy coves & the palm trees of the English Riviera. This is one of England's great holiday coasts with a string of popular resorts; Seaton, Sidmouth, Budleigh Salterton, Exmouth, Dawlish, Teignmouth & the trio of Torquay, Paignton & Brixham thatmake up Torbay. To the south, beyond Berry Head are Dartmouth, rich in navy tradition, & Salcombe, a premiere sailing centre in the deep inlet of the Kingsbridge estuary. Plymouth is a happy blend of holiday resort, tourist centre, historic & modern city, & the meeting-point for the wonderful old sailing vessels for the Tall Ships Race.

Inland the magnificent wilderness of Dartmoor National Park offers miles of sweeping moorland, granite tors, clear streams & wooded valleys, ancient stone circles & clapper bridges. The tors, as the Dartmoor peaks, are called are easily climbed & the views from the tops are superb. Widecombe-in-the-Moor, with its imposing church tower, & much photographed Buckland-in-the-Moor are only two of Dartmoor's lovely villages.

The Exmoor National Park straddles the Devon/Somerset border. It is a land of wild heather moorland above deep wooded valleys & sparkling streams, the home of red deer, soaring buzzards & of legendary Lorna Doone from R.D. Blackmore's novel. The south west peninsula coastal path follows the whole of the Exmoor coastline affording dramatic scenery & spectacular views, notably from Countisbury Hill.

The seafaring traditions of Devon are well-known. Sir Walter Raleigh set sail from Plymouth to Carolina in 1584; Sir Francis Drake began his circumnavigation of the world at Plymouth in the "Golden Hind" & fought the Spanish Armada off Plymouth Sound. The Pilgrim Fathers sailed from here & it was to here that Sir Francis Chichester returned having sailed around the world in 1967.

Exeter's maritime tradition is commemorated in an excellent museum located in converted riverside warehouses but the city's chief glory is the magnificent 13th century cathedral of St. Mary & St. Peter, built in an unusual decorated Gothic style, with its west front covered in statues.

The River Dart near Dittisham.

Devon

Devon
Gazeteer
Areas of outstanding natural beauty. North, South, East Devon.

Houses & Castles
Arlington Court - Barnstaple
Regency house, collection of shell, pewter & model ships.
Bickleigh Castle - Nr. Tiverton
Thatched Jacobean wing. Great Hall & armoury. Early Norman chapel, gardens & moat.
Buckland Abbey - Nr. Plymouth
13th century Cistercian monastery - 16th century alterations. Home of Drake - contains his relics & folk gallery.
Bradley Manor - Newton Abbot
15th century Manor house with perpendicular chapel.
Cadhay - Ottery St. Mary
16th century Elizabethan Manor house.
Castle Drogo - Nr. Chagford
Designed by Lutyens - built of granite, standing over 900 feet above the gorge of the Teign river.
Chambercombe Manor - Illfracombe
14th-15th century Manor house.
Castle Hill - Nr. Barnstaple
18th century Palladian mansion - fine furniture of period, pictures, porcelain & tapestries.
Hayes Barton - Nr. Otterton
16th century plaster & thatch house. Birthplace of Walter Raleigh.
Oldway - Paignton
19th century house having rooms designed to be replicas of rooms at Palace of Versailles.
Powederham Castle - Nr. Exeter
14th century mediaeval castle much damaged in Civil War. Altered in 18th & 19th centuries. Fine music room by Wyatt.
Saltram House - Plymouth
Some remnants of Tudor house built into George II house, with two rooms by Robert Adam. Excellent plasterwork & woodwork.
Shute Barn - Nr. Axminster
Interesting architecturally - built over several centuries & finished in 16th.
Tiverton Castle - Nr. Tiverton
Fortress of Henry I. Chapel of St. Francis. Gallery of Joan of Arc.
Torre Abbey Mansion - Torquay
Abbey ruins, tithe barn. Mansion house with paintings & furniture.

Cathedrals & Churches
Atherington (St. Mary)
Perpendicular style - mediaeval effigies & glass, original rood loft. Fine screens, 15th century bench ends.
Ashton (St. John the Baptist)
15th century - mediaeval screens, glass & wall paintings. Elizabethan pulpit with canopy, 17th century altar railing.
Bere Ferrers (St. Andrew)
14th century rebuilding - 14th century glass, 16th century benches, Norman font.
Bridford (St. Thomas a Becket)
Perpendicular style - mediaeval glass & woodwork. Excellent rood screen c.1530.
Cullompton (St. Andrew)
15th century perpendicular - Jacobean west gallery - fan tracery in roof, exterior carvings.
Exeter Cathedral
13th century decorated - Norman towers. Interior tierceron ribbed vault (Gothic) carved corbets & bosses, moulded piers & arches. Original pulpitum c.1320. Choir stalls with earliest misericords in England c.1260.
Haccombe (St. Blaize)
13th century effigies, 14th century glass, 17th century brasses, 19th century screen, pulpit & reredos.
Kentisbeare (St. Mary)
Perpendicular style - checkered tower. 16th century rood screen.
Ottery St. Mary (St. Mary)
13th century, 14th century clock, fan vaulted roof, tomb with canopy, minstrel's gallery, gilded wooded eagle. 18th century pulpit.
Parracombe (St. Petrock)
Unrestored Georgian - 16th century benches, mostly perpendicular, early English chancel.
Sutcombe (St. Andrew)
15th century - some part Norman. 16th century bench ends, restored rood screen, mediaeval glass & floor tiles.
Swimbrige (St. James)
14th century tower & spire - mediaeval stone pulpit, 15th century rood screen,

Devon

font cover of Renaissance period.
Tawstock (St. Peter)
14th century, Italian plasterwork ceiling, mediaeval glass, Renaissance memorial pew, Bath monument.
Buckfast Abbey
Living Benedictine monastery, built on mediaeval foundation. Famous for works of art in church, modern stained glass, tonic wine & bee-keeping.

Museums & Galleries
Bideford Museum - Bideford
Geology, maps, prints, shipwright's tools, North Devon pottery.
Burton Art Gallery - Bideford
Hubert Coop collection of paintings etc.
Butterwalk Museum - Dartmouth
17th century row of half timbered buildings, nautical museum. 140 model ships.
Newcomen Engine House - Nr. Butterwalk Museum
Original Newcomen atmospheric/pressure steam engine c.1725.
Royal Albert Memorial Museum Art Gallery - Exeter
Collections of English watercolours, paintings, glass & ceramics, local silver, natural history & anthropology.
Rougemont House Museum - Exeter
Collections of archaeology & local history. Costume & lace collection
Guildhall - Exeter
Mediaeval structure with Tudor frontage - City regalia & silver.
Exeter Maritime Museum - Exeter
Largest collection in the world of working boats, afloat, ashore & under cover.
The Steam & Countryside Museum - Exmouth
Very large working layout - hundreds of exhibits, including Victorian farmhouse - farmyard pets for children.
Shebbear - North Devon
Alcott Farm Museum with unique collections of agricultural implements & photographs, etc.
The Elizabethan House - Totnes
Period costumes & furnishings, tools, toys, domestic articles, etc.
The Elizabethan House - Plymouth
16th century house with period furnishings.

City Museum & Art Gallery - Plymouth
Collections of pictures & porcelain, English & Italian drawing. Reynolds' family portraits, early printed books, ship models.
Cookworthy Museum - Kingsbridge
Story of china clay. Local history, shipbuilding tools, rural life.
Honiton & Allhallows Public Museum - Honiton
Collection of Honiton lace, implements etc. Complete Devon Kitchen.
Lyn & Exmoor Museum - Lynton
Life & history of Exmoor.
Torquay & Natural History Society Museum - Torquay
Collection illustrating Kent's Cavern & other caves - natural history & folk culture.

Historic Monuments
Okehampton Castle - Okehampton
11th -14th century chapel, keep & hall.
Totnes Castle - Totnes
13th - 14th century ruins of Castle.
Blackbury Castle - Southleigh
Hill fort - well preserved.
Dartmouth Castle - Dartmouth
15th century castle - coastal defence.
Lydford Castle - Lydford
12th century stone keep built upon site of Saxon fortress town.
Hound Tor - Manaton
Ruins of mediaeval hamlet.

Other things to see & do
The Big Sheep - Abbotsham
Sheep-milking parlour, with gallery, dairy & production rooms. Exhibition & play area.
Dartington Crystal - Torrington
Watch skilled craftworkers make lead crystalware. Glass centre & exhibition.
Dartmoor Wildlife Park - Sparkwell Nr. Plymouth
Over 100 species, including tigers, lions, bears, deer, birds of prey & waterfowl.
The Devon Guild of Craftsmen - Riverside Mill, Bovey Tracey
Series of quality exhibitions throughout the year.
Paignton Zoological & Botanical Gardens - Paignton
Third largest zoo in England. Botanical gardens, tropical house, "The Ark" family activity centre.

DEVON
Map reference

#	Name	#	Name
01	Hopewell	22	Chudley
02	Payne	49	Bassett
03	Ogle	24	Ward
04	Seymour-Lee	25	Bell
05	Taylor	26	Gregson
06	Tunnicliffe	27	Johnson-King
07	Barnes	28	Tucker
08	Thompson	29	Harvey
09	Wroe	30	Roberts
10	P. Lees	30	Griffiths
10	Kingsley	32	P. J. Lee
11	Wagg	33	Wilkens
12	Hyde	34	Bryan
13	Jiggins	35	Butler
13	Braund	36	Tucker
14	Maskell	36	Vaissiere
15	Yot	37	Lee
16	Bidder	38	Jaques
16	Gable	39	Cameron
17	Balkwill	40	Hayes
17	Lancaster	41	Farr
18	Kinder	42	Graeme
19	Murphy	43	Ellis
19	Trueman	44	Hill-King
19	Kamp	46	Allnutt
20	Keen	47	Edwards
21	Chilcott	48	Eastwood
22	Landor	49	Ashford

Devon

		minimum £ per person	children taken	evening meals	animals taken
Mrs Helga Hopewell **Lambley Brook** **The Street** **Kilmington** **Axminster S30 1AA** Tel: (0297) 35033 Open: FEB-DEC Map Ref No. 01	Nearest Road: A.35 A warm & friendly atmosphere is found at this delightful, secluded 19th century converted cottage. Standing in its own grounds surrounded by open countryside & woodland on the outskirts of this picturesque village. Offering comfortable & spacious accommodation in 4 pleasant bedrooms with tea/coffee makers, lovely views. An idyllic retreat for nature lovers. Close to the Devon/Somerset, Dorset border. 7 miles from the coast. Children over 10 years.	£14.00	N	N	N
Mrs Jackie Payne **Huxtable Farm** **West Buckland** **Barnstable** **EX32 0SR** Tel: (05986) 254 Open: MAR-DEC Map Ref No. 02	Nearest Road: A.361 Relax at Huxtable Farm a mediaeval longhouse with listed barn & round house. Carefully restored & furnished with antiques. This secluded sheepfarm (2 miles from M.5 link road) is ideally situated for Exmoor & the North Devon coast. Offering 6 rooms, most with private facilities, T.V. & tea/coffee makers. Enjoy 4-course candlelit dinners using farm/local produce served with homemade wine. Award-winning cook. Games room. Children welcome. Ideal base with riding & golf nearby.	£16.00	Y	Y	Y
Mrs Margaret Ogle **Lower Winsford House** **Abbotsham Road** **Bideford EX39 3QP** Tel: (0237) 475083 Fax 0237 425802 Open: MAY - SEPT Map Ref No. 03	Nearest Road: A.39 Everyone made very welcome at Lower Winsford to share our family home, tastefully furnished having a relaxing atmosphere, surrounded by lovely countryside. There are 3 rooms, 2 doubles & 1 twin, with wash basins, 2 bathrooms. Children over 5 welcome. Baby sitting arranged. Caring service at all times. Exmoor & Dartmoor within easy reach. The beach at Westward Ho! 3 miles, with lovely coastal walks.	£13.50	N	N	N
Petre Josephine Tunnicliffe **Henaford Manor Farm** **Welcombe** **Bideford** **EX39 6HE** Tel: (028883) 252 Open: ALL YEAR Map Ref No. 06	Nearest Road: A.39 Henaford Manor is a 13th century farmhouse set in 226 acres; retaining many traditional features including beamed ceilings & large fireplaces. Offering 4 tastefully furnished bedrooms, 1 en-suite, all with modern amenities including telephone, radio, colour T.V. & tea/coffee making facilities. Guests can relax in the spacious garden or lounge, available throughout the day. Excellent meals. Within 3 miles of Devon's Atlantic coast where there are several beaches & delightful small coves.	£15.00	Y	Y	Y

When booking your accommodation please mention

The Best Bed & Breakfast

Devon

		minimum £ per person	children taken	evening meals	animals taken
Penelope Seymour-Lee Tower House Abbotsham Court Bideford EX39 5BH Tel: (0237) 472418 Open: ALL YEAR Map Ref No. 04	Nearest Road: B. 3236 A unique 15th century listed building standing in a superb setting surrounded by cliffs & heaths in an area of outstanding beauty, with its own orchard with donkeys, sheep & a spring. Offering accommodation in 3 pleasant comfortable rooms, all en-suite, with T.V. & tea/coffee making facilities. An elegant dining room where delicious meals are prepared & served by your hostess, who is an enthusiastic cook. Vegetarian & low calorie diets catered for.	£36.00 see PHOTO over	Y	Y	Y
Mrs Jean Barnes Denham Farm North Buckland Braunton EX33 1HY Tel: (0271) 890297 Open: ALL YEAR (excl. Xmas) Map Ref No. 07	Nearest Road: A.361 Denham is a beautiful country house situated in the heart of the countryside with 160 acres of its own farmland. Only a short drive away are superb beaches, breathtaking scenery & lovely coastal walks. Situated only 3 miles from a championship golf course this delightful house offers 10 en-suite bedrooms with colour T.V. & tea/coffee making facilities. The inglenook fireplace & bread oven are a part of the character of this country home built in the 1700's.	£18.00	Y	Y	N
Mr & Mrs G. B. Thompson Bly House Hotel Nattadon Hill Chagford TQ13 8BW Tel: (0647) 432404 Open: JAN - NOV Map Ref No. 08	Nearest Road: A.30 A 100 year-old former rectory in a quiet position close to village in Dartmoor National Park. There are sweeping lawns, woodland walks, splendid views. Elegantly furnished with antiques, the 6 bedrooms all have private bathrooms, colour T.V. & tea making facilities & have antique 4-poster, half-tester or twin beds. Two quiet lounges with log fires, full C.H. Access to moor from the garden. Minimum age of children is 10 years.	£22.00	Y	N	Y
Mrs H . S. Wroe The Old Rectory Northleigh Colyton EX13 6BS Tel: (040487) 300 Open: ALL YEAR Map Ref No. 09	Nearest Road: A.30, A.35 Set in an idyllic south facing situation on the slopes of a peaceful unspoilt valley with beautiful & extensive rural views. The Old Rectory offers comfortable, attractive rooms, each with T.V., washbasin & tea/coffee making facilities, some en-suite. Within 20 minutes of the sea at Seaton, Beer, Branscombe & the charming Regency resort of Sidmouth. An ideal base for exploring or just relaxing in blissful peace & quiet.	£17.00	N	N	N
Peter & Edna Lees Wheel Farm Country Guest House Berrydown Combe Martin EX34 0NT Tel: (027188) 2550 Open: ALL YEAR Map Ref No. 10	Nearest Road: A.39 A really delightful old farm house in beautiful grounds on the edge of Exmoor. Offering 6 spacious & comfortable rooms, 3 have bath en-suite. All have modern amenities & tea/coffee makers. Each room has wonderful views. Excellent food with home grown produce. Wholefoods & vegetarian. Pony trekking, riding & golf arranged. Garden for guests.	£14.00	Y	Y	Y

Tower House. Bideford

Devon

		minimum £ per person	children taken	evening meals	animals taken
Jackie & John Kingsley Brinscott Farmhouse Berry Down Combe Martin EX34 0PA Tel: (0271) 883146 Open: ALL YEAR Map Ref No. 10	Nearest Road: B.3343 Delightful 16th century listed longhouse with many features, garden, peaceful setting of 5 acres. Exmoor & sea 2 miles. Offering 5 comfortable rooms, 3 en-suite, all with tea/coffee making facilities & central heating. A large oak-beamed lounge has inglenook fireplace with woodburner, colour T.V. Plentiful breakfasts & an optional choice of candlelit dinners by an enthusiastic cook. Good touring centre.	£14.50	Y	Y	N
Louisa & David Wagg Fair Park Exeter Road Crediton EX17 3BJ Tel: (0363) 772686 Open: ALL YEAR (Excl. Xmas & New Year) Map Ref No. 11	Nearest Road: A.377 A comfortable Georgian family home located on the edge of town with beautiful rural views. Decorated & furnished to a high standard with full central heating & log fires in the drawing room. All the bedrooms have private facilities & tea/coffee makers. No smoking in the bedrooms please. There is a solar heated swimming pool & table tennis for guests' enjoyment. Delicious home cooking using garden produce. This makes an excellent touring base.	£13.00	Y	Y	N
R.J. & S.A. Hyde Raffles 11 Blackall Road Exeter EX4 4HD Tel: (0392) 70200 Open: ALL YEAR Map Ref No. 12	Nearest Road: M.5 This small Victorian hotel is situated minutes from the heart of one of England's Roman cities. Accommodation in is 7 spacious bedrooms, all with private facilities, colour T.V., tea/coffee making facilities & central heating. Attractively furnished in the Victorian style & retaining many original features. Home cooked 3 course meals using local produce are available with advance notice. Raffles offers an excellent standard of comfort & care.	£17.00	Y	Y	Y
Alan & Vicky Jiggins Down House Whimple Exeter EX5 2QR Tel: (0404) 822860 Open: MAR-OCT Map Ref No. 13	Nearest Road: A.30 Down House offers peace, quiet & seclusion, being a lovely Edwardian farmhouse set in 5 acres of gardens & paddocks. Personal service, home produce & a family atmosphere are priorities. Single, family & en-suite rooms are available including a twin downstairs room suitable for handicapped guests. A good base for discovering the richness of the East Devon countryside. No smoking in the public rooms.	£13.00	Y	Y	N
Mrs L. L. Braund Woodside Wood Hayes Lane Whimple Exeter EX5 2QR Tel: (0404) 822340 Open: APR - OCT Map Ref No. 13	Nearest Road: A.30 Lovely accommodation in a spacious, elegantly furnished Edwardian house, delightfully situated with a beautiful garden & panoramic views over Exeter to Dartmoor. Pleasant bedrooms with modern amenities, T.V. lounge, dining room & flower lounge. Choice of 5 inns all within 3 miles for evening meals. This makes an excellent base for a touring holiday.	£13.00	N	N	N

Devon

		minimum £ per person	children taken	evening meals	animals taken
Mr & Mrs J. H. Maskell **Bridford Guest House** **Bridford** **Exeter** **EX6 7HS** Tel: (0647) 52563 Open: Easter - DEC Map Ref No. 14	Nearest Road: B.3212 A warm welcome awaits you at this 350 year-old house in the centre of a charming village on Dartmoor. 5 bedrooms with modern amenities, & tea/coffee making facilities. Lounge with colour T.V. has a large granite fireplace & there are lots of beamed ceilings. Plentiful home cooking, lovely Devon cream teas. Delicious 3-course evening meals are also available with advance notice. Exeter 8 miles, Torbay & the coast 20 miles.	£14.00	Y	Y	Y
Mrs Jacqueline Yot **Colestocks House** **Colestocks** **Honiton** **EX14 0JR** Tel: (0404) 850633 Open: ALL YEAR Map Ref No. 15	Nearest Road: A.30 Pink-washed & newly rethatched, a lovely 16th century grade II listed country house in 2 acres of gardens. Tranquil rural situation, & well placed for touring the West Country. All rooms have en-suite bath/shower, colour T.V. & tea making facilities. Many antiques, one 4-poster, one canopied brass bed & 2 half testers. Log fires in the huge inglenook fireplace. Excellent restaurant, all home cooking. French wines personally chosen & imported by the proprietor. Minimum age of children is 10 years.	£24.50 see PHOTO over	Y	Y	N
Ellen & Ray Bidder **Lyncott** **56 St. Brannock's Road** **Ilfracombe** **EX34 8EQ** Tel: (0271) 862425 Open: APR- OCT Map Ref No. 16	Nearest Road: A.361 A friendly family guest house situated only 200 yards from Bicclescombe Park. A most attractive rose garden at the front makes a welcoming sight. 9 nicely decorated & comfortable rooms with modern amenities & tea/coffee making facilities, 2 with en-suite facilities. A T.V. lounge & garden for guests. This house is very suited to families & the evening meals are good value, with delicious home cooking & a varied menu. Children are welcome & well catered for.	£11.00	Y	Y	Y
Roy & Barbara Gable **Varley House** **Chambercombe Park** **Ilfracombe EX34 9QW** Tel: (0271) 863927 Open: MAR-OCT Map Ref No. 16	Nearest Road: A.399 A spacious Victorian character house on the outskirts of Ilfracombe, having both sea & country views. Our aim is quality, comfort, courtesy & care with our personal touch. Accommodation is in 9 attractive rooms: all fully en-suite with C.T.V., tea/coffee making facilities. The house is elegantly furnished: the food served is imaginative & plentiful. An excellent base for exploring this lovely area.	£16.00	Y	Y	Y
Mrs Jill Balkwill **Court Barton Farmhouse** **Aveton Gifford** **Kingsbridge** **TQ7 4LE** Tel: (0548) 550312 Open: JAN - DEC Map Ref No. 17	Nearest Road: A.379 An absolutely delightful 16th century, listed manor farmhouse situated on a 300 acre arable farm. Accommodation is in a choice of 7 comfortable bedrooms, all with ensuite facilities. A comfortable, well furnished T.V. lounge with lots of books. Delicious country breakfasts are served in the sunny breakfast room. Full central heating & log fires in cooler weather. Close to moorland & beaches. Ideal for walking, sailing fishing & birdwatching.	£16.00	Y	N	N

Devon

	minimum £ per person	children taken	evening meals	animals taken
Mrs Christine Lancaster **Helliers Farm** **Ashford** **Aveton Gifford** **Kingsbridge TQ7 4ND** Tel: (0548) 550689 Open: ALL YEAR Map Ref No. 17	Nearest Road: A.379 Set in the heart of South Hams countryside, this recently modernised farmhouse offers accommodation in 4 pleasant bedrooms with tea/coffee making facilities, a spacious dining room where good farmhouse breakfasts are served & a comfortable lounge with T.V. & games room. Close to the beaches, moors, golf courses, National Trust walks & the city of Plymouth. A non-smoking establishment.	£14.50	Y	N	N
David & Georgiana Kinder **Trebles Cottage Hotel** **Kingston** **Kingsbridge** **TQ7 4PT** Tel: (0548) 810268/ (0831) 558222 Open: ALL YEAR Map Ref No. 18	Nearest Road: A.379 Originally a family cottage built in 1801, now a small hotel set in secluded grounds on the edge of an attractive unspoilt village. Trebles offers 5 bedrooms all en-suite, tastefully & individually furnished with colour T.V., radio/alarm, tea/coffee makers & hair dryers. Small cocktail bar compliments the excellent restaurant. Lovely coastal walks, picturesque beach & golf nearby. David & Georgiana offer a warm welcome, personal service & a high standard of comfort & good food.	£25.00	N	Y	Y
Brian & Dorothy Murphy **Neubia House Hotel** **Lydiate Lane** **Lynton EX35 6AH** Tel: (0598) 52309 Open: FEB - NOV Map Ref No. 19	Nearest Road: A.39 A very charming former farmhouse, built in 1840, set in private courtyard/car park in Old Lynton, 12 very comfortable bedrooms all with en-suite facilities, colour T.V. & tea/coffee making facilities. Proprietor-chef welcomes vegetarians. Situated in a very pleasant village, it is an ideal base for touring this lovely region. Riding, fishing & walking all superb & beaches are close by.	£27.75	Y	Y	Y
Mr & Mrs C. J. Trueman **Gordon House Hotel** **31 Lee Road** **Lynton** **EX35 6BS** Tel: (0598) 53203 Open: MAR - NOV Map Ref No. 19	Nearest Road: A.39 A warm & friendly welcome awaits you at Gordon House Hotel. This gracious Victorian house provides charming period features with modern conveniences. Accommodation is in 7 pretty bedrooms, all en-suite, with colour T.V. & tea/coffee making facilities. 2 attractive lounges for relaxation after roaming Exmoor. Dine by candlelight & enjoy delicious home-cooking & good wine. Conveniently located with secluded beaches, quaint harbours & picturesque villages close by.	£21.50	Y	Y	Y
June & Adrian Kamp **Southcliffe** **Lee Road** **Lynton EX35 6BS** Tel: (0598) 53328 Open: MAR-OCT Map Ref No. 19	Nearest Road: A.39 Charming private hotel of the Victorian era. Modernised throughout yet retaining many original features such as the natural pitch-pine staircase & doors. Beautifully appointed bedrooms - all with private bathrooms, colour T.V. & beverage makers. June & Adrian Kamp have been at Southcliffe since 1978 & have a reputation for good food, comfort, cleanliness & value for money.	£18.50	Y	Y	Y

Devon

			minimum £ per person	children taken	evening meals	animals taken
Sybil Keen **Glen Doone** **Oare** **Lynton EX35 6NU** Tel: (05987) 202 Open: ALL YEAR(Excl. Xmas) Map Ref No. 20	Nearest Road: A.39 Glen Doone, beautifully re-furbished Victorian Rectory at Oare, tucked into a valley between Porlock & Lynmouth, with lovely Exmoor at its back. The 1000 ft. cliffs, well supplied with paths, roll down to the sea through woods, streams & waterfalls. Accommodation is in 4 bedrooms, 3 with private facilities, all with modern amenities. The house is elegantly furnished, food imaginative, well presented & mostly home-produced. Children & pets welcome.		£16.00	Y	Y	Y
Stephen Paul Chilcott **Wigham** **Morchard Bishop** **EX17 6RJ** Tel: (03637) 350 Open: ALL YEAR Map Ref No. 21	Nearest Road: A.377 Wigham is a 16th century Devon longhouse with a 30 acre farm which provides fresh fruit, vegetables & dairy produce for imaginative meals. Accommodation is in 5 double rooms, including a 4-poster suite. All with colour T.V. & video & full private bathroom. There are 2 sitting rooms in which guests may relax & a snooker lounge & outdoor heated pool for pleasure. Licenced. Stabling - livery by arrangement.		£37.00 *see PHOTO over*	N	Y	N
Stephen & Phyllis Landor **Cross Tree House** **Moretonhampstead** **TQ13 8NL** Tel: (0647) 40726 Open: MAR - FEB Map Ref No. 22	Nearest Road: A.38, B.3212 Cross Tree House is a tastefully restored listed Queen Anne house located on the village edge in Dartmoor Narional Park. Offering guests every comfort. There are 3 large south-facing double bedrooms, 1 with en-suite facilities. Good English & Cordon Bleu cuisine is served. A delightful walled garden for relaxation & a nearby children's play area. An excellent base for walks & touring Devon.		£18.00	Y	Y	Y
Owen & Kathleen Chudley **Great Doccombe Farm** **Doccombe** **Moretonhampstead** **TQ13 8SS** Tel: (0647) 40694 Open: FEB - DEC Map Ref No. 22	Nearest Road: A.30, B3212 Great Doccombe is a lovely 300 year old farm-house, situated in a pretty village within Dartmoor National Park. 3 comfortable bedrooms, 1 en-suite, 1 on the ground floor, all with modern amenities & tea/coffe making facilities. Cosy lounge with woodburning fire & colour T.V. In the dining room enjoy a good farmhouse break-fast. Ideal for walking in the Teign Valley & Dartmoor.		£13.00	Y	Y	Y

When booking your accommodation please mention

The Best Bed & Breakfast

Wigham.   Morchard Bishop.

Devon

	minimum £ per person	children taken	evening meals	animals taken
Peter & Celia Ward **The Thatched Cottage Restaurant** 9 Crossley Moor Rd. Kingsteignton Newton Abbot TQ12 3LE Tel: (0626) 65650 Open: ALL YEAR Map Ref No. 24	Nearest Road: A.380 A beautiful 400 year-old thatched longhouse with enclosed garden & large car park. Many original features including a wealth of oak beams & a large fireplace create a cosy, intimate atmosphere. Accommodation is in 5 bedrooms with modern amenities including T.V. & tea/coffee making facilities. Comfortable cocktail bar & restaurant with excellent cuisine. Delightful garden available for guests. A warm welcome & personal attention are guaranteed by Peter & Celia.	£15.00	Y	Y	N
Mrs Madeleine Gregson **Penpark** Bickington Newton Abbot TQ12 6LH Tel: (0626) 821314 Open: ALL YEAR Map Ref No. 26	Nearest Road: A.38 In the Dartmoor National Park, with secluded, beautiful woodland gardens, tennis court & glorious panoramic views, Penpark is an elegant, charming country house, a gem of its period, designed by famous architect Clough Williams Ellis. Your lovely, spacious twin room has a balcony, sofa, chairs, colour T.V., tea/coffee facilities & handbasin. Adjoining is a single room & bathroom. A warm welcome awaits you.	£18.00 see PHOTO over	Y	N	N
Peter & Patricia Johnson-King **Oakfield** Exeter Road, Chudleigh Newton Abbot TQ13 0DD Tel: (0626) 852194 Open: APR - OCT Map Ref No. 27	Nearest Road: A.38 This lovely old family home, beautifully furnished with antiques, surrounded by 20 acres of delightfully landscaped gardens, orchards & paddocks with glorious views of the Devon countryside, offers perfect peace & tranquillity. Peter & Patricia treat their guests as friends & emphasise comfort, relaxation & excellent food. Accommodation is in 3 very attractive en-suite bedrooms. Guests may also enjoy the drawing room, billards room, library & heated pool.	£20.00	Y	Y	N
Margaret & John Tucker **The Gate House** North Bovey Newton Abbot TQ13 8RB Tel: (0647) 40479 Open: ALL YEAR(Excl.Xmas) Map Ref No. 28	Nearest Road: A.38, A.382 A listed mediaeval thatched house, with beamed ceilings, granite fireplace & bread oven. All bedrooms have en-suite/private bathrooms, colour T.V. & tea/coffee making facilities. There is a secluded garden, swimming pool & delightful views. North Bovey is a classic Dartmoor village with a green surrounded by thatched cottages. 2 miles from Moretonhampstead. Lovely walks on Dartmoor & golf & riding nearby.	£21.50	Y	Y	Y
Mrs J. Harvey **Budleigh Farm** Moretonhampstead Newton Abbot TQ13 8SB Tel: (0647) 40835 Open: FEB-DEC Map Ref No. 29	Nearest Road: A.382, A.38 Budleigh, a delightful old thatched farmhouse, nestles in a wooded valley in the Dartmoor National Park half a mile from Moretonhampstead. All bedrooms have tea/coffee making facilities & handbasins. Small apartments, with every comfort, are available out of season, making stays a real treat. Board games, paperbacks & magazines, maps & books are available. A delightful garden, with outdoor swimming pool, croquet & barbeque make this the perfect touring base.	£12.00	Y	N	N

Penpark. Bickington.

Devon

		minimum £ per person	children taken	evening meals	animals taken
N. & C. Bell **Sampsons Farm** **Restaurant** **Preston** **Newton Abbot TQ12 3PP** Tel: (0626) 54913 Open: ALL YEAR Map Ref No. 25	Nearest Road: A.38, B.3193 A super relaxed family atmosphere is found at this traditional Devon thatched longhouse. It retains much of its original charm & character with oak beams, panelling & inglenook fireplaces. 5 comfortable bedrooms are available, including a honeymoon suite with 4-poster bed. A delicious breakfast is served & an extensive a la carte menu is offered in the evening. Only a short distance from lovely thatched villages. Fishing & golf are within easy reach.	£14.00 *see PHOTO over*	Y	Y	Y
Hilary Roberts **Willmead Farm** **Lustleigh** **Bovey Tracey** **Newton Abbot TQ13 9NP** Tel: (06477) 214 Open: ALL YEAR (excl. Xmas & New Year) Map Ref No. 30	Nearest Road: A.38, A.382 Willmead Farm dates back to 1437. The hall has a minstrels gallery & there is an attractive drawing room with a large stone fireplace decked with gleaming copper & brass. A full English breakfast is served in the beamed dining room. Accommodation is in 3 attractive bedrooms, 1 with private facilities. Set in 31 acres of fields, woodland, duckpond & streams, an excellent base where peace & tranquility are guaranteed.	£19.00	Y	N	Y
Mrs Pauline Griffiths **Lower Elsford Cottage** **Bovey Tracey** **Newton Abbot** **TQ13 9NY** Tel: (06477) 408 Open: JAN - DEC Map Ref No. 30	Nearest Road: A.38, A.382 A 17th century stone cottage in magical woodland setting, with spectacular views over glorious countryside in an area of outstanding natural beauty. Complete peace and quiet, every home comfort, central heating. 1 double room with en-suite facilities, 1 single room h&c, both south facing. Situated within the Dartmoor National Park ideal for touring, riding, golf, fishing and walking.	£15.00	Y	N	Y
Peter J. Lee **Barracott** **Manaton** **Newton Abbot** **TQ13 9XA** Tel: (0647) 22312 Open: APR - OCT Map Ref No. 32	Nearest Road: A.382, A.38 A charming 16th century Dartmoor farmhouse set in an ancient beautiful & magical landscape with magnificent views to heatherclad granite hill tops. 2 comfortable south-facing guest rooms with private bath/shower. Colour T.V. & tea making facilities & lovely sitting room for guests' use. Situated in the National Park, Barracott is ideal for touring, riding & golf as well as marvellous walking country.	£20.00	N	N	Y
The Wilkens Family **Poltimore Country Hotel** **Ramsley** **South Zeal** **Okehampton EX20 2PD** Tel: (0837) 840209 Open: ALL YEAR Map Ref No. 33	Nearest Road: A.30 Delightfully located country hotel on the fringe of Dartmoor with a warm & friendly atmosphere. Comfortable oak beamed lounge with inglenook fireplace & licenced bar. Ideally situated as a base for walking or touring. Accomodation is in 7 comfortable bedrooms, 4 en-suite, each with tea/coffee making facilities & colour T.V. Home cooking using garden produce in season offering a varied menu, 4 course dinners & packed lunches.	£14.00	Y	Y	Y

Sampsons Farm Restaurant. Newton Abbot

Devon

	minimum £ per person	children taken	evening meals	animals taken
Ellen Bryan **Lower Gorhuish Farm** **Northlew** **Okehampton EX20 3BU** Tel: (0837) 810272 Open: FEB - DEC Map Ref No. 34 Nearest Road: A.30 A warm welcome is assured here. Accommodation is in 4 comfortable rooms, 2 ensuite, each with modern amenities, radio & tea/coffee making facilities. Plus T.V. lounge & garden. Good home cooking. Opportunities for pony trekking/riding nearby, also Okehampton 18-hole golf course. This mixed farm provides a super base for touring Devon, Cornwall Dartmoor National Park & National Trust homes & castles.	£13.00	Y	Y	N
Mrs Josephine Butler **Four Chimneys** **Bratton Clovelly** **Okehampton Ex20 4JS** Tel: (083787) 409 Open: MAR - NOV Map Ref No. 35 Nearest Road: A.30 Four Chimneys, originally 2 18th century cottages restored with taste & charm in one acre garden, skirts a pretty village. Guests needs are sympathetically catered for. Special attention paid to quality, variety & presentation of meals. Homemade bread, packed lunches. Modern amenities including teasmade in warm attractive bedrooms. Guests lounge with colour T.V., piano, inglenook logfires. Private suite by arrangement. Babysitting, cots, highchairs.	£17.00	Y	Y	Y
Mrs Tricia Tucker **Courtenay House** **Moult Hill** **Salcombe TQ8 8LF** Tel: (0548) 842761 Open: ALL YEAR Map Ref No. 36 Nearest Road: A.38 A beautiful Victorian house overlooking Salcombe estuary to sea. Accommodation is in 3 comfortable bedrooms with modern amenities. A residents' T.V. lounge & garden are also available. Special diets can be catered for with advance notice. This makes a delightful base for visiting the many interesting villages in the area. Guests at Courtenay House also benefit from good advice about all the local amenities.	£21.00	Y	N	N
Patricia Vaissiere **The Wood** **De Courcy Road** **South Sands** **Salcombe TQ8 8LQ** Tel: (054884) 2778 Open: ALL YEAR Map Ref No. 36 Nearest Road: A.38, A.381 This is a Victorian house with luxurious bedrooms & en-suite facilities. Dramatic views over one of Englands most beautiful estuaries may be enjoyed whilst savouring Pat's traditional English cooking using local & home produce. Salcombe is one of south Devon's most delightful resorts with a climate favoring palms, orange & lemon trees. This makes an excellent centre for sailing, walking & golf.	£19.00	Y	Y	Y
John & Diana Lee **Cheriton Guest House** **Vicarage Road** **Sidmouth EX10 8QU** Tel: (0395) 513810 Open: JAN - DEC Map Ref No. 37 Nearest Road: M.5 This large town house stands in a secluded, prize winning garden that reaches down to the River Sid with parkland beyond, and the seafront just half a mile away. The 8 bedrooms are mostly en-suite and all have T.V. and hot drinks facilities. Cheriton is renowned for its fine cooking and varied menu. Comfortable T.V. lounge. Private parking.	£12.00	Y	Y	N

Devon

			minimum £ per person	children taken	evening meals	animals taken
Allan & Bunny Jaques Coombe House North Huish South Brent TQ10 9NJ Tel: (054882) 277 Open: MAR - mid DEC Map Ref No. 38		Nearest Road: A.38 This Country House, originally a Georgian farmhouse, offers a friendly welcome to a small number of guests. Its tranquil valley setting is home to Heron, Owls etc. Nearby Dartmoor offers walking, riding, fishing; several golf courses locally; quick and easy access to other parts of Devon & Cornwall. The four bedrooms have own bath and/or shower, w.c., and tea/coffee facilities. Spacious lounge with Minster fireplace. Licensed bar.	£23.00	Y	N	N
Mrs C.G. Cameron Rowden House Brentor Tavistock PL19 0NG Tel: (0822) 810230 Fax 0822 810230 Open: JAN - DEC Map Ref No. 39		Nearest Road: A.30 An Edwardian country residence with large, magnificent garden ideally situated on the edge of the Dartmoor National Park, with extensive views of the surrounding countryside and St. Michael's Church on the Tor. Beautiful, unspoilt rural area, noted for its peacefulness and easy access. One comfortable twin room with h/c, colour T.V., radio alarm, electric blankets, tea/coffee facilities. Dogs accepted by arrangement only.	£17.50	N	N	Y
Jeanne & Martin Hayes Colcharton Gulworthy Tavistock PL19 8HU Tel: (0822) 613047 Open: ALL YEAR Map Ref No. 40		Nearest Road: A.390 A warm welcome & an informal family atmosphere await you at this charming 16th century farmhouse. Located in a quiet valley within easy reach of the moors. Accommodation in 3 pleasant bedrooms, including a family room, with modern amenities & tea/coffee makers. This makes a good base for touring both Devon & Cornwall. A short drive away are Tavistock, Plymouth, Cotehele House, Lydford Gorge & the historic part of Morwelham.	£14.00	Y	N	Y
Gill & Andrew Farr Moorland Hall Hotel Brentor Road Mary Tavy Tavistock PL19 9PY Tel: (0822) 810466 Open: ALL YEAR Map Ref No. 41		Nearest Road: A.386 Standing in 5 acres of gardens & paddocks, including a croquet lawn. Moorland Hall is a delightful country house with some parts over 200 years old. Accommodation is in 8 ensuite bedrooms, 2 have four-poster beds, all with T.V. & tea/coffee making facilities. There are 2 lounges & a small bar. The excellent menu is changed daily & includes vegetarian dishes. The coasts of Devon & Cornwall are all within easy reach & the hotel itself is situated on the edge of the Dartmoor National Park.	£25.00	Y	Y	Y
Mrs Jennifer Graeme Fonthill Torquay Road Shaldon Teignmouth TQ14 0AX Tel: (0626) 872344 Open: FEB - DEC Map Ref No. 42		Nearest Road: A.379 Visitors are warmly welcomed to this lovely Georgian house for a peaceful holiday in charming & very comfortable accommodation. Fonthill stands in 20 acres of beautiful gardens, woodland & fields on the edge of Shaldon, a pretty village on the South Devon coast. 3 delightful rooms with every comfort. The lovely garden is for guests' enjoyment & there is also a tennis court in the grounds. Several sandy beaches nearby & an excellent golf course.	£16.50 🚭 *see PHOTO over*	Y	N	N

Fonthill, Shaldon

Devon

			minimum £ per person	children taken	evening meals	animals taken
Mrs Eileen Ellis Hill Rise Hotel Winterbourne Road Teignmouth TQ14 8JT Tel: (0626) 773108 Open: ALL YEAR Map Ref No. 43		Nearest Road: A.381, A.379 Hill Rise is an elegant Edwardian house located in a quiet residential area only a few minutes walk from the sea & town centre. Accommodation is in 8 attractive warm rooms all with modern amenities & tea/coffee making facilities. Many rooms have sea views. A T.V. lounge, bar & attractive garden are also available for guests. Excellent centre for touring South Devon & Dartmoor. Private parking.	£15.00	Y	Y	N
Mrs Ruth Hill-King Little Holwell Collipriest Tiverton EX16 4PT Tel: (0884) 258741 Fax 0884 258741 Open: ALL YEAR Map Ref No. 44		Nearest Road: M.5, A.361 Little Holwell is a delightful 'olde worlde' farmhouse standing in beautiful Devon coutryside, surrounded by rolling hills & woodland. This 13th century home has many oak beams, inglenook fireplace & spiral staircase. Accommodation is in 3 rooms with tea/coffee making facilities. A lounge is also available. Home-made bread, eggs & vegetables are used whenever possible. Good for touring as Tiverton, Exeter, Exmouth & Torbay are within easy reach. Phone for directions.	£11.50 🚭	Y	Y	N
Jeannie & Peter Allnutt The Old Forge at Totnes Seymour Place Totnes TQ9 5AY Tel: (0803) 862174 Open: ALL YEAR Map Ref No. 46		Nearest Road: A.381 - 50yds Totnes Route Centre. The Old Forge at Totnes is a delightfully converted working 600 year-old smithy. This family-run hotel, located in the centre of Totnes, offers visitors a choice of 8 comfortable well-equipped bedrooms. some en-suite, all with radio, colour T.V. & tea/coffee making facilities. Cottage suite also available for families. There is also a pleasant walled garden for guests' use, where delicious cream teas are served. The Old forge is ideally located for touring Torbay coast & Dartmoor. Licensed.	£17.50 🚭 see PHOTO over	Y	N	N
Sheila Edwards Ford Farm Guest House Ford Farm Harberton Totnes TQ9 7SJ Tel: (0803) 863539 Open: ALL YEAR Map Ref No. 47		Nearest Road: A.381 A 16th century village house, situated on the edge of a typical Devonshire village. It stands in a small, secluded 'olde worlde' garden with a stream. Accommodation is very comfortable with antique furnishings, log fires & beamed ceilings. Offering 3 bedrooms,1 ensuite, with hairdryers, electric blankets & a bathroom courtesy chest; asprins, razors etc.. Tea/cofee facilities in the guest lounge. A warm, friendly atmosphere prevails at all times.	£16.50	Y	N	Y
Ann & David Eastwood 'Sandunes' Guest House Beach Road Woolacombe EX34 7BT Tel: (0271) 870661 Open: APR - OCT Map Ref No. 48		Nearest Road: A.361 'Sandunes' is a very pleasant, most comfortable modern guest house where you are assured of a friendly welcome, relaxed atmosphere & courteous service. Conveniently located for Woolacombe Sands & village. The comfortable accommodation is in 6 en-suite bedrooms, many with lovely sea views. The well appointed guest lounge & sun patio have marvellous panoramic views out to sea. This is an ideal base for touring with sandy beaches, Illfracombe, Lynton, Lynmouth & Exmoor within easy reach.	£13.00 🚭	N	Y	N

The Old Forge at Totnes.   Totnes.

Devon

		minimum £ per person	children taken	evening meals taken	animals taken
Marian & Richard Ashford **The Cleeve House Hotel** **Mortehoe** **Woolacombe** **EX34 7ED** **Tel: (0271) 870719** **Open: MAR - NOV** **Map Ref No. 49**	Nearest Road: A.361 Marian and Richard extend a warm welcome to their newly refurbished Edwardian Hotel set in its own grounds, in the centre of Mortehoe village, and surrounded by National Trust coastline and walks. 5 minutes from Woolacombe's 3 miles of golden, sandy beach. After your day out, go back to a comfortable room, imaginative home cooking and a cosy bar where you can hear tales of old Morte.	£17.00	Y	Y	Y
Mr & Mrs V. W. Bassett **Sunnycliffe Hotel** **Chapel Hill** **Mortehoe** **Woolacoombe** **EX34 7EB** **Tel: (0271) 870597** **Open: FEB - NOV** **Map Ref No. 49**	Nearest Road: A.361 Sunnycliffe is a small, select hotel located on a hillside position with wonderful views of both coast & countryside. Accommodation is in 8 rooms, all with private facilities, T.V. & tea/coffee. All rooms have sea views. Sunnycliffe's proprietor-chef. This makes a good base for any kind of holiday. Nearby are golden sands, safe swimming, surfing, riding, & walking along the coastal paths. Sea fishing & boat trips. Potteries, market towns & stately homes are within easy reach.	£20.00	N	Y	N

If you have any comments regarding your accommodation please send them to us using the form at the back of the guide

Dorset

Dorset
(West Country)

The unspoilt nature of this gem of a county is emphasised by the designation of virtually all of the coast & much of the inland country as an Area of Outstanding Natural Beauty. Along the coast from Christchurch to Lyme Regis there are a fascinating variety of sandy beaches, towering cliffs & single banks, whilst inland is a rich mixture of downland, lonely heaths, fertile valleys, historic houses & lovely villages of thatch & mellow stone buildings.

Thomas Hardy was born here & took the Dorset countryside as a background for many of his novels. Few writers can have stamped their identity on a county more than Hardy on Dorset, forever to be known as the "Hardy Country". Fortunately most of the area that he so lovingly described remains unchanged, including Egdon Heath & the county town of Dorchester, famous as Casterbridge.

In the midst of the rolling chalk hills which stretch along the Storr Valley lies picturesque Cerne Abbas, with its late mediaeval houses & cottages & the ruins of a Benedictine Abbey. At Godmanstone is the tiny thatched "Smiths Arms" claiming to be the smallest pub in England.

The north of the county is pastoral with lovely views over broad Blackmoor Vale. Here is the ancient hilltop town of Shaftesbury, with cobbled Gold Hill, one of the most photographed streets in the country.

Coastal Dorset is spectacular. Poole harbour is an enormous, almost circular bay, an exciting mixture of 20th century activity, ships of many nations & beautiful building of the 15th, 18th & early 19th centuries.

Westwards lies the popular resort of Swanage, where the sandy beach & sheltered bay are excellent for swimming. From here to Weymouth is a marvellous stretch of coast with scenic wonders like Lulworth Cove & the arch of Durdle Door.

Chesil Beach is an extraordinary bank of graded pebbles, as perilous to shipping today as it was 1,000 years ago. It is separated from the mainland by a sheltered lagoon known as the Fleet. From here a range of giant cliffs rises to 617 feet at Golden Gap & stretches westwards to Lyme Regis, beloved by Jane Austen who wrote "Persuasion" whilst living here.

Dorset has many interesting archaeological features. Near Dorchester is Maiden Castle, huge earthwork fortifications on a site first inhabited 6,000 years ago. The Badbury rings wind round a wooded hilltop near Wimborne Minster; legend has it that King Arthur's soul, in the form of a raven, inhabited this "dread" wood. The giant of Cerne Abbas is a figure of a man 180 feet high carved into the chalk hillside. Long associated with fertility there is still speculation about the figures' origins, one theory suggesting it is a Romano-British depiction of Hercules. A Roman amphitheatre can be seen at Dorchester, & today's road still follows the Roman route to Weymouth.

Corfe Castle.

Dorset

Dorset
Gazeteer
Areas of outstanding natural beauty. The Entire County.

Houses & Castles
Athelthampton
Mediaeval house - one of the finest in all England. Formal gardens.
Barneston Manor - Nr. Church Knowle
13th - 16th century stone built manor house.
Forde Abbey - Nr. Chard
12th century Cistercian monastery - noted Mortlake tapestries.
Manor House - Sandford Orcas
Mansion of Tudor period, furnished with period furniture, antiques, silver, china, glass, paintings.
Hardy's Cottage - Higher Bockampton
Birthplace of Thomas Hardy, author (1840-1928).
Milton Abbey - Nr. Blandford
18th century Georgian house built on original site of 15th century abbey.
Purse Caundle Manor - Purse Caundle
Mediaeval Manor - furnished in style of period.
Parnham House - Beaminster
Tudor Manor - some later work by Nash. Leaded windows & heraldic plasterwork. Home of John Makepeace & the International School for Craftsmen in Wood. House, gardens & workshops.
Sherborne Castle - Sherborne
16th century mansion - continuously occupied by Digby family.
No. 3 Trinity Street - Weymouth
Tudor cottages now converted into one house, furnished 17th century.
Smedmore - Kimmeridge
18th century manor.
Wolfeton House - Dorchester
Mediaeval & Elizabethan Manor. Fine stone work, great stair. 17th century furniture - Jacobean ceilings & fireplaces.

Cathedrals & Churches
Bere Regis (St. John the Baptist)
12th century foundation - enlarged in 13th & 15th centuries. Timber roof & nave, fine arcades, 16th century seating.
Blandford (St. Peter & St. Paul)
18th century - ashlar - Georgian design. Galleries, pulpit, box pews, font & mayoral seat.
Bradford Abbas (St. Mary)
14th century - parapets & pinnacled tower, panelled roof. 15th century bench ends, stone rood screen. 17th century pulpit.
Cerne Abbas (St. Mary)
13th century - rebuilt 15th & 16th centuries, 14th century wall paintings, 15th century tower, stone screen, pulpit possibly 11th century.
Chalbury (dedication unknown)
13th century origin - 14th century east windows, timber bellcote. Plastered walls, box pews, 3-decker pulpit, west gallery.
Christchurch (Christ Church)
Norman nave - ribbed plaster vaulting - perpendicular spire. Tudor renaissance Salisbury chantry - screen with Tree of Jesse: notable misericord seats.
Milton Abbey (Sts. Mary, Michael, Sampson & Branwaleder)
14th century pulpitum & sedilla, 15th century reredos & canopy, 16th century monument, Milton effigies 1775.
Sherborne (St. Mary)
Largely Norman but some Saxon remains - excellent fan vaulting, of nave & choir. 12th & 13th century effigies - 15th century painted glass.
Studland (St. Nicholas)
12th century - best Norman church in the country. 12th century font, 13th century east windows.
Whitchurch Canonicorum (St. Candida & Holy Cross)
12th & 13th century. 12th century font, relics of patroness in 13th century shrine, 15th century painted glass, 15th century tower.
Wimbourne Minster (St. Cuthberga)
12th century central tower & arcade, otherwise 13th-15th century. Former collegiate church. Georgian glass, some Jacobean stalls & screen. Monuments & famed clock of 14th century.
Yetminster (St. Andrew)
13th century chancel - 15th century rebuilt with embattled parapets. 16th century brasses & seating.

Dorset

Museums & Galleries

Abbey Ruins - Shaftesbury
Relics excavated from Benedictine Nunnery founded by Alfred the Great.
Russell-Cotes Art Gallery & Museum - Bournemouth
17th-20th century oil paintings, watercolours, sculptures, ceramics, miniatures, etc.
Rothesay Museum - Bournemouth
English porcelain, 17th century furniture, collection of early Italian paintings, arms & armour, ethnography, etc.
Bournemouth Natural Science Society's Museum
Archaeology & local natural history.
Brewery Farm Museum - Milton Abbas
Brewing & village bygones from Dorset.
Dorset County Museum - Dorchester
Geology, natural history, pre-history. Thomas Hardy memorabilia
Philpot Museum - Lyme Regis
Old documents & prints, fossils, lace & old fire engine.
Guildhall Museum - Poole
Social & civic life of Poole during 18th & 19th centuries displayed in two-storey Georgian market house.
Scapolen's Court - Poole
14th century house of local merchant exhibiting local & archaeological history of town, also industrial archaeology.
Sherborne Museum - Sherborne
Local history & geology - abbey of AD 705, Sherborne missal AD 1400, 18th century local silk industry.
Gallery 24 - Shaftesbury
Art exhibitions - paintings, pottery, etc.
Red House Museum & Art Gallery - Christchurch
Natural history & antiques of the region. Georgian house with herb garden.
Priest's House Museum - Wimbourne Minster
Tudor building in garden exhibiting local archaeology & history.

Other things to see & do

Abbotsbury Swannery - Abbotsbury
Unique colony of Swans established by monks in the 14th century. 16th century duck decoy, reed walk, information centre.
Dorset Rare Breeds Centre - Park Farm, Gillingham
Poole Potteries - the Quay, Poole
Sea Life Centre - Weymouth
Variety of displays, including Ocean Tunnel, sharks, living "touch" pools.

West Bay.

DORSET

Map reference

01 Dearlove
02 Farmer
02 Smith
02 Du Faur
03 Game
04 Walker
05 Allan
06 Jennings
07 Slocock
07 Hipwell
08 Tomblin
09 Willis
10 Haggett
11 Walford
12 Griffin
13 Powell
14 Mayo
15 Partridge
16 McCallum
17 Hookham-Bassett
18 Newson-Smith
19 Dick
19 Wingate-Saul
20 Norman
21 Gregory
22 Spender

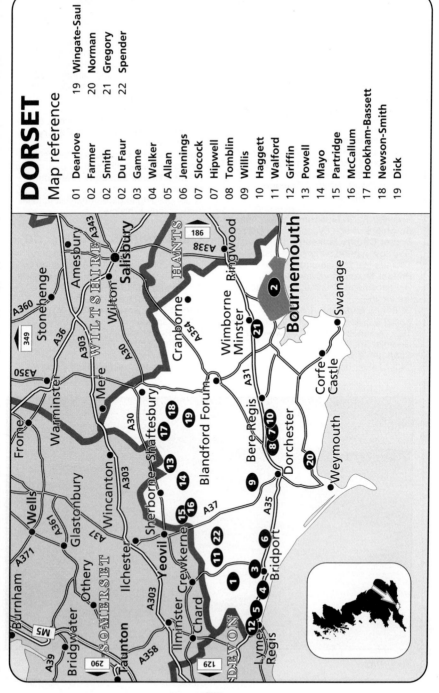

Dorset

			minimum £ per person	children taken	evening meals	animals taken
Judy & Giles Dearlove **Hams Plot** **Bridport Road** **Beaminster DT8 3LU** Tel: (0308) 862979 Open: ALL YEAR Map Ref No. 01	Nearest Road: A.3066 Hams Plot, in the middle of its colourful garden, looks like a continental summer villa. French windows open onto a veranda with potted pink oleanders & a fringe of flower beds. Beyond are a tennis court & swimming pool. Upstairs the big bedrooms have private bathrooms, patchwork quilts & family antiques. Downstairs guests can browse in the library among the guides, walkers' maps & umpteen books.		£21.00	N	N	N
Madeline & David Farmer **Wenmaur House Hotel** **14 Carysfort Road** **Boscombe** **Bournemouth BH1 4EJ** Tel: (0202) 395081 Open: ALL YEAR Map Ref No. 02	Nearest Road: A.35, A.338 A comfortable small hotel with friendly atmosphere, offering good accommodation in 12 rooms. All rooms have T.V., tea/coffee making facilities & are fully centrally heated. Cots are provided. Centrally located for the beaches & sporting facilities are available locally. The evening meal offers a choice of menu & late night refreshments are available. Licenced. This makes a pleasant holiday base.		£13.50	Y	Y	Y
Jo & Bill Smith **Silver Trees Hotel** **57 Wimbourne Road** **Bournemouth** **BH3 7AL** Tel: (0202) 556040 Open: ALL YEAR Map Ref No. 02	Nearest Road: A.347 A charming Victorian house standing in its own wooded grounds with sweeping lawns, colourful flowers & shrubs. Offering comfortable accommodation in 8 bedrooms, 6 en-suite with colour T.V. Breakfast is cooked to order in the elegant dining room overlooking the garden. Early morning tea, evening snacks & refreshments are available on request & served in your room or in the lounge. Ideally located for visiting the New Forest & Dorset.		£18.50	Y	N	N
Colin & Jean Du Faur **Sandhurst Hotel** **16 Southern Road** **Southbourne** **Bournemouth BH6 3SR** Tel: (0202) 423748 Open: MAR - OCT Map Ref No. 02	Nearest Road: A.35 Guests' comfort is a priority at this friendly welcoming hotel. There's a choice of 9 comfortable rooms each with colour T.V. & tea/coffee makers. Some also have en-suite facilities. Good home-cooked breakfasts with evening meals available. Situated 2 mins. from the beach in a quiet suburb of Bournemouth. An ideal centre for touring, with Christchurch, Beaulieu, The New Forest, Salisbury & Dorchester a short drive. Private parking.		£13.00	Y	Y	N
Michael & Sandra Game **Riverdale** **168 St. Andrews Road** **Bridport** **DT6 3BW** Tel: (0308) 27721 Open: ALL YEAR Map Ref No. 03	Nearest Road: A.35 Riverdale is an early Victorian House, retaining most of the original features. Guests' breakfast in a beautiful room overlooking the garden, or on the patio if weather permits. The food is of the highest quality, with the emphasis on home cooking, using the freshest produce. Vegetarians are welcome, as are children of all ages. The rooms are beautifully decorated, with coffee/tea making facilities. Most have en-suite facilities. Private parking.		£18.00 🚭	Y	Y	N

Dorset

			minimum £ per person	children taken	evening meals	animals taken
Mrs C. Jennings **The Loders Arms** Loders Bridport DT6 3SA Tel: (0308) 22431 Open: ALL YEAR Map Ref No. 06	Nearest Road: A.35 The Loders Arms is a delightful country pub set in the centre of the picturesque & tranquil village, yet only 1 mins. drive from Bridport & the sea. There are 3 pretty, comfortable en-suite bedrooms with colour T.V.. Delicious home-cooked meals are available most evenings at the inn's restaurant. A riding establishment & golf course are close by as well as glorious country & coastal walks.		£17.50	N	Y	Y
Ann & Dan Walker MHCIMA **Britmead House** 154 West Bay Road Bridport DT6 4EG Tel: (0308) 22941 Open: ALL YEAR Map Ref No. 04	Nearest Road: A.35 A friendly & pleasant small hotel renowned for superb facilities, delightful food & personal service; situated between Bridport & the quaint little fishing harbour of West Bay with its beaches, golf course & walks. 7 spacious bedrooms, 5 en-suite (1 ground floor), all with colour T.V., tea- making facilities, hair dryers & mini bar. Full C/H. South facing lounge & garden. Private parking. Table d'hote dinner menu, incorporating local fish & produce. Children over 5 years welcome.		£15.75	Y	Y	Y
Alistair & Clemency Allan **Humbers** Chideock Bridport DT6 6JW Tel: (0297) 89310 Open: ALL YEAR Map Ref No. 05	Nearest Road: A.35 This 17th century home is set in a beautiful West Dorset village. A lane leads to the sea & there is fine walking country over coastal hills with breath-taking views. A warm welcome awaits, spacious accommodation in two rooms with modern amenities, traditional English breakfast. Information & advice on local walks & drives in the Hardy Country & nearby Devon & Somerset. Minimum age of children is 2 years.		£14.00	Y	N	N
Michael & Terry Slocock **Southover House** Tolpuddle Dorchester DT2 7HF Tel: (0305) 848220 Fax 0305 848516 Open: JAN - DEC Map Ref No. 07	Nearest Road: A.35 Large period country house with extensive grounds and spacious rooms. Luxurious double bedroom with massive bathroom. Large, comfortable twin bedroom with marble-lined bathroom. Both have southerly views over rolling fields and woodland, colour T.V. and easy chairs. (Single bedroom at £15.00) Use of downstairs reception room and hard tennis court. Tolpuddle Trout Fishery (separate, but family management) for fly fishing and tuition 250 yards.		£15.00	Y	N	N
Mrs Anthea Hipwell **The Old Vicarage** Affpuddle Dorchester DT2 7HH Tel: (0305) 848315 Open: JAN - DEC Map Ref No. 07	Nearest Road: A.35 The Old Vicarage is a traditional country house standing in a large mature garden in the charming Piddle Valley, at the heart of the Dorset countryside. Accommodation is in 3 comfortable and attractively furnished rooms, one en-suite, with all facilities at hand at your request. Your hosts will be pleased to help with advice on the numerous places of interest and places to dine.		£17.50	Y	N	N

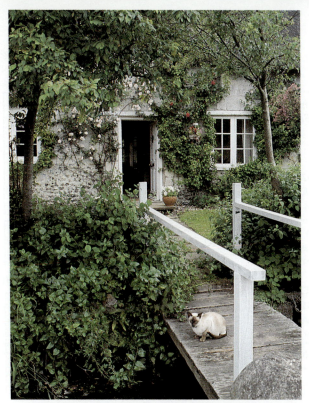

Lamperts Cottage.   Sydling St. Nicholas.

Dorset

		per person minimum £	children taken	evening meals	animals taken
Marian Tomblin **Lower Lewell Farmhouse** **West Stafford** **Dorchester** **DT2 8AP** Tel: (0305) 267169 Open: ALL YEAR Map Ref No. 08	Nearest Road: A.35 Lower Lewell Farmhouse dates from the 17th century & is situated in the delightful Frome Valley in the midst of Thomas Hardy country - indeed the house is reputed to be the Talbothays Dairy portrayed in Hardy's novel "Tess of the D'Urbervilles". 3 bedrooms are available equipped with tea/coffee making facilities & a full English breakfast is served. There is a sitting room with colour T.V. A delightful touring centre.	£14.00	Y	N	N
Mrs V. I. Willis **Lamperts Cottage** **Sydling St. Nicholas** **Cerne Abbas** **Dorchester DT2 9NU** Tel: (0300) 341659 Open: ALL YEAR Map Ref No. 09	Nearest Road: A.37 Lamperts Cottage is a charming 16th century thatched cottage, standing in fields with streams running front & back, on the outskirts of the village. Roses climb around the windows & door. 3 bedrooms are available, equipped with tea/coffee making facilities. Full English breakfast, or Continental if preferred. Ideal for visiting Dorset's many beauty spots.	£15.00 *see PHOTO over*	Y	N	N
Mrs D. M. Haggett **Vartrees House** **Moreton** **Crossways** **Dorchester DT2 9NU** Tel: (0305) 852704 Open: ALL YEAR Map Ref No. 10	Nearest Road B.3390 off A.35 A peaceful & secluded character country house set in 3 acres of picturesque woodland gardens. Built by Hermon Lee, friend of Thomas Hardy. Accommodation throughout is spacious & comfortable. Tea/coffee makers in all rooms. T.V. lounge. Situated near the pretty village of Moreton with its renowned church & burial place of Lawrence of Arabia. Coast 4 miles. Station 1/4 of mile. Excellent local pubs.	£16.00	Y	N	Y
Mrs Chris Walford **Rectory House** **Fore Street** **Evershot** **DT2 0JW** Tel: (0935) 83273 Open: JAN - NOV Map Ref No. 11	Nearest Road: A.37 Rectory House is an 18th century listed building set in the picturesqe village of Evershot. 6 delightfully appointed bedrooms with en-suite bathrooms, colour T.V. & tea/coffee makers. Superb home cooking of traditional & exotic dishes. Delicious breakfasts include freshly baked bread & locally made sausages. Melbury estate adjoins the village with beautiful walks & scenery. Ideally located for visiting Bath, Bournemouth & Lyme Regis.	£25.00 *see PHOTO over*	N	Y	N
Geoffrey & Elizabeth Griffin **The Red House** **Sidmouth Road** **Lyme Regis** **DT7 3ES** Tel: (0297) 442055 Open: MAR-NOV Map Ref No. 12	Nearest Road: A.3052 This distinguished house, abutting open countryside enjoys commanding views over spectacular Dorset coastline, yet is only a short walk to the centre of Lyme Regis. The house offers 3 en-suite bedrooms (1 for family use) & facilities include tea/coffee making, colour T.V., clock radio, desk, armchairs & drink refrigerator, central heating plus electric heaters. Breakfast can be taken on the garden balcony. Private parking in house grounds. Minimum age children: 5 years	£18.00	Y	N	N

Dorset

		minimum £ per person	children taken	evening meals	animals taken
Mrs Vivienne Powell 'Strawberry Cottage' Packers Hill Holwell Sherborne DT9 5LN Tel: (0963) 23629 Open: ALL YEAR Map Ref No. 13	Nearest Road: A.3030 'Strawberry Cottage' is a part 16th century (listed) thatched cottage, situated in quiet countryside near Sherborne, in Hardy's Wessex & within easy reach of the coast. Guest's accommodation is in a choice of 3 bedrooms. There is a cheerful guests' T.V. lounge & the garden is also available. Children over 10 welcome. Plenty of reading material & local information provided for touring beautiful Dorset.	£15.50	Y	N	N
Mrs Jenny Mayo Almshouse Farm Hermitage Sherborne DT9 6HA Tel: (096321) 296/ (0963) 210296 Open: MAR - OCT Map Ref No. 14	Nearest Road: A.352 This charming old farmhouse was a monastery during the 16th century, restored in 1849 & now a listed building. It is surrounded by 140 acres overlooking the Blackmore Vale. Accommodation is in 3 comfortable rooms with tea/coffee making facilities. Dining room with inglenook fireplace. The garden & lawns are available for guests' use at all times. Situated only 6 miles from Sherborne with its beautiful Abbey & Castle	£13.50	Y	N	N
Ann & Jack Partridge Manor Farmhouse High Street Yetminster Sherborne DT9 6LF Tel: (0935) 872247 Open: ALL YEAR(Excl. Xmas/New Year) Map Ref No. 15	Nearest Road: A.37 This 17th century farmhouse with oak panelling, beams & inglenook fireplaces offers every comfort to the discerning visitor. There are 4 bedrooms all with private facilities & modern amenities including T.V. & tea/coffee makers. Delicious meals served, made from traditional recipes using fresh local produce. Village described as the "best 17th century stone-built village in the south of England". An excellent centre for visiting Sherborne, Glastonbury, New Forest & Hardy's Dorset.	£23.75 *see PHOTO over*	N	Y	N
Mrs G.M. McCallum Foys Chetnole Sherborne DT9 6PD Tel: (0935) 872686 Open: JAN - DEC Map Ref No. 16	Nearest Road: A.37, A.352 Foys is a gracious family home standing in 3 acres of peaceful country garden. The main house, built in 1888, is a typical Hamstone building with stone mullioned windows etc. Many places of historical and natural interest within easy reach. 2 twin bedrooms available for guests. Evening meals by arrangement only.	£14.00	N	N	N
Mary Ann Newson-Smith Lovells Court Marnhull Sturminster Newton DT10 1JJ Tel: (0258) 820652 Open: JAN - DEC Map Ref No. 18	Nearest Road: A.30, A.303 Lovells Court is a large family house (used as The Prince of Wales' hunting lodge in the 19th century), standing in peaceful Marnhull village. Fine views over Blackmore Vale. Market town of Sturminster Newton and Abbeys of Sherborne and Milton Abbass nearby. 2 en-suite rooms & 1 with private bathroom; all with T.V., radio and tea/coffee facilities. Swimming pool in grounds. Excellent evening meals in local Inns.	£17.50	Y	N	N

Halstock Mill. Halstock.

Manor Farmhouse. Yetminster.

Dorset

Name / Address	Description	minimum £ per person	children taken	evening meals	animals taken
Jill & Ken Hookham-Bassett Stourcastle Lodge Goughs Close DT10 1BU Sturminster Newton Tel: (0258) 72320 Open: ALL YEAR Map Ref No. 19	Nearest Road: A.357 Visitors to Stourcastle Lodge can expect a relaxing stay & a very warm welcome in a pleasant house built in 1739. Located in a quiet part of the town. There are 5 charming bedrooms with modern amenities, 4 en-suite. Tea/coffee/soft drinks are available all day. Exposed beams throughout the house. A pretty lounge with open log fire & colour T.V. Super food here & good value. Regional Award Winners 1986.	£18.00	Y	Y	N
Ann Dick Romaynes Lydlinch Sturminster Newton DT10 2HU Tel: (0258) 72508 Open: ALL YEAR Map Ref No. 19	Nearest Road: A.357 Romaynes is a spacious country house with an acre of garden. Ideally situated for touring beautiful Dorset. Guests from home & abroad are warmly welcomed. Double, twin, or single bedrooms all with modern amenities. Enjoy an excellent breakfast in the pleasant dining room overlooking the sun terrace & garden with views across the Dorset countryside. Children over 12 welcome. Colour brochure available.	£15.00	N	N	N
Charles & Sally Wingate-Saul Holebrook Farm Lydlinch Sturminster Newton DT10 2JB Tel: (0258) 817348 Open: ALL YEAR Map Ref No. 19	Nearest Road: A.357 Holebrook farm is a family run mixed farm located in the heart of Hardy Country. Accommodation is in the Georgian stone farmhouse or the delightfully converted stables with own siting room, colour T.V., shower room & kitchen. Breakfast is served in the lovely old farmhouse kitchen with its flagstone floors, original fire place & bread oven. A small swimming pool & games room with darts, pool table & table tennis are available for guests' use. Clay shooting can also be arranged.	£17.00	Y	Y	N
Mrs Joyce Norman Dingle Dell Osmington Weymouth DT3 6EW Tel: (0305) 832378 Open: MAR - OCT Map Ref No. 20	Nearest Road: A.353 Dingle Dell is a mellow stone house set in a garden of roses & ancient apple trees. Offering 2 spacious & comfortable bedrooms, 1 ensuite, attractively furnished with views of the gardens & fields. Full English breakfast served. Osmington has changed little since 1816 when the painter John Constable spent his honeymoon there. A comfortable & friendly holiday base in the beautiful Dorset countryside. Only 5 miles from the seaside & harbour town of Weymouth. Children over 5 yrs.	£15.00	Y	N	N
Peter & Jane Spender Halstock Mill Halstock Yeovil BA22 9SJ Tel: (0935) 891278 Open: JAN-NOV Map Ref No. 22	Nearest Road: A.37 At the end of a 1/2 mile private lane is the 17th century Halstock Mill. The 400 acres of pastureland surrounding it ensure a peaceful relaxing stay. Accommodation is in 4 spacious en-suite bedrooms with colour T.V. & tea/coffee makers. The beamed drawing room has an inglenook log fire. Jane offers a superb 4 course dinner prepared with home/local produce. An ideal base for touring Dorset, Somerset & Devon.	£20.00 see PHOTO over	Y	Y	N

Dorset

	minimum £ per person	children taken	evening meals	animals taken
Mrs Margaret Gregory **Ashton Lodge** **10 Oakley Hill** **Wimborne** **BH21 1QH** **Tel: (0202) 883423** **Open: ALL YEAR** **Map Ref No. 21** Nearest Road: A.349, A.31 Detached family residence with relaxed & friendly atmosphere. The dining room overlooks an attractively laid out garden. Full English breakfast with freshly ground coffee. The 4 bedrooms are light & spacious with colour T.V. & tea/coffee making facilities & hair dryers. Ironing facilities are available on request. Ashton Lodge is conveniently situated for the coast, New Forest & Kingston Lacy House. Baby sitting service can be arranged.	£14.50	Y	N	N

All the establishments mentioned in this guide are members of

The Worldwide Bed & Breakfast Association

When booking your accommodation please mention

The Best Bed & Breakfast

Essex

Essex
(East Anglia)

Essex is a county of commerce, busy roads & busier towns, container ports & motorways, yet it is also a landscape of mudflats & marshes, of meadows & leafy lanes, villages & duckponds. Half timbered buildings & thatched & clapboard cottages stand among rolling hills topped by orange brick windmills.

The coast on the east, now the haunt of wildfowl, sea-birds, sailors & fishermen has seen the arrival of Saxons, Romans, Danes, Vikings & Normans. The names of their settlements remain - Wivenhoe, Layer-de-la-Haye, Colchester & Saffron Walden - the original Saxon name was Walden, but the Saffron was added when the crocus used for dyes & flavouring was grown here in the 15th century.

The seaside resorts of Southend & Clacton are bright & cheery, much-loved by families for safe beaches. Harbours here are great favourites with anglers & yachtsmen.

Inland lie the watermeadows & windmills, willows & cool green water which shaped the life & work of John Constable, one of the greatest landscape painters. Scenes are instantly recognisable today as you walk from Dedham to Flatford Mill with the swift River Stour flowing by.

Colchester is England's oldest recorded town, once the Roman capital of Britain trading in corn & cattle, slaves & pearls. Roman remains are still to be seen & their original street plan is the basis of much of modern Colchester. A great feast is held here annually to celebrate the famous oyster - the "Colchester native".

South Essex, though sliced through by the M.25 motorway is still a place of woodland & little rivers. The ancient trees of Epping Forest, hunting ground for generations of monarchs, spread 6,000 acres of leafy glades & heathland into the London suburbs.

Flatford Mill.

Essex

Essex Gazeteer
Areas of outstanding natural beauty.
Dedham Vale (part), Epping Forest.

Houses & Castles
Audely End House - Saffron Walden
1603 - Jacobean mansion on site of Benedictine Abbey. State rooms & Hall.
Castle House - Dedham
Home of the late Sir A. Munnings. President R.A. Paintings & other works.
Hedingham Castle - Castle Hedingham
Norman keep & Tudor bridge.
Layer Marney Tower - Nr. Colchester
1520 Tudor brick house. 8 storey gate tower. Formal yew hedges & lawns.
Payecock's - Coggeshall
1500 - richly ornamented - merchant's house - National Trust.
St. Osyth's Priory - St. Osyth
Was Augustinian Abbey for 400 years until dissolution in 1537, 13th-18th century buildings. 13th century chapel. Wonderful gatehouse containing works of art including ceramics & Chinese Jade.
Spains Hall - Finchingfield
Elizabethan Manor incorporating parts of earlier timber structure. Paintings, furniture & tapestries.

Cathedrals & Churches
Brightlingsea (All Saints)
15th century tower - some mediaeval painting fragments. Brasses.
Castle Hedingham (St. Nicholas)
12th century doorways, 14th century rood screen, 15th century stalls, 16th century hammer beams, altar tomb.
Copford (St. Michael & All Angels)
12th century wall paints. Continuous vaulted nave & chancel
.**Finchingfield** (St. John the Baptist)
Norman workmanship. 16th century tomb -18th centuary tower & cupola.
Layer Marney (St. Mary)
Tudor brickwork, Renaissance monuments, mediaeval screens, wall paintings.
Little Maplestead (St. John the Baptist)
14th century, one of the five round churches in England, having hexagonal nave, circular aisle, 14th century arcade.

Newport (St. Mary the Virgin)
13th century. Interesting 13th century altar (portable) with top which becomes reredos when opened. 15th century chancel screen. Pre-Reformation Lectern. Some old glass.

Museums & Galleries
Dutch Cottage Museum - Canvey Island
17th century thatched cottage of octagonal Dutch design. Exhibition of models of shipping used on the Thames through the ages.
Ingatestone Hall - Ingatestone
Documents & pictures of Essex.
The Castle - Colchester
Norman Keep now exhibiting archeological material from Essex & especially Roman Colchester.
Southchurch Hall - Southend-on-Sea
14th century moated & timber framed manor house - Tudor wing, furnished as meiaeval manor.
Thurrock - Grays
Prehistoric, Romano-British & pagan Saxon archaeology.

Other things to see & do
Colchester Oyster Fishery - Colchester
Tour showing cultivating, harvesting, grading & packing of oysters. Talk, tour & sample.

Burnham on Crouch.

ESSEX
Map reference

- 01 Mesnard
- 02 Crawshaw
- 03 Tritton
- 05 Bredin
- 06 Bishop
- 07 Mitchell
- 08 Sloan
- 09 Collins

Essex

		minimum £ per person	children taken	evening meals	animals taken
Mrs Margaret Mesnard Oakwood House 126 Norsey Road Billericay CM11 1BH Tel: (0277) 655865 Open: JAN - DEC Map Ref No. 01	Nearest Road: B.1007 A detached Tudor-style house with a large rear garden backing onto 150 acre Nature Reserve. Accommodation is offered in a choice of two double en-suite bedrooms or single room with adjacent bathroom. Each room is equipped with colour T.V., hospitality tray and radio. Guests may relax in the conservatory or attractive garden. Ideal location for visiting London or touring East Anglia. Children over 5.	£16.00	Y	N	N
Mrs Penny Crawshaw The Old School House St James Street Castle Hedingham CO9 3EW Tel: (0787) 61370 Open: JAN - DEC Map Ref No. 02	Nearest Road: A.604, A.131 Charming terracotta-and-white Georgian house in Mediaeval village. Oak beamed, pamment-tiled hall/dining room; entrancing walled garden with many interesting plants including old-fashioned roses, and a lily pond. Bedrooms have private bath or shower, radio and tea/coffee facilities. 2 are in attractive converted coach-house; one fully en-suite with sitting room and T.V. Evening meals by prior arrangement. Children over 12.	£18.50	Y	Y	N
Mrs Linda Tritton The Wick Hatfield Peverel Chelmsford CM3 2EZ Tel: (0245) 380705 Open: JAN - NOV (Excl.AUG) Map Ref No. 03	Nearest Road: A.12 Grade II listed 16th century farmhouse in pleasant rural setting. Large garden, duck ponds and stream. 2 attractive comfortable bedrooms, 1 single ,1 twin (own basin) sharing large bathroom. Cosy drawing-room with log fire, books, games, T.V., video. Delicious home-cooked meals served in dining room or large pine kitchen. Easy access to London and East Coast ports.	£15.00	Y	Y	N
Mrs A. F. Bredin Bovills Hall Ardleigh Colchester CO7 7RT Tel: (0206) 230217 Open: FEB - NOV Map Ref No. 05	Nearest Road: A.137 A friendly host & a relaxing atmosphere are found at this delightful manor house. Listed in the Domesday Book, Bovills Hall offers interesting & comfortable accommodation in a choice of 3 rooms, 1 en-suite, all with modern amenities. T.V. & radio. There's a colour T.V. lounge for guests' use, open fires, & 14 acres of garden, making a pleasant & delightful spot to relax in after a day's touring. This makes a perfect base for a holiday.	£17.00	Y	N	N

When booking your accommodation please mention
The Best Bed & Breakfast

Essex

		minimum £ per person	children taken	evening meals	animals taken
Chris & Graham Bishop Hodgenolls Farmhouse Pork Lane Gt. Holland Frinton CO13 0ES Tel: (0255) 672054 Open: APR - OCT Map Ref No. 06	Nearest Road: A.133, B.1033 Chris & Graham welcome you to their home, a 17th century timber framed farmhouse in two and a half acres, surrounded by farmland, close to sandy beaches, Constable country and historic Colchester. Within easy reach of Harwich. 3 rooms, each with hot & cold, T.V., and tea making facilities. Guests are requested not to smoke in the house.	£16.00	Y	N	N
Mrs H. P. Mitchell New Farm House Spinnell's Lane Wix Manningtree CO11 2VJ Tel: (0255) 870365 Open: ALL YEAR Map Ref No. 07	Nearest Road: A.120 Modern farmhouse set in picturesque garden welcomes visitors with its warm homely atmosphere. The location offers close proximity to both Constable Country & within 10 minutes drive of Harwich Port. 12 bedrooms with modern amenities, the option of en-suite facilities & colour T.V. 2 guests' lounges incorporating well equipped kitchenette for preparing snacks. Children welcome. Cot, high chair, baby sitting & play area provided.	£16.50	Y	Y	Y
P. D. & J. A. Sloan Stanford Rivers Hall Stanford Rivers Ongar CM5 9QG Tel: (0277) 362997 Open: ALL YEAR Map Ref No. 08	Nearest Road: A.113 Stanford Rivers Hall is a very fine example of Georgian architecture, in a pleasant rural location yet within easy reach of London, Cambridge, Stanstead, M.25 & M.11. Lovely accommodation in 6 characterful rooms all en-suite, & a friendly atmospheric lounge with oak beams & a wood burning stove. Spacious dining room where English or Continental breakfast is served. 10 minutes from Epping tube, Central Line.	£20.00	Y	N	N
Susan Collins The Stow Great Sampford Saffron Walden CB10 2RG Tel: (079986) 354 Open: ALL YEAR Map Ref No. 09	Nearest Road: B.1053 The Stow is a lovely 16th century farmhouse, situated in the centre of the delightfully attractive village of Great Sampford. The house itself is a real treat, featuring beamed ceilings, buttoned chairs, Persian rugs, patchwork & embroidered cushions. The kitchen is pinewood & delicious meals are prepared on the large Aga cooker. Accommodation is in 2 rooms with modern amenities & tea/coffee making facilities. There is also a residents' colour T.V. lounge & a super garden.	£20.00	Y	Y	N

When booking your accommodation please mention The Best Bed & Breakfast

Gloucestershire

Gloucestershire
(Heart of England)

The landscape is so varied the people speak not of one Gloucestershire but of three - Cotswold, Vale & Forest. The rounded hills of the Cotswolds sweep & fold in graceful compositions to form a soft & beautiful landscape in which nestle many pretty villages. To the east there are wonderful views of the Vale of Berkeley & Severn, & across to the dark wooded slopes of the Forest of Dean on the Welsh borders.

Hill Forts, ancient trackways & long barrows of neolithic peoples can be explored, & remains of many villas from late Roman times can be seen. A local saying "Scratch Gloucester & find Rome" reveals the lasting influence of the Roman presence. Three major roads mark the path of invasion & settlement. Akeman street leads to London, Ermine street & the Fosse Way to the north east. A stretch of Roman road with its original surface can be seen at Blackpool Bridge in the Forest of Dean, & Cirencester's museum reflects its status as the second most important Roman city in the country.

Offa's Dyke, 80 miles of bank & ditch on the Welsh border was the work of the Anglo-Saxons of Mercia who invaded in the wake of the Romans. Cotswold means "hills of the sheepcotes" in the Anglo-Saxon tongue, & much of the heritage of the area has its roots in the wealth created by the wool industry here.

Fine Norman churches such as those at Tewkesbury & Bishops Cleeve were overshadowed by the development of the perpendicular style of building made possible by the growing prosperity. Handsome 15th century church towers crown many wool towns & villages as at Northleach, Chipping Camden & Cirencester, & Gloucester has a splendid 14th century cathedral. Detailing on church buildings gives recognition to the source of the wealth- cloth-workers shears are depicted on the north west buttresses of Grantham church tower & couchant rams decorate church buttresses at Compton Bedale.

Wool & cloth weaving dominated life here in the 14th & 15th centuries with most families dependent on the industry. The cottage craft of weaving was gradually overtaken by larger looms & water power. A water mill can be seen in the beautiful village of Lower Slaughter & the cottages of Arlington Row in Bibury were a weaving factory. The Cotswold weaving industry gave way to the growing force of the Lancashire mills but a few centres survive. At Witney you can still buy the locally made blankets for which the town is famous.

From the 16th century the wealthy gentry built parks & mansions. Amongst the most notable are the Jacobean Manor house at Stanway & the contrasting Palladian style mansion at Barnsley Park. Elizabethan timber frame buildings can be seen at Didbrook, Dymock & Deerhurst but houses in the local mellow golden limestone are more common, with Chipping Camden providing excellent examples.

Cheltenham was only a village when, in 1716 a local farmer noticed a flock of pigeons pecking at grains of salt around a saline spring in his fields. He began to bottle & sell the water & in 1784 his son-in-law, Henry Skillicorne, built a pump room & the place received the name of Cheltenham Spa. Physicians published treatises on the healing qualities of the waters, visitors began to flock there & Cheltenham grew in style & elegance.

Gloucestershire

Gloucestershire Gazeteer

Areas of outstanding natural beauty
The Cotswolds, Malvern Hills & the Wye Valley

Houses & Castles

Ashleworth Court - Ashleworth
15th century limestone Manor house. Stone newel staircase.
Berkeley Castle - Berkeley
12th century castle - still occupied by the Berkeley family. Magnificent collections of furniture, paintings, tapestries & carved timber work. Lovely terraced gardens & deer park.
Chavenage - Tetbury
Elizabethan Cotswold Manor house, Cromwellian associations.
Clearwell Castle - Nr. Coleford
A Georgian neo-Gothic house said to be oldest in Britain, recently restored.
Court House - Painswick
Cotswold Manor house - has original court room & bedchamber of Charles I. Splendid panelling & antique furniture.
Kelmscott Manor - Nr. Lechlade
16th century country house - 17th century additions. Examples of work of William Morris, Rosetti & Burne-Jones.
Owlpen Manor - Nr. Dursley
Historic group of traditional Cotswold stone buildings. Tudor Manor house with church, barn, court house & a grist mill. Holds a rare set of 17th century painted cloth wall hangings.
Snowshill Manor - Broadway
Tudor house with 17th century facade. Unique collection of musical instruments & clocks, toys, etc. Formal garden.
Sudeley Castle - Winchcombe
12th century - home of Katherine Parr, is rich in historical associations, contains art treasures & relics of bygone days.

Cathedrals & Churches

Gloucester Cathedral
Birthplace of Perpendicular style in 14th century. Fan vaulting, east windows commemorate Battle of Crecy - Norman Chapter House.
Prinknash Abbey - Gloucester
14th & 16th century - Benedictine Abbey.
Tewkesbury Abbey - Tewkesbury
Dates back to Norman times, contains Romanesque & Gothic styles. 14th century monuments.
Bishops Cleeve (St. Michael & All Saints)
12th century with 17th century gallery. Magnificent Norman West front & south porch. Decorated chancel. Fine window.
Bledington (St.Leonards)
15th century glass in this perpendicular church--Norman bellcote. Early English east window.
Buckland (St. Michael)
13th century nave arcades. 17th century oak panelling, 15th century glass.
Cirencester (St. John the Baptist)
A magnificent church - remarkable exterior, 3 storey porch, 2 storey oriel windows, traceries & pinnacles. Wine-glass pulpit c.1450. 15th century glass in east window, monuments in Lady chapel.
Hailes Abbey - Winchcombe
14th century wall paintings, 15th century tiles, glass & screen, 17th century pulpit. Elizabethan benches.
Newland (All Saints)
13th century, restored 18th century. Pinnacled west tower; effigies.

Museums & Galleries

Bishop Hooper's Lodgings - Gloucester
3 Tudor timber frame buildings - museum of domestic life & agriculture in Gloucester since 1500.
Bourton Motor Museum - Bourton-on-the-Water
Collection of cars & motor cycles - also vintage advertising.
Cheltenham Art Gallery - Cheltenham
Gallery of Dutch paintings, collection of oils, watercolours, pottery, porcelain, English & Chinese; furniture.
City Wall & Bastion - Gloucester
Roman & mediaeval city defences in an underground exhibition room.
Stroud Museum - Cirencester
Depicts earlier settlements in the area & has a very fine collection of Roman antiquities.

Gloucestershire

Lower Slaughter.

Historic Monuments

Chedworth Roman Villa - Yanworth
Remains of Romano-British villa.
Belas Knap Long Barrow - Charlton Abbots
Neolithic burial ground - three burial chambers with external entrances.
Hailes Abbey - Stanway
Ruins of beautiful mediaeval abbey built by son of King John, 1246.
Witcombe Roman Villa - Nr. Birdlip
Large Roman villa - Hypocaust & mosaic pavements preserved.
Hetty Pegler's Tump - Uley
Long Barrow - fairly complete, chamber is 120 feet long.

Ashleworth Tithe Barn - Ashleworth
15th century tithe barn - 120 feet long - stone built, interesting roof timbering.
Odda's Chapel - Deerhurst
Rare Saxon chapel dating back to 1056.

Other things to see & do

Cheltenham International Festival of Music & Literature - Annual event.
Cotswolds Farm Park - dozens of rare breeds of farm animals
The Three Choirs Festival - music festival staged in alternating years at Gloucester, Hereford & Worcester Cathedrals.
Slimbridge - Peter Scott's Wildfowl Trust.

GLOUCESTERSHIRE
Map reference

- 01 Spiers
- 01 Price
- 02 Farley
- 02 Adams
- 02 Minchin
- 03 Kirkpatrick
- 03 Leach
- 04 Gisby
- 05 Milton
- 05 Price
- 05 Berg
- 07 Burrough
- 08 Brown
- 08 Loving
- 09 Eastman
- 11 Robinson
- 12 St. John Mildmay
- 13 Reid
- 14 Helm
- 15 Dean
- 16 Wiliams - Allen
- 17 Thompson
- 18 Swinley
- 19 Wells
- 20 Peacock
- 21 Axon
- 21 Keyte
- 22 Chambers
- 23 Simmonds
- 23 Hassell
- 24 Mills
- 25 Tremellen
- 26 Virr
- 27 Wainwright
- 28 Sparks
- 28 Saunders

Gloucestershire

		minimum £ per person	children taken	evening meals	animals taken
Mrs Patsy Spiers The Green Farm Wainlodes Lane Bishops Norton GL2 9LN Tel: (0452) 730252 Open: MAR - NOV Map Ref No. 01	Nearest Road: A.38, M.5 A very attractive 300 year-old half-timbered farmhouse, standing on a 200 acre mixed farm. There are 3 beautifully decorated bedrooms with modern amenities. Exposed beams, inglenook fireplaces with brasses & very comfortably furnished rooms. There are most attractive lawns with masses of flowers. Ideal for touring Gloucester, Cheltenham, Tewkesbury, the Forest of Dean & the Cotswolds.	£12.50	Y	N	N
Mrs Farley Rooftrees Rissington Road Bourton-on-the-Water GL54 2EB Tel: (0451) 21943 Open: ALL YEAR Map Ref No. 02	Nearest Road: A.429, A.424 Warmth, comfort & hospitality are offered in the relaxed atmosphere of this detached Cotswold stone guest house, situated on the edge of the famous village of Bourton-on-the-Water. Offering 4 bedrooms, 1 has a 4-poster bed & is en-suite. Children welcome. Traditional English home-cooking using fresh produce. An enjoyable stay is assured here while visiting the Cotswolds. No smoking in bedrooms.	£14.00	Y	Y	N
Mrs Helen Adams Upper Farm Clapton-on-the-Hill Bourton-on-the-Water GL54 2LG Tel: (0451) 20453 Open: MAR-NOV Map Ref No. 02	Nearest Road: A.40, A.429 If peace & tranquility is what you require, then this charming undiscovered village 2 miles from Bourton is certainly the spot. Clapton enjoys one of the finest Cotswold views from its hill position. Here you will find Upper Farm with its 17th century stone farmhouse, lovingly restored & retaining a wealth of original charm. Delightful accommodation, commanding views & personal attention are complimented with fresh farmhouse fayre.	£13.50	Y	N	N
Mrs C. J. Kirkpatrick Little Rissington Manor Bourton-on-the-Water GL54 2NB Tel: (0451) 21078 Open: MAR - SEPT Map Ref No. 03	Nearest Road: A.424 A 19th century Victorian Manor House set in 11 acres of grounds with superb views. Accommodation is in 5 attractive & tastefully furnished rooms, 2 with private bathroom, all have tea/coffee making facilities. A full English breakfast is served. Outdoor swimming pool & tennis court. Children most welcome, cot & highchair available. A charming residence where guests can relax in peaceful surroundings. A non-smoking establishment.	£16.00	Y	N	N
Sybil Gisby College House Chapel Street Broadwell GL56 0TW Tel: (0451) 32351 Open: ALL YEAR (Excl. Xmas/New Year) Map Ref No. 04	Nearest Road: A.429 Hidden in an enchanting & unspoilt Cotswold village, College house offers the most luxurious accommodation in lovely bedrooms with en-suite facilities. Exposed beams & ancient flagstone floors, mullioned windows with hand painted shutters. Tranquil sitting room with massive stone fireplace. Every comfort is provided & Mrs Gisby enjoys spending time with her guests.	£16.50	N	Y	N

Gloucestershire

		minimum £ per person	children taken	evening meals	animals taken
Stephanie & St.John Milton Milton House Hotel 12 Royal Parade Bayshill Road Cheltenham GL50 3AY Tel: (0242) 582601 Fax 0242 222326 Open: ALL YEAR Map Ref No. 05	Nearest Road: A.40, M.5 Milton House stands in a quiet tree-lined avenue of elegant Regency homes. Situated just a 4 mins. stroll from the imposing promenade, restaurants & the Imperial Gardens. Guests have a choice of 9 en-suite individually styled & decorated bedrooms, colour T.V., 'phone & tea/coffee makers. A choice of healthy & generously proportioned breakfasts are available together with the morning papers. There is also a pretty sun lounge with bar & T.V. An ideal base from which to explore the lovely Cotswolds.	£25.00	Y	N	N
Eric & Kath Price Stretton Lodge Western Road Cheltenham GL50 3RN Tel/Fax: (0242) 570771 Telex 444337 Open: ALL YEAR Map Ref No. 05	Nearest Road: M.5, A.40 Quiet, central period home with relaxing welcome, comfort & good food. 9 spacious, thoughtfully equipped rooms, each with private bathroom, colour T.V., telephone, trouser press, beverages & mini bar. Most non-smoking. Hosts have a wealth of information available to help you enjoy Cheltenham, the Regency Spa with its elegant buildings, gardens & superb shopping, the Cotswolds, 'Royal' Gloucestershire & the Wye Valley.	£27.50	Y	Y	N
Mr & Mrs J. Berg Hollington House Hotel 115 Hales Road Cheltenham GL52 6ST Tel: (0242) 519718 Fax 0242 570280 Open: ALL YEAR Map Ref No. 05	Nearest Road: A.40, M.5, A late victorian house with a large garden & ample parking just a few mins. from the town centre. Guests will enjoy the pleasant relaxed atmosphere & the personal attention of the proprietors. There are 9 spacious bedrooms with en-suite facilities, tea/coffee makers & colour T.V. A comfortable lounge with bar is also available. Good food is enjoyed here and a choice of menu is offered.	£22.00	Y	Y	N
Michael & Pamela Minchin The Ridge Whiteshoots Hill Bourton-on-the-Water Cheltenham GL54 2LE Tel: (0451) 20660 OpenALL YEAR(Excl Xmas) Map Ref No. 02	Nearest Road: A.429, A.40 The Ridge stands in 2 acres of beautiful secluded grounds just 1 mile from the centre of Bourton-on-the-Water. A large country house with 5 individually decorated centrally heated bedrooms, most of which are en-suite & 1 is on the ground floor. This house provides an extremely pleasant & comfortable base for touring the Cotswolds. A delicious full English breakfast is served. Good restaurants & pubs nearby serve excellent evening meals.	£13.00	Y	N	N
Viv & Robin Leach Bobble Barn Little Rissington Bourton-on-the-Water Cheltenham GL54 2ND Tel: (0451) 20340 Open: ALL YEAR Map Ref No. 03	Nearest Road: A.429, A.424 Bobble Barn is a most delightful & comfortable farmhouse converted from an ancient listed Costswold barn with magnificent views of Bourton-on-the-Water & the surrounding countryside. This lovely house offers well furnished centrally heated bedrooms with colour T.V. & tea/coffee making facilities. Some rooms have en-suite facilities. A pleasant & peaceful atmosphere at this beautiful farm. A perfect base for the Costswolds. Children over 6 welcome.	£14.00	Y	N	N

Gloucestershire

	minimum £ per person	children taken	evening meals	animals taken
Jenny & David Burrough **Windrush Farm** **Bourton-on-the-Water** **Cheltenham** **GL54 3BY** Tel: (0451) 20419 Open: ALL YEAR Map Ref No. 07	Nearest Road: A.436 This 150 acre farm is situated in the heart of the glorious Cotswolds renowned for its beauty & interest. The traditional stone mullioned farmhouse has a lovely garden & commands superb views yet is only 2 miles from Bourton. Our guest rooms are tastefully furnished & comprise 1 twin-bedded & 1 double room with en-suite bathrooms & beverage making facilities. A delicious English breakfast is served. Jenny & David enjoy helping to plan your day. Children over 10 welcome.	£15.00 (no smoking)	Y	N	N
Patricia Powell **Cotteswold House** **Market Place** **Northleach** **Cheltenham GL54 3EG** Tel: (0451) 60493 Open: ALL YEAR Map Ref No. 08	Nearest Road: A.40, A.429 This is a fine listed Costwold stone house, & having been carefully renovated to a high standard, it shows some architectural features of note. The bedrooms, of individual character, are comfortably furnished. Private facilities are available at most times. Northleach is a quiet town of historical interest & an ideal base from which to tour the surrounding area.	£14.50	Y	N	N
Mr T. Eastman **Market House** **The Square** **Northleach** **Cheltenham GL54 3EJ** Tel: (0451) 60557 Open: ALL YEAR Map Ref No. 09	Nearest Road: A.40, A.429 A 400 year-old Cotswold stone house of 'olde worlde' charm characterised by exposed beams, inglenook fireplace & flagstone floors. Located in the centre of a quiet, unspoilt Cotswold town. Offering 3 cosy bedrooms, with handbasins, tea/coffee facilities as well as map & guide information. Full central heating throughout makes for a very comfortable stay. A choice of farmhouse breakfasts will sustain you for a day's tour in the Cotswolds, Bath & Stratford.	£14.00	N	N	N
Pauline Loving **Northfield** **Cirencester Road** **Northleach** **Cheltenham GL54 3JL** Tel: (0451) 60427 Open: ALL YEAR Map Ref No. 08	Nearest Road: A.429, A.40 Detached family house in the country with large gardens & own garden produce to compliment home-cooking. Close to all local services in the small market town of Northleach. Offering 3 comfortable bedrooms, 1 en-suite. Excellent centre for visiting lovely Cotswold villages & easily reached by car are Cheltenham, Oxford, Cirencester & Stratford.	£13.00 (no smoking)	Y	Y	N
Mrs S. Simmonds **Gower House** **16 North Street** **Winchcombe** **Cheltenham GL54 5LH** Tel: (0242) 602616 Open: ALL YEAR (ExclXmas) Map Ref No. 23	Nearest Road: A.40, B.4632 Mick & Sally will welcome you to their handsome 17th century town house, situated centrally in Winchcombe, convenient for shops & restaurants. Car parking at rear of house, 3 attractive bedrooms, 1 double & 2 twin are available. Full English breakfast served with Continental alternative if requested. Pretty garden for guests' use. Baby sitting can be arranged.	£15.00	Y	N	N

Gloucestershire

			minimum £ per person	children taken	evening meals	animals taken
Mr Nick Brown The Malt House Broad Campden Chipping Campden Tel: (0386) 840295 Fax 0386 841334 Open: ALL YEAR Map Ref No. 11	Nearest Road: A.44 A personal welcome to this distinguished 17th century country house in the heart of rural England. Dinner is served on 'table d'hote' basis, the kitchen garden supplies us with fruit & vegetables in season, the cellar offers a wide choice of fine wines, spirits & liqueurs. Guests can walk in the gardens & orchards where rare breeds of poultry & Jacob sheep are kept. Croquet lawn. Children over 12 years.		£32.50 see PHOTO over	Y	Y	N
Hugh & Crystal St. John Mildmay Drakestone House Stinchcombe Dursley GL11 6AS Tel: (0453) 542140 Open: APR - OCT Map Ref No. 12	Nearest Road: A.38, B.4060 A delightful country manor house where guests receive a warm, friendly welcome & personal attention from Hugh & Crystal. The house is beautifully located on the edge of beech woods surrounded by garden, overlooking the Vale of Berkeley. This elegantly furnished & well maintained home offers most comfortable accommodation in 3 bedrooms each with individual charm. A cosy residents' lounge is also available. The formal Edwardian gardens are lovely & guests are welcome to use them.		£18.00	Y	Y	N
Mrs Sheila Reid Edale house Folly Road Parkend Lydney GL15 4JF Tel: (0594) 562835 Open: ALL YEAR Map Ref No. 13	Nearest Road: A.48, B.4234 Built in 1850, Edale House is a fine Georgian style residence facing the cricket green in the village of Parkend at the centre of the Royal Forest of Dean. To the rear is the RSPB Nagshead Nature Reserve, a delight for bird-watchers and walkers alike. Great care has been taken in providing all rooms with en-suite facilities and every comort for the discerning traveller.		£18.00	Y	Y	N
Margaret Helm Hunters Lodge Dr. Brown's Road Minchinhampton Tel: (0453) 883588 Open: All Year Map Ref No. 14	Nearest Road: A.419 A friendly and helpful welcome is assured for guests at this beautifully furnished Cotswold stone Country House situated adjoining 600 acres of National Trust common land and golf course. Central heating throughout. All bedrooms have colour T.V., tea/coffee facilities, h/c, and private bathrooms. Visitors lounge with colour T.V. adjoins delightful conservatory overlookinng large garden. Ideal centre for Bath, Cheltenham, Cirencester and South Cotswold.		£15.00	Y	N	Y
Mrs E. Dean Treetops London Road Moreton-in-Marsh GL56 0HE Tel: (0608) 51036 Open: FEB - DEC Map Ref No. 15	Nearest Road: A.44 A beautiful family home offering traditional Bed &Breakfast. 6 attractive bedrooms, 4 with bathroom en-suite, 2 of which are on the ground floor and suitable for disabled persons or wheelchair users. All rooms have T.V., radio and tea/coffee facilities. Cots and high chairs available. Delightful secluded gardens to relax in. Ideally situated for exploring the Cotswolds. A warm and homely atmosphere awaits you here.		£13.50	Y	Y	Y

The Malt House, Broad Campden.

Gloucestershire

			minimum £ per person	children taken	evening meals	animals taken
Richard & Lesley Wiliams - Allen The Laurels Guest House Inchbrook Nailsworth GL5 5HA Tel: (0453) 834021 Open: FEB - DEC Map Ref No. 16	Nearest Road: A.46 The Laurels is a lovely Georgian country house with a warm atmosphere. Attractive walled garden borders a stream and fields beyond. Heated swimming pool. Older converted buildings house family's hand-made furniture business. 3 double and 1 family room, all en-suite or private facilities, radio alarms, T.V., tea/coffee trays. Lounge with T.V. and snooker table, conservatory, and panelled study for guests' use.	£14.00	Y	Y	Y
Mrs Anne Thompson Orchard House Kilcot Newent GL18 1NP Tel: (0989) 82417 Open: ALL YEAR Map Ref No. 17	Nearest Road: M50, B.4221 This beautiful country house is completely surrounded by five acres of extensive grounds including well tended lawns, paddocks & woodland paths. A relaxed & friendly atmosphere with every modern comfort & delicious food. The elegant & finely furnished rooms include 4 attractive double bedrooms overlooking the gardens, a beamed colour T.V. lounge with log fire in winter & a spacious dinning room. Well located for visiting the Wye Valley, Cotswolds & Malverns.	£19.50	Y	Y	N
Mrs Jenny Swinley Broughtons Newnham-on-Severn GL14 1JW Tel: (045276) 328 Open: ALL YEAR Map Ref No. 18	Nearest Road: A.48 A lovely Georgian Country House built by your host's ancestors 200 years ago in an idyllic pastoral setting. As a Naval family, the Swinleys have enjoyed living overseas & welcome all their guests with friendly hospitality, offering 2 spacious twin bedrooms with private bathrooms & sitting room en-suite, also tennis, fully equipped laundry, & if required, chauffeured day trips to Bath, Cotswolds, Stratford, Wales. Good pubs & country restaurants nearby	£18.00	N	N	N
Judith Price Merrivale Tewkesbury Road Norton GL2 9LQ Tel: (0452) 730412 Open: ALL YEAR Map Ref No. 01	Nearest Road: A.38, M.5 A warm, friendly welcome awaits the visitor to Merrivale. This large homely guest house offers 6 charming, comfortable rooms. It has a nice garden for visitors to enjoy. It is well located for easy access to Gloucester & for touring the magnificent Cotswolds with their super historic villages & the surrounding countryside. Small dogs only, please. Cots provided.	£14.00	Y	N	N
Mrs Joan Wells Painswick Mill Painswick GL6 6SA Tel: (0452) 812245 Open: ALL YEAR Map Ref No. 19	Nearest Road: A.46 Painswick, a Grade II listed Cotswold stone mill dating from 1634, is situated in 4 acres of lawn & natural garden - traversed by 2 streams complete with trout. Offering 2 beamed bedrooms with tea/coffee facilities & colour T.V. Lounge, garden & hard tennis court available to guests. Painswick, "the Queen of the Cotswolds" is a good base for touring & walking. Superb local pub serves delicious meals. Steep stairs - unsuitable for young children & disabled.	£19.50	Y	N	N

Gloucestershire

	minimum £ per person	children taken	evening meals	animals taken
Gillie Peacock **Cinderhill House** **St. Briavels** **GL15 6RH** Tel: (0594) 530393 Open: ALL YEAR Map Ref No. 20	Nearest Road: A.466 A pretty 14th century house tucked into the hill below the castle in St. Briavels with magnificent views across the Wye Valley to the Brecon Beacons & Black Mountains. A comfortable, lovingly restored & tastefully furnished house, offering 6 bedrooms, 1 four-poster, with either private or en-suite bathroom. Tea/coffee making facilities. Host is a professional cook & takes delight in ensuring that all meals are well cooked using local produce.	£20.00	Y	Y	N
Mrs Barbara Axon **Croyde** **Evesham Road** **Stow on the Wold** **GL54 1EJ** Tel: (0451) 31711 Open: APR - OCT Map Ref No. 21	Nearest Road: A.429 A warm and friendly welcome awaits you at this detached Cotswold stone guest house. Ground floor accommodation, offering 2 double rooms. Just 4 minutes walk from the centre of Stow, which makes an excellent base from which to visit the many Cotswold attractions, including Warwick Castle, Blenheim Palace, Stratford upon Avon, and the beautiful Cotswold villages. Car parking. Children over 10.	£13.00	Y	N	N
Mrs V. Keyte **The Limes** **Tewkesbury Road** **Stow-on-the-Wold** **GL54 1EN** Tel: (0451) 30034 Open: ALL YEAR (Excl. Xmas & New Year) Map Ref No. 21	Nearest Road: A.424 A large family house offering excellent accommodation with 3 rooms, 1 with 4-poster, all having modern facilities, 2 en-suite. Situated only 4 minutes walk from the centre of town, it overlooks the countryside in a quiet area. Large attractive garden with ornamental pool & waterfall. A choice of good English breakfasts. From here Bourton-on-the-Water, Broadway, Burford, Chipping Campden & Moreton-in-Marsh are just a short drive.	£14.00	Y	N	N
Margaret Fraser & **Dennis Chambers** **The Old Vicarage** **167 Slad Road** **Stroud GL5 1RD** Tel: (0453) 752315 Open: FEB - DEC Map Ref No. 22	Nearest Road: M.5 Facing south overlooking the beautiful Slad Valley in the central Cotswolds, The Old Vicarage offers elegant comfort in 3 en-suite bedrooms with colour T.V., central heating & tea/coffee making facilities. Delicious meals are served in the licenced dining room. An ideal base for visiting the Cotswolds, Berkley Vale, Bath, Cheltenham, Gloucester & the Royal Forest of Dean. Pony trekking & golf nearby.	£14.00	Y	Y	Y
Queenie Mary Hassell **Burleigh Cottage** **Burleigh** **Stroud GL5 2PW** Tel: (0453) 884703 Open: ALL YEAR Map Ref No. 23	Nearest Road: A.419 Situated on 600 acres of Minchinhampton Common, designated as an area of outstanding natural beauty - Burleigh Cottage offers 3 attractively decorated rooms with private bathroom, tea/coffee making facilities, colour T.V. & beautiful views. Ideal for walking, horse riding, golf or mere relaxation; wandering around the many tranquil villages nearby, stopping for refreshment in the delightful tea shops.	£16.00	N	N	N

The Moat House Stud. Longdon.

Gloucestershire

		minimum £ per person	children taken	evening meals	animals taken
Mrs Anne Mills Down Court Slad Stroud GL6 7QE Tel: (0452) 812427 Open: ALL YEAR Map Ref No. 24	Nearest Road: A.46, B.4070 Down Court, formerly 5 farm-labourers' cottages situated at the head of the beautiful Slad valley standing in an acre of cottage garden. Down Court still retains many of its original features, inglenook fireplaces & oak beams with modern day comforts. Uninterrupted views & an ideal centre for touring the Cotswolds, Bath, Cheltenham, Gloucester, Royal Forest of Dean & the Severn Vale. A relaxing atmosphere in homely accommodation awaits guests.	£15.00	N	Y	Y
Tim & Janet Tremellen Tavern House Willesley Tetbury GL8 8QU Tel: (0666) 880444 Open: ALL YEAR Map Ref No. 25	Nearest Road: A.433 A Grade II listed, part 17th century former staging post, Tavern House has been sympathetically refurbished to provide a high standard of Bed & Breakfast accommodation. All rooms with bath & shower en-suite, direct-dial telephones, T.V., etc. Delightful gardens in which to relax. Ideally situated for the Arboretum, Badminton Horse Trials, Cheltenham Races. A genuine country house atmosphere & an excellent base from which to explore the Cotswolds.	£21.50 see PHOTO over	Y	N	N
Sue Virr The Moat House Longdon Tewkesbury GL20 6AT Tel: (068481) 313 Fax 068481 686 Open: FEB - NOV Map Ref No. 26	Nearest Road: A.438, A38 An absolutely marvellous Elizabethan, moated manor house standing in 8 secluded acres of wonderful countryside. This heavily beamed 15th century house offers delightful accommodation in a choice of 3 sumptuously appointed rooms with antique furnishings including half-tester beds & en-suite facilities. An oak pannelled guest lounge is also available. Sue, an ex-jockey runs a vetenary hospital for horses at the Moat House. Ducks, guinea fowl, peacocks & rare breeds of sheep can also be found here.	£23.00 see PHOTO over	Y	N	N
Jack & Doris Wainwright Personal Touch 37 Tirle Bank Way Newtown Tewkesbury GL20 8ES Tel: (0684) 297692 Open: ALL YEAR Map Ref No. 27	Nearest Road: M.5 A modern house overlooking farmland offering cosy & homely accommodation. 2 twin bedded rooms with modern amenities including colour T.V., shaver points & tea/coffee making facilities. A full English breakfast is served. Lounge & garden available for guests to relax in. Within walking distance of the town centre. Ideally situated for visiting Cheltenham, Cirencester, Oxford & the Cotswolds.	£13.50	Y	Y	N
Mrs J. G. Saunders Great House Castle Street Winchcombe GL54 5JA Tel: (0242) 602490 Open: ALL YEAR Map Ref No. 28	Nearest Road: A.46 A superb Jacobean house offering comfortable accommodation with modern facilities. A warm welcome awaits the visitor here. It is only half a mile walking distance to Sudeley Castle, in the heart of the Cotswolds. 2 rooms are available with T.V., & 1 with 4-poster bed. There is a garden for guests' use. Ideal touring centre.	£14.00	Y	N	N

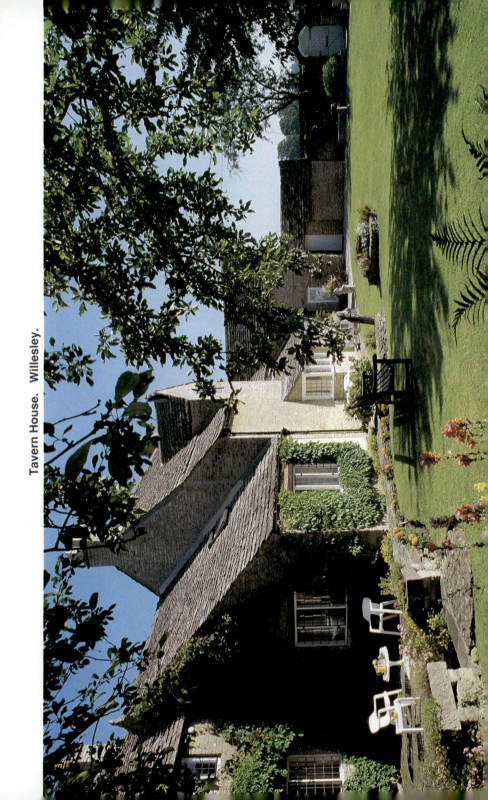

Tavern House. Willesley.

Gloucestershire

		minimum £ per person	children taken	evening meals	animals taken
Mary & Paul Sparks Postlip House Winchcombe GL54 5AH Tel: (0242) 602390 Open: ALL YEAR Map Ref No. 28	Nearest Road: A.46 B.4632 This delightful Cotswold manor house has been tastefully refurbished to a very high standard by award winning hoteliers Mary & Paul Sparks. The house is set in 7 acres of beautiful gardens & wooded grounds. There are 2 comfortable bedrooms both with ensuite facilities & a T.V. lounge. Breakfast is served in the billiard room, now a beautiful kitchen with views over the gardens & countryside. Delicious food prepared by the experienced proprietors. A warm & friendly welcome assured.	£21.00 see PHOTO over	Y	Y	N

All the establishments mentioned in this guide
are members of
The Worldwide Bed & Breakfast Association

If you have any comments regarding your accommodation
please send them to us
using the form at the back of the guide.
We value your comments

Postlip House. Winchcombe.

Hampshire

Hampshire (Southern)

Hampshire is located in the centre of the south coast of England & is blessed with much beautiful & unspoilt countryside. Wide open vistas of rich downland contrast with deep woodlands. Rivers & sparkling streams run through tranquil valleys passing nestling villages. There is a splendid coastline with seaside resorts & harbours, the cathedral city of Winchester & the "jewel" of Hampshire, the Isle of Wight.

The north of the county is known as the Hampshire Borders. Part of this countryside was immortalised by Richard Adams & the rabbits of 'Watership Down'. Beacon Hill is a notable hill-top landmark. From its slopes some of the earliest aeroplane flights were made by De Haviland in 1909. Pleasure trips & tow-path walks can be taken along the restored Basingstoke Canal.

The New Forest is probably the area most frequented by visitors. It is a landscape of great character with thatched cottages, glades & streams & a romantic beauty. There are herds of deer & the New Forest ponies wander at will. To the N.W. of Beaulieu are some of the most idyllic parts of the old forest, with fewer villages & many little streams that flow into the Avon. Lyndhurst, the "capital" of the New Forest offers a range of shops & has a contentious 19th century church constructed in scarlet brickwork banded with yellow, unusual ornamental decoration, & stained glass windows by William Morris.

The Roman city of Winchester became the capital city of Saxon Wessex & is today the capital of Hampshire. It is famous for its beautiful mediaeval cathedral, built during the reign of William the Conquerer & his notorious son Rufus. It contains the great Winchester Bible.

William completed the famous Domesday Book in the city, & Richard Coeur de Lion was crowned in the cathedral in 1194.

Portsmouth & Southampton are major ports & historic maritime cities with a wealth of castles, forts & Naval attractions from battleships to museums.

The channel of the Solent guarded by Martello towers, holds not only Southampton but numerous yachting centres, such as Hamble, Lymington & Bucklers Hard where the ships for Admiral Lord Nelson's fleet were built.

The River Test.

The Isle of Wight

The Isle of Wight lies across the sheltered waters of the Solent, & is easily reached by car or passenger ferry. The chalk stacks of the Needles & the multi-coloured sand at Alum Bay are among the best known of the island's natural attractions & there are many excellent beaches & other bays to enjoy. Cowes is a famous international sailing centre with a large number of yachting events throughout the summer. Ventnor, the most southerly resort is known as the "Madeira of England" & has an exotic botanic garden. Inland is an excellent network of footpaths & trails & many castles, manors & stately homes.

Hampshire

Hampshire
Gazeteer
Areas of outstanding natural beauty.
East & South Hampshire, North Wessex Downs & Chichester Harbour.

Houses & Castles
Avington Park - Winchester
16th century red brick house, enlarged in 17th century by the addition of two wings & a classical portico. Stateroom, ballroom with wonderful ceiling. Red drawing room, library, etc.
Beaulieu Abbey & Palace House - Beaulieu
12th century Cistercian abbey - the original gatehouse of abbey converted to palace house 1538. Houses historic car museum.
Breamore House - Breamore
16th century Elizabethan Manor House, tapestries, furniture, paintings. Also museum.
Jane Austen's Home - Chawston
Personal effects of the famous writer.
Broadlands - Romsey
16th century - park & garden created by Capability Brown. Home of the Earl Mountbatten of Burma.
Mottisfont Abbey - Nr. Romsey
12th century Augustinian Priory until Dissolution. Painting by Rex Whistler trompe l'oeil in Gothic manner.
Stratfield Saye House - Reading
17th century house presented to the Duke of Wellington 1817. Now contains his possessions - also wild fowl sanctuary.
Sandham Memorial Chapel - Sandham, Nr. Newbury
Paintings by Stanley Spencer cover the walls.
The Vyne - Sherbourne St. John
16th century red brick chapel with Renaissance glass & rare linenfold panelling. Alterations made in 1654 - classical portico. Palladian staircase dates form 1760.
West Green House - Hartley Wintney
18th century red brick house set in walled garden.

Appuldurcombe House - Wroxall, Isle of Wight
The only house in the 'Grand Manner' on the island. Beautiful English baroque east facade. House now an empty shell standing in fine park.
Osbourne House - East Cowes, Isle of Wight
Queen Victoria's seaside residence.
Carisbrooke Castle - Isle of Wight
Oldest parts 12th century, but there was a wooden castle on the mound before that. Museum in castle.

Cathedrals & Churches
Winchester Cathedral
Largest Gothic church in Europe. Norman & perpendicular styles, three sets of mediaeval paintings, marble font c.1180. Stalls c.1320 with 60 misericords. Extensive mediaeval tiled floor.
Breamore (St. Mary) - Breamore
10th century Saxon. Double splayed windows, stone rood.
East Meon (All Saints)
15th century rebuilding of Norman fabric. Tournai marble front.
Idsworth (St. Hubert)
16th century chapel - 18th century bell turret. 14th century paintings in chancel.
Pamber (dedication unknown)
Early English - Norman central tower, 15th central pews, wooden effigy of knight c.1270.
Romsey (St. Mary & St. Ethelfleda)
Norman - 13th century effigy of a lady - Saxon rood & carving of crucifixion, 16th century painted reredos.
Silchester (St. Mary)
Norman, perpendicular, 14th century effigy of a lady, 15th century screen, Early English chancel with painted patterns on south window splays, Jacobean pulpit with domed canopy.
Winchester (St. Cross)
12th century. Original chapel to Hospital. Style changing from Norman at east to decorated at west. Tiles, glass, wall painting.

Hampshire

Museums & Galleries

Browning Barracks - Aldershot
Airbourne Forces Exhibition of weapons from war, dioramas of battles, models, equipment, medals, photographs, etc.

Bargate Guildhall Museum - Southampton
Former Hall of Guilds - exhibition of local history, etc.

Southsea Castle - Portsmouth
Local history & military history, archeaology.

Cumberland House Museum & Aquarium - Southsea
Natural history & geology of district.

Portsmouth Royal Naval Museum - Portsmouth
Relics of Nelson, H.M.S. Victory, ship models, figureheads, etc.

Dickens' Birthplace Museum - Portsmouth
House where the author was born in 1812.

Southampton Art Gallery - Southampton
British & French paintings, particularly contemporary British.

Tudor House Museum - Southampton
Tudor mansion - historical antiquarian exhibits.

Westgate Museum - Winchester
Mediaeval West Gate - exhibition illustrating history of Winchester, collection of weights & measures from mediaeval time onwards.

Winchester Cathedral Treasury - Winchester
Silver from churches & parishes, etc. in Hampshire.

Winchester College Museum - Winchester
English Watercolours - collections of Greek pottery.

Museum of the Iron Age - Andover
Comprehensive view of Iron Age culture & society

Historic Monuments

Bishop Waltham's Palace - Bishops Waltham
12th & 15th centuries. Flint ruins of the palace of the Bishops of Winchester.

Basing House - Nr. Basingstoke
16th century - ruined Tudor palace - originally Saxon fortress, then Norman Castle.

Porchester Castle - Porchester
4th century - Saxon fort, 12th century keep & Assheton's tower, 1368.

Netley Abbey - Nr. Hamble
13th century - remains of Cistercian abbey.

Hurst Castle - Nr. Milford-on-Sea
Fortress built for Henry VIII - restored in 1800's.

Mary Rose Museum - Portsmouth
Almost complete Tudor Warship. Flagship of Henry VIII. Thousands of artifacts from the wreck including complete ship's surgeon's implements & the largest collection of Tudor arrows in the world. Possibly the most important archaeological discovery of this century.

Rockbourne Roman Villa - Nr. Fordingbridge
Mosaics & museum.

Other things to see & do

Cholderton Rare Breeds Farm - Cholderton

Hillier Arboretum - Nr. Romsey
World famous collection of hardy, woody plants.

The Needles Old Battery - Isle of Wight
Former fort built 1862, 250 feet above sea level. Tunnel to spectacular view of the Needles.

New Forest Museum & Visitor Centre - Lyndhurst
Displays & information

Queen Elizabeth Country Park - Nr. Petersfield
Forest drive & walking, ponytrekking, grass - skiing

Mid-Hants Railway - "The Watercress Line"
Alresford station to Alton. 10 miles of steam railway.

HAMPSHIRE
Map reference

01 Pritchard
02 Cadman
03 Hill
03 Watts
04 Harris
05 Skelton
06 Harris
07 Poulter
08 Cutmore
08 Gallagher
09 Mayle
10 Baigent
11 Nixon
12 Humphryes
13 Taylor
14 Talbot
15 Coombe
16 Farrell

Hampshire

Listing	Description	minimum £ per person	children taken	evening meals	animals taken
David & Judith Pritchard Abbotts Law Abbotts Ann Andover SP11 7DW Tel: (0264) 710350 Open: APR-OCT Map Ref No. 01	Nearest Road: A.303 A delightful country house in a picturesque village, set in 3 acres of grounds. 3 extremely attractive, large bedrooms with private facilities, colour T.V. & tea/coffee makers. 1 single room suitable for child over 10 years. Log fires & excellent cuisine. Judith is a Cordon Bleu cook & uses fresh garden produce. Heated pool, tennis court, croquet & sauna. Fishing arranged on the Test & Avon. An ideal stop on route from London to the West Country & for exploring Wessex.	£20.00 see PHOTO over	Y	Y	N
Rosemary Taylor Moortown Farm Soberton Droxford SO3 1QU Tel: (0489) 877256 Open: ALL YEAR Map Ref No. 13	Nearest Road: A.32 A friendly atmosphere is found at Moortown in the heart of the Meon Valley just by the Wayfarers Walk. Offering 2 rooms with radio, T.V. & tea & coffee making facilities. Situated in a peaceful village within easy reach of areas of outstanding beauty & historical interest such as Winchester, ancient capital of Wessex & home of King Arthurs Round Table, Portsmouth & The Mary Rose & Nelsons Flagship, Chichester & the New Forest.	£13.50	Y	N	N
Mrs G. Cadman Cottage Crest Castle Hill Woodgreen Fordingbridge SP6 2AX Tel: (0725) 22009 Open: ALL YEAR Map Ref No. 02	Nearest Road: A.338 Woodgreen, a typical New Forest village with cottages surrrounded by thick hedges to keep out the cattle & ponies. Cottage Crest is a Victorian Drover's Cottage set high in its own 4 acres enjoying superb views of the River Avon & the valley below. Bedrooms are spacious, decorated to a very high standard, all with private bathroom/shower & w.c.	£18.00	Y	N	N
Mrs Jean Harris Colt Green North End Damerham Fordingbridge SP6 3HA Tel: (07253) 240 Open: MAR - NOV Map Ref No. 04	Nearest Road: A.354, A.338 Damerham is a downland village. The part 12th century Church, with ring of 6 bells (practice Fridays), is surrounded by drifts of Snowdrops in Spring. Local footpaths by meadows, river, woods and downs. Numerous places of interest/activity within one hours drive. Colt Green, built of Cedarwood in the family's walled kitchen garden, is pleasant and comfortable. 3 double/twin rooms (1 en-suite) Children over 8.	£17.00	Y	Y	Y
Mrs P. H. Hill Priory Cottage Rockbourne Fordingbridge SP6 3NAA Tel: (07253) 246 Open: ALL YEAR Map Ref No. 03	Nearest Road: A.354, A.338 A charming house offering 3 delightful, comfortable rooms for guests. Mrs. Hill is well known for her hospitality & the house is very popular. Situated in a lovely village, it is an ideal base for visiting the numerous stately homes, museums & beauty spots in the surrounding area. Evening meals are also available, offering good cooking & home produce. Children over 12 years.	£15.00	Y	Y	N

Abbotts Law. Abbotts Ann.

Hampshire

		minimum £ per person	children taken	evening meals	animals taken
Brigadier & Mrs A.C. Watts Shearings Rockbourne Fordingbridge SP6 3NA Tel: (07253) 256 Open: Mid FEB - Mid DEC Map Ref No. 03	Nearest Road: A.354, A.338 Shearings is a much-photographed, warm, comfortable, exceptionally picturesque 16th century listed timber-framed thatched cottage. Located beside a stream in one of the prettiest villages in Hampshire, on the edge of the New Forest. The oak beams, some nearly 1000 years old & inglenook fireplaces, lend 'olde worlde' charm. The bedrooms have their own bath or shower & are prettily furnished with every comfort in mind. A lovely sitting room is available for guests where they can relax with colour T.V. & plan their visits. Children over 12.	£20.00	N	Y	N
David & Diane Skelton Cockle Warren Hotel 36 Seafront Hayling Island Havant PO11 9HL Tel: (0705) 464961/464838 Open: ALL YEAR Map Ref No. 05	Nearest Road: M.27, A delightful cottage hotel on Hayling seafront set in a large garden with hens & ducks & white picket fencing. Lovely en-suite bedrooms facing out to sea or overlooking the swimming pool, all with colour T.V., phones, etc. Some with 4-poster & Victorian beds. Enjoy French & English country cooking with home-made bread & French wine & relax by the open log fire to the sound of the sea just a few yards away. National Award Winners.	£19.00 see PHOTO over	Y	Y	Y
The Harris Family The Nodes Country Hotel Alum Bay Old Road Totland Bay Isle of Wight PO39 OHZ Tel: (0983) 752859 Open: ALL YEAR Map Ref No. 06	Nearest Road: B.3322 Set in two & a half acres of grounds at the foot of Tennyson Downs, this lovely old country house hotel offers 11 charming bedrooms with en-suite facilities, tea/coffee makers, radio & baby listening service. There are beautiful walks & views all around the hotel & the nearby beaches are superb. Some facilities of this delightful hotel are: Courtyard bar, T.V. lounge, log fires, badminton, table tennis, swings, etc.	£18.00	Y	Y	Y
Mrs Sylvia Poulter 'Quinces' Cranmore Avenue Yarmouth Isle of Wight PO41 OXS Tel: (0983) 760080 Open: ALL YEAR Map Ref No. 07	Nearest Road: A.3054 An attractive modern house set between a vineyard & a dairy farm, on a private road 2 miles from Yarmouth. 2 delightful bedrooms both with hand basins, heating & tea/coffee making facilities. It offers an ideal base for exploring the beautiful & varied countryside & coastline of West Wight. The delightful 1 acre garden with ponds, merges into a larger nature reserve where nightingales sing. Meals are good using home grown produce. Children over 6.	£13.00	Y	N	Y
Jennifer & Peter Cutmore Wheatsheaf House Gosport Street Lymington SO41 9BG Tel: (0590) 679208 Open ALL YEAR (excl. Xmas) Map Ref No. 08	Nearest Road: A.337 A beautifully appointed early 17th century former tavern, Wheatsheaf House is close to the centre of this charming Georgian market town & only 3 minutes walk from the historic town quay. Tea/coffee available on request in choice of 3 comfortable rooms. Ideally placed for sailing, the New Forest & touring the whole region, you are assured of a warm welcome. Self-catering accommodation also available.	£16.00	Y	N	Y

Cockle Warren Cottage Hotel.   Hayling Island.

Hampshire

			minimum £ per person	children taken	evening meals	animals taken
Wendy M. Gallagher Albany House Highfield Lymington SO41 9GB Tel: (0590) 671900 Open: ALL YEAR Map Ref No. 08	Nearest Road: A.337 This fine Regency house built in 1842 provides a warm welcoming atmosphere in a traditionally furnished home. There are views over the town of Solent & the Isle of Wight. Accommodaton is in 5 very comfortably furnished bedrooms most with private or en-suite facilities, colour T.V. & tea/coffee makers. Delicious meals are served in the elegant dining room using freshly prepared ingredients. In season shellfish & New Forest game will be provided.		£18.50	Y	Y	Y
Mrs G. W. Baigent Trotton Farm Trotton Rogate Petersfield GU31 5EN Tel: (0730) 813618 Open: ALL YEAR Map Ref No. 10	Nearest Road: A.272 This charming home set in 200 acres of farmland offers comfortable accommodation in 2 twin bedded rooms with en-suite shower & 1 single room. All have modern amenities including tea/coffee making facilities. A residents' lounge is available throughout the day. Games room & pretty garden for guests' relaxation. Ideally situated for visiting many local, historical, sporting attractions. 1 hour from Gatwick & Heathrow.		£17.50	Y	N	N
Mrs Yvonne Nixon The Nest 10 Middle Lane Ringwood BH24 1LE Tel: (0425) 476724 Open: ALL YEAR Map Ref No. 11	Nearest Road: A.31, B.3347 Charming Victorian family home, offering high standard of character accommodation. Quietly situated close to the centre of this riverside market town. Ideal base for exploring New Forest, River Avon fishing & South Coast beaches. Bournemouth, Salisbury & Southampton nearby. The "Laura Ashley" style rooms are fresh & comfortable with hand basins, tea/coffee facilities & colour T.V. Breakfast is served in delightful conservatory overlooking the garden. Parking available.		£14.00	Y	N	N
Mrs A. Humphryes Belmont House Gilbert Street Ropley SO24 0BY Tel: (0962) 772344 Open: ALL YEAR (Excl. Xmas/Easter) Map Ref No. 12	Nearest Road: A.31 Belmont, dating back to the 19th century, is situated on a quiet country lane, set in an acre of beautiful garden with rural views from the house. Offering 1 bedroom with private facilities, T.V. & tea/coffee makers. Short walk to village with ancient church, shop & 3 pubs. Within easy reach of Petersfield, Salisbury & Winchester by car. Approx. 1 hour from London airports		£15.00	N	N	N
Mrs Carole Mayle Rose Cottage Otterbourne Winchester SO21 2EQ Tel: (0962) 713926 Open: JAN - DEC (Excl. Xmas) Map Ref No. 09	Nearest Road: A.33, M.3 Rose Cottage, circa 1783, once owned by authoress Charlotte Young, has oak beamed lounge with inglenook fireplace, retaining original character of times past. Accommodation is offered in two charmingly furnished bedrooms; 1 double, 1 family room, both with T.V., tea/coffee facilities. Conveniently situated for visiting historic Winchester, Salisbury and the New Forest. Children over 5 please.		£18.00	Y	N	N

Hampshire

		minimum £ per person	children taken	evening meals	animals taken
Mr & Mrs J. R. Talbot Church Farm Barton Stacey Winchester SO21 3RR Tel: (0962) 760268 Open: ALL YEAR Map Ref No. 14	Nearest Road: A.303, A.34, Church Farm is a 15th century tythe barn, having Georgian & modern additions. Adjacent coach house & groom's cottage, recently converted, where guests may be totally self-contained or be welcomed to the log-fired family drawing room to dine on locally produced fresh food. 7 beautiful bedrooms for guests, most with en-suite, T.V., tea/coffee making facilities. Horses are kept. Swimming pool & croquet. Tennis court adjacent.	£25.00	Y	Y	Y
Mrs M. J. Coombe Yew Tree Cottage Lower Baybridge Lane Baybridge Winchester SO21 3RR Tel: (0962) 777254 Open: ALL YEAR Map Ref No. 15	Nearest Road: M.3 Charming 17th century thatched cottage with inglenook fireplace, log fires & antique furniture. There is a lovely cottage garden set in quiet countryside yet only 6 miles from Winchester. Accommodation is in 2 pretty bedrooms, 1 with private facilities, T.V., 'phone, radio & tea/coffee makers. Sitting room. Only 1 room is let unless to a family or party of friends ensuring complete privacy. Superb dinner is served in a typical country setting.	£18.00	Y	Y	N
Ann & Tony Farrell The Farrells 5 Ranelagh Road St Cross Winchester SO23 9TA Tel: (0962) 869555 Open: ALL YEAR Map Ref No. 16	Nearest Road: A.33, M.3 A friendly atmosphere & warm welcome are found at number 5. A pleasant Victorian house retaining many of its original features. Accommodation is in 3 rooms; 1 double, 1 twin & 1 family room, with modern amenities & tea/coffee making. There is also a T.V. lounge for guests to use. Conveniently located, only 15 minutes walk from the Cathedral.	£15.00	Y	N	N

When booking your accommodation please mention

The Best Bed & Breakfast

Hereford & Worcester

Hereford & Worcester
(Heart of England)

Hereford is a beautiful ancient city standing on the banks of the River Wye, almost a crossing point between England & Wales. It is a market centre for the Marches, the border area which has a very particular history of its own.

Hereford Cathedral has a massive sandstone tower & is a fitting venue for the Three Choirs festival which dates from 1727, taking place yearly in one or the other of the three great cathedrals of Hereford, Worcester & Gloucester.

The country is fortunate in having many well preserved historic buildings. Charming "black & white" villages abound here, romantically set in a soft green landscape.

The Royal Forest of Dean spreads its oak & beech trees over 22,000 acres. When people first made their homes in the woodlands it was vaster still. There are rich deposits of coal & iron mined for centuries by the foresters, & the trees have always been felled for charcoal. Ancient courts still exist where forest dwellers can & do claim their rights to use the forest's resources.

The landscape alters dramatically as the land rises to merge with the great Black Mountain range at heights of over 2,600 feet. It is not possible to take cars everywhere but a narrow mountain road, Gospel Pass, takes traffic from Hay-on-Wye to Llanthony with superb views of the upper Wye Valley.

The Pre-Cambrian Malvern Hills form a natural boundary between Herefordshire & Worcestershire & from the highest view points you can see over 14 counties. At their feet nestle pretty little villages such as Eastonor with its 19th century castle in revived Norman style that looks quite mediaeval amongst the parklands & gardens.

There are, in fact, five Malverns. The largest predictably known as Great Malvern was a fashionable 19th century spa & is noted for the purity of the water which is bottled & sold countrywide.

The Priory at Malvern is rich in 15th century stained glass & has a fine collection of mediaeval tiles made locally. William Langland, the 14th century author of "Piers Ploughman", was educated at the Priory & is said to have been sleeping on the Malvern Hills when he had the visionary experience which led to the creation of the poem. Sir Edward Elgar was born, lived & worked here & his "Dream of Gerontius" had its first performance in Hereford Cathedral in 1902.

In Worcestershire another glorious cathedral, with what remains of its monastic buildings, founded in the 11th century, stands beside the River Severn. College Close in Worcester is a lovely group of buildings carefully preserved & very English in character.

The Severn appears to be a very lazy waterway but flood waters can reach astonishing heights, & the "Severn Bore" is a famous phenomenon.

A cruise along the river is a pleasant way to spend a day seeing villages & churches from a different perspective, possibly visiting a riverside inn. To the south of the county lie the undulating Vales of Evesham & Broadway - described as the show village of England.

The Malvern Hills.

Hereford & Worcester

Hereford & Worcester Gazeteer

Areas of outstanding natural beauty.
The Malvern Hills, The Cotswolds, The Wye Valley

Historic Houses & Castles

Berrington Hall - Leominster
18th century - painted & plastered ceilings. Landscape by Capability Brown.
Brilley - Cwmmau Farmhouse - Whitney-on-Wye
17th century timber-framed & stone tiled farmhouse.
Burton Court - Eardisland
14th century great hall. Exhibition of European & Oriental costume & curios. Model fairground.
Croft Castle - Nr. Leominster
Castle on the Welsh border - inhabited by Croft family for 900 years.
Dinmore Manor - Nr. Hereford
14th century chapel & cloister.
Eastnor Castle - Nr. Ledbury
19th century - Castellated, containing pictures & armour. Arboretum.
Eye Manor - Leominster
17th century Carolean Manor house - excellent plasterwork, paintings, costumes, books, secret passage. Collection of dolls.
Hanbury Hall - Nr. Droitwich
18th century red brick house - only two rooms & painted ceilings on exhibition.
Harvington Hall - Kidderminster
Tudor Manor house with moat, priest's hiding places.
The Greyfriars - Worcester
15th century timber-framed building adjoins Franciscan Priory.
Hellen's - Much Marcle
13th century manorial house of brick & stone. Contains the Great hall with stone table - bedroom of Queen Mary. Much of the original furnishings remain.
Kentchurch Court - Hereford
14th century fortified border Manor house. Paintings & Carvings by Grinling Gibbons.
Moccas Court - Moccas
18th century - designed by Adam - Parklands by Capability Brown - under restoration.
Pembridge Castle - Welsh Newton
17th century moated castle.
Sutton Court - Mordiford
Palladian mansion by Wyatt, watercolours, embroideries, china.

Cathedrals & Churches

Amestry (St. John the Baptist & St.Alkmund)
16th century rood screen.
Abbey Dore (St. Mary & Holy Trinity)
17th century glass & great oak screen - early English architecture.
Brinsop (St. George)
14th century, screen & glass, alabaster reredos, windows in memory of Wordsworth, carved Norman tympanum.
Bredon (St. Giles)
12th century - central tower & spire. Mediaeval heraldic tiles, tombs & early glass.
Brockhampton (St. Eadburgh)
1902. Central tower & thatched roof.
Castle Frome (St. Michael & All Angles)
12th century carved font, 17th century effigies in alabaster.
Chaddesley Corbett (St. Cassian)
14th century monuments, 12th century font.
Elmley (St. Mary)
12th century & 15th century font, tower, gargoyles, mediaeval.
Great Witley (St. Michael)
Baroque - Plasterwork, painted ceiling, painted glass, very fine example.
Hereford (All Saints)
13th-14th centuries, spire, splendid choir stalls, chained library.
Hereford Cathedral
Small cathedral - fine central tower c.1325, splendid porch, brasses, early English Lady Chapel with lancet windows. Red sandstone.
Kilpeck (St. Mary & St. David)
Romanesque style - mediaeval windows - fine carvings.
Leominster (St. Peter & St. Paul)
12th century doorway, fine Norman arches, decorated windows.
Much Marcle (St. Bartholomew)
13th century. 14th & 17th century monuments.

Hereford & Worcester

Worcester Cathedral
11th-16th century. Fine cloisters & crypt. Tomb of King John.
Worcester (St. Swithun)
18th century - furnishings untouched. Ceiling vaulted in plaster.

Museums & Galleries

Hereford City Museum & Art Gallery
Collections of natural history & archeology, costumes, textiles, embroideries, toys, agricultural bygones. Paintings by local artists, examples of applied art, silver, pottery & porcelain.
The Old House - Hereford
Jacobean period museum with furnishings of time.
Churchill Gardens Museum - Hereford
Extensive costume collection, fine furniture, work by local artists.
Almonry Museum - Evesham
Anglo-British, Roman-British, mediaeval & monastic remains.

Avoncroft Museum of Buildings - Stoke Heath
Open air museum showing buildings of reconstructed iron-age dwelling to 15th century merchant's homes.
City Museum & Art Gallery - Worcester
Local history, archaeology, natural history, environmental studies.
Dyson Perins Museums of Worcester Porcelain - Worcester
Most comprehensive collection of old Worcester in the world.
The Commandery - Sidbury
15th century timber-framed building, was originally a hospital. Royalist H.Q. during Battle of Worcester 1651.

Other things to see & do

Three Choirs Festival - an annual event, held in the cathedrals of Hereford, Worcester & Gloucestershire, alternately.

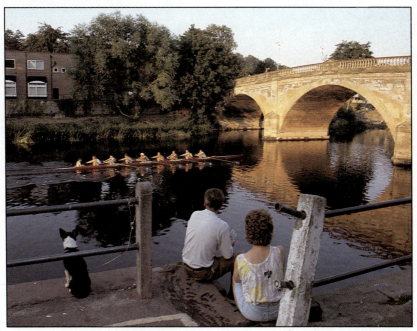

The River Severn at Bewdley.

HEREFORD & WORCESTER

Map reference

01 Barrell
02 Hart
03 R. Price
04 Lee
05 Jancey
06 Carter
06 Mears
07 Fothergill
08 Williams
08 van Gelderen
09 Blunt
10 Denne
11 Webb
12 Meekings
12 Jones
13 Page
14 Chugg
15 Teuma
16 Keel
17 Dunand
18 Neath

Herefordshire

		minimum £ per person	children taken	evening meals	animals taken

Mrs Marjorie Barrell Orchard Farm Mordiford Hereford HR1 4EJ Tel: (0432) 870253 Open: JAN - DEC Map Ref No. 01	Nearest Road: A.438, B.4224 You will be made very welcome at this delightful 17th century stone built farmhouse with large natural garden and superb views, in the Wye Valley Area of Outstanding Natural beauty. Guests return for the tranquillity and the imaginative traditional and Cordon Bleu food. 3 cosy bedrooms, furnished with period furniture and antiques, have tea-trays and wash basins. 2 guest bathrooms (1 can be private). Residential licence. Children over 10.	£14.00	Y	Y	Y
Mr & Mrs W.A. Jancey Bredwardine Hall Bredwardine Hereford HR3 6DB Tel: (09817) 596 Open: MAR - OCT Map Ref No. 05	Nearest Road: A.438 A charming 19th century Manor House with immense character and literary interest standing in secluded wooded gardens, providing elegant and well-appointed accommodation. 5 delightful bedrooms; spacious en-suite bathrooms; full central heating; tea/coffee facilities; colour T.V.s; ample parking. Excellent food and wine; relaxed, friendly atmosphere; personal service. Set in the tranquil Wye Valley, near Hay-on-Wye and its world famous bookshops.	£21.00	N	Y	N
Mrs Carol Hart The Bowens Country House Fownhope Hereford HR1 4PS Tel: (0432) 860430 Open: ALL YEAR Map Ref No. 02	Nearest Road: M.50 A delightful early Georgian, 17th century farmhouse, offering accommodation in 12 well furnished rooms, 7 ensuite, 3 with super king size beds. 4 ground floor rooms suitable for disabled guests. Each has colour T.V. & tea trays. Good home cooking using fresh local produce. Vegetarian meals available. Grass tennis court & putting green. Set in a lovely village with lovely views & walks. Within easy reach of Iron Age hill forts, Capler Hill & Cherry Hill.	£19.25	Y	Y	Y
Rosemary Price Dinedor Court Dinedor Hereford HR2 6LG Tel: (0432) 870481 Open: MAR - NOV Map Ref No. 03	Nearest Road: A.49, B.4399 Receive a friendly welcome & feel at home in this spacious 16th century farmhouse set beside the River Wye yet only 3 miles from the cathedral city of Hereford. Standing in an acre of garden with views over rolling farmland. The elegant oak panelled dining hall overlooks the cider apple orchard. Guests' own sitting room with log fires in season. 3 charming bedrooms with tea/coffee making facilities. Ideal base for touring.	£14.00	Y	N	Y
Mrs Gladys W. Lee Cwm Craig Farm Little Dewchurch Hereford HR2 6PS Tel: (0432) 840250 Open: ALL YEAR Map Ref No. 04	Nearest Road: A.49 Spacious Georgian farmhouse, surrounded by superb unspoilt countryside. Situated between the Cathedral city of Hereford & Ross-on-Wye, just a few minutes drive from the Wye Valley. Ideal base for touring the Forest of Dean. All 3 bedrooms have modern amenities, shaver points & tea/coffee facilities. There is a lounge & seperated dining room both with colour T.V. A full English breakfast is served.	£12.00	Y	N	N

Herefordshire

Details	Description	minimum £ per person	children taken	evening meals	animals taken
Mrs Mary Carter **Kimbolton Court** Kimbolton Leominster HR6 0HH Tel: (056887) 259 Open: ALL YEAR (Excl.Xmas/ New Year) Map Ref No. 06	Nearest Road: A.4112, A.49 You can be assured of a very warm welcome in this stone built farmhouse at the end of a peaceful lane which passes through a shallow ford. Offering 3 rooms, 2 double/twin with en-suite facilities & tea/coffee makers. Large lounge with colour T.V. , small library & woodburning stove. A garden room for Cordon Bleu meals which overlooks the patio & lawns. Special diets. Natural springs provide the water supply.	£13.00	Y	Y	N
Mrs Evelyn Mears **Ratefield Farm** Kimbolton Leominster HR6 0JB Tel: (0568) 612507 Open: ALL YEAR Map Ref No. 06	Nearest Road: A.49 Located in the heart of the beautiful unspoilt countryside, with 25 acres of pasture & woodland designed by Capability Brown. This 200 year-old house offers 3 bedrooms with modern amenities & tea/coffee making facilities. Comfortable colour T.V. lounge with log fire & good selection of tourist literature. Good home cooking using farm produce including beef, lamb, eggs & vegetables.Vegetarians catered for.	£15.50	Y	Y	Y
C. & M. Fothergill **'Highfield'** Newtown Ivington Road Leominster HR6 8QD Tel: (0568) 613216 Open: ALL YEAR Map Ref No. 07	Nearest Road: A.44, A.49 Twins Catherine & Marguerite are eager to make you feel welcome & at home in their elegant Edwardian house in a rural tranquil location. You will be very comfortable in any of the 3 attractive bedrooms all with a bathroom (one being en-suite). There is a large garden, T.V. lounge with crackling fire & the home-made food is absolutely delicious. Residential licence.	£18.00	Y	Y	N
Peggy & Geoff Williams **Sunnymount Hotel** Ryefield Road Ross-on-Wye HR9 5LU Tel: (0989) 63880 Open: ALL YEAR Map Ref No. 08	Nearest Road: M.50, A.40 Quietly situated on the edge of the town, this attractive Edwardian house is warm & inviting. Offering 9 well appointed bedrooms, 6 en-suite, all with tea/coffee facilities. The sitting rooms (1 with colour T.V.) & dining room overlook the pretty garden. Wide choice of breakfasts using home & local produce freshly prepared for each meal. English/French cooking. Licenced. Ample private parking. An ideal base from which to explore this fascinating area.	£17.50	Y	Y	N
Val & Tony Blunt **Woodlea Hotel** Symonds Yat West Ross-on-Wye HR9 6BL Tel: (0600) 890206 Open: MAR - DEC Map Ref No. 09	Nearest Road: A.40 A delightful family-owned Victorian guest house, set amid glorious scenery with wonderful valley views. The house has a priviliged position & overlook the famous Wye Rapids. Accommodation is in 9 rooms, with modern amenities & radio. Most rooms have en-suite facilities. There is a colour T.V. lounge, reading lounge & lounge bar where guests can relax comfortably with a drink. In the spacious dining room imaginative & delicious meals are served, accompanied by wine from the well stocked cellar. Outdoor swimming pool.	£21.50	Y	Y	Y

Herefordshire & Worcestershire

		minimum £ per person	children taken	evening meals	animals taken
Jeanne & Mike Denne Peterstow Country House Peterstow Ross-on-Wye HR9 6LB Tel: (0989) 62826 Fax 0989 67264 Open: JAN - DEC Map Ref No. 10	Nearest Road: A.49 Peterstow House is a magnificent Georgian Rectory set in 25 acres of pastures, woodlands & paddocks. 9 bedrooms with private facilities, telephone, radio, T.V. & tea/coffee makers. Fishing, clay pigeon shooting & pony trekking in the Forest of Dean available. Within the grounds of Peterstow lies The Flann Farmhouse where the fresh produce used in the restaurant is grown. An excellent base with Hereford, Monmouth, Gloucester & Chepstow close by. Children over 7.	£20.50	Y	Y	N
Renate van Gelderen Edde Cross House Edde Cross Street Ross-on-Wye HR9 7BZ Tel: (0989) 65088 Open: FEB - NOV Map Ref No. 08	Nearest Road: A.40, M.50 Edde Cross House, once the home of Sybil the Dame of Sark, is a Georgian town house of great charm & character overlooking the river. Offering 5 beautifully decorated & comfortable furnished bedrooms. 2 en-suite, each with tea/coffee makers, colour T.V. & hairdryer. Extensive breakfast menu including vegetarian. This is an ideal base from which to explore the Wye Valley & Forest of Dean. Children over 10.	£17.00	Y	N	N
Anne & Jack Webb Queen's House Wigmore HR6 9UN Tel: (056886) 451 Open: ALL YEAR Map Ref No. 11	Nearest Road: A.4110 Three Elizabethan cottages have been altered & extended to make a comfortable, rambling house. Guest accommodation comprises 4 bedrooms with h & c & tea/coffee making facilities. A comfortable & well appointed guests' lounge with open fire & colour T.V. is available. Delicious meals served in the spacious stone flagged dining hall with inglenook fireplace & exposed beams. An ideal base for touring. Offa's Dyke & Welsh border 8 miles away.	£12.00	Y	Y	Y

Worcestershire

Mrs Barbara Meekings Leasow House Laverton Meadows Broadway WR12 7NA Tel: (0386) 73526 Open: ALL YEAR Map Ref No. 12	Nearest Road: A.46, B.4632 Leasow is a charming 17th century Cotswold stone farmhouse. Recently renovated, it now offers guests a choice of 7 delightful spacious bedrooms, each with shower/bath en-suite, T.V. & tea/coffee making faclities. Set in the peaceful tranquility of the open countryside, it is only two & a half miles from Broadway village. The house has wonderful panoramic views of the Cotswold escarpment. Ideally situated for touring the Cotswolds & the Vale of Evesham. A warm welcome, friendly hosts & comfortable accommodation ensure an enjoyable & memorable stay.	£23.00 *see PHOTO over*	Y	N	Y

Leasow House.   Broadway.

Worcestershire

		minimum £ per person	children taken	evening meals	animals taken
Frances & Jim Page **Crofton Lodge** **80 New Road** **Bromsgrove B60 2LA** Tel: (0527) 74136 Open: FEB-NOV Map Ref No. 13	Nearest Road: A.38, M5. Crofton Lodge is an attractive Victorian town house, with a walled garden, built in 1880. 1 double & 1 twin room, with the usual coffee & tea making facilities, are available together with a sitting room, with colour T.V., available for guests' use. Stratford, Worcester & Birmingham are within half an hour, the Cotswolds, Malvern Hills, Shropshire & Herefordshire within an hour's drive. Leaflet available.	£13.50	Y	N	N
Mrs Jacqueline Chugg **Little Lodge Farm** **Broughton Green** **Hanbury** **Droitwich WR9 7EE** Tel: (0527) 821305 Open: APRIL - OCT Map Ref No. 14	Nearest Road: A.38, B.4090 This charming grade II listed Black & White Tudor farmhouse, once a hunting lodge in the Deer Park of Feckenham Forest, is now surrounded by 330 acres of farmland. A lovely country home with exposed beams, inglenook fireplaces, dried flowers & beautiful fabrics complement the antique furniture. 3 guest bedrooms with ensuite or private bathroom.. Home-made bread & preserves. An unusually quiet & scenic spot to stay. Central for Stratford, Worcester & Cotswolds.	£18.50 *see PHOTO over*	Y	N	N
Rosalind Teuma **The Nupend** **Cradley** **Malvern** **WR13 5NP** Tel: (0886) 880881 Open: ALL YEAR Map Ref No. 15	Nearest Road: A.4103 Elegant Georgian former farmhouse in grounds of 2 acres in Area of Outstanding Natural Beauty. Ideal for nature lovers, walkers, painters or as touring base for Welsh Marches, Cotswolds, Wye Valley, Shakespeare Country. All 4 bedrooms have views of Malvern Hills, en-suite bathroom, colour T.V., tea/coffee making facilities. Choice of breakfast, optional 4-course dinner or high tea, all freshly cooked in traditional manner using only finest ingredients. Vegetarians catered for. French & German spoken.	£20.00	N	Y	N
Mrs Carolyn Dunand **49 Britannia Square** **Worcester** **WR1 3HP** Tel: (0905) 22756 Open: ALL YEAR Map Ref No. 17	Nearest Road: A.38, M.5 Charming home in quiet & pleasant Georgian square near the city centre. Cathedral, Theatre, Royal Worcester Porcelain & many places of historic interest in this 'Faithful City' are within walking distance. An ideal centre for touring. Spacious comfortable rooms all with tea/coffee making facilities & T.V. One double with bathroom en-suite. One twin & one single with shared bathroom. Lovely walled garden. Parking.	£17.00	Y	N	Y
Helen & John Jones **The Old Rectory** **Church Street** **Willersey** **Broadway WR12 7PN** Tel: (0386) 853729 Open: ALL YEAR Map Ref No. 12	Nearest Road: B.4632 Guests can be assured of a warmth of welcome second to none at this 300 year old Georgian rectory. Set in 1/2 acre of beautiful walled gardens the Old Rectory retains its original charm & character with many old beams & open fireplaces. Accommodation is in a choice of 6 rooms with en-suite or private facilities with 'phone, radio, colour T.V. & tea/coffee makers. This is a delightful home to rest & relax in.	£39.50	Y	N	N

Little Lodge Farm, Hanbury.

Worcestershire

		minimum £ per person	children taken	evening meals	animals taken
Jane Keel **Hunthouse Farm** **Frith Common** **Tenbury Well WR15 8JY** Tel: (029983) 2277 / (029922) 277 Open: ALL YEAR Map Ref No. 16	Nearest Road: A.456, A.443 Relax and enjoy comfort, peace and hospitality in this beautiful 16th century timbered farmhouse ideally situated amidst 180 acre arable/sheep farm, commanding memorable views. The 3 comfortable bedrooms are all en-suite with tea-making facilities. There is a colour television in the guest sitting room where guests are welcomed with tea and home-made cake. Excellent local eating houses. Children over 8 years please.	£15.00	Y	N	N
Sally Neath **Church Farm** **Abberley** **Worcester WR6 6BB** Tel: (0299) 896316 Open: APR -OCT Map Ref No. 18	Nearest Road: A.443, B.4202 You will find Church Farm 12 miles west of Worcester in a setting that delights visitors, nestling against the backdrop of the Abberley Hills. This is complemented by the attractive, individually decorated bedrooms which are all en-suite. Evening meals are no problem as you can stroll from the door across the fields to the village Inn. Ideally situated to vist some of England's most beautiful countryside.	£15.00	Y	N	N

All the establishments mentioned in this guide

are members of

The Worldwide Bed & Breakfast Association

Kent

Kent
(South East)

Kent is best known as "the garden of England". At its heart is a tranquil landscape of apple & cherry orchards, hop-fields & oast-houses, but there are also empty downs, chalk sea-cliffs, rich marshlands, sea ports, castles & the glory of Canterbury Cathedral.

The dramatic chalk ridgeway of the North Downs links the White Cliffs of Dover with the north of the county which extends into the edge of London. It was a trade route in ancient times following the high downs above the Weald, dense forest in those days. It can be followed today & it offers broad views of the now agricultural Weald.

The pilgrims who flocked to Canterbury in the 12th-15th centuries, (colourfully portrayed in Chaucer's Canterbury Tales), probably used the path of the Roman Watling Street rather than the high ridgeway.

Canterbury was the cradle of Christianity in southern England & is by tradition the seat of the Primate of All England. This site, on the River Stour, has been settled since the earliest times & became a Saxon stonghold under King Ethelbert of Kent. He established a church here, but it was in Norman times that the first great building work was carried out, to be continued in stages until the 15th century. The result is a blending of styles with early Norman work, a later Norman choir, a vaulted nave in Gothic style & a great tower of Tudor design. Thomas Becket was murdered on the steps of the Cathedral in 1170. The town retains much of its mediaeval character with half-timbered weavers' cottages, old churches & the twin towers of the west gate.

Two main styles of building give the villages of Kent their special character. The Kentish yeoman's house was the home of the wealthier farmers & is found throughout the county. It is a timber-frame building with white lath & plaster walls & a hipped roof of red tiles. Rather more modest in style is a small weatherboard house, usually painted white or cream. Rolvenden & Groombridge have the typical charm of a Kentish village whilst Tunbridge Wells is an attractive town, with a paved parade known as the Pantiles & excellent antique shops.

There are grand houses & castles throughout the county. Leeds Castle stands in a lake & dates back to the 9th century. It has beautifully landscaped parkland. Knowle House is an impressive Jacobean & Tudor Manor House with rough ragstone walls, & acres of deer-park & woodland.

Kent is easily accessible from the Channel Ports, Gatwick & London.

Ightham Mote

Kent

Kent Gazeteer
Areas of outstanding natural beauty.
Kent Downs.

Historic Houses & Castles
Aylesford, The Friars - Nr. Maidstone
13th century Friary & shrine of Our Lady, (much restored), 14th century cloisters - original.
Allington Castle - Nr. Maidstone
13th century. One time home of Tudor poet Thomas Wyatt. Restored early 20th century. Icons & Renaissance paintings.
Black Charles - Nr. Sevenoaks
14th century Hall house - Tudor fireplaces, beautiful panelling.
Boughton Monchelsea Place - Nr. Maidstone
Elizabethan Manor House - grey stone battlements - 18th century landscaped park, wonderful views of Weald of Kent.
Chartwell - Westerham
Home of Sir Winston Churchill.
Chiddingstone Castle - Nr. Edenbridge
18th century Gothic revival building encasing old remains of original Manor House - Royal Stuart & Jacobite collection. Ancient Egyptian collection - Japanese netsuke, etc.
Eyehorne Manor - Hollingbourne
15th century Manor house with 17th century additions.
Cobham Hall - Cobham
16th century house - Gothic & Renaissance - Wyatt interior. Now school for girls.
Fairfield - Eastry, Sandwich
13th-14th centuries - moated castle. Was home of Anne Boleyn. Beautiful gardens with unique collection of classical statuary.
Knole - Sevenoaks
15th century - splendid Jacobean interior - 17th & 18th century furniture. One of the largest private houses in England.
 Leeds Castle - Nr. Maidstone
Built in middle of the lake, it was the home of the mediaeval Queens of England.
Lullingstone Castle - Eynsford
14th century mansion house - frequented by Henry VIII & Queen Anne. Still occupied by descendants of original owners.
Long Barn - Sevenoaks
14th century house - said to be home of William Caxton. Restored by Edwin Lutyens; 16th century barn added to enlarge house. Galleried hall - fine beaming & fireplaces. Lovely gardens created by Sir Harold Nicholson & his wife Vita Sackville-West.
Owletts - Cobham
Carolean house of red brick with plasterwork ceiling & fine staircase.
Owl House - Lamberhurst
16th century cottage, tile hung; said to be home of wool smuggler. Charming gardens.
Penshurst Place - Tonbridge
14th century house with mediaeval Great Hall perfectly preserved. English Gothic. Birthplace of Elizabethan poet, Sir Philip Sidney
Fine staterooms, splendid picture gallery, famous toy museum. Tudor gardens & orchards.
Saltwood Castle - Nr. Hythe
Mediaeval - very fine castle & is privately occupied. Was lived in by Sir Ralph de Broc, murderer of Thomas a Becket.
Squerreys Court - Westerham
Manor house of William & Mary period, with furniture, paintings & tapestries of time. Connections with General Wolfe.
Stoneacre - Otham
15th century yeoman's half-timbered house.

Cathedrals & Churches
Brook (St. Mary)
11th century paintings in this unaltered early Norman church.
Brookland (St. Augustine)
13th century & some later part. Crown-post roofs, detached wooden belfry with conical cap. 12th century lead font.
Canterbury Cathedral
12th century wall paintings, 12th & 13th century stained glass. Very fine Norman crypt. Early perpendicular nave & cloisters which have heraldic bosses. Wonderful central tower.
Charing (St. Peter & St. Paul)
13th & 15th century interior with 15th century tower. 17th century restoration.

Kent

Cobham (St. Mary)
16th century carved & painted tombs - unequalled collection of brasses in county.
Elham (St. Mary the Virgin)
Norman wall with 13th century arcades, perpendicular clerestory. Restored by Eden.
Lullingstone (St. Botolph)
14th century mainly - 16th century wood screen. Painted glass monuments.
Newington-on-the-Street (St. Mary the Virgin)
13th & 14th century - fine tower. 13th century tomb. Wall paintings.
Rochester Cathedral
Norman facade & nave, otherwise early English. 12th century west door. 14th century doorway to Chapter room.
Stone (St. Mary)
13th century - decorated - paintings, 15th century brass, 16th century tomb.
Woodchurch (All Saints)
13th century, having late Norman font & priest's brass of 1320. Arcades alternating octagonal & rounded columns. Triple lancets with banded marble shafting at east end.

Museums & Galleries

Royal Museums - Canterbury
Archaeological, geological, mineralogical exhibits, natural history, pottery & porcelain. Engravings, prints & pictures.
Westgate - Canterbury
Museum of armour, etc. in 14th century gatehouse of city.
Dartford District Museum - Dartford
Roman, Saxon & natural history.
Deal Museum - Deal
Prehistoric & historic antiquities.
Dicken's House Museum - Broadstairs
Personalia of Dickens; prints, costume & Victoriana.
Down House - Downe
The home of Charles Darwin for 40 years, now his memorial & museum.
Dover Museum - Dover
Roman pottery, ceramics, coins, zoology, geology, local history, etc.
Faversham Heritage Society - Faversham
1000 years of history & heritage.
Folkestone Museum & Art Gallery - Folkestone
Archeology, local history & sciences.
Herne Bay Museum - Herne Bay
Stone, Bronze & Early Iron Age specimens. Roman material from Reculver excavations. Items of local & Kentish interest.
Museum & Art Gallery - Maidstone
16th century manor house exhibiting natural history & archaeolgical collections. Costume Gallery, bygones, ceramics, 17th century works by Dutch & Italian painters. Regimental museum

Historic Monuments

Eynsford Castle - Eynsford
12th century castle remains.
Rochester Castle - Rochester
Storied keep - 1126-39
Roman Fort & Anglo-Saxon Church - Reculver
Excavated remains of 3rd century fort & Saxon church.
Little Kit's Coty House - Aylesford
Ruins of burial chambers from 2 long barrows.
Lullingstone Roman Villa - Lullingstone
Roman farmstead excavations.
Roman Fort & Town - Richborough
Roman 'Rutupiae' & fort
Tonbridge Castle - Tonbridge
12th century curtain walls, shell of keep & 14th century gatehouse.
Dover Castle - Dover
Keep built by Henry II in 1180. Outer curtain built 13th century.

Gardens

Chilham Castle Gardens - Nr. Canterbury
25 acre gardens of Jacobean house, laid out by Tradescant. Lake garden, fine trees & birds of prey. Jousting & mediaeval banquets.
Great Comp Gardens - Nr. Borough Green
Outstanding 7 acre garden with old brick walls.
Owl House Gardens - Lamberhurst
16th century smugglers cottage with beautiful gardens of roses, daffodils & rhododendrons.
Sissinghurst Castle Gardens - Sissinghurst
Famous gardens created by Vita Sackville-West around the remains of an Elizabethan mansion.

KENT
Map reference

01	Scrivens	14	Piper
02	Towner	15	Harman
03	Swatland	16	Brooks
04	Pellay	17	Coleman
04	Jenkins	18	Bannock
04	Dellaway	19	Earl
04	Hall	20	Dakin
06	Hilary	21	Lindsay
06	Kirk	22	Scott
07	Wilton	23	Rawlinson
07	Tennent	24	Emanuel
08	Stearns	25	Wotton
08	Oaten	25	Dakin
09	Alexander	25	Carrell
10	Oakley	26	Godbold
10	Reidy		
10	Howarth		
10	Robbins		
11	Chesterfield		
12	Latham		
13	Coleman		

207

Anns House. Canterbury.

Kent

			per person minimum £	children taken	evening meals	animals taken
Pam & Alan Scrivens **Tram Hatch** **Charing Heath** **Ashford** **TN27 0BN** Tel: (023371) 3373 Open: ALL YEAR Map Ref No. 01	Nearest Road: A.20 Tram Hatch is a lovely 14th century manor house, standing in seven & a half acres of grounds including 2 acres of formal gardens, with the River Stour flowing through half a mile. The many original dark oak beams & inglenook fireplaces lend great charm & character to this super house. Now carefully refurbished, the accommodation offered is very spacious & comfortable, with en-suite facilities, one 4-poster bed, T.V. & radio. Guests may also like to use the swimming pool. Close by are Leeds & Chilham castles.		£19.00	N	Y	N
Mrs Dianne Towner **Hill Cottage** **Pluckley** **Ashford TN27 0PE** Tel: (023384) 448 Open: APR - OCT Map Ref No. 02	Nearest Road: A.20 Hill Cottage is a lovely 17th century cottage with Dering windows, interior beams and inglenook fireplaces. Soft country furnishings and antiques create a warm atmosphere. Two twin rooms with colour T.V. and tea/coffee making facilities. Guests are welcome to enjoy the exceptionally beautiful garden. Attention to detail assures you of an enjoyable stay. Children over 8 please.	🚭	£15.00	Y	N	N
Mrs Anne Swatland **Groome Farm** **Newland Green** **Egerton** **Ashford TN27 9EP** Tel: (023376) 260 Open: APR - SEPT Map Ref No. 03	Nearest Road: A.20 Groome Farm is a superb 15th century half timbered farmhouse. The rooms are quite delightful; heavily beamed with inglenook fireplaces & decorated with many lovely antiques, creating a charming 'olde worlde' atmosphere. Offering 3 rooms, each with private facilities, a residents' lounge & a fabulous garden. A plantsman's paradise beautifully tended with every kind of herb & shrub. A first class spot for a break.		£16.00	Y	N	N
David & Jill Jenkins **Thanington Hotel** **140 Wincheap** **Canterbury** **CT1 3RY** Tel: (0227) 453227 Open: JAN - DEC Map Ref No. 04	Nearest Road: A.28, A.2 Bed & Breakfast in style. Five minutes stroll to Cathedral and city centre. !0 en-suite bedrooms, with telephone, colour T.V., tea/coffee facilities, hairdryer, trouser-press, even your own wall safe. There is an elegant dining room, lounge, garden room and pretty walled garden with large terrace for relaxing. Private car park. A warm welcome and efficient service await you at Thanington Hotel.		£20.00	Y	N	Y
Lisa Dellaway **Anns House** **63 London Road** **Canterbury** **CT2 8JZ** Tel: (0227) 768767 Open: ALL YEAR Map Ref No. 04	Nearest Road: A.2 Furnished to a high standard this delightful Victorian house offers 19 tastefully decorated bedrooms, some with 4 posters, many en-suite with colour T.V. & tea/coffee making facilities (3 on the ground floor). Delicious breakfast menu. Situated only 3 minutes walk from the city centre, Anns House is an excellent base from which to visit Canterbury Cathedral & many other attractions. Good local pubs & restaurants. Ample parking.		£18.00 *see PHOTO over*	Y	N	Y

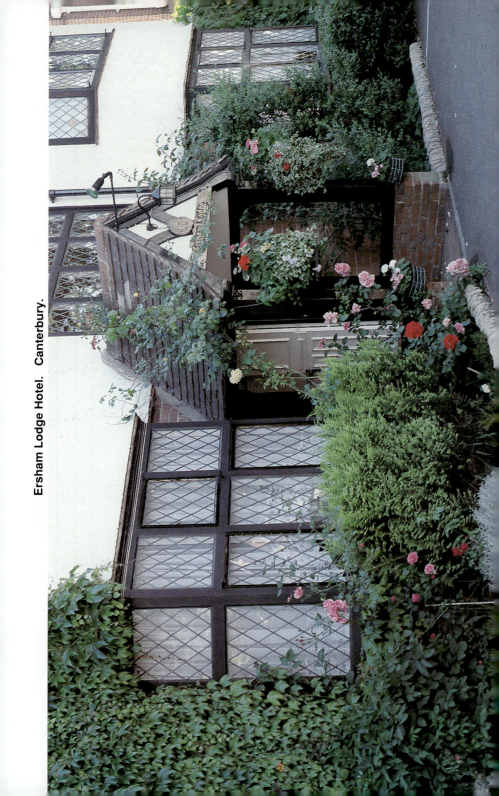

Ersham Lodge Hotel. Canterbury.

Kent

per person minimum £ / children taken / evening meals / animals taken

A. & K. Pellay **Ersham Lodge Hotel** 12 New Dover Road Canterbury CT1 3AP Tel: (0227) 463174 Fax 0227 455 482 Open: JAN-OCT Map Ref No. 04	Nearest Road: A.2, M2 This well established Tudor Lodge is run professionally to high standards & is furnished with exquisite taste & elegance. Its delightfully appointed bedrooms offer modern amenities, colour T.V., radio, telephone, hairdryer, en-suite facilities. Public areas include a well stocked bar, a bright breakfast room & a pleasant patio. Ersham Lodge is a leisurely 5 minute walk from the Cathedral. Parking & lock-up garage.	£22.00 see PHOTO over	Y	N	Y
Robin Hall **Yorke Lodge** 50 London Road Canterbury CT2 8LF Tel: (0227) 451243 Fax 0227 451243 Open: JAN - DEC Map Ref No. 04	Nearest Road: A.2, M.2 A spacious, elegant, Victorian house close to the city centre, Yorke Lodge has been completely refurbished in 1989. All rooms have private facilities, plus radio & 'phone. Each is beautifully decorated, echoing the Victorian features & character of the house. Robin enjoys offering a very special English Bed & Breakfast to his guests & provide all the comforts of a home away from home. Fax & boardroom style conference facilities are also available.	£15.00 see PHOTO over	Y	N	N
Hilary Harper **East Bridge Country Hotel** Bridge Hill Bridge Canterbury CT4 5AS Tel: (0227) 830808 Open: ALL YEAR Map Ref No. 06	Nearest Road: A.2, M.2 A friendly, elegant & comfortable Georgian house in a pretty village. 15 minutes from sea ports of Dover & Folkstone. Overlooking open countryside of outstanding beauty, the house offers acccommodation in 8 rooms, 4 en-suite, all with modern amenities, T.V. & tea/coffee making facilities. Ideal for walking, riding, fishing. Close to Kent's historic castles. Tasty English breakfasts. Licenced restaurant available to residents & non residents.	£21.00	Y	Y	N
Barry & Pleasance Kirk **Wych Elm Guest House** 13 High Street Bridge Canterbury CT4 5JY Tel: (0227) 830242 Open: ALL YEAR Map Ref No. 06	Nearest Road: A.2, M.2 This pretty Regency house is delightfully situated in the small village of Bridge. Accommodation is in a choice of 3 comfortable rooms with modern amenities, 1 with private shower, all with tea making facilities. A very comfortable lounge/dining room, decorated with antiques is available as is the very attractive walled garden. The food here is delicious. Evening meals are well prepared & nicely served along with a complimentary glass of wine. Ideal as a base for touring.	£15.00	Y	Y	N
Sheila Wilton **Walnut Tree Farm** Lynsore Bottom Upper Hardres Canterbury CT4 6EG Tel: (022787) 375 Open: ALL YEAR Map Ref No. 07	Nearest Road: A.2 Set in 6 acres of its own land, this delightful 14th century thatched farmhouse offers peace & tranquility in unspoilt countryside. Offering family accommodation or friends wishing to share, in 2 double adjacent bedrooms with shower rooms en-suite or double en-suite, in dormer of cottage. Good farmhouse breakfast, home-made bread, marmalade, preserves & fresh eggs. Ideal base for walking, bird watching & en-route to Continent. Excellent pub food 2 miles away.	£16.00	Y	N	N

211

Yorke Lodge. Canterbury.

Kent

			minimum £ per person	children taken	evening meals	animals taken
Mrs Patricia Tennent **Little Mystole** **Mystole Park** **Canterbury CT4 7DB** Tel: (0227) 738210 Open: ALL YEAR (Excl. Xmas) Map Ref No. 07	Nearest Road: A.28 Small Georgian house of great charm with pretty, secluded walled garden amongst parkland, orchards and hop gardens in area of unspoilt natural beauty. Canterbury 5 miles; Dover and the Channel ferries 30 minutes drive. Beautiful castles and gardens nearby, Hever, Leeds and Sissinghurst to name but a few. Guests will enjoy peace and comfort in a relaxed, cosy atmosphere. 3 rooms with en-suite or private facilities.		£25.00	Y	Y	Y
James & Pat Stearns **Sissinghurst Castle Farm** **Sissinghurst** **Cranbrook TN17 2AB** Tel: (0580) 712885 Open: ALL YEAR (excl. Xmas) Map Ref No. 08	Nearest Road: A.262 This Victorian farmhouse is delightfully situated in the grounds of the famous Sissinghurst Castle. All rooms are spacious with beautiful views & have tea making facilities. One bedroom has en-suite facilities & one a private shower. A guests' colour T.V. lounge & garden are available. Evening meals provided by arrangement. Vegetarians can be catered for. This makes a good base for touring the many historic sites of Kent.		£19.00	Y	Y	N
Mr & Mrs A. T. R. Oaten **Hancocks Farmhouse** **Tilsden Lane** **Cranbrook** **TN17 3PH** Tel: (0580) 714645 Open: ALL YEAR Map Ref No. 08	Nearest Road: A.229. A. 262 Extended in the late 16th century, Hancocks Farmhouse is now a lovely grade II listed building, surrounded by farmland on the edge of the Wealdon town of Cranbrook. Comfortably furnished with antiques, the accommodation is in 3 beautifully decorated bedrooms, 1 with four poster, modern amenities including radio & tea/coffee making facilities. Dinner here is delicious & all the bread, rolls, cakes & jams are home made. A lounge is available & guests may relax in the pretty country garden.		£16.00	Y	Y	Y
Mrs Sarah Alexander **Home Farm** **Riverside** **Eynsford** **Dartford DA4 0AE** Tel: (0322) 866193 Open: MAR - NOV Map Ref No. 09	Nearest Road: M.25, M20 Situated in a picturesque village within an area of outstanding natural beauty. This 18th century farmhouse set on a dairy/arable farm offers 3 attractively furnished en-suite bedrooms with modern amenities including tea/coffee making facilities. Ideal for London, Gatwick & the Channel ports. Only 2 miles from the M.25/M.20 junction. Leeds Castle, Brands Hatch & many National Trust properties within easy reach. There are many places to eat in the village.		£17.00	Y	N	N
Mr & Mrs C. P. Oakley **Wallett's Court Manor** **West Cliffe** **St Margarets-at-Cliffe** **Dover CT15 6EW** Tel: (0304) 852424 Open: ALL YEAR Map Ref No. 10	Nearest Road: A.258, B.2058 A wonderful 17th century manor house, home of William Pitt the Younger, situated in countryside above the White Cliffs of Dover. 7 luxury bedrooms, all en-suite. Oak beams & inglenook fireplaces. True 17th century atmosphere. Homemade produce for breakfast & Saturday is 'Gourmet Evening' in the restaurant. Kingsdown Golf Course close by. A very warm welcome awaits all visitors to this lovely house.		£22.00	Y	Y	N

Kent

			minimum £ per person	children taken	evening meals	animals taken
John & Adeline Reidy **Number One Guest House** **1 Castle Street** **Dover CT16 1QH** Tel: (0304) 202007 Open: ALL YEAR Map Ref No. 10	Nearest Road: A20, A2 An attractive guest house dating back to 1800 & one of Dover's oldest homes. Dominated by the imposing castle, it is ideally situated for both town & ferries. 5 very comfortable rooms all with bath or shower en-suite, colour T.V., tea/coffee makers. Breakfast is a real pleasure as it is served in your room. A pleasant lounge for guests & a high walled garden-a perfect sun trap on summer evenings. Lock up garage.		£14.00	Y	N	N
Nona Howarth **Castle Guest House** **10 Castle Hill Road** **Dover CT16 1QW** Tel: (0304) 201656 Fax 0304 210197 Open: FEB - NOV Map Ref No. 10	Nearest Road: A.2, M.2, A20 Castle House is situated in the foothills of Dover Castle & is a few minutes from the town centre, ferries & hoverport. Accommodation is in 6 comfortable bedrooms 3 with private shower, all with modern amenities, including colour T.V. & tea/coffee making facilities. A hearty English or Continental breakfast is served. Residents' lounge available throughout the day. A lovely family guest house with warm & welcoming hosts. No smoking in public rooms.		£14.00	Y	N	N
Mr & Mrs L. Robbins **Dell Guest House** **233 Folkestone Road** **Dover CT17 9SL** Tel: (0304) 202422 Open: ALL YEAR Map Ref No. 10	Nearest Road: A.20, M.20 A friendly welcome is extended to all guests, together with comfort & cleanliness, at this pleasant Victorian house. Offering a choice of 6 bedrooms with modern facilities. A colour T.V. lounge is also available. The Robbins' serve breakfast from 6a.m. every morning so that those catching the early morning cross channel ferries get a good early start. Conveniently located close to docks & station. Parking.		£12.50	Y	N	N
Mrs Susan Chesterfield **Frith Farm House** **Otterden** **Faversham ME13 0DD** Tel: (0795) 89701/ 890701 Open: ALL YEAR Map Ref No. 11	Nearest Road: A.2, A.20, M.2 A warm welcome awaits guests at this restored Georgian farmhouse, surrounded by lovely cherry trees. It stands in an area of outstanding natural beauty. Accommodation is in a choice of 3 en-suite rooms with radio, T.V. & tea/coffee making facilities. This makes a pleasant base from which to tour the whole of Kent. Leeds Castle, Rochester, Chilam & Canterbury are nearby. Children over 10 years only.		£19.50	Y	Y	N
Prudence Latham **Tenterden House** **209 The Street** **Boughton** **Faversham ME13 9BL** Tel: (0227) 751593 Open: ALL YEAR Map Ref No. 12	Nearest Road: A.2, M.2 Tenterden House is a listed Tudor building in the village of Boughton which is 6 miles from Canterbury, 1 mile from the M.2 & within 5 miles of the coast. The old gardener's cottage has been renovated to provide 2 comfortable bedrooms (1 double & 1 twin) with modern amenities including h&c, T.V. & tea/coffee making facilities. A full English breakfast is served in the main house. An ideal spot for touring.		£13.00	Y	N	N

Kent

		minimum £ per person	children taken	evening meals	animals taken
Mrs S. Coleman Crowbourne Farm House Goudhurst TN17 1ET Tel: (0580) 211226 Open: FEB - DEC Map Ref No. 13	Nearest Road: A.262 Crowbourne is a delightful 17th century farmhouse in a 125 acre fruit & sheep farm, peacefully situated with glorious views just outside the charming village of Goudhurst. Accommodation is in 3 lovely comfortable rooms with bath (1 en-suite) sitting room with T.V. & tea/coffee making facilities. Delicious evening meals, using local produce, by arrangement only. Ideal for visiting Kent castles especially Sissinghurst. Golf, fishing & sailing nearby. Gatwick 1 hour.	£18.00	Y	Y	N
Mrs Rosemary Piper Conghurst Farm Conghurst Lane Hawkhurst TN18 4RW Tel: (0580) 753331 Open: MAR - OCT Map Ref No. 14	Nearest Road: A.268, A.229 Conghurst is a 500 acre sheep/arable farm on the Kent/Sussex border in beautiful, unspoilt countryside. Excellent holiday base. Many historic houses and gardens in area; Tunbridge Wells, Rye, Hastings nearby; Canterbury an hours drive. 3 bedrooms, all with private bathrooms, radio, tea/coffee facilities. Separate T.V. and sitting rooms for guests use. Outdoor swimming pool. Evening meals by prior arrangement.	£16.50	Y	Y	N
Mrs Jane Harman Vine Farm Waterman Quarter Headcorn TN27 9JJ Tel: (0622) 890203 Open: MAR - NOV Map Ref No. 15	Nearest Road: A.274, M.20 Quietly situated on its own drive and surrounded by its farmland, Vine Farmhouse is a 16th century Wealden residence. It is heavily beamed and provides comfortable accommodation in 3 rooms with en-suite or private bathrooms. T.V., & tea/coffee facilities. Headcorn is 2 miles away, and this central position makes for easy access to all the attractions of the county and much of East Sussex.	£17.50	N	Y	N
Mrs Diana Brooks Lucy's Lucy's Hill Hythe CT21 5ES Tel: (0303) 262018 Open: ALL YEAR Map Ref No. 16	Nearest Road: M.20 Lucy's, built in 1883 for Sir Henry Lucy, first editor of Punch, has panoramic sea views and lovely terraced gardens. The owners previously ran an excellent restaurant and provide a homely atmosphere in a beautiful house. 3 bedrooms with private bathrooms, T.V., tea/coffee facilities. Children over 10 welcome. Two golf courses one mile. Under 3 miles from M.20; close to Channel Ports and Tunnel terminal. Canterbury 25 minutes drive.	£17.50	Y	Y	N
Mrs Lisa Coleman Warwick House 64 Tonbridge Road Maidstone ME16 8SE Tel: (0622) 756096 Open: ALL YEAR Map Ref No. 17	Nearest Road: A.20, M.20 A marvellous 16th century Tudor house standing in a huge garden. 3 super rooms with modern facilities. The proprietors extend a warm welcome & arrange theatres, outings, restaurants, plus a guided car tour to many interesting places. Leeds Castle, Knowle Castle, Hever Castle, Sissinghurst & Canterbury within comfortable driving distance. French & German spoken. No babies, please. Hostess is accredited guide to Leeds Castle & area.	£16.00	Y	N	N

The Greswolde Hotel. Margate.

Kent

			minimum £ per person	children taken	evening meals	animals taken
Mrs Rosemarie Bannock **Court Lodge Farm** **The Street** Teston Maidstone ME18 5AQ Tel/Fax: (0622) 814200/ Open ALL YEAR (Excl Xmas) Map Ref No. 18	Nearest Road: M.20, A.26 With lovely views overlooking the River Medway Valley with its hop gardens & orchards, this 16th century oak beamed farmhouse offers warm & friendly hospitality. All 4 attractively furnished rooms, 2 with private facilities are spacious & comfortable. Only 4 miles from Maidstone & M.20 & convenient for visiting Leeds Castle, Igtham Mote & Chartwell, yet London, Heathrow, Gatwick, Sheerness & Dover are only 1 hour by car.		£15.00 🚭	Y	N	N
Mrs Ann Earl **The Greswolde Hotel** **20 Surrey Road** Cliftonville Margate CT9 2LA Tel: (0843) 223956 Open: ALL YEAR Map Ref No. 19	Nearest Road: M.2, A.299 The Greswolde, a 6 bedroomed Victorian Hotel retaining much of its original character & charm. All rooms have en-suite facilities, with colour T.V. & tea makers. There is a quiet, relaxing lounge/reading room. Located 100 yds. from the promenade, close to championship indoor & outdoor bowling greens with many golf courses in easy reach. Pubs & eating places are nearby. Ideal for touring with Channel ports close by.		£15.50 see PHOTO over	Y	N	Y
Cynthia Dakin **Swale Cottage** **Old Swaylands Lane** off Poundsbridge Lane Penshurst TN11 8AH Tel: (0892) 870738 Open: ALL YEAR Map Ref No. 20	Nearest Road: B.2176, M.25 Swale Cottage is a charmingly converted Kentish barn of architectural merit. A Grade II listed building. Formerly part of a 13th century Yeoman farm. 3 beautifully furnished en-suite guest rooms with T.V. & modern amenities. Four poster suite & twin bedded rooms available. Idyllic tranquil setting with views over a hilly wooded valley & rose garden. Near to Penshurst Place & Hever & Chartwell Castles. Within easy reach of both London airports.		£20.00 🚭	N	N	N
Mrs Jo Lindsay A.T.D.N.D.D. **Jordans** **Sheet Hill** Plaxtol Sevenoaks TN15 0PU Tel: (0732) 810379 Open: Mid MAR - Mid DEC Map Ref No. 21	Nearest Road: M.25, Beautiful picture-postcard 15th century Tudor house, awarded a 'Historic Building of Kent' plaque & situated in the picturesque village of Plaxtol, among orchards & parkland. The house is beautifully furnished, has leaded windows, inglenook fireplaces, massive oak beams & an enchanting old English garden, with rambler roses & espalier trees. Within easy reach are Ightham Mote, Leeds Castle, Penshurst, Hever Castle, Chartwell & Knole. 3 lovely rooms, 2 with en-suite facilites. London 35 mins by train & easy access to airports.		£19.00 🚭 see PHOTO over	Y	N	N
Mrs Josephine Scott **Munk's Farm** **Smarden** TN27 8PN Tel: (023377) 265 Open: JAN - DEC Map Ref No. 22	Nearest Road: A.274 Munk's Farm is a listed 17th century, oak beamed, weatherboarded farmhouse with inglenook fireplaces. It is set in a large attractive garden with swimming pool , and surrounded by farmland. There are 3 charming, comfortably furnished twin-bedded rooms with en-suite or private bathrooms, and guests' lounge. Sissinghurst, Leeds Castle and many other castles and gardens nearby; Canterbury, Rye and the Channel Ports within easy reach.		£15.00 🚭	N	Y	N

217

Jordans. Plaxtol.

Kent

		minimum £ per person	children taken	evening meals	animals taken
Maureen Rawlinson **Brattle House** **Cranbrook Road** **Tenterden** **TN30 6UL** Tel: (05806) 3565 Open: ALL YEAR Map Ref No. 23	Nearest Road: A.28 A handsome Georgian farmhouse dating from the 17th century, surrounded by a large garden & the Wealden countryside. Accommodation is in 3 luxuriously furnished en-suite bedrooms providing every comfort. Evening meals are served by candlelight in the elegant dining room furnished with antiques. The cooking is of a high standard & vegetarians can be catered for. Close by are Sissinghurst, Bodiam & Leeds Castles. Ideal centre for touring Kent & Sussex. Children over 12 years only.	£19.50	Y	Y	N
Mrs A. Emanuel **Little Pagehurst** **Staplehurst** **Tonbridge TN12 OJD** Tel: (0580) 891486 Open: ALL YEAR Map Ref No. 24	Nearest Road: M.20 Situated near Staplehurst in the Weald of Kent, this fine listed Elizabethan house set in mature grounds close to several gardens & castles. The interior combines modern & traditional furnishings. Superb breakfasts & fine English cooking. Tennis court, heated pool & croquet lawn available. A relaxed atmosphere awaits you at Little Pagehurst. An excellent base for a weekend break or an overnight stay. Children over 10 years welcome.	£20.00 *see PHOTO over*	Y	Y	N
Mrs R. Wotton **Town House** **64 Dudley Road** **Tunbridge Wells** **TN1 1LF** Tel: (0892) 35130/35100 Open: JAN - NOV Map Ref No. 25	Nearest Road: A.26 One of the original principal houses of Tunbridge Wells, Town House offers spacious & well-fitted rooms close to the town centre, entertainments & the beautiful common, with many restaurants nearby. Overnight parking is adjacent & main bus routes just a short stroll away. Each bedroom is very comfortable, having full central heating, colour T.V. & tea/coffee making facilities. Many historic attractions are nearby, including Chartwell, Penshurst Place, Knowle Park & the castles of Scotney, Hever, Leeds & Bodiam. 45 minutes drive from Gatwick.	£17.00	Y	N	N
Mrs C. M. Carrell **Rowden House Farm** **Frant** **Tunbridge Wells** **TN3 9HS** Tel: (0892) 750259 Open: APR - OCT Map Ref No. 25	Nearest Road: A.267 A delightful Elizabethan house standing on a 15 acre small-holding with sheep, horses & chickens. Surrounded by the beautiful, rolling ,wooded countryside of Sussex it is perfectly placed for visiting Kent, Sussex & the south coast. Accommodation is in 1 twin bedded room, with private facilities & 2 singles, with radio & tea/coffee making facilities. An attractive drawing room with colour T.V.. Gatwick 1 hour, London one & a half hours drive. Children over 10 yrs. .	£17.00	Y	N	N
Angela Jane Godbold **Danehurst House Hotel** **41 Lower Green Road** **Rusthall** **Tunbridge Wells TN4 8TW** Tel: (0892) 27739 Open: JAN - DEC Map Ref No. 26	Nearest Road: A.264 Danehurst is an attractive Victorian character house. 6 tastefully furnished bedrooms, 4 with en-suite facilities, afford you excellent accommodation. Breakfast is served in a delightful conservatory, and intimate candle-lit dinners in the elegant dining room. Your hosts welcome you most warmly to their home, and would like to feel you can relax and enjoy everything they and the area have to offer.	£24.00	Y	Y	N

Little Pagehurst. Staplehurst.

Kent

	minimum £ per person	children taken	evening meals	animals taken
Tony & Mary Dakin The Old Parsonage Church Lane Frant Tunbridge Wells TN3 9DX Tel: (0892) 750773 Open: ALL YEAR Map Ref No. 25	Nearest Road: A.267 The Old Parsonage is a classic Georgian rectory built by Lord Abergavenny for his son who was the parish priest between 1820 & 1846. The house is located in one of Southern England's prettiest villages, 2 miles from Royal Tunbridge Wells. Accommodation is in 3 en-suite rooms, 1 with four poster, all with colour T.V.. The reception rooms are beautifully furnished with antiques. Within a short drive of 15 historic houses. Gatwick 40 mins., Heathrow 70 mins., London 40 mins. by train.	£19.00 *see PHOTO over*	Y	N	Y

All the establishments mentioned in this guide
are members of
The Worldwide Bed & Breakfast Association

When booking your accommodation please
mention
The Best Bed & Breakfast

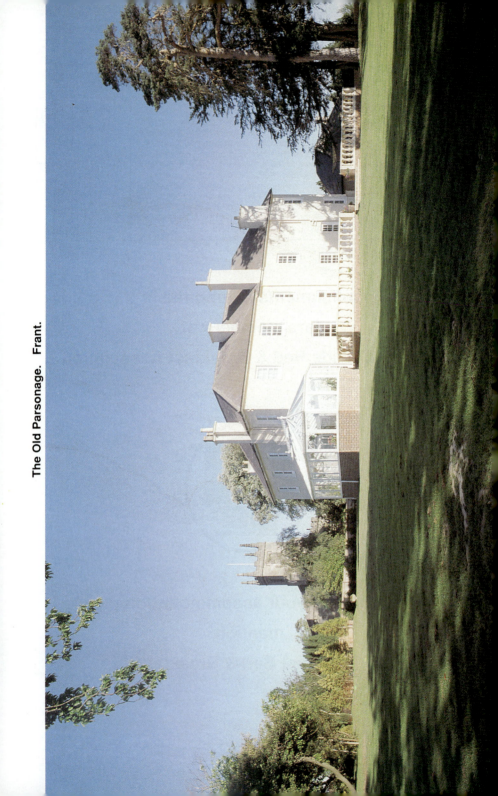

The Old Parsonage. Frant.

Lancashire

Lancashire (North West)

Lancashire can prove a surprisingly beautiful county. Despite its industrial history of cotton production, there is magnificent scenery & there are many fine towns & villages. Connections with the Crown & the clashes of the Houses of Lancaster & York have left a rich heritage of buildings with a variety of architecture. There are old stone cottages & farmhouses, as well as manor houses from many centuries.

For lovers of the countryside, Lancashire has the sweeping hills of Bowland, the lovely Ribble Valley, the moors of Rossendale & one mountain, mysterious Pendle Hill.

The Royal Forest of Bowland is a forest without trees, which has provided rich hunting grounds over the centuries. An old windswept pass runs over the heights of Salter Fell & High Cross Fell from Slaidburn, where the Inn, the "Hark to Bounty", was named after the noisiest hound in the squire's pack & used to be the courtroom where strict forest laws were enforced.

Further south, the Trough of Bowland provides an easier route through the hills, & here is the beautiful village of Abbeystead in Wynesdale where monks once farmed the land. The church has stained glass windows portraying shepherds & their flocks & there are pegs in the porch where shepherds hung their crooks.

Below the dramatic hills of Bowland, the green valley of the Ribble climbs from Preston to the Yorkshire Dales. Hangridge Fell, where the tales of witches are almost as numerous as those of Pendle Hill, lies at the beginning of the valley.

Pendle Hill can be reached from the pretty village of Downham which has Tudor, Jacobean & Georgian houses, village stocks & an old inn. Old Pendle rises abruptly to 1831 feet & is a strange land formation. It is shrouded in legend & stories of witchcraft.

Between Pendle Hill & the moors of Rossendale are the textile towns of Nelson, Colne, Burnley, Accrington & Blackburn. The textile industry was well established in Tudor times & the towns grew up as markets for the trading of the cloth woven in the Piece Halls.

The moors which descend to the very edges of the textile towns are wild & beautiful & have many prehistoric tumuli & earthworks. Through the towns & the countryside, winds the Liverpool & Leeds canal, providing an excellent towpath route to see the area.

Lancaster is an historic city boasting the largest castle in England, dating back to Norman times.

Lancashire's coastal resorts are legendary, & Blackpool is Queen of them all with her miles of Illuminations & millions of visitors.

Downham Village.

Lancashire

Lancashire Gazeteer

Areas of outstanding natural beauty.
The Forest of Bowland, Parts of Arnside & Silverdale.

Historic Houses & Castles

Rufford Old Hall - Rufford
15th century screen in half-timbered hall of note. Collection of relics of Lancashire life.
Chingle Hall - Nr. Preston
13th century - small manor house with moat. Rose gardens. Haunted!
Astley Hall - Chorley
Elizabethan house reconstructed in 17th century. Houses pictures, tapestries, pottery & furniture.
Gawthorpe Hall - Padiham
17th century manor house with 19th century restoration. Moulded ceilings & some fine panelling. A collection of lace & embroidery.
Bramall Hall - Bramall
Fine example of half-timbered (black & white) manor house built in 14th century & added to in Elizabethan times. Fine grounds.
Lancaster Castle - Lancaster
Largest of English castles - dates back to Norman era.
Astley Hall - Chorley
16th century half-timbered grouped around central court. Rebuilt in the Jacobean manner with long gallery. Unique furniture.
Hoghton Tower - Nr. Preston
16th century - fortified hill-top mansion - magnificent banquet hall. Dramatic building - walled gardens & rose gardens.
Thurnham Hall - Lancaster
13th century origins. 16th century additions & 19th century facade. Beautiful plasterwork of Elizabethan period. Jacobean staircase.

Cathedrals & Churches

Lancaster (St. Mary)
15th century with 18th century tower. Restored chapel - fine stalls.
Whalley (St. Mary)
13th century with 15th century tower, clerestory & aisle windows. Fine wood carving of 15th century canopied stalls.
Halsall (St. Cuthbert)
14th century chancel, 15th century perpendicular spire. 14th century tomb. Original doors, brasses & effigies. 19th century restoration.
Tarleton (St. Mary)
18th century part 19th century.
Great Mitton (All Hallows)
15th century rood screen, 16th century font cover, 17th century pulpit.

Museums & Galleries

Blackburn Museum - Blackburn
Extensive collections relating to local history archeology, ceramics, geology & natural history. One of the finest collection of coins & fine collection of mediaeval illuminated manuscripts & early printed books.
Bury Museum & Art Gallery - Bury
Houses fine Victorian oil & watercolours. Turner, Constable, Landseer, de Wint
City Gallery - Manchester
Pre-Raphaelites, Old Masters, Impressionists, modern painters all represented in this fine gallery; also silver & pottery collections.
Higher Mill Museum - Helmshaw
One of the oldest wool textile finishing mills left in Lancashire. Spinning wheels, Hargreave's Spinning Jenny, several of Arkwrights machines, 20 foot water wheel.
Townley Hall Art Gallery & Museum, & Museum of Local Crafts & Industries - Burnley

LANCASHIRE

Map reference

01 Yeomans
02 Dodgson
03 Edwards
04 Townend
05 Ireland

Sunray. Blackpool.

Lancashire

			minimum £ per person	children taken	evening meals	animals taken
Jean & John Dodgson Sunray Private Hotel 42 Knowle Avenue Blackpool FY2 9TQ Tel: (0253) 51937 Fax 0253 862357 Open: Map Ref No. 02	Nearest Road: A.585 A 16th century Manor House standing in 4 acres of grounds overlooking the banks of the River Wyre. Once the home of the Hesketh Family & Prince George IV. This grade II listed house retains much of its period detail including oak panelling, open fire places & four-poster beds. All rooms have private facilities, colour T.V., radio, 'phone, trouser press & tea/coffee makers. Convenient for Blackpool & the Lake District.	£24.00 *see PHOTO over*		Y	Y	Y
Roger & Pamela Yeomans Mains Hall Country House Mains Lane Little Singleton Blackpool FY6 7LE Tel: (0253) 885130 Fax 0253 894132 Open: ALL YEAR Map Ref No. 01	Nearest Road: A.6, M.6 Ex 35 Guests will find a comfortable, friendly atmosphere in this delightful 17th century farmhouse. Situated on a small sheep & beef-rearing farm of 52 acres, it is conveniently located between Carnforth & Bolton-le-Sands. Accommodation is in 4 pleasant rooms 2 with en-suite facilities & tea/coffee making facilities. There are 2 comfortable lounges, one with colour T.V. Hot drinks & biscuits are served. Breakfast is served in the attractive dining room.	£30.00	Y	Y	Y
Mark & Patricia Edwards Lindeth House Lindeth Road Silverdale Carnforth LA5 0TX Tel: (0524) 701238 Open: FEB-DEC Map Ref No. 03	Nearest Road A.6, M.6 Ex 35 Pleasant country house situated within an area of outstanding natural beauty surrounded by woodland walks, yet only a few minutes from the coast. All 3 bedrooms are individually furnished with private facilities, colour T.V., clock-radio, tea/coffee makers & hairdryer. Enjoy a five course, candle-lit dinner in the elegant, licenced dining room. A relaxed & friendly atmosphere makes this an ideal base for a quiet break or touring the Lake District.	£18.50	Y	Y	N
Mrs Adelaide Ireland Thwaite End Farm Bolton-le-Sands Carnforth LA5 9TN Tel: (0524) 732551 Open: ALL YEAR Map Ref No. 05	Nearest Road: A.6, M.6 Ex. 35 Absolute peace & comfort are found in this enchanting 17th century house, with its many low ceilings & ancient oak beams. Enjoy the cosiness of the lounge, an excellent candle-lit dinner & retire to one of three charming fully equipped bedrooms with en-suite/private facilities & colour T.V.. 3 miles from the M.6 in superb countryside. Ideal for the Lake District/Yorkshire Dales or stopover London-Scotland. N.W. Regional Winner. Best Bed & Breakfast Award for Excellence. No smoking in the bedrooms Children over 10 welcome.	£17.50	N	N	N
Mrs Sally Townend New Capernwray Farmhouse Capernwray Carnforth LA6 1AD Tel: (0524) 734284 Open: ALL YEAR Map Ref No. 04	Nearest Road: M.55 Situated in the seaside resort of Blackpool, Sunray Private Hotel offers attractive accommodation in 9 bedrooms each with private bathroom, radio, colour T.V. & tea/coffee making facilities. Excellent English breakfast & evening meals served. Guests may relax in the residents' lounge available throughout the day. An ideal base for a holiday or for visiting the many places of interest in Lancashire.	£26.00 *see PHOTO over*	Y	Y	Y

New Capernwray Farm. Carnforth.

Leicester & Notts

Leicestershire
(East Midlands)

Rural Leicestershire is rich in grazing land, a peaceful, undramatic landscape broken up by the waterways that flow through in the south of the county.

The River Avon passes on its way to Stratford, running by 17th century Stanford Hall & its motorcycle museum. The Leicester section of the Grand Union Canal was once very important for the transportation of goods from the factories of the Midlands to London Docks. It passes through a fascinating series of multiple locks at Foxton. The decorative barges, the 'narrow boats' are pleasure craft these days rather than the life-blood of the closed community of boat people who lived & worked out their lives on the canals.

Rutland was formerly England's smallest county, but was absorbed into East Leicestershire in the 1970's. Its name lives on in Rutland Water, one of Europe's largest reservoirs & an attractive setting for sailing, fishing or enjoying a trip on the pleasure cruiser. There is also the Rutland Theatre at Tolethorpe Hall, where a summer season of Shakespeare's plays is presented in the open air.

Melton Mowbray is famous for its pork pies & it is also the centre of Stilton cheese country. The "King of Cheeses" is made mainly in the Vale of Belvoir where Leicestershire meets Nottinghamshire, & the battlements & turrets of Belvoir Castle overlook the scene from its hill-top.

To the north-west the Charnwood Forest area is pleasantly wooded & the deer park at Bradgate surrounding the ruined home of Lady Jane Grey, England's nine-day queen, is a popular attraction.

Nottinghamshire
(East Midlands)

Nottinghamshire has a diversity of landscape from forest to farmland, from coal mines to industrial areas.

The north of the county is dominated by the expanse of Sherwood Forest, smaller now than in the time of legendary Robin Hood & his Merry Men, but still a lovely old woodland of Oak & Birch.

The Dukeries are so called because of the numerous ducal houses built in the area & there is beautiful parkland on these great estates that can be visited. Clumber Park, for instance has a huge lake & a double avenue of Limes.

Newstead Abbey was a mediaeval priory converted into the Byron family home in the 16th century. It houses the poet Byron's manuscripts & possessions & is set in wonderful gardens.

More modest is the terraced house in Eastwood, where D.H. Lawrence was born into the mining community on which his novels are based.

Nottingham was recorded in the Domesday Book as a thriving community & that tradition continues. It was here that Arkwright perfected his cotton-spinning machinery & went on to develop steam as a power source for industry.

Textiles, shoes, bicycles & tobacco are all famous Nottingham products, & the story of Nottingham Lace can be discovered at the Lace Hall, housed in a former church.

Nottingham Castle, high on Castle Rock, was built & destroyed & rebuilt many times during its history. It now houses the city's Art Gallery & Museum. The Castle towers over the ancient 'Trip to Jerusalem' Inn, said to be so named because crusaders stopped there for a drink on their way to fight in the Holy Land.

Leicester & Notts

Leicestershire Gazeteer
Areas of outstanding natural beauty.
Charnwood Forest, Rutland Water.

Historic Houses & Castles
Belvoir Castle - Nr. Grantham
Overlooking the Vale of Belvoir, castle rebuilt in 1816, with many special events including jousting tournaments. Home of the Duke of Rutland since Henry VIII. Paintings, furniture, historic armoury, military museums, magnificent stateroom

Oakham Castle - Oakham
Norman banqueting hall of late 12th century

Stanford Hall - Nr Lutterworth
17th century William & Mary house - collection of Stuart relics & pictures, antiques & costumes of family from Elizabeth I onward. Motor cycle museum.

Stapleford Park - Nr. Melton Mowbray
Old wing dated 1500, restored 1663. Extended to mansion in 1670. Collection of pictures, tapestries, furniture & Balston's Staffordshire portrait figures of Victorian age.

Cathedrals & Churches
Breedon-on-the-Hill (St. Mary & St. Hardulph)
Norman & 13th century. Jacobean canopied pew, 18th century carvings.
Empingham (St. Peter)
14th century west tower, front & crocketed spire. Early English interior - double piscina, triple sedilla.
Lyddington (St. Andrew)
Perpendicular in the main - mediaeval wall paintings & brasses.
Staunton Harol (Holy Trinity)
17th century - quite unique Cromwellian church - painted ceilings.

Belvoir Castle

Belgrave Hall - Leicester
18th century Queen Anne house - furnishing of 18th & 19th centuries.
Langton Hall - Nr. Market Harborough
Privately occupied - perfect English country house from mediaeval times - drawing rooms have 18th century Venetian lace.

Museums & Galleries
Bosworth Battlefield Visitor Centre - Nr Market Bosworth
Exhibitions, models, battlefield trails at site of 1485 Battle of Bosworth where Richard III lost his life & crown to Henry.
Leicestershire Museum of Technology - Leicester
Beam engines, steam shovel, knitting machinery & other aspects of the county's industrial past.
Leicester Museum & Art Gallery - Leicester
Painting collection. 18th & 19th century, watercolours & drawings, 20th century French paintings, Old Master & modern prints, English silver & ceramics, special exhibitions.
Jewry Wall Museum & Site - Leicester
Roman wall & baths site adjoining museum of archaeology.

Leicester & Notts

Melton Carnegie Museum-Melton Mobray Displays on Stilton cheese, pork pies & other aspects of the past & present life of the area.
Rutland County Museum - Oakham Domestic & agricultural life of Rutland, formerly England's smallest county.
Donnington Collection of Single-Seater Racing Cars - Castle Donington Large collection of grand prix racing cars & racing motorcycles, adjoining Donington Park racing circuit..
Wygson's House Museum of Costume - Leicestershire Costume, accessories & shop settings in late mediaeval buildings.
The Bellfoundry Museum - Loughborough Moulding, casting, tuning & fitting of bells, with conducted tours of bellfoundry.

Historic Monuments

The Castle - Ashby-de-la-Zouch 14th century with tower added in 15th century.
Kirby Muxloe Castle - Kirby Muxloe 15th century fortified manor house with moat ruins.

Other things to see & do

Rutland Farm Park - Oakham Rare & commercial breeds of livestock in 18 acres of park & woodland, with early 19th century farm buildings.
Stoughton Farm Park - Nr. Leicester Shire horses, rare breeds, small animals & modern 140 dairy herd. Milking demonstrations, farm museum, woodland walks, adventure playground.
Twycross Zoo - Nr. Atherstone Gorillas, orang-utans, chimpanzees, gibbons, elephants, giraffes, lions & many other animals.
The Battlefield Line - Nr. Market Bosworth Steam railway & collection of railway relics, adjoining Bosworth Battlefield.
Great Central Railway - Loughborough Steam railway over 5-mile route in Charnwood Forest area, with steam & diesel museum.
Rutland Railway Museum - Nr. Oakham Industrial steam & diesel locomotives & wagons from quarries, mines & factories.

Nottinghamshire Gazeteer

Historic Houses & Castles

Holme Pierrepont Hall - Nr. Nottingham Outstanding red brick Tudor manor, in continuous family ownership, with 19th century courtyard garden.
Newark Castle - Newark Dramatic castle ruins on riverside site, once one of the most important castles of the north.
Newstead Abbey - Nr. Mansfield Priory converted to coutry mansion, home of poet Lord Byron with many of his possessions & manuscripts on display. Beautiful parkland, lakes & gardens.
Nottingham Castle - Nottingham 17th century residence on site of mediaeval castle. Fine collections of ceramics, silver, Nottingham alabaster carvings, local historical displays. Art gallery. Special exhibitions & events.
Wollaton Hall - Nottingham Elizabethan mansion now housing natural history exhibits. Stands in deer park, with Industrial Museum in former stables, illustrating the city's bicycle, hosiery, lace, pharmaceutical & other industries.

Cathedrals & Churches

Egmanton (St. Mary) Magnificent interior by Comper. Norman doorway & font. Canopied rood screen, 17th century altar.
Newark (St. Mary Magdalene) 15th century. 2 painted panels of "Dance of Death". Reredos by Comper.
Southwell Cathedral Norman nave, unvaulted, fine early English choir. Decorated pulpitum, 6 canopied stalls, fine misericords. Octagonal chapter house..
Terseval (St. Catherine) 12th century - interior 17th century unrestored

Museums & Galleries

Castlegate Museum - Nottingham Row of Georgian terraced houses showing costume & textile collection. Lace making equipment & lace collection.
Nottingham Castle Museum - Nottingham Collections of ceramics, glass & silver. Alabaster carvings.

Leicester & Notts

D.H. Lawrence Birthplace - Eastwood
Home of the novelist & poet, as it would have been at time of his birth, 1885.
Millgate Museum of Social & Folk Life - Newark
Local social & folk life, with craft workshops.
Brewhouse Yard Museum - Nottingham
Daily life in Nottingham, displayed in 17th century cottages & rock-cut cellars.
The Lace Hall - Nottingham
The story of Nottingham Lace audio-visual display & exhibition with lace shops, in fine converted church.
Museum of Costume & Textiles - Nottingham
Costumes, lace & textiles on display in fine Georgian buildings.
Bassetlaw Museum - Retford
Local history of north Nottinghamshire.
Canal Museum - Nottinghamshire
History of the River Trent & canal history, in former canal warehouse.
Ruddington Framework Knitters' Museum - Ruddington
Unique complex of early 19th-century framework knitters' buildings with over 20 hand frames in restored workshop.

Other things to see & do

The Tales of Robin Hood - Nottingham
A 'flight to adventure' from mediaeval Nottingham to Sherwood Forest through the tales of the world's most famous outlaw.
Clumber Park - Nr. Worksop
Landscaped parkland with double avenue of limes, lake, chapel. One of the Dukeries' estates, though the house no longer remains.
Rufford - Nr. Ollerton
Parkland, lake & gallery with fine crafts, around ruin of Cistercian abbey.
Sherwood Forest Visitor Centre - Nr. Edwinstowe
Robin Hood exhibition & 450 acres of ancient oak woodland associated with the outlaw & his merry men.
Sherwood Forest Farm Park - Nr. Edwinstowe
Rare breeds of cattle, sheep, pigs & goats. Lake with wildfowl.
White Post Farm Centre - Farnsfield, Nr Newark
Working modern farm with crops & many animals, including cows, sheep, pigs, hens, geese, ducks, llamas, horses. Indoor displays & exhibits.

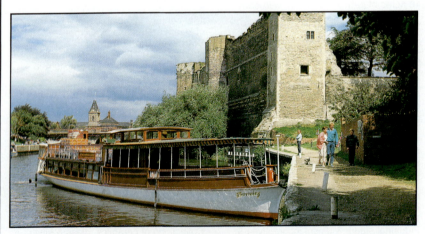

Newark Castle.

LEICESTERSHIRE & NOTTINGHAMSHIRE

Map reference

01 Hitchen
01 Hackney
02 Hinchley
03 Ibbotson
05 Need
06 Brammer
07 Stewart-Smith

Leicestershire & Nottinghamshire

			per person minimum £	children taken	evening meals	animals taken
Mrs J. Hitchen Rutland House 61 High Street Uppingham LE15 9PY Tel: (0572) 822497 Open: ALL YEAR Map Ref No. 01	Nearest Road: A.47 Rutland House offers excellent accommodation in 4 guest rooms. Double, single & twin rooms are available, all with private bathrooms, central heating, colour T.V. & tea making facilities. Being a small establishment, the rooms are quiet & homely. Children are well provided for. Full English breakfast, or Continental alternative is served. Packed lunches can be prepared.		£18.50	Y	N	Y
Christine & Ian Hackney Garden Hotel High Street Uppingham LE15 9QD Tel: (0572) 822352 Fax 0572 821156 Open: ALL YEAR Map Ref No. 01	Nearest Road: A.47 Regarded as Uppingham's best kept secret, this historic hotel has a reputation for friendly, homely service. All rooms en-suite with colour T.V., telephone, radio and tea/coffee facilities. Comfortable lounge and separate bar, together with large well-tended garden provide country home comforts. The restaurant is renowned for traditional British home cooking. Good wine list. Summer barbeques in the garden.		£21.00	Y	Y	Y

Nottinghamshire

Peter, Marjorie & Nicky Need Peacock Farm Guesthouse & Restaurant Redmile NG13 0GQ Tel: (0949) 42175 Open: ALL YEAR Map Ref No. 05	Nearest Road: A.1, A.52 Situated within sight of Belvoir Castle, Peacock Farm is a 280 year old farmhouse with all modern conveniences. Most rooms have unbroken views of the nearby village & Belvoir Castle set on wooded hills. A warm welcome is extended to house guests who are offered a first class service with old fashioned English hospitality. The restaurant offers home cooking with local fresh produce.		£14.50	Y	Y	Y
Mrs B. Hinchley Titchfield House 300/302 Chesterfield Road North Mansfield NG19 7QU Tel: (0623) 810356 Open: ALL YEAR Map Ref No. 02	Nearest Road: M.1, A.617 This is two houses, converted into one family-run guest house, offering 8 comfortable rooms, lounge with T.V., kitchen for guests' use, bathroom & showers. It also has an adjoining garage. Near to Mansfield, which is a busy market town. Sherwood Forest & the Peak District easily accessible. Very handy for touring this lovely area & onward travel. A warm & friendly welcome is assured here.		£14.00	Y	Y	N

When booking your accommodation please mention
The Best Bed & Breakfast

Nottinghamshire

		minimum £ per person	children taken	evening meals	animals taken
June M. Ibbotson Blue Barn Farm Langwith Mansfield NG20 9JD Tel: (0623) 742248 Open: ALL YEAR Map Ref No. 03	Nearest Road: A.616 An enjoyable visit is guaranteed at this family run 250 acre farm, set in tranquil countryside on the edge of Sherwood Forest (Robin Hood country). Accommodation is in 3 guest bedrooms with modern amenities including h&c, tea/coffee making facilities & guest bathroom with shower. Colour T.V. lounge & garden are also available. Guests are very welcome to walk around the farm. Many interesting places catering for all tastes, only a short journey away.	£13.50	Y	N	Y
Roslie Brammer 'The Barns ' Morton Farm Babworth Retford DN22 8HA Tel: (0777) 706336 Open: ALL YEAR Map Ref No. 06	Nearest Road: A.1, B.6420 A delightfully warm welcome & pleasant relaxed atmosphere await you at 'The Barns'. This beautifully converted 18th century barn boasts open fires & many oak beams & offers guests a choice of 6 comfortable rooms, all with en-suite facilities, radio, T.V. & tea/coffee makers. An interesting base for touring. It is located at Babworth - home of the Pilgrim Fathers - only 2 miles from Robin Hood country.	£18.00	Y	N	N
Mrs C. Stewart-Smith Yews Farm Firbeck Worksop S81 8JW Tel: (0909) 731458 Open: MAR-OCT Map Ref No. 07	Nearest Road: A1, M.1 Dating from the 16th century this charming country house faces south with lovely views overlooking garden & fields bordered by a stream. The pretty bedrooms all have tea/coffee trays, colour T.V., radio alarm clocks & electric blankets, & with the elegant drawing & dining rooms are mainly furnished with antiques. Within an hours' drive are Yorkshire & Derbyshire dales, Sherwood Forest Lincoln & York. M.1,M.18, A.1 motorways are all conveniently nearby.	£20.00	Y	Y	Y

All the establishments mentioned in this guide are members of
The Worldwide Bed & Breakfast Association

Lincolnshire

Lincolnshire (East Midlands)

Lincolnshire is an intriguing mixture of coast & country, of flat fens & gently rising wolds.

There are the popular resorts of Skegness & Mablethorpe as well as quieter coastal regions where flocks of wild birds take food & shelter in the dunes. Gibraltar Point & Saltfleetby are large nature reserves.

Fresh vegetables for much of Britain are produced in the rich soil of the Lincolnshire fens, & windmills punctuate the skyline. There is a unique 8-sailed windmill at Heckington. In spring the fields are ablaze with the red & yellow of tulips. The bulb industry flourishes around Spalding & Holbeach, & in early May tulip flowers in abundance decorate the huge floats of the Spalding Flower Parade.

The city of Lincoln has cobbled streets & ancient buildings & a very beautiful triple-towered Cathedral which shares its hill-top site with the Castle, both dating from the 11th century. There is a 17th century library by Wren in the Cathedral, which has amongst its treasures one of the four original copies of Magna Carta.

Boston has a huge parish church with a distincive octagonal tower which can be seen for miles across the surrounding fenland, & is commonly known as the 'Boston Stump'. The Guildhall Museum displays many aspects of the town's history, including the cells where the early Pilgrim Fathers were imprisioned after their attempt to flee to the Netherlands to find religious freedom. They eventually made the journey & hence to America.

One of England's most outstanding towns is Stamford. It has lovely churches, ancient inns & other fine buildings in a mellow stone.

Sir Isaac Newton was born at Woolsthorpe Manor & educated at nearby Grantham where there is a museum which illustrates his life & work.

The poet Tennyson was born in the village of Somersby, where his father was Rector.

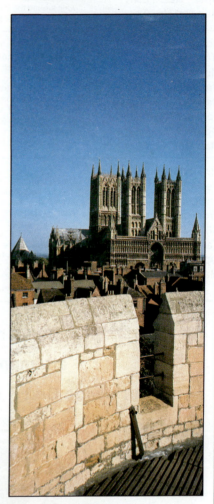

Lincoln Cathedral.

Lincolnshire

Lincolnshire Gazeteer

Areas of outstanding natural beauty.
Lincolnshire Wolds.

Historic Houses & Castles

Auborn House - Nr. Lincoln
16th century house with imposing carved staircase & panelled rooms.
Belton House - Grantham
House built 1684-88 - said to be by Christopher Wren - work by Grinling Gibbons & Wyatt also. Paintings, furniture, porcelain, tapestries, Duke of Windsor mementoes. A great English house with formal gardens & extensive grounds with orangery.
Doddington Hall - Doddington, Nr. Lincoln
16th century Elizabethan mansion with elegant Georgian rooms & gabled Tudor gatehouse. Fine furniture, paintings, porcelain, etc. Formal walled knot gardens, roses & wild gardens.
Burghley House - Stamford
Elizabethan - England's largest & grandest house of the era. Famous for its beautiful painted ceilings, silver fireplaces & art treasures.
Gumby Hall - Burgh-le-Marsh
17th century manor house. Ancient gardens.
Harrington Hall - Spilsby
Mentioned in the Domesday Book - has mediaeval stone base - Carolinean manor house in red brick. Some alterations in 1678 to mullioned windows. Panelling, furnishings of 17th & 18th century.
Marston Hall - Grantham
16th century manor house. Ancient gardens.
The Old Hall - Gainsborough
Fine mediaeval manor house built in 1480's with original kitchen, rebuilt after original hall destroyed during Wars of the Roses. Tower & wings, Great Hall. It was the first meeting place of the "Dissenters", later known as the Pilgrim Fathers.
Woolsthorpe Manor - Grantham
17th century house. Birthplace of Sir Isaac Newton.
Fydell House - Boston
18th century house, now Pilgrim College.

Lincoln Castle - Lincoln
William the Conqueror castle, with complete curtain wall & Norman shell keep. Towers & wall walk. Unique prisoners' chapel.
Tattershall Castle - Tattershall
100 foot high brick keep of 15th century moated castle, with fine views over surrounding country.

Cathedrals & Churches

Addlethorpe (St. Nicholas)
15th century - mediaeval stained glass - original woodwork.
Boston (St. Botolph)
14th century decorated - very large parish church. Beautiful south porch, carved stalls.
Brant Broughton (St. Helens)
13th century arcades - decorated tower & spire - perpendicular clerestory. Exterior decoration.
Ewerby (St. Andrew)
Decorated - splendid example of period - very fine spire. 14th century effigy.
Fleet (St. Mary Magdalene)
14th century - early English arcades - perpendicular windows - detached tower & spire.
Folkingham (St. Andrew)
14th century arcades - 15th century windows - perpendicular tower - early English chancel.
Gedney (St. Mary Magdalene)
Perpendicular spire (unfinished). Early English tower. 13th-14th century monuments, 14th-15th century stained glass.
Grantham (St. Wulfram)
14th century tower & spire - Norman pillars - perpendicular chantry - 14th century vaulted crypt.
Lincoln Cathedral - Lincoln
Magnificent triple-towered Gothic building on fine hill-top site. Norman west front, 13th century - some 14th century additions. Norman work from 1072. Angel choir - carved & decorated pulpitum - 13th century chapter house - 17th century library by Wren (containing one of the four original copies of Magna Carta)

Lincolnshire

St. Botolph's Church - Boston
Fine parish church, one of the largest in the country, with 272 foot octagonal tower dominating the surrounding fens.
Long Sutton (St. Mary)
15th century south porch, mediaeval brass lectern, very fine early English spire.
Louth (St. James)
Early 16th century - mediaeval Gothic - wonderful spire.
Scotter (St. Peter)
Saxon to perpendicular - early English nave - 15th century rood screen.
Stow (St. Mary)
Norman - very fine example, particularly west door. Wall painting.
Silk Willoughby (St. Denis)
14th century - tower with spire & flying buttresses. 15th-17th century pulpit.
Stainfield (St. Andrew)
Queen Anne - mediaeval armour & early needlework.
Theddlethorpe (All Saints)
14th century - 15th century & rerodos of 15th century, 16th century parcloses, 15th century brasses - some mediaeval glass.
Wrangle (St. Mary the Virgin & St. Nicholas)
Early English - decorated - perpendicular - Elizabethan pulpit. 14th century east window & glass.

Museums & Galleries

Alford Manor House - Alford
Tudor manor house - thatched - folk museum. Nearby windmill.
Boston Guildhall Museum - Boston
15th century building with mayor's parlour, court room & cells where Pilgrim Fathers were imprisoned in 1607. Local exhibits.
Lincoln Cathedral Library - Lincoln
Built by Wren housing early printed books & mediaeval manuscripts.
Lincoln Cathedral Treasury - Lincoln
Diocesan gold & silver plate.
Lincoln City & Country Museum - Lincoln
Prehistoric, Roman & mediaeval antiquities with local associations. Armour & local history.
Museum of Lincolnshire Life - Lincoln
Domestic, agricultural, industrial & social history of the county. Edwardian room settings, shop settings, agricultural machinery.
Usher Gallery - Lincoln
Paintings, watches, miniatures, porcelain, silver, coins & medals. Temporary exhibitions. Tennyson collection. Works of English watercolourist Peter de Wint.
Grantham Museum - Grantham
Archeology, prehistoric, Saxon & Roman. Local history with special display about Sir Isaac Newton, born nearby & educated in Grantham.
Church Farm Museum - Skegness
Farmhouse & buildings with local agricultural collections & temporary exhibitions & special events.
Stamford Museum - Stamford
Local history museum, with temporary special exhibitions.
Battle of Britain Memorial Flight - Coningsby
Lancaster bomber, five Spitfires & two Hurricanes with other Battle of Britain memorabilia.
National Cycle Museum - Lincoln
Development of the cycle.
Stamford Steam Brewery Museum - Stamford
Complete Victorian steam brewery with 19th century equipment.

Other things to see & do

Springfield - Spalding
Show gardens of the British bulb industry, & home of the Spalding Flower Parade each May. Summer bedding plants & roses.
Butlins Funcoast World - Skegness
Funsplash Water World with amusements & entertainments
Castle Leisure Park - Tattershall
Windsurfing, water-skiing, sailing, fishing & other sports & leisure facilities.
Long Sutton Butterfly Park - Long Sutton
Walk-through tropical butterfly house with outdoor wildflower meadows & pets corner.
Skegness Natureland Marine Zoo - Skegness
Seal sanctuary with aquaria, tropical house, pets corner & butterfly house.
Windmills - at Lincoln (Ellis Mill - 4 sails), Boston (Maud Foster - 5 sails), Burgh-le-Marsh (5 sails), Alford (5 sails), Sibsey (6 sails), Heckington (8 sails).

LINCOLNSHIRE
Map reference

01 **Beresford**
02 **Robinson**
03 **Pritchard**
04 **Brown**
05 **Higginbottom**
06 **Wade**
07 **Gosse**

Lincolnshire

		minimum £ per person	children taken	evening meals	animals taken
Gill & John Pritchard **Carline Guest House** 1/3 Carline Road Lincoln LN1 1HW Tel: (0522) 530422 Open: ALL YEAR (Excl. Xmas & New Year) Map Ref No. 03	Nearest Road: A.57, A.46, Gill & John Pritchard extend a warm welcome & excellent accommodation. Offfering 12 attractively furnished bedrooms, most with ensuite facilities, each with T.V., radio alarms, tea/coffee facilities & hair dryers. All public rooms & some bedrooms are totally non-smoking. The Carline is a pleasant five minute walk from the historic 'uphill' area of Lincoln. There are several restaurants & public houses nearby for your lunch or evening meal. Ask for Jill & Johns recommendations.	£14.00	Y	N	N
Dr. & Mrs J. Wade **The Manor House** Nocton Road Potterhanworth Lincoln LN4 2DN Tel: (0522) 791288 Open: JAN - NOV Map Ref No. 04	Nearest Road: B.1188, A.15 A peaceful 19th century Manor House clad in wisteria, honeysuckle & virginia creeper, in a pretty village 6 miles south of Lincoln. Large drawing room overlooking 8 acres of grounds, majestic trees, stream, pond & weir. Outdoor swimming pool, large summer house with table tennis, croquet & garden furniture. Cosy book-lined sitting room with T.V. In all the pretty bedrooms there are tea/coffee making facilities.	£17.00	Y	N	N
Mrs Ann Higginbottom **Dunston Manor** Dunston Lincoln LN4 2EN Tel: (0526) 20463 Open: ALL YEAR Map Ref No. 05	Nearest Road: A.15, B.1188 A delightful old manor house dating back to 1750. The oldest house in the small, unspoilt village of Dunston is built of local stone & has huge walls up to 32 inches thick. Accommodation is in 3 comfortable rooms with separate bathroom. Private lounge & dining room. Good home-cooked Lincolnshire food. Excellent for an overnight stop or for touring. Golf & coarse fishing nearby. Children over 12 years. Evening meals provided with prior notice only.	£16.50	Y	Y	N
Mrs Peter Gosse **Rookery Farm** Castle Carlton Louth LN11 8JF Tel: (0507) 450357 Open: ALL YEAR Map Ref No. 06	Nearest Road: A.157 Rookery Farm is a delightful, traditional, late 18th century farmhouse. Restored to a high standard of comfort & convenience, while maintaining many of the original features, including low beamed ceilings & original interior brick walls. The main features outside are the old-fashioned shrub roses & herb garden. Accommodation is in 3 nice rooms with modern amenities. A residents' lounge is available. The food here is delicious, mainly wholefood with organically grown vegetables from the garden. Homemade bread is a speciality.	£14.50	Y	Y	N
Mrs Sue Robinson **Sycamore Farm** Bassingthorpe Grantham NG33 4ED Tel: (047685) 274 Open: APR-OCT Map Ref No. 01	Nearest Road: B.6403, A1 A warm welcome & comfortable accommodation is assured at Sycamore Farm. A large, peaceful Victorian farmhouse set on a 450 acre farm, situated approximately 4 1/2 miles from the A.1, & within easy reach of Stamford, Belvoir Castle, Belton House & Lincoln. Comfortable guest lounge with open fire, colour T.V. & piano. Accommodation is in 3 attractively decorated bedrooms with lovely views across open countryside. Tea/coffee makers.	£12.00	Y	Y	N

Stoke Cottage. Stoke Rochford.

Lincolnshire

		minimum £ per person	children taken	evening meals	animals taken
Norman & Doreen Beresford Stoke Cottage Stoke Rochford Grantham NG33 5EP Tel: (0476) 83 453 Open: ALL YEAR Map Ref No. 02	Nearest Road: A.1 A warm welcome is extended to all guests by Doreen & Norman Beresford in this lovely thatched country house, situated in the beautiful private park of Stoke Rochford - 5 miles south of Grantham. The house is set in 4 acres of garden & woodland which guests can explore at their leisure. Adjacent is an 18 hole golf course where the first green is a "sand iron" away from the house.	£27.50 see PHOTO over	Y	Y	Y
Mr Raymond H. Brown Minster Lodge Hotel 3 Church Lane Lincoln LN2 1QJ Tel: (0522) 513220 Fax 0522 513220 Open: ALL YEAR Map Ref No. 03	Nearest Road: A.15 Minster Lodge is a delightful small hotel refurbished to a high standard. Offering 5 en-suite bedrooms with radio, colour T.V. & beverage facilities. Ideally situated within 50 yards of Newport Arch - the only remaining Roman Arch still in use & 5 minutes walk from Lincoln's major tourist attractions of Lincoln Cathedral & Castle & a colourful mixture of antique shops, gift shops & boutiques which are situated in the mediaeval area surrounding the cathedral & castle.	£24.00	Y	N	N
Roger Allston Cross Keys Hotel 4 Cross Key Yard Eastgate Sleaford NE34 7DH Tel: (0529) 305463 Fax 0529 414495 Open: JAN - DEC Map Ref No. 07	Nearest Road: A.15, A.17 A delightful patio garden, wecoming residents' lounge and cosy pine dining room all add to the exceptional charm of this totally renovated, licensed, town centre private hotel. Quietly situated around a picturesque mews, the 12 superb bedrooms are at ground and first-floor levels, each fully equipped with all usual comforts plus satellite T.V. & direct dial telephones. Choice between en-suite or standard de-luxe rooms.	£17.00	Y	Y	N

When booking your accommodation please mention

The Best Bed & Breakfast

Norfolk

Norfolk
(East Anglia)

One of the largest of the old counties, Norfolk is divided by rivers from neighbouring counties & pushes out into the sea on the north & east sides. This is old East Anglia.

Inland there is great concentration on agriculture where fields are hedged with hawthorn which blossoms like snow in summer. A great deal of land drainage is required & the area is crisscrossed by dykes & ditches - some of them dating back to Roman times.

Holkham Hall.

The Norfolk Broads were formed by the flooding of mediaeval peat diggings to form miles & miles of inland waterways, navigable & safe. On a bright summer's day, on a peaceful backwater bounded by reed & sedge, the Broads seem like paradise. Here are hidden treasures like the Bittern, that shyest of birds, the Swallowtail butterfly & the rare Marsh orchid.

Contrasting with the still inland waters is a lively coastline which takes in a host of towns & villages as it arcs around The Wash. Here are the joys of the seaside at its best, miles of safe & sandy golden beaches to delight children, dunes & salt marshes where birdlife flourishes, & busy ports & fishing villages with pink-washed cottages.

Cromer is a little seaside town with a pier & a prom, cream teas & candy floss, where red, white & blue fishing boats are drawn up on the beach.

Hunstanton is more decorous, with a broad green sweeping down to the cliffs. Great Yarmouth is a boisterous resort. It has a beach that runs for miles, with pony rides & almost every amusement imaginable.

It is possible to take a boat into the heart of Norwich, past warehouses, factories & new penthouses, & under stone & iron bridges. Walking along the riverbank you reach Pulls Ferry where a perfectly proportioned grey flint gateway arcs over what was once a canal dug to transport stone to the cathedral site. Norwich Cathedral is magnificent, with a sharply soaring spire, beautiful cloisters & fine 15th century carving preserved in the choir stalls. Cathedral Close is perfectly preserved, as is Elm Hill, a cobbled street from mediaeval times. There are many little shops & narrow alleys going down to the river.

Norfolk is a county much loved by the Royal family & the Queen has a home at Sandringham. It is no castle, but a solid, comfortable family home with red brick turrets & French windows opening onto the terrace.

Norfolk

Norfolk Gazeteer
Areas of outstanding beauty.
Norfolk coast (part)

Historic Houses & Castles
Anna Sewell House - Great Yarmouth
17th century Tudor frontage. Birthplace of writer Anna Sewell.
Blicking Hall - Aylsham
Great Jacobean house. Fine Russian tapestry, long gallery with exceptional ceiling. Formal garden.
Felbrigg Hall - Nr. Cromer
17th century, good Georgian interior. Set in wooded parklands.
Holkham Hall - Wells
Fine Palladian mansion of 1734. Paintings, statuary, tapestries, furnishings & formal garden by Berry.
Houghton Hall - Wells
18th century mansion. Pictures, china & staterooms.
Oxburgh Hall - Swafftham
Late 15th century moated house. Fine gatehouse tower. Needlework by Mary Queen of Scots.
Wolterton Hall - Nr. Norwich
Built in 1741 contains tapestries, porcelain, furniture.
Trinity Hospital - Castle Rising
17th century, nine brick & tile almshouses, court chapel & treasury.

Cathedrals & Churches
Attleborough (St. Mary)
Norman with late 14th century. Fine rood screen & frescoes.
Barton Turf (St. Michael & All Angles)
Magnificent screen with painting of the Nine Orders of Angles.
Beeston-next-Mileham (St. Mary)
14th century. Perpendicular clerestory tower & spire. Hammer Beam roof, parclose screens, benches, front cover. Tracery in nave & chancel windows.
Cawston (St. Agnes)
Tower faced with freestone. Painted screens, wall paintings, tower, screen & gallery. 15th century angel roof.
East Harding (St. Peter & St. Paul)
14th century, some 15th century alterations. Monuments of 15th-17th century. Splendid mediaeval glass.
Erpingham (St. Mary)
14th century military brass to John de Erpingham, 16th century Rhenish glass. Fine tower.
Gunton (St. Andrew)
18th century. Robert Adam - classical interior in dark wood - gilded.
King's Lynn (St. Margaret)
Norman foundation. Two fine 14th century Flemish brasses, 14th century screens, reredos by Bodley, interesting Georgian pulpit with sounding board.
Norwich Cathedral
Romanesque & late Gothic with 15th century spire. Perpendicular lierne vaults in nave, transeptsand presbytery.
Ranworth (St. Helens)
15th century screen, very fine example. Sarum Antiphoner, 14th century illuminated manuscript - East Anglian work.
Salle (St. Peter & St. Paul)
15th century. Highly decorated west tower & porches. Mediaeval glass, pulpit with 15th century panels & Jacobean tester. Stalls, misericords, brasses & monuments, sacrament font.
Terrington (St. Clement)
Detached perpendicular tower. Western front has fire-light window & canopied niches. Georgian panelling west of nave. 17th century painted font cover. Jacobean commandment boards.
Trunch (St. Botolph)
15th century screen with painted panels, mediaeval glass, famous font canopy with fine carving & painting, ringer's gallery, Elizabethan monument.
Wiggenhall (St. Germans)
17th century pulpit, table, clerk's desk & chair, bench ends 15th century.
Wymondham (St. Mary & St. Thomas of Canterbury)
Norman origins including arcades & triforium windows, 13th century font fragments, complete 15th century font. 15th century clerestory & roof. Comper reredos, famous Corporas Case, rare example of 13th century Opus Anglicanum.

Museums & Galleries
Norwich Castle Museum
Art collection, local & natural history,

Norfolk

Strangers Hall - Norwich
Mediaeval mansion furnished as museum of urban domestic life in 16th-19th centuries.

St. Peter Hungate Church Museum - Norwich
15th century church for the exhibition of ecclesiastical art & East Anglican antiquities.

Sainsbury Centre for Visual Arts - University, Norwich
Collection of modern art, ancient, classical & mediaeval art, Art Nouveau, 20th century constructivist art.

Bridewell Museum of Local Industries - Norwich
Crafts, industries & aspects of city life.

Museum of Social History - King's Lynn
Exhibition of domestic life & dress, etc., noted glass collection.

Bishop Bonner's Cottages
Restored cottages with coloured East Anglia pargetting, c. 1502, museum of archaeological discoveries, exhibition of rural crafts.

The Guildhall - Thetford
Duleep Singh Collection of Norfolk & Suffolk portraits.

Shirehall Museum - Walsingham
18th century court room having original fittings, illustrating Walsingham life.

Historic Monuments

Binham Priory & Cross - Binham
12th century ruins of Benedictine foundation.

Caister Castle - Great Yarmouth
15th century moated castle - ruins. Now motor museum.

The Castle - Burgh Castle
3rd century Saxon fort - walls - ruin.

Mannington Hall - Saxthorpe
Saxon church ruin in gardens of 15th century moated house.

Castle Rising - Castle Rising
Splendid Norman keep & earthworks.

Castle Acre Priory & Castle Gate - Swaffham

Other things to see & do

African Violet Centre - Terrington St. Clements.
60 varieties of African Violets. Talks & Tours.

Norfolk Lavender Centre - Heacham
Open to the public in July & August. Demonstrations of harvesting & distilling the oil.

Thetford Forest
Forest walks, rides & picnic places amongst conifers, oak, beech & birch.

The Broads.

NORFOLK
Map reference

- 01 Morfoot
- 02 Dawson
- 03 Webb
- 04 Atkins
- 05 Gillam
- 06 Gent
- 07 Wells
- 08 Fieldsend
- 09 Tweedy Smith
- 09 Porter
- 10 Nightingale
- 11 Nott
- 12 Hickey
- 13 Muddle
- 14 Earp
- 15 Ford
- 16 Clarke
- 16 Leeming
- 17 Parker
- 18 Goff
- 19 Wace
- 20 Coe
- 21 Thompson
- 22 Lovatt
- 22 Peters
- 24 Garnier
- 25 Carr
- 26 Collins
- 27 Whittley

Norfolk

			minimum £ per person	children taken	evening meals	animals taken
Mrs E. M. Morfoot **Church Cottage** **Breckles** **Attleborough MR17 1EW** Tel: (0953) 498286 Open: ALL YEAR (Excl. Xmas & New Year) Map Ref No. 01	Nearest Road A.11. A friendly welcome awaits visitors to this charming 18th century house situated in beautiful Breckland overlooking typical Norfolk farmland. Centrally located for touring East Anglia. Offering 2 double & 1 single bedroom each with modern amenities. Visitors' own sitting/dining room with colour T.V. Home made bread & own eggs. Heated outdoor swimming pool. Own coarse fishing. Children over 10 years.		£16.00	Y	N	N
A. Dawson & C.Tyler **Sherbourne Country House** **Norwich Road** **Attleborough NR17 2JX** Tel: (0953) 454363 Fax 0953 453509 Open: ALL YEAR Map Ref No. 02	Nearest Road: A.11 Set in mature grounds, this delightful 17th century house has a friendly, family atmosphere. Accommodation is offered in 3 four-poster, en-suite rooms, 2 twins, 1 double & 2 singles. A charming lounge & lovely bar for guests. The evening meals are super & great value. The house has a fine reputation for cuisine & Australian wine list. This is an excellent base for touring Norwich & the Broads. Riding is available locally.		£22.00	Y	Y	Y
Ken & Brenda Webb **Strenneth Farmhouse** **Old Airfield Road** **Fersfield** **Diss IP22 2BP** Tel/Fax: (037988) 8182 Open: ALL YEAR Map Ref No. 03	Nearest Road: A.1066 A 16-17th century former farmhouse located close to the small market town of Diss. Renovated to a high standard. The heavily beamed house now offers guests very pleasant comfortable accommodation in a choice of 9 bedrooms, most with en-suite facilities. A separate lounge for non-smokers. An excellent 3-course meal is available & special diets can be catered for. Children are welcome. Licenced.		£20.00	Y	Y	Y
Connie & Doug Atkins **Ingleneuk Lodge** **Hopton Road** **Garboldisham** **Diss IP22 2RQ** Tel: (095381) 541 Open: ALL YEAR Map Ref No. 04	Nearest Road: A.11 A.1066 A warm welcome is extended to visitors at Ingleneuk, a large modern family-run bungalow standing in 10 acres of quiet wooded countryside with riverside walks. A variety of rooms, most en-suite, all centrally heated, double-glazed, with colour T.V., telephone, electric blankets & hot drink facilities. Children well provided for. Residents' lounge, licenced bar, evening meals by prior arrangement. Morning coffee & cream teas daily. Wheelchair disabled welcome		£16.25	Y	Y	Y
Jill & Ian Gillam **The Old Rectory** **Gissing** **Diss IP22 3XB** Tel: (037977) 575 Fax 037977 4427 Open: ALL YEAR Map Ref No. 05	Nearest Road: A.140 This delightful Victorian house stands in grounds of mature gardens & woodland & is a haven of peace, comfort & elegance. Bedrooms are spacious with private or en-suite facilities. Every effort has been made to ensure a memorable stay - tea/coffee making facilities, colour T.V., notepaper, fresh flowers & an extensive range of toiletries. Breakfast is copious & beautifully presented. Candlelit dinner is available by prior arrangement. Amenities - croquet, indoor swimming pool (heated). Smoking restrictions.		£22.00 *see PHOTO over*	Y	Y	Y

The Old Rectory. Gissing.

Norfolk

	minimum £ per person	children taken	evening meals	animals taken

Tessa & Tony Gent The Old Brick Kilns Little Barney Fakenham NR21 0NL Tel: (0328) 878305 Open: FEB-DEC (Excl. xmas/ New Year) Map Ref No. 06	Nearest Road: A.148 A warm welcome awaits you at these charmingly converted cottages. Situated in a quiet rural area. Yet convenient for the coast. Accommodation is in 3 rooms, all with en-suite facilities, colour T.V., radio, hair dryers & tea/coffee makers. A lounge & garden is available for guests at any time. Conveniently located as a touring base for visiting many places of local interest.	£19.00	Y	Y	N
Mrs B. Wells 'Spindrift' Private Hotel 36 Wellesley Road Great Yarmouth NR30 1EU Tel: (0493) 858674 Open: ALL YEAR Map Ref No. 07	Nearest Road: A.47 Good food & comfortable accommodation are the by-words at 'Spindrift'. Attractively situated adjacent to the sea front, the Golden Mile, bowling greens, tennis courts & the water ways. Easy going atmosphere with keys provided for access at all times. A selection of 8 bedrooms, some with excellent sea views & 4 bedrooms with en-suite facilities, all with modern amenities, colour T.V. & tea/coffee making facilites. Good on road parking, public car park at rear if space allows.	£14.00	Y	Y	N
Mrs Jane Fieldsend Windmill Guest House 56 The Street Hindolveston Holt NR20 5DF Tel: (0263) 861095 Open: ALL YEAR Map Ref No. 08	Nearest Road: A.1067, The Windmill, originally 2 farm cottages dating from 1830, has been restored & renovated & retains all its original charm & character, including an oak beamed living room with wood burning stove. Offering accommodation in the pleasantly decorated twin or double bedroom each with tea/coffee making facilities. This is a good base for visiting rural North Norfolk's nature reserves & Blickling Hall, Holkham Hall, Mannington Hall & gardens & Sandringham.	£15.00	Y	N	Y
Sheila Tweedy Smith Fieldsend House Homefields Road Hunstanton PE36 5HL Tel: (0485) 532593 Open: ALL YEAR (Excl. Xmas) Map Ref No. 09	Nearest Road: A.149 Fieldsend is a large Carrstone house, built at the turn of the century enjoying lovely sea views. There are canopied beds including 1 four-poster en-suite bedroom. Colour T.V. & tea/coffee makers & an oak panelled sitting room. Guests will enjoy a leisurely stay at this country house style home while being only 4 mins from the centre of town. Delicious breakfasts served by a Cordon Bleu cook. Parking.	£15.00	Y	N	N
Mrs Susan Porter Pinewood Hotel 26 Northgate Hunstaton PE36 6AP Tel: (0485) 533068 Open: ALL YEAR Map Ref No. 09	Nearest Road: A.149 Enjoy warmth, comfort & hospitality in this friendly family run Victorian Hotel, with a natural pine look. 8 delightfully decorated bedrooms, 1 with Victorian bedstead & Laura Ashley decor. Some with sea views, 4 en-suite, all with colour T.V. & tea/coffee making facilties. Enjoy delicious home cooking & good wines, or relax in front of a log fire in the bar/lounge.	£16.50	Y	Y	Y

Norfolk

	minimum £ per person	children taken	evening meals	animals taken
Dawn Nightingale **The White House** **44 Hunstanton Road** **Dersingham** **King's Lynn PE31 6HQ** **Tel: (0485) 541895** **Open: ALL YEAR** **Map Ref No. 10**	Nearest Road: A.149, B.1440 Comfortable detached centrally heated house built in 1901 on land once owned by Edward VII & only one & a half miles from Sandringham, the Queen's Norfolk home. Accommodation is in 5 rooms all with tea/coffee making facilities. A ground floor double en-suite room, suitable for the disabled by arrangement. Guests lounge with colour T. V.. Centrally located for many historic houses, bird reserves, museums, working windmills & beautiful beaches. Parking.	£13.50	Y	N	Y
Mr & Mrs R. E. Nott **The Mill House** **Station Road** **Snettisham** **King's Lynn PE31 7QJ** **Tel: (0485) 542180** **Open: ALL YEAR** **Map Ref No. 11**	Nearest Road: A.149 Located along a private drive, set by the millpool in a beautiful garden with waterfall, river & 18th century working watermill. The Mill House offers 3 charming bedrooms, 1 of which is en-suite/shower. Hospitality tray in each room. Breakfast is in the pine morning room which has colour T.V. & is available to guests in the evening. Guest rooms have views over the millpool & gardens. Ideally placed for Sandringham. No smoking.	£14.50	N	N	N
Linda & Martin Hickey **Corfield House** **Sporle** **Nr. Swaffham** **King's Lynn PE32 2DR** **Tel: (0760) 23636** **Open: APR - DEC** **Map Ref No. 12**	Nearest Road: A.47 This family-run country guest house is set in peaceful surroundings 3 miles from the attractive market town of Swaffham. 5 comfortable & well-equipped bedrooms, with en-suite bath or shower, all offer colour T.V., radio, tea/coffee making facilities & full central heating. Separate guest lounge & dining room, public telephone. Good home cooking, licenced. An ideal base for touring North Norfolk.	£16.50	Y	Y	Y
B.A. & R.I.D. Muddle **Russet House Hotel** **53 Goodwins Road** **Kings Lynn PE30 5PE** **Tel: (0553) 773098** **Open: Mid-JAN - DEC** **Map Ref No. 13**	Nearest Road: A.10, A.47, A friendly old Victorian house with a very pretty garden in attractive area of Kings Lynn, only a short walk from the town centre. The twelve bedrooms are comfortable, light and pleasant with private facilities, T.V. etc. Intimate bar with a real fire on cold nights. Meals are served in lovely dining room (no smoking). Rae & Barry Muddle try not to live up to their name!	£31.50	Y	Y	N
Mrs Philippa Earp **Mornington House** **33 Church Plain** **Loddon NR14 6EX** **Tel: (0508) 28572** **Open: APR - OCT** **Map Ref No. 14**	Nearest Road: A.146 Delightful Grade II listed character residence in market town centre. Dating back in parts to 1570, it was originally believed to be an Inn and it is reputed that Charles Wesley once stayed here. Beams and inglenooks abound. 2 Guest bedrooms. Both Norwich and the Heritage Coast are within easy reach. Loddon is on the river Chet, with boat hire or trips available.	£14.00	N	Y	Y

Norfolk

			minimum £ per person	children taken	evening meals	animals taken
Mrs Marion Ford Old Bottle House Lynn Road Cranwich Mundford IP26 5JL Tel: (0842) 878012 Open: JAN - DEC Map Ref No. 15	Nearest Road: A.134 Old Bottle House is a 275-year old former coaching inn, on the edge of Thetford Forest. Guests have a choice of 3 spacious, colour co-ordinated bedrooms with tea/coffee making facilities & colour T.V. Delicious meals are served in the dining room which has an inglenook fireplace. A charming house with every comfort and a warm, friendly welcome. Children over 5 please.		£15.00	Y	Y	N
Sally Clarke Kingsley Lodge 3 Kingsley Road Norwich NR1 3RB Tel: (0603) 615819 Open: ALL YEAR Map Ref No. 16	Nearest Road: A.11, A.140 A friendly Edwardian house in the city centre yet surprisingly quiet, very close to the bus station, shops & restaurants. All 4 rooms (1 twin, 2 double, 1 single) have en-suite bathrooms, colour T.V., tea/coffee making facilities & are comfortably furnished. Traditional English breakfasts are cooked to order & served in the large lounge or in the conservatory during the summer. An ideal location for exploring historic Norwich & Norfolk.		£18.00	Y	N	N
W.R. & A.E. Parker Elm Farm Chalet Hotel St. Faith Norwich NR10 3HH Tel: (0603) 898366 Fax 0603 897129 Open: ALL YEAR (excl. Xmas & New Year) Map Ref No. 17	Nearest Road: A.140 Attractive, comfortable accommodation is offered at the 17th century farmhouse & chalet hotel. Most rooms have en-suite shower, all with tea/coffee making facilities, radio alarms, telephone & colour T.V. Large licenced dining room & T.V. lounge. Situated in the attractive village of St. Faith, 4 miles north of Norwich & ideal for visiting the Broads & touring Norfolk & Suffolk.		£25.50	Y	Y	N
Mrs Gill Goff Rookery Farm Church Street Reepham Norwich NR10 4JW Tel: (0603) 871847 Open:ALL YEAR(Excl. Xmas) Map Ref No. 18	Nearest Road: A.1067 A warm welcome awaits at Rookery Farm. Situated on the edge of a small market town this listed farmhouse, built in the 17th century, renovated in 1810 & modernised in the 20th century retains a wealth of fascinating period features. It now offers peaceful accommodation in one of the loveliest corners of Norfolk. There are 3 attractive guest rooms, each with en-suite facilities. In short, comfort & character with a hearty farmhouse breakfast.		£15.00	Y	N	N
Jean Wace Gables Farm Hemblington Hall Rd Hemblington Norwich NR13 4PT Tel: (060549) 548 Open: ALL YEAR Map Ref No. 19	Nearest Road: A.47 This delightful 17th century thatched farmhouse stands in a large garden surrounded by a 300 acre farm. There is a twin room & a family room, each with private facilities, colour T.V. & tea makers. A traditional breakfast is served in the dining room. Guests are invited to enjoy the nearby Broads & nature reserves. Both Norwich & the beautiful coast are within easy reach.		£16.00	Y	N	N

Norfolk

		minimum £ per person	children taken	evening meals	animals taken
Phil & Ray Coe Brooksbank Lower Street Salhouse Norwich NR13 6RW Tel: (0603) 720420 Open: JAN - DEC Map Ref No. 20	Nearest Road: 18th century Brooksbank stands in the centre of Salhouse village in the heart of Broadland, 2 miles from Wroxham, 7 miles from the lovely Cathedral city of Norwich. Guests have own private accommodation with T.V. lounge. Bedrooms have colour T.V., tea/coffee facilities, and all have private bathrooms. Phil & Ray Coe extend you a warm welcome to their home. Their pleasure is your comfort!	£14.00	Y	Y	N
Mrs R Thompson Oakfield Yelverton Road Framingham Earl Norwich NR14 7SD Tel: (05086) 2605 Open: JAN - DEC Map Ref No. 21	Nearest Road: A.146 Oakfield is set in a quiet, picturesque village 4 miles from Norwich, in four acres of meadowland and garden. Accommodation is in 3 comfortable rooms (one en-suite), each with washbasins, shaver point, tea/coffee facilities. Residents lounge with colour T.V. Superb breakfasts. Several local pubs serving excellent evening meals. Ample car parking. Children over 12 welcome.	£13.00	Y	N	N
Eddie & Margaret Lovatt Edmar Lodge 64 Earlham Road Norwich NR2 3DF Tel: (0603) 615599 Fax 0603 615515 Open: ALL YEAR Map Ref No. 22	Nearest Road: B.1108 A large corner house with parking for 6 cars, situated in a quiet area, only 10 minutes walk from the city centre. There are 5 very attractive, comfortable rooms with every modern amenity, including tea/coffee makers & colour T.V., 3 rooms have private facilities. Mrs Lovatt makes all her guests very welcome & serves wonderful breakfasts in a pretty dining room. Help is readily given on tour plannning & advice on Norwich City & its' many gourmet restaurants.	£15.00	Y	N	N
P.M. & A.E. Leeming Earlham Guest House 147 Earlham Road Norwich NR2 3RG Tel: (0603) 54169 Open: ALL YEAR Map Ref No. 16	Nearest Road: B.1108 A delightful Victorian residence on major road from city centre to the University (B.1108). All rooms have modern amenities including colour T.V. & hot drinks tray, some with private facilities & keys are provided for freedom of access. Our visitors book reflects the satisfaction of guests & our attention to their needs, including wholefoods as an alternative to a generous full English breakfast if required. Visa accepted.	£15.00	N	N	N
Carol & Donald Peters Linden House 557 Earlham Road Norwich NR4 7HW Tel: (0603) 51303 Fax 0603 250641 Open: ALL YEAR Map Ref No. 22	Nearest Road: B.1108, A.11, Lovely house with all new facilities, ample parking and attractive gardens. University 5 minutes walk; frequent mini-bus from house to city centre. Luxury all en-suite hotel accommdation but with cosy, friendly atmosphere at inexpensive prices. Washing machine & dryer, Fax, photocopier, metered telephone. Colour T.V., tea/coffee facilities in all rooms. Full central heating; double glazing. Reduced terms for weekends or extended visits.	£19.00	Y	N	N

Norfolk

			minimum £ per person	children taken	evening meals	animals taken
Lavender Garnier College Farm Thompson Thetford IP24 1QG Tel: (095383) 318 Open: ALL YEAR Map Ref No. 24	Nearest Road: A.1075 Built 600 years ago as a College of Priests & becoming a manor house when Henry VIII dismissed the monasteries. College Farm has been modernised to provide 4 comfortable rooms all with colour T.V. & have superb views over farmland & mature trees. Delicious breakfasts are served in the panelled dining room. An excellent thatched pub in the village offers tasty meals. Norfolk coast, Norwich, Cambridge & Sandringham within easy reach by car.		£15.00	Y	N	N
Mrs D.G. Carr White Hall Carbrooke Thetford IP25 6SG Tel: (0953) 885950 Open: JAN - DEC Map Ref No. 25	Nearest Road: B.1108 Elegant Georgian country house in delightful grounds of 3 acres with large natural pond. Offering 3 attractive, comfortable bedrooms (one en-suite), a spacious, sunny drawing room with colour T.V., traditional breakfast served in the fine dining room. Early morning tea, evening drinks, full central heating, log fires etc. ensure your stay is enjoyable and relaxing. Ideal touring centre, lots of local interest. Good food, golf, swimming nearby.		£15.50	Y	N	N
Mrs Christine Collins Cedar Lodge West Tofts Thetford IP26 5DB Tel: (0842) 878281 Open: ALL YEAR Map Ref No. 26	Nearest Road: A.134 Guests receive a true country welcome at this cedar Colt house. Standing in a well kept garden it is located in the heart of Thetford Forest. Traditionally furnished & offering comfortable guest rooms, 1 with private bathroom, each with T.V. & tea/coffee making facilities. Christine is Cordon Bleu trained & loves entertaining her guests & is pleased to provide packed lunches. The North Norfolk coast, Cambridge, Norwich & Newmarket are within 45 minutes drive.		£16.50	Y	Y	Y
Mr & Mrs M. Whittley The Grange Northwold Thetford IP26 5NF Tel: (0366) 728240 Open: ALL YEAR (Excl. Xmas & New Year) Map Ref No. 27	Nearest Road: A.134 Guests will enjoy the real family atmosphere at The Grange. This beautiful Regency rectory stands in 5 acres of mature garden with a stream running through the grounds. The accommodation is in 4 rooms with use of a drawing room, tea/coffee facilities & a T.V. room. There is also an outdoor heated swimming pool. Good home cooking. Centrally located for Norfolk, Suffolk & Cambridge. Children over 12 only.		£15.00 *see PHOTO over*	Y	Y	N

When booking your accommodation please mention

The Best Bed & Breakfast

The Grange.   Northwold.

Northumbria

Northumbria

Mountains & moors, hills & fells, coast & country are all to be found in this Northern region which embraces four counties - Northumberland, Durham, Cleveland & Tyne & Wear.

Saxons, Celts, Vikings, Romans & Scots all fought to control what was then a great wasteland between the Humber & Scotland.

Northumberland

Northumberland is England's Border country, a land of history, heritage & breathtaking countryside. Hadrian's Wall, stretching across the county from the mouth of the Tyne in the west to the Solway Firth, was built as the Northern frontier of the Roman Empire in 122 AD. Excavations along the Wall have brought many archaeological treasures to light. To walk along the wall is to discover the genius of Roman building & engineering skill. They left a network of roads, used to transport men & equipment in their attempts to maintain discipline among the wild tribes.

Through the following centuries the Border wars with the Scots led to famous battles such as Otterburn in 1388 & Flodden in 1513, & the construction of great castles including Bamburgh & Lindisfarne. Berwick-on-Tweed, the most northerly town, changed hands between England & Scotland 13 times.

Northumberland's superb countryside includes the Cheviot Hills in the Northumberland National Park, the unforgettable heather moorlands of the Northern Pennines to the west, Kielder Water (Western Europe's largest man-made lake), & 40 miles of glorious coastline.

Holy Island, or Lindisfarne, is reached by a narrow causeway that is covered at every incoming tide. Here St. Aidan of Iona founded a monastery in the 7th century, & with St. Cuthbert set out to Christianise the pagan tribes. The site was destroyed by the Danes, but Lindisfarne Priory was built by the monks of Durham in the 11th century to house a Benedictine community. The ruins are hauntingly beautiful.

Durham

County Durham is the land of the Prince Bishops, who with their armies, nobility, courts & coinage controlled the area for centuries. They ruled as a virtually independent State, holding the first line of defence against the Scots.

In Durham City, the impressive Norman Castle standing proudly over the narrow mediaeval streets was the home of the Prince Bishops for 800 years.

Durham Cathedral, on a wooded peninsula high above the River Wear, was built in the early 12th century & is undoubtably one of the world's finest buildings, long a place of Christian pilgrimage.

The region's turbulent history led to the building of forts & castles. Some like Bowes & Barnard Castle are picturesque ruins whilst others, including Raby, Durham & Lumley still stand complete.

The Durham Dales of Weardale, Teesdale & the Derwent Valley cover about one third of the county & are endowed with some of the highest & wildest scenery. Here are High Force, England's highest waterfall, & the Upper Teesdale National Nature Reserve.

The Bowes Museum at Barnard Castle is a magnificent French-style chateau & houses an important art collection.

In contrast is the award-winning museum at Beamish which imaginatively recreates Northern life at the turn of the century.

Northumbria

Cleveland

Cleveland, the smallest 'shire' in England, has long been famous for its steel, chemical & shipbuilding industries but it is also an area of great beauty. The North Yorkshire National Park lies in the south, & includes the cone-shaped summit of Roseberry Topping, "Cleveland's Matterhorn".

Cleveland means 'land of cliffs', & in places along the magnificent coastline, cliffs tower more than 600 feet above the sea, providing important habitat for wild plants & sea-birds.

Pretty villages such as Hart, Elwick & Staithes are full of steep, narrow alleys. Marton was the birthplace of Captain James Cook & the museum there traces the explorer's early life & forms the start of the 'Cook Heritage Trail'.

The Tees estuary is a paradise for birdwatchers, whilst walkers can follow the Cleveland Way or the 38 miles of the Langbaurgh Loop. There is surfing, windsurfing & sailing at Saltburn, & for the less energetic, the scenic Esk Valley Railway runs from Middlesbrough to Whitby.

Tyne & Wear

Tyne & Wear takes its name from the two rivers running through the area, & includes the large & lively city of Newcastle-on-Tyne.

Weardale lies in a beautiful valley surrounded by wild & bleak fells. Peaceful now, it was the setting for a thriving industry mining coal & silver, zinc & lead. Nature trails & recreation areas have been created among the old village & market towns.

The county was the birthplace of George Stephenson, railway engineer, who pioneered the world's first passenger railway on the Stockton to Darlington Line in 1825.

Durham Cathedral.

Northumbria

Northumbria Gazeeter

Areas of Outstanding Natural Beauty
The Heritage Coast, the Cheviot Hills, the North Pennine chain.

Historic Houses & Castles

Alnwick Castle - Alnwick
A superb mediaeval castle of the 12th century.
Bamburgh Castle-Bamburgh
A resorted 12th century castle with Norman keep.
Callaly Castle - Whittingham
A 13th century Pele tower with 17th century mansion. Georgian additions.
Durham Castle - Durham
Part of the University of Durham - a Norman castle.
Lindisfarne Castle - Holy Island
An interesting 14th century castle.
Ormesby Hall - Nr. Middlesbrough
A mid 18th century house.
Raby Castle - Staindrop, Darlington
14th century with some later alteration. Fine art & furniture. Large gardens.
Wallington Hall -Combo
A 17th century house with much alteration & addition.
Washington Old Hall-Washington
Jacobean manor house, parts of which date back to 12th century.

Cathedrals & Churches

Brancepeth (St. Brandon)
12th century with superb 17th century woodwork. Part of 2 mediaeval screens. Flemish carved chest.
Durham Cathedral
A superb Norman cathedral. A unique Galilee chapel & early 12th century vaults.
Escombe
An interesting Saxon Church with sundial.
Hartlepool (St. Hilda)
Early English with fine tower & buttresses.
Hexham (St. Andrews)
Remains of a 17th century church with Roman dressing. A unique night staircase & very early stool. Painted screens.
Jarrow (St. Pauls)
Bede worshipped here. Strange in that it was originally 2 churches until 11th century. Mediaeval chair.
Newcastle (St. Nicholas)
14th century with an interesting lantern tower. Heraldic font. Roundel of 14th century glass.
Morpeth (St. Mary the Virgin)
Fine mediaeval glass in east window - 14th century.
Pittington (St. Lawrence)
Late Norman nave with wall paintings. Carved tombstone - 13th century.
Skelton (St. Giles)
Early 13th century with notable font, gable crosses, bell-cote & buttresses.
Staindrop (St. Mary)
A fine Saxon window. Priests dwelling. Neville tombs & effigies.

Museums & Galleries

Aribea Roman Fort Museum - South Shields
Interesting objects found on site.
Berwick-on-Tweed Museum - Berwick
Special exhibition of interesting local finds.
Bowes Museum - Bernard Castle
European art from mediaeval to 19th century.
Captain Cook Birthplace Museum - Middlesbrough
Cook's life & natural history relating to his travels.
Clayton Collection - Chollerford
A collection of Roman sculpture, weapons & tools from forts.
Corbridge Roman Station - Corbridge
Roman pottery & sculpture.
Dormitory Musuem - Durham Cathedral
Relics of St. Cuthbert. Mediaeval seats & manuscripts.
Gray Art Gallery - Hartlepool
19th-20th century art & oriental antiquities.
Gulbenkian Museum of Oriental Art - University of Durham
Chinese pottery & porcelain, Chinese jade & stone carvings, Chinese ivories, Chinese textiles, Japenese & Tibetan art. Egyptian & Mesopotamian antiquities.
Jarrow Hall - Jarrow
Excavation finds of Saxon & mediaeval monastery. Fascinating information room dealing with early Christian sites in England.

Northumbria

Keep Museum - Newcastle-upon-Tyne
Mediaeval collection.
Laing Art Gallery - Newcastle-upon-Tyne
17th-19th century British arts, porcelain, glass & silver.
National Music Hall Museum - Sunderland
19th-20th century costume & artefacts associated with the halls.
Preston Hall Museum - Stockton-on-Tees
Armour & arms, toys, ivory period room
University - New Castle -Upon -Tyne
The Hatton Gallery - housing a fine collection of Italian paintings.
Museum of Antiquities
Prehistoric, Roman & Saxon collection with an interesting reconstruction of a temple.
Beamish North of England Open Air Museum - European Museum of the Year
Chantry Bagpipe Museum - Morpeth
Darlington Museum & Railway Centre.

Historic Monuments

Ariiea Roman Fort - South Shields
Remains which include the gateways & headquarters.
Barnard Castle - Barnard Castle
17th century ruin with interesting keep.
Bowes Castle - Bowes
Roman Fort with Norman keep.
The Castle & Town Walls - Berwick-on-Tweed
12th century remains, reconstructed later.
Dunstanburgh Castle - Alnwick
14th century remains.
Egglestone Abbey - Barnard Castle
Remains of a Poor House.
Finchdale Priory - Durham
13 th century church with much remaining.
Hadrian's Wall - Housesteads
Several miles of the wall including castles & site museum.
Mithramic Temple - Carrawbrough
Mithraic temple dating back to the 3rd century.
Norham Castle - Norham
The partial remains of a 12th century castle.
Prudhoe Castle - Prudhoe
From the 12th century with additions. Bailey & gatehouse well preserved.

The Roman Fort - Chesters
Extensive remains of a Roman bath house.
Tynemouth Priory & Castle - Tynemouth
11th century priory - ruin - with 16th century towers & keep.
Vindolanda - Barton Mill
Roman fort dating from 3rd century.
Warkworth Castle - Warkworth
Dating from the 11th century with additions - a great keep & gatehouse.
Warkworth Hermitage - Warkworth
An interesting 14th century Hermitage.
Lindisfarne Priory - Holy Island (Lindisfarne)
11th century monastery. Island accessible only at low tide.

Other things to see & do

Botanical Gardens - Durham University
Bird & Seal Colonies - Farne Islands
Conducted tours by boat
Marine Life Centre & Fishing Museum - Seahouses
Museum of sealife, & boat trips to the Farne Islands.
Tower Knowe Visitor Centre - Keilder Water

Saltburn Victorian Festival.

NORTHUMBERLAND, DURHAM & TYNE & WEAR

Map reference

- 01 Finn
- 02 Jackson
- 03 Davison
- 04 Wood
- 04 Clarke
- 04 Wilson
- 04 Jones
- 05 Weightman
- 05 Graham-Tomlinson
- 05 Elliott
- 06 Courage
- 08 Gay
- 09 Close
- 10 Reed
- 11 Osterman
- 12 Mullins
- 13 Bewick
- 14 Hagerty

Northumbria
Northumberland

		minimum £ per person	children taken	evening meals	animals taken
Eileen Finn Thornley House Allendale NE47 9NH Tel: (0434) 683255 Open: JAN - DEC Map Ref No. 01	Nearest Road: A.69 Large country house in spacious and peaceful grounds, surrounded by fields and woods one mile out of Allendale village. Relaxed and comfortable accommodation here; 3 roomy and light bedrooms (1 en-suite). 2 lounges, one with colour T.V., one with Steinway Grand. Good food & home baking; unlicensed, but guests are welcome to bring their own wine. Marvellous walking country. Hadrian's Wall, Keilder Forest, & stately houses nearby.	£14.00	Y	Y	Y
Dorothy Jackson Bilton Barns Farmhouse Bilton Barns Alnmouth Alnwick NE66 2TB Tel: (0665) 830427 Open: EASTER- OCT Map Ref No. 02	Nearest Road: A.1 This spacious & well furnished farmhouse has beautiful, panoramic views over Alnmouth & Warkworth Bay, only one & a half miles away. Set in lovely countryside, excellently situated for the many magnificent beaches, castles, walks & recreational activities that Northumberland can offer. All rooms are centrally heated & the large bedrooms have their own washbasin, T.V. & tea/coffee making facilities. Dorothy makes many dishes with a distinctly local flavour. Brian is pleased to show any interested visitors around the farm.	£16.00	Y	Y	N
Mrs Anne I. Davison Alndyke Farmhouse Alnwick NE66 3PB Tel: (0665) 602193 Open: APR - OCT Map Ref No. 03	Nearest Road: A.1068 This charming, listed Georgian farmhouse, with panoramic views, is an excellent base for touring Northumberland, with miles of golden sands, castles, country homes & all sporting activities, only 1 mile from the historical market town of Alnwick. The bedrooms are superbly furnished, having washbasins, hot drink facilities, clock/radios & hairdryers. In the elegant dining room Anne serves beautiful traditional, home-made meals.	£16.00	N	Y	N
Mrs K. S. Wood Fellcroft Station Road Corbridge NE45 5AY Tel: (0434) 632384 Open: MAR-OCT Map Ref No. 04	Nearest Road: A.68 A.69. A friendly welcome is assured at this well appointed Edwardian house set in a quiet cul-de-sac with open countryside to the front & rear. Fellcroft offers 2 delightful twin rooms, 1 with en-suite facilities, the other with private bathroom, both have colour T.V. & tea/coffee makers. There are excellent eating places in the village a short walk away.	£14.00	Y	N	N
Mrs E.Clarke Clive House Appletree Lane Corbridge NE45 5DN Tel: (0434) 632617 Open: ALL YEAR Map Ref No. 04	Nearest Road: A.68, A.69 A lovely house dating back 150 years, offering delightful accommodation in comfortable rooms with bathrooms en-suite. 2 rooms have 4-poster bed & all rooms have tea/coffee facilities, hair dryers, electric blankets & T.V. Residents' lounge also has colour T.V. The breakfast room has exposed beams, a gallery & log fires. The warm welcome given by Mrs Clarke extends to small touches like fresh flowers in the bedrooms. No children under 12 years. Evening meals are by prior arrangement only.	£20.00	N	N	N

Northumberland

		minimum £ per person	children taken	evening meals	animals taken
Dorothy Margaret Wilson **Town Barns** **Corbridge** **NE45 5HP** Tel: (0434) 633345 Open: FEB - NOV Map Ref No. 04	Nearest Road: A.68, A.69 A warm welcome always awaits you at Town Barns, an impressive detached stone house, once the home of authoress Catherine Cookson. Uninterrupted views over the Tyne valley, yet only 2 minutes walk to village centre. Attractive double staircase to balcony and 3 luxurious bedrooms, 2 en-suite, all with tea/coffee making and T.V. Superb Lounge. Indoor heated pool (seasonal). Lovely walled garden. Ample private parking.	£16.00	Y	N	Y
Tom & Sue Jones **Low Barns** **Thornbrough** **Corbridge** **NE45 5LX** Tel: (0434) 632408 Open: ALL YEAR Map Ref No. 04	Nearest Road: A.68, A.69 Set in 2 acres of garden & paddock, this handsome 18th century farmhouse is surrounded by open countryside. It makes an ideal base for walking the Roman Wall & discovering the delights of rural Northumberland. All 3 rooms have en-suite or private facilities, tea/coffee makers & colour T.V. Evening meals are prepared using home grown produce whenever possible. Clothes washing machine & drying room available. Dogs welcome by arrangement.	£18.00	Y	Y	Y
Mrs Margaret Weightman **Kitty Frisk House** **Corbridge Road** **Hexham** **NE46 1UN** Tel: (0434) 606850 Open: MAY-OCT Map Ref No. 05	Nearest Road: A.69 Kitty Frisk House, built at the turn of the century as a gentleman's country residence, is a beautiful family home retaining all the style of the era. The en-suite master bedroom is a delight with a fine ebony four poster bed. Standing in 3 acres of gardens & woodland, 1 mile from Hexham market town, 3 miles from the charming historic village of Corbridge. An ideal retreat from which to visit Hadrian's Wall & explore the unspoilt Northumbrian countryside, after, of course, a lovely traditional English breakfast.	£20.00	Y	N	N
P. Graham-Tomlinson **West Close House** **Hextol Terrace** **Hexham NE46 2AD** Tel: (0434) 603307 Open: ALL YEAR Map Ref No. 05	Nearest Road: B.6305, A.69 West Close House is a charming detached 1920's residence set in pretty prize-winning secluded gardens & situated in a quiet cul-de-sac with private parking (half a mile from Hexham town centre). 4 beautifully appointed bedrooms, offer washbasins radio/alarms & tea/coffee making facilities. There is a choice of full English or wholefood Continental breakfast & suppers are served in a lovely dining/T.V. lounge.	£17.00	Y	N	Y
Eileen Elliott **Middlemarch** **Hencotes** **Hexham** **NE46 2EB** Tel: (0434) 605003 Open: ALL YEAR Map Ref No. 05	Nearest Road: A.68, A.69 Listed Georgian town house in centre of mediaeval market town overlooking the Sele (Park) & Abbey. Awarded Civic Society Award for Restoration 1990. Good stop for Roman Wall, exploring Northumberland or going to & from Scotland. Spacious bedrooms, 1 four-poster with en-suite facilities, 1 double, 1 twin & 1 family room each with w.h.b. All rooms have tea/coffee making makers, remote colour T.V., clock radio alarms & hairdryers. Private parking.	£20.00	Y	N	Y

Northumberland & Durham

			minimum £ per person	children taken	evening meals	animals taken
Elizabeth Courage Rye Hill Farm Slaley Hexham NE47 0AH Tel: (0434) 673259 Open: ALL YEAR Map Ref No. 06	Nearest Road: B.6306 Rye Hill Farm dates back some 300 years & is a traditional livestock unit in beautiful countryside just 5 miles south of Hexham. Recently some of the stone barns adjoining the farmhouse have been converted into superb modern guest accommodation. 6 bedrooms, all with private facilities, all have radio, colour T.V. & tea/coffee making facilities. Delicious home-cooked meals. Perfect for a "get away from it all" holiday.		£16.00	Y	Y	Y
Stephen & Celia Gay Shieldhall Wallington Kirkharle Morpeth NE61 4AQ Tel: (0830) 40387 Open: MAR - NOV Map Ref No. 08	Nearest Road: A.696 Within acres of well kept gardens, offering unimpeded views & overlooking the National Trust's Wallington estate, this meticulously restored 18th century farmhouse is built around a pretty courtyard. All bedrooms are beautifully furnished & have en-suite facilities. There are very comfortable lounges & an extremely charming inglenooked dining room where home produce is often used for delicious meals which are especially prepared when booked in advance.		£17.50	Y	Y	Y

Durham

Helene P. Close Grove House Hamsterley Forest Bishop Auckland DL13 3NL Tel: (038888) 203 Open: ALL YEAR Map Ref No. 09	Nearest Road: A.68 Grove House, once an aristocrats' shooting lodge, is set in 5,000 acres of woodland, moors & becks. A walkers paradise where much wildlife can be seen. If you tire of walking then simply relax & breathe the pure air. Within easy reach of England's highest waterfall, Durham City, Beamish Museum, Hadrian's Wall & Raby Castle. Golf, horseriding, bicycle hire nearby.		£18.50	Y	Y	N
Mrs B Reed Lands Farm Westgate-in-Weardale Bishop Auckland DL13 1SN Tel: (0388) 517210 Open: APR - OCT Map Ref No. 10	Nearest Road: A.689 You will be warmly welcomed to Lands Farm, an old stone-built farmhouse within walking distance of Westgate village. Walled garden with stream meandering by. Accommodation is in centrally heated double & family rooms with luxury en-suite facilities, T.V., tea/coffee making. Full English breakfast or Continental alternative served in attractive dining room. Ideal base for touring (Durham, Hadrian's Wall, Beamish Museum etc.) & for walking.		£15.00	Y	N	N

When booking your accommodation please mention The Best Bed & Breakfast

Durham & Tyne & Wear

			minimum £ per person	children taken	evening meals	animals taken
Elsie Osterman Little Holmside Hall Burnhope DH7 0DS Tel: (0207) 284740 Open: ALL YEAR Map Ref No. 11	Nearest Road: A.691 Little Holmside Hall is an Elizabethan Manor House dating from 1668. Winner of a prestigious environment award for its recent restoration. There are 2 delightful, comfortable guest rooms, both with en-suite bathroom, T.V., & tea/coffee making facilities. The guest lounge has panoramic views of the glorious countryside. A haven of peace & tranquility is found in this easy going, friendly atmosphere. Conveniently located for Durham City, Beamish museum & the Metro Centre.		£16.00	Y	N	N
David E. Mullins The Gables South View Middlestone Moor Spennymoor DL16 7DF Tel: (0388) 817544 Open: ALL YEAR Map Ref No. 12	Nearest Road: A.1(M) The Gables is a spacious Victorian detached house in a tranquil residential area, 10 mins. to A.1(M) & only 7 miles from Durham City Centre & "Beamish" 1990 European Museum of the Year. Ideal touring centre for North Yorks., Moors, Teesdale, Weardale, Cumbria & Hadrian's Wall. Destinations within 30 mins'. drive - Newcastle, Darlington, Sunderland, Middlesborough & Richmond Gateshead Metro centre. Colour T.V./welcome tray in each room.		£13.00	Y	N	Y

Tyne & Wear

Mrs Lyn S. Bewick The Gables Ogle Ponteland Newcastle-upon-Tyne NE20 0AU Tel: (067075) 392 Open: ALL YEAR Map Ref No. 13	Nearest Road: A.696 A warm welcome awaits you at The Gables. This large, ranch-style bungalow is located in the delightful, quiet village of Ogle. Accommodation is in a choice of 4 comfortable, spacious, tastefully decorated bedrooms 2 with ensuite facilities, all with radio, T.V., tea/coffee makers, hairdryer & trouser press. Relax in the comfortable oak beamed lounge with open log fire & enjoy the country garden. Parking.		£20.00	Y	N	N
Capt. Keith J. Hagerty Chirton House Hotel 46 Clifton Road Newcastle-upon-Tyne NE4 6XH Tel: (091) 2730407 Open: ALL YEAR Map Ref No. 14	Nearest Road: A.1, A.186 An imposing elegant house standing in its own pleasant grounds, offering 11 very comfortable rooms, 5 with private facilities, each with colour T.V. & tea/coffee making facilities available. A T.V. lounge & cocktail bar with friendly country house atmosphere. Situated within a few minutes of the city centre it is a good base for touring the countryside including Hadrian's Wall. The beaches are not far away & there are many places of great interest close by.		£18.00	Y	Y	Y

When booking your accommodation please mention
The Best Bed & Breakfast

All the establishments mentioned in this guide are members of the
Worldwide Bed & Breakfast Association.

If you have any comments regarding your accommodation please send them to us using the form at the back of the book.
We value your comments.

Oxfordshire

Oxfordshire
(Thames & Chilterns)

Oxfordshire is a county rich in history & delightful countryside. It has prehistoric sites, early Norman churches, 15th century coaching inns, Regency residences, distinctive cottages of black & white chalk flints & lovely Oxford, the city of dreaming spires.

The countryside ranges from lush meadows with willow-edged river banks scattered with small villages of thatched cottages, to the hills of the Oxfordshire Cotswolds in the west, the wooded Chilterns in the east & the distinctive ridge of the Berkshire Downs in the south. "Old Father Thames" meanders gently across the county to Henley, home of the famous regatta.

The ancient track known as the Great Ridgeway runs across the shire, & a walk along its length reveals barrows, hill forts & stone circles. The 2,000 year old Uffington Horse cut into the chalk of the hillside below an ancient hill fort site, is some 360 feet in length & 160 feet high.

The Romans built villas in the county & the remains of one, including a magnificent mosaic can be seen at North Leigh. In later centuries lovely houses were built. Minster Lovell stands beside the Windrush; Rousham house with its William Kent gardens is situated near Steeple Aston & beside the Thames lies Elizabethan Mapledurham House with its working watermill.

At Woodstock is Blenheim Palace, the largest private house in Britain & birthplace of Sir Winston Churchill. King Alfred's statue stands at Wantage, commemorating his birth there, & Banbury has its cross, made famous in the old nursery rhyme.

Oxford is a town of immense atmosphere with fine college buildings around quiet cloisters, & narrow cobbled lanes. It was during the 12th century that Oxford became a meeting place for scholars & grew into the first established centre of learning, outside the monasteries, in England.

The earliest colleges to be founded were University College, Balliol & Merton. Further colleges were added during the reign of the Tudors, as Oxford became a power in the kingdom. There are now 35 university colleges & many other outstanding historic buildings in the city. Christ Church Chapel is now the Cathedral of Oxford, a magnificent building with a deservedly famous choir.

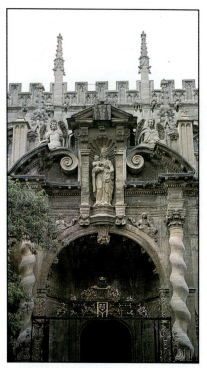

St. Mary's Church.

Oxfordshire

Oxfordshire Gazeteer

Areas of Oustanding Natural Beauty
The North Wessex Downs. The Chiltern Hills. The Cotswolds.

Historic Houses & Castles

Ashdown House - Nr. Lambourn
17th century, built for Elizabeth of Bohemia, now contains portraits associated with her. Mansard roof has cupola with golden ball.
Blenheim Palace - Woodstock
Sir John Vanbrugh's classical masterpiece. Garden designed by Vanbrugh & Henry Wise. Further work done by Capability Brown who created the lake. Collection of pictures & tapestries.
Broughton Castle- Banbury.
14th century mansion with moat - interesting plaster work fine panelling & fire places
Chasleton House-Morton in Marsh
17th century, fine examples of plaster work & panelling. Still has original furniture & tapestries. topiary garden from 1700.
Grey Court - Henly-on-Thames
16th century house containing 18th century plasterwork & furniture. Mediaeval ruins. Tudor donkey-wheel for raising water from well.
Mapledurham House - Mapledurham
16th century Elizabethan house. Oak staircase, private chapel, paintings, original moulded ceilings. Watermill nearby.
Milton Manor House - Nr. Abingdon
17th century house designed by Inigo Jones - Georgian wings, walled garden, pleasure grounds.
Rousham House - Steeple Ashton
17th century - contains portraits & miniatures.

University of Oxford Colleges

University college,	1249
Balliol,	1263
Merton,	1264
Hertford,	1284
Oriel,	1326
New,	1379
All Souls,	1438
Brasenose,	1509
Christ Church,	1546
St. John's,	1555
Pembroke,	1624
Worcester,	1714
Nuffield,	1937
St. Edmund Hall,	1270
Exeter,	1314
The Queen's,	1340
Lincoln,	1427
Magdalen,	1458
Corpus Christi,	1516
Trinity,	1554
Jesus,	1571
Wadham,	1610
Keble,	1868

Cathedrals & Churches

Abingdon (St. Helen)
14th-16th century perpendicular. Painted roof. Georgian stained & enamelled glass.
Burford (St. John the Baptist)
15th century. Sculptured table tombs in churchyard.
Chislehampton (St. Katherine)
18th century. Unspoilt interior of Georgian period. Bellcote.
Dorchester (St. Peter & St. Paul)
13th century knight in stone effigy. Jesse window.
East Hagbourne (St. Andrew)
14th -15th century. Early glass, wooden roofs, 18th century tombs.
North Moreton (All Saints)
13th century with splendid 14th century chantry chapel - tracery.
Oxford Cathedral
Smallest of our English cathedrals. Stone spire form 1230. Norman arcade has double arches, choir vault.
Ryecote (St. Michael & All Angels)
14th century benches & screen base. 17th century altar-piece & communion rails, old clear glass, good ceiling.
Stanton Harcourt (St. Michael)
Early English - old stone & marble floor. Early screen with painting, monuments of 17th -19th century.
Yarnton (St. Bartholomew)
13th century - late perpendicular additions. Jacobean screen. 15th century alabaster reredos.

Oxfordshire

Museums & Galleries

The Ashmolean Museum of Art & Archaeology - Oxford
British, European, Mediterranean, Egyptian & Near Eastern archaeology. Oil paintings of Italian, Dutch, Flemish, French & English schools. Old Master watercolours, prints, drawings, ceramics, silver, bronzes & sculptures. Chinese & Japanese porcelain, lacquer & painting, Tibetan, Islamic & Indian art.

Christ Church Picture Gallery - Oxford
Old Master drawings & paintings.

Museum of Modern Art - Oxford
Exhibitions of contemporary art.

Museum of Oxford
Many exhibits depicting the history of Oxford & its University.

The Rotunda - Oxford
Privately owned collection of dolls' houses 1700-1900, with contents such as furniture, china, silver, dolls, etc.

Oxford University Museum
Entomological, zoological, geological & mineralogical collections.

Pendon Museum of Miniature Landscape & Transport - Abingdon.
Showing in miniature the countryside & its means of transport in the thirties, with trains & thatched village. Railway relics.

Town Museum - Abingdon
17th century building exhibiting fossil, archaeological items & collection of charters & documents.

T olsey Museum - Burford
Seals, maces, charters & bygones - replica of Regency room with period furnishings & clothing.

Historic Monuments

Uffington Castle & White Horse - Uffington
White horse cut into the chalk - iron age hill fort.

Rollright Stones - Nr. Chipping Norton
77 stones placed in circle - an isolated King's stone & nearby an ancient burial chamber.

Minster Lovell House - Minster Lovell
15th century mediaeval house - ruins.

Deddington Castle - Deddington

Other things to see & do

Didcot railway centre -a large collection of locomotives etc., from Brunel's Great Western Railway.

Filkins -a working wool mill where rugs & garments are woven in traditional way.

Blenheim Palace. Woodstock.

OXFORDSHIRE
Map reference

- 01 Crowther
- 02 J. Rouse
- 02 M. Rouse
- 03 Ritter
- 04 Hearne
- 05 Wills
- 06 Grove-White
- 08 Scavuzzo
- 09 Howden-Ferme
- 09 Ovey
- 10 Fulford-Dobson
- 11 Johnston
- 12 Naylor
- 13 Sykes
- 14 Ellis
- 15 Trafford
- 15 Cotmore
- 15 Welham
- 15 Barrett
- 15 Downes
- 15 Butler
- 15 Morris
- 15 Tong
- 15 Edwards
- 16 Naylor
- 17 Wadsworth
- 18 Simpson
- 19 Claridge

Oxford

		minimum £ per person	children taken	evening meals	animals taken
Mrs A. Y. Crowther **Fallowfields** Southmoor Abingdon OX13 5BH Tel: (0865) 820416 Fax 0865 820629 Open: APR - SEPT Map Ref No. 01	Nearest Road: A.420 Fallowfields, the former home of Begum Aga Khan, is an absolutely delightful 300 year-old Gothic-style manor house. Beautifully furnished with the emphasis on gracious elegance. The 2 lounges are spacious & comfortable. The pleasant bedrooms have pretty linens, tea/coffee making facilities, hairdryer, radio,' phone & valet press. The elegant dining room befits the super cuisine served. Guests are also encouraged to use the tennis court, croquet lawn & the outdoor swimming pool. Children over 10 years.	£26.00 see PHOTO over	Y	Y	Y
Janet Rouse **'Morar' Farmhouse** Weald Street Bampton OX18 2HL Tel: (0993) 850162 Fax 0993 851738 Open ALL YEAR(Excl. Xmas) Map Ref No. 02	Nearest Road: A.4095 A warm country welcome & comfortable accommodation is assured at 'Morar'. This spacious farmhouse stands on a 500 acre dairy farm. Offering a choice of 3 pleasant bedrooms with modern amenities & teasmade. There's also a comfortable lounge with colour T.V., piano & a lovely open log fire. Breakfast is delicious with a wide choice of home-made preserves. A super 4-course dinner is also available from October to April.	£16.00	Y	Y	N
Mrs M. J. Rouse **Farmhouse Hotel** University Farm Lew Bampton OX8 2AU Tel: (0993) 850297 Open: ALL YEAR (Excl. Xmas & New Year) Map Ref No. 02	Nearest Road: A.40, A.4095 A charming 17th century farmhouse standing in 216 acres. Heavily beamed throughout, with a huge inglenook fireplace in the lounge. 6 prettily decorated bedooms, all with bath or shower en-suite. Honeymoon suite available. A superb timbered dining room & a most attractive lounge with colour T.V. There is a large sun terrace for guests' use. Situated in a small peaceful village, 3 miles from Witney, it is an ideal base for touring.	£22.00	Y	Y	N
Patti Ritter **La Madonette Country Guest House** North Newington Banbury OX15 6AA Tel: (0295) 730212 Open: ALL YEAR Map Ref No. 03	Nearest Road: B.4035, M.40 A charming 17th century mill house situated in peaceful country surroundings. Conveniently located for the Cotswolds, Oxford, Warwick & Stratford-upon-Avon. Accommodation consists of 6 comfortable & well furnished double rooms, all en-suite with colour T.V. Radio direct telephone and tea/coffee facilities. Delicious breakfasts served. Local pubs & reastaurants offering evening meals nearby. Lounge & garden for guests' use. Licenced.	£20.00	Y	N	N
M. & G. Hearne **Easington House Hotel** 50 Oxford Road Banbury OX16 9AN Tel: (0295) 270181 Open: ALL YEAR Map Ref No. 04	Nearest Road: A.41 Easington House is a family-run, listed 16th century farmhouse located only 300 yards from Banbury Cross, the town centre shops. Accommodation is in a choice of 11 rooms, 7 en-suite, all with modern amenities, 'phone, T.V. & tea/coffee making facilities. A residents' lounge is also available. This makes a good base from which to tour Oxford & the Cotswolds. Evening meals Monday-Friday with prior notice.	£20.00	Y	Y	Y

Fallowfields. Abingdon.

Oxford

		minimum £ per person	children taken	evening meals	animals taken
Mr & Mrs Stephen Wills **Fulford House** **The Green** **Culworth** **Banbury OX17 2BB** **Tel: (029576) 355** **Fax 029576 8304** **Open: FEB - DEC** **Map Ref No. 05**	Nearest Road: A.422, M40 A house party atmosphere prevails in this charming, 17th century country home with its acres of grounds & beautiful terraced gardens in which to wander, play croquet or watch the training of horses & riders. Personal attention is top priority & with just 3 spacious double/twin rooms, delightfully furnished with en-suite or private facilities & T.V., there is an air of exclusivity. Dinners by arrangement. Licenced. Only 1 hr. from London/ Heathrow on the M.40.	£18.50 *see PHOTO over*	Y	Y	Y
Mrs R J Grove-White **Home Farmhouse** **Charlton** **Banbury** **OX17 3DR** **Tel: (0295) 811683** **Open: JAN - DEC** **Map Ref No. 06**	Nearest Road: A.43 A.41, This charming listed stone house dating from 1637 with its attractive colourful paved courtyard provides an excellent base for visiting Oxford, Blenheim, Stratford-upon-Avon, Warwick & the beautiful Cotswold villages. Mrs Grove-White has used her expertise as a professional interior designer to ensure that the 3 double/twin bedded rooms, with en-suite or private bathroom & colour T.V. are comfortable & elegantly furnished. Evening meals by arrangement only.	£20.00	Y	N	Y
Mr & Mrs E. E. Trafford **Tilbury Lodge Hotel** **5 Tilbury Lane** **Eynsham Road** **Botley OX2 9NB** **Tel: (0865) 862138** **Open: ALL YEAR** **Map Ref No. 15**	Nearest Road: B.4044 Tilbury Lodge is a pleasant, family-run private hotel situated in a quiet country lane. Offering 9 en-suite rooms with radio, T.V., 'phone, hairdryer & tea/coffee making facilities. 1 4-poster suite & 2 ground floor rooms. A pleasant jacuzzi bath is also available. Residents' lounge & garden. Located 2 miles west of the city centre with good pubs & restaurants a few minutes walk away.	£25.50	Y	N	N
Mrs Audrey Scavuzzo **The Forge House** **Churchill** **Chipping Norton** **OX7 6NJ** **Tel: (0608) 658173** **Open: JAN - DEC** **Map Ref No. 08**	Nearest Road: A.44 The Forge House is a 150 year old, traditional Cotswold stone cottage, with inglenook log fires & exposed beams, combining the charm of tradition with the comfort of contemporary living. Accommodation is in 4 tastefully furnished en-suite rooms, 2 with 4-poster beds & 1 with jacuzzi. All have radio, colour T.V. & tea/coffee making facilities. Lounge & garden available for guests' use. Convenient for Stratford-upon-Avon & the Cotswolds.	£25.00	Y	N	N
Mrs J.L. Howden-Ferme **Pennyford House** **Peppard Common** **Henley on Thames** **RE9 5JE** **Tel: (04917) 272** **Open: ALL YEAR** **Map Ref No. 09**	Nearest Road: B.481 In the heart of the Thames Valley, Pennyford House is a traditional English home full of warmth and family memories. Acre of mature garden with heated pool. Pretty bedrooms, all with en-suite or private bathrooms. Evening meals if requested in advance. Well situated for visiting London, Windsor and Eton to the east, and Oxford, Blenheim and the edge of the Cotswolds to the west. Heathrow 25 miles, by car or rail/air link coach from Reading.	£15.00	Y	Y	Y

Fulford House.   Banbury.

Oxford

	minimum £ per person	children taken	evening meals	animals taken

Richard & Gillian Ovey **Hernes** **Henley-on-Thames** **RG9 4NT** Tel: (0491) 573245 Open: Mid JAN - Mid DEC Map Ref No. 09	Nearest Road: A.423 A part 16th century home situated in the heart of the Thames & Chilterns. Ideal for London, Windsor, Oxford & The Cotswolds & Bath. Spacious gardens overlook fields & parkland. Large warm comfortable rooms full of family history, offer a welcome traditional to Hernes for five generations. Bedrooms, including a four poster, have private ensuite bathrooms, tea/coffee facilities. Children over 13 yrs. welcomed. Evening meals by arrangement.	£27.50	N	Y	N
Mrs Susan Fulford-Dobson **'Shepherds'** **Shepherds Green** **Rotherfield Greys** **Henley-on-Thames** **RG9 4QL** Tel: (04917) 413 Open ALL YEAR (Excl. Xmas) Map Ref No. 10	Nearest Road: B.481 An attractive, part 18th century house, standing on peaceful village green in its own lovely gardens & paddocks, covered in roses, wisteria, clematis & jasmine. 3 pretty guest rooms, 2 with private facilites. Some have T.V., all have clock-radios & tea/coffee facilities. Delightful drawing room for guests with antiques & open fire. An ideal centre for exploring Chilterns, Windsor & Oxford. Accessible to Heathrow. Children over 12 only. Evening meals by prior arrangement.	£18.00	Y	N	N
Ginnie & Peter Johnston **Chessall Shaw** **Newnham Hill, Nettlebed** **Henley-on-Thames** **RG9 5TN** Tel: (0491) 641311 Fax 0491 641819 Open: ALL YEAR Map Ref No. 11	Nearest Road: A.423 Delightfully located, 10 minutes from Henley-on-Thames, 40 minutes from Heathrow, Windsor & Oxford. Beautifully positioned in the peaceful idyllic Oxfordshire countryside. This charming welcoming house offers 2 pretty en-suite rooms with every creature comfort including tea/coffee making facilities, refrigerator, iron, shoe-cleaning, T.V., radio, electric blankets, etc. A colour T.V. lounge, garden & swimming pool. Delicious cordon bleu cuisine using fresh, home-grown produce whenever possible. Evening meals by arrangement.	£17.50	Y	Y	Y
Keith & Eve Naylor **Bowood House Hotel** **238 Oxford Road** **Kidlington OX5 1EB** Tel: (0865) 842288 Fax 0865 841858 Open ALL YEAR (Excl. Xmas) Map Ref No. 12	Nearest Road: A.423 Situated on the A423, only 4 miles from Oxford city centre. Bowood House offers accommodation of a high standard in a warm, friendly atmosphere. There is a licenced 'a la carte' menu open to non-residents. Offering 20 en-suite rooms with colour T.V., 'phone, hairdryers & tea/coffee makers. An ideal touring centre for the Cotswolds, Stratford, Warwick, Blenheim Palace, Bladon & of course Oxford's numerous attractions. Heathrow 60 miles.	£36.00	Y	Y	N
Brian Sykes **Conygree Gate Country** **House Hotel** **Church Street** **Kingham OX7 6YA** Tel: (0608) 658389 Open: FEB - DEC Map Ref No. 13	Nearest Road: A.429, A.361 Small family run country house in Kingham village, set in heart of glorious Cotswold countryside. Converted from a farmhouse, this is a 16th century building with leaded windows, oak beams and inglenook fireplaces. Large rear garden for sitting out. 10 guest bedrooms, mostly en-suite, with colour T.V., tea/coffee facilities. 2 sitting rooms, dining room and licensed bar. Central heating and log fires throughout. Ample parking.	£22.00	Y	Y	Y

Oxford

		minimum £ per person	children taken	evening meals	animals taken
Tom & Carol Ellis **Wynford House** 79 Main Road Long Hanborough OX7 2JX Tel: (0993) 881402 Open: ALL YEAR Map Ref No. 14	Nearest Road: A.4095 Wynford House is situated in the charming village of Long Hanborough. Accommodation is in 3 guest rooms, 1 with private facilities. All have modern amenities, including colour T.V. & tea/coffee makers & are comfortably furnished. Delicious breakfasts are served with local pubs & restaurants offering tasty evening meals. Conveniently located on the doorstep of the Cotswolds, with Bladon 1 mile, Woodstock & Blenheim Palace 3 miles & Oxford 12 miles.	£15.00	Y	Y	Y
Derek & Audrey Cotmore **The Lawns** 12 Manor Road South Hinksey Oxford OX1 5AS Tel: (0865) 739980 Open: ALL YEAR Map Ref No. 15	Nearest Road: A34. Situated in an 'olde worlde' village, walking distance of the city. The Lawns offers 3 bedrooms with unique views of the dreaming spires, overlooking the garden. All are attractively furnished, with modern amenities, T.V., tea/coffee making facilities, some en-suite. Garden & swimming pool for guests enjoyment. Relax in the dining room & enjoy a varied selection of breakfast foods. Local pub serves tasty meals. Easy access to Blenheim Palace & Cotswolds.	£16.00	Y	N	N
Mr & Mrs P. Welham **Norham Guest House** 16 Norham Road Oxford OX2 6SF Tel: (0865) 515352 Open: JAN - DEC Map Ref No. 15	Nearest Road: A.423 A delightful Victorian house situated in a conservation area yet convenient for the many attractions of Oxford. Accommodation is in 8 tastefully furnished guest rooms, including 2 family rooms with modern amenities, h&c, T.V. & tea/coffee making facilites. Delicious breakfasts are served. Vegetarian diets provided by arrangement. Children over 5 years welcome. Convenient for the city centre. Ideal for visiting the Cotswolds & Stratford-upon-Avon.	£19.00	Y	N	N
Tina & Robin Barrett **Highfield West Guest House** 188 Cumnor Hill Oxford OX2 9PJ Tel: (0865) 863007 Open: ALL YEAR Map Ref No. 15	Nearest Road: A.420 Tina & Robin invite guests to enjoy Bed & Breakfast in the comfort of their home, set in a quiet residential area of Oxford, within walking distance of Cumnor village where 2 inns both serve food. Guest rooms have excellent facilities - 1 double, 1 twin, 1 family, all en-suite, & 2 singles sharing a separate bathroom. There is a lounge, dining room, & garden with swimming pool, heated in season. Fire certificate & car parking.	£17.00	Y	N	Y
Bernadette Downes **Bravalla** 242 Iffley Road Oxford OX4 1SE Tel: (0865) 241326 or 250511 Open: ALL YEAR Map Ref No. 15	Nearest Road: A.4158, M.40 A late Victorian house situated half a mile from Magdalen College & the river. 5 comfortable rooms. Pleasantly decorated with modern amenities. All rooms have T.V. & tea/coffee making facilities, 4 are en-suite. Oxford has so much to see & the Downes family will not only make you welcome but help plan the most interesting tour so as not to miss the best places. 'The Dreaming Spires' begin at the bottom of Iffley Road.	£17.00	Y	N	Y

Oxford

		minimum £ per person	children taken	evening meals	animals taken
M. S. & P. H. Butler Melcombe House 227 Iffley Road Oxford OX4 1SQ Tel: (0865) 249520 Open: ALL YEAR (Excl. Xmas) Map Ref No. 15	Nearest Road: A.4158 A super family atmosphere is found at this delightful architect-designed 100 year-old residence. Accommodation in 9 comfortable bedrooms with modern amenities, T.V. & tea/coffee makers. Situated in the East of the city, conveniently placed for the centre with all its historic sites & colleges. Blenheim Palace, Woodstock, Stratford-upon-Avon, Windsor & the Cotswolds are an easy drive away. Vegetarians catered for.	£17.00	Y	N	Y
Mr & Mrs P. Morris Pine Castle Hotel 290 Iffley Road Oxford OX4 4AE Tel: (0865) 241497 Open: ALL YEAR (excl. Xmas) Map Ref No. 15	Nearest Road: A.423, M.40 A warm welcome awaits you at this Edwardian guest house which still retains many of its period features. It is conveniently situated on a main bus route into the city centre. An alternative route is a short walk along the tow path beside the Thames which is both convenient & picturesque. Cots are provided, T.V. & tea/coffee making facilities in all rooms. Breakfasts vary from the healthy to the positively indulgent. Evening meals with prior notice.	£16.00	Y	N	N
Catherine Tong Courtfield Private Hotel 367 Iffley Road Oxford OX4 4DP Tel: (0865) 242991 Open: ALL YEAR Map Ref No. 15	Nearest Road: A.423 Courtfield Guest House has been recently refurbished to provide accommodation for guests in 6 rooms, most with en-suite facilities. A lounge & the garden are also available for visitors to relax in. Ample parking in mews-style forecourt. Situated on good bus route, one & a half miles from the centre of Oxford. Children over 3 years. No single availability.	£19.00	Y	N	N
Mrs Doreen Edwards Highfield House 91 Rose Hill Oxford OX4 4HT Tel: (0865) 774083/ 718524 Open: ALL YEAR Map Ref No. 15	Nearest Road: A.423, A.4158 A pleasing & friendly house with good access to the City Centre & Ring road. Accommodation is in 7 spacious bedrooms, 5 with en-suite bathroom, all have colour T.V. & tea/coffee making facilites. A short walk brings you to the old attractive village of Iffley, where there are good pubs & food. An excellent base for exploring the historic delights of Oxford. Evening meals by arrangement.	£20.00	Y	Y	N
A.R. Naylor Essex House Chinnor Road Thame OX9 3LS Tel: (084421) 7567 Open: ALL YEAR Map Ref No. 16	Nearest Road: M.40, A.418 Essex House was built in 1870 as Thame Railway Station Hotel & is a perfect base for visiting Oxford, Windsor, London & the Cotswolds. All rooms have satellite T.V., direct dial telephones, tea/coffee making facilities & most rooms have bath/shower en-suite. There is an extensive wine list & the restaurant is open to non-residents. Large private car park.	£27.50	Y	Y	N

The Craven.   Uffington.

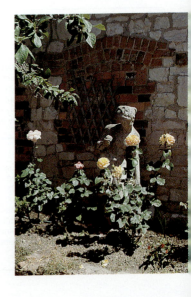

Oxford

	minimum £ per person	children taken	evening meals	animals taken
Mrs C. A. Wadsworth **The Craven** **Fernham Road** **Uffington SN7 7RD** Tel: (036782) 449 Open: ALL YEAR Map Ref No. 17	Nearest Road: A.420 An extremely attractive 17th century thatched farmhouse with exposed beams & open log-burning fire. Accommodation is very comfortable in 7 bedrooms, 1 with 4-poster bed & private bathroom. Good home cooking with fresh local produce. The Craven offers a friendly, relaxed atmosphere. The perfect base for touring this fascinating area.	£16.00 *see PHOTO over*	Y	Y	Y
Liz & John Simpson **Field View** **Wood Green** **Witney OX8 6DE** Tel: (0993) 705485 Open: ALL YEAR Map Ref No. 18	Nearest Road: A.40, A.4095 Attractive Cotswold stone house set in 2 acres, situated on picturesque "Wood Green", midway between Oxford University & the Cotswolds. It is an ideal centre for touring yet only 8 minutes walk from the centre of this lively Oxfordshire market town. A peaceful setting & a warm, friendly atmosphere await you. Accommodation is in 3 comfortable ensuite rooms with modern amenities & tea/coffee making facilities.	£16.00	N	N	N
Bob & Pat Claridge **The Old Rectory** **Church End** **Standlake** **Witney OX8 7SG** Tel: (0865) 300559 Open: FEB-NOV Map Ref No. 19	Nearest Road: A.415, This listed old rectory is a charming Cotswold stone family house ideally situated on the banks of the river Windrush in its own grounds of 5 acres. The 4 delightful bedrooms have private facilities with the 4-poster suite having magnificent views of the river & garden. Oxford, Blenheim, Stratford & the Cotswolds are within easy reach. A very warm welcome by Bob & Pat Claridge is guaranteed.	£25.00 *see PHOTO over*	Y	N	N

All the establishments mentioned in this guide are members of

The Worldwide Bed & Breakfast Association

The Old Rectory.   Standlake.

Shropshire

Shropshire
(Heart of England)

Shropshire is a borderland with a very turbulent history. Physically it straddles highlands & lowlands with border mountains to the west, glacial plains, upland, moorlands & fertile valleys & the River Severn cutting through. It has been quarrelled & fought over by rulers & kings from earliest times. The English, the Romans & the Welsh all wanted to hold Shropshire because of its unique situation. The ruined castles & fortifications dotted across the county are all reminders of its troubled life. The most impressive of these defences is Offa's Dyke, an enormous undertaking intended to be a permanent frontier between England & Wales.

Shropshire has great natural beauty, countryside where little has changed with the years. Wenlock Edge & Clun Forest, Carding Mill Valley, the Long Mynd, Caer Caradoc, Stiperstones & the trail along Offa's Dyke itself, are lovely walking areas with magnificent scenery.

Shrewsbury was & is a virtual island, almost completely encircled by the Severn River. The castle was built at the only gap, sealing off the town. In this way all comings & goings were strictly controlled. In the 18th century two bridges, the English bridge & the Welsh bridge, were built to carry the increasing traffic to the town but Shrewsbury still remains England's finest Tudor city.

Massive Ludlow Castle was a Royal residence, home of Kings & Queens through the ages, whilst the town is also noted for its Georgian houses.

As order came out of chaos, the county settled to improving itself & became the cradle of the Industrial Revolution. Here Abraham Darby discovered how to use coke (from the locally mined coal) to smelt iron. There was more iron produced here in the 18th century than in any other county. A variety of great industries sprang up as the county's wealth & ingenuity increased. In 1781 the world's first iron bridge opened to traffic.

There are many fine gardens in the county. At Hodnet Hall near Market Drayton, the grounds cover 60 acres & the landscaping includes lakes & pools, trees, shrubs & flowers in profusion. Weston Park has 1,000 acres of parkland, woodland gardens & lakes landscaped by Capability Brown.

The house is Restoration period & has a splendid collection of pictures, furniture, china & tapestries.

Shrewsbury hosts an annual poetry festival & one of England's best flower shows whilst a Festival of Art, Music & Drama is held each year in Ludlow with Shakespeare performed against the castle ruins.

Coalbrookedale Museum.

Shropshire

Shropshire Gazeteer

Areas of Outstanding Natural Beauty
The Shropshire Hills.

Historic Houses & Castles

Stokesay Castle - Craven Arms
13th century fortified manor house. Still occupied - wonderful setting - extremely well preserved. Fine timbered gatehouse.
Weston Park - Nr. Shifnal
17th century - fine example of Restoration period - landscaping by Capability Brown. Superb collection of pictures.
Shrewsbury Castle - Shrewsbury
Built in Norman era - interior decorations - painted boudoir.
Benthall Hall - Much Wenlock
16th century. Stone House - mullioned windows. Fine wooden staircase - splendid plaster ceilings.
Shipton Hall - Much Wenlock
Elizabethan. Manor House - walled garden - mediaeval dovecote.
Upton Cressett Hall - Bridgnorth
Elizabethan. Manor House & Gatehouse. Excellent plaster work. . 14th century great hall.

Cathedrals & Churches

Ludlow (St. Lawrence)
14th century nave & transepts. 15th century pinnacled tower. Restored extensively in 19th century. Carved choir stalls, perpendicular chancel - original glass. Monuments.
Shrewsbury (St. Mary)
14th, 15th, 16th century glass. Norman origins.
Stottesdon (St. Mary)
12th century carvings. Norman font. Fine decorations with columns & tracery.
Lydbury North (St. Michael)
14th century transept, 15th century nave roof, 17th century box pews and altar rails. Norman font.
Longor (St. Mary the Virgin)
13th century having an outer staircase to West gallery.
Cheswardine (St. Swithun)
13th century chapel - largely early English. 19th century glass and old brasses. Fine sculpture.

Tong (St. Mary the Virgin with St. Bartholomew)
15th century. Golden chapel of 1515, stencilled walls, remains of paintings on screens, gilt fan vaulted ceiling. Effigies, fine monuments

Museums & Galleries

Clive House - Shrewsbury
Fine Georgian House - collection of Shropshire ceramics. Regimental museum of 1st Queen's Dragoon Guards.
Rowley's House Museum - Shrewsbury
Roman material from Viroconium and prehistoric collection.
Coleham Pumping Station - Old Coleham
Preserved beam engines
Acton Scott Working Farm Museum - Nr. Church Stretton
Site showing agricultural practice before the advent of mechanization.
Ironbridge Gorge Museum - Telford
Series of industrial sites in the Severn Gorge.
CoalBrookdale Museum & Furnace Site
Showing Abraham Darby's blast furnace history. Ironbridge information centre is next to the world's first iron bridge.
Mortimer Forest Museum - Nr. Ludlow
Forest industries of today and yesterday. Ecology of the forest.
Whitehouse Museum of Buildings & Country life - Aston Munslow
4 houses together in one, drawing from every century 13th to 18th, together with utensils and implements of the time.
The Buttercross Museum - Ludlow
Geology, natural & local history of area.
Reader's House - Ludlow
Splendid example of a 16th century town house. 3 storied porch.
Much Wenlock Museum. - Much Wenlock
Geology, natural & local history.
Clun Town Museum - Clun
Pre-history earthworks, rights of way, commons & photographs.

Historic Monuments

Acton Burnell Castle - Shrewsbury
13th century fortified manor house - ruins only.

Shropshire

Boscobel House - Shifnal
17th century house.
Bear Steps - Shrewsbury
Half timbered buildings. Mediaeval.
Abbot's House - Shrewsbury
15th century half-timbered.
Buildwas Abbey - Nr. Telford
12th century - Savignac Abbey - ruins. The church is nearly complete with 14 Norman arches.
Haughmond Abbey - Shrewsbury
12th century - remains of house of Augustinian canons.
Wenlock Priory - Much Wenlock
13th century abbey - ruins.
Roman Town - Wroxeter
2nd century - remains of town of Viroconium including public baths and colonnade.
Moreton Corbet Castle - Moreton Corbet
13th century keep, Elizabethan features - gatehouse altered 1519.
Lilleshall Abbey
12th century - completed 13th century, West front has notable doorway.
Bridgnorth Castle - Bridgnorth
Ruins of Norman castle whose angle of incline is greater than Pisa.
Whiteladies Priory - Boscobel
12th century cruciform church - ruins.
Old Oswestry - Oswestry
Iron age hill fort covering 68 acres; five ramparts and having an elaborate western portal.

Other things to see & do

Ludlow Festival of Art and Drama - annual event
Shrewsbury Flower Show - every August
Severn Valley Railway - the longest full guage steam railway in the country.

Kings Head Inn. Shrewsbury.

SHROPSHIRE
Map reference

02 Rowlands
03 Rogers
04 Davies
06 Spencer
07 Lloyd
08 Royce
09 Thomas
10 Russell
11 Pashen
12 Stening-Rees
13 Bovill
14 Baly
15 Grundey
16 Jones
17 Anderson
18 Mitchell
19 Savage
20 Evans

Shropshire

		minimum £ per person	children taken	evening meals	animals taken
Mary Rowlands **Middleton Lodge** **Middleton Priors** **Bridgnorth WV16 6UR** Tel: (074634) 228 Open: ALL YEAR Map Ref No. 02	Nearest Road: B.4268 Middleton Lodge is set in 20 acres of beautiful rural Shropshire countryside overlooking Brown Clee Hill. Offering 3 extremely attractive en-suite bedrooms, 1 with four poster. There are many places of interest within easy reach of Middleton, the scenic Severn Valley Railway, Ironbrige, Stokesay Castle, the breath-taking beauty of the Long Mynd & the picturesque Carding Mill Valley.	£20.00 🚭	Y	N	N
Don & Rita Rogers **Belvedere Guest House** **Burway Road** **Church Stretton** **SY6 6DP** Tel: (0694) 722232 Open: ALL YEAR Map Ref No. 03	Nearest Road: A.49 A comfortable, relaxed atmosphere prevails in this centrally heated house, set on the slopes of the Long Mynd in the delightful village of Church Stretton. It is an ideal base for exploring Shropshire & the borders on foot or by car. All 12 bedrooms (6 en-suite) have tea making facilities & two lounges are available to guests. Cots & packed lunches are available & there is a drinks license.	£18.00	Y	Y	Y
Mrs Jeanette Davies **Rectory Farm** **Woolstaston** **Church Stretton SY6 6NN** Tel: (0694) 751306 Open: MAR - NOV Map Ref No. 04	Nearest Road: A.49 An extremely attractive half-timbered farmhouse dating back to 1620, offering 3 charming rooms, all with bath en-suite. Situated on the edge of the National Trust Long Mynd Hills, it has marvellous views & superb walking right from the door. There is much for the sportsman here: golf, riding, fishing & gliding. Many historic houses & wonderful beauty spots are a short drive. Children over 12 years.	£16.00	N	N	N
Hayden & Yvonne Lloyd **Upper Buckton Farm** **Leintwardine** **Craven Arms SY7 0JU** Tel: (05473) 634 Open: ALL YEAR Map Ref No. 07	Nearest Road: A.4113 A delightful riverside farmhouse with spectacular views over unspoilt countryside, Upper Buckton, a lovely home with many antiques & beautiful fabrics. Superb traditional & "Cordon bleu" dinners served in the dining room using fresh local produce. Excellent shower room. Pre-breakfast drink brought to your room. Electric blankets & heaters in all rooms. Log fires. A no smoking home	£18.00 🚭	Y	Y	N
Mr & Mrs Graham Spencer **The Old Rectory** **Hopesay** **Craven Arms** **SY7 8HD** Tel: (05887) 245 Open: JAN-DEC Map Ref No. 06	Nearest Road: A.49, B.4348 The Old Rectory dating from the 17th century is set in beautiful landscaped gardens of one & a half acres with croquet lawn. Offering 3 spacious en-suite bedrooms, 2 with Emperor-size beds, all have radio, colour T.V. & tea/coffee makers. Comfortable drawing room & spacious dining room. Tastefully furnished throughout with antiques & many period pieces. Superb home cooking using garden produce. Unlicenced but own wine welcome. An excellent base for touring with easy access to Ludlow, Offa's Dyke & Stokesay Castle. Restricted smoking.	£24.00	N	Y	N

Shropshire

			minimum £ per person	children taken	evening meals	animals taken
Mary & Arthur Royce Woodville Clun Road Craven Arms SY7 9AA Tel: (0588) 672476 Open: ALL YEAR Map Ref No. 08		Nearest Road: A.49, B.4368 A restful holiday in friendly, relaxed surroundings is assured at Woodville. This large family house is set in 3/4 of an acre, surrounded by the hills & woods of the Long Mynd, Wenlock Edge, Clee Hills & Clun Forest. Accommodation is in a choice of 3 pleasant bedrooms, 2 en-suite, the other has private facilities, both with tea/coffee makers. This is an excellent base for touring the region with Stokesay Castle, Ludlow & Church Stretton nearby.	£15.00	Y	Y	N
Mike & Julia Thomas Stoke Manor Stoke-on-Tern Market Drayton TF9 2DU Tel: (063084) 222 Open: JAN-NOV Map Ref No. 08		Nearest Road: A.41, A.53 A warm welcome awaits guests at Stoke Manor, a 250 acre arable farm with farm trail & vintage tractor collection. Ironbrige & Cosford Aerospace Museums, Wedgewood Potteries, ancient towns of Shrewsbury & Chester are only a few of the many palces to visit locally. Each bedroom has bathroom, colour T.V., tea/coffee trays. Abundance of good eating places nearby. Residents' licence.	£20.00	Y	N	N
Mrs Julia Russell Brockton Grange Brockton Much Wenlock TF13 6JR Tel: (074636) 443 Open: JAN - DEC Map Ref No. 10		Nearest Road: B.4378 Idyllically set in 25 acres including private lake & woodland, this fine Country House combines the cosiness of old oak beams & log fires with later Victorian splendour. Bedrooms are en-suite with T.V., tea/coffee facilities. A friendly, relaxed atmosphere created in one of Shropshire's finest dales, where wildlife flourishes in carefully tended tranquillity. Near Ironbridge Gorge, Church Stretton, Shrewsbury. Trout & coarse fishing available.	£20.00	Y	N	N
Lorraine Pashen Bron Heulog Waterfall Road Llanrhaeadr-y-m Oswestry SY10 0JX Tel: (069189) 521 Open: JAN-DEC Map Ref No. 11		Nearest Road: A.5, B.4396 Bron Heulog is a large Victorian home with a mixture of antique and traditional furnishings where good food and a warm welcome awaits. Although not en-suite, the three bedrooms are very comfortable, with wasbasins, radio, colour T.V., tea/coffee facilities. Guests may play the grand piano or relax with one of the many books. Area of Natural Beauty with Pistyll Rhaeadr waterfall; ideal for walking, birdwatching, or just getting away from it all!	£13.00	Y	Y	Y
Carol & Norman Stening - Rees Roseville 12 Berwick Road Shrewsbury SY1 2LN Tel: (0743) 236470 Open: FEB - DEC Map Ref No. 12		Nearest Road: A.458, B.5067 Roseville, a late Victorian detached town-house with own parking. 10 minutes easy walk to town centre, rail/bus stations. Offering comfortable, centrally heated & tastefully furnished accommodation (en-suite available) in a no-smoking environment. Relaxed atmosphere encouraged. Tea, coffee, non-alcoholic drinks served on request at all reasonable times in guests' lounge. Wide choice of excellent food. Children over 12.	£14.00	Y	N	N

Shropshire

		minimum £ per person	children taken	evening meals	animals taken
H. C. Bovill **Mytton Hall** **Montford Bridge** **Shrewsbury SY4 1EU** Tel: (0743) 850 264 Open: ALL YEAR Map Ref No. 13	Nearest Road: A.5 An elegant white Georgian house built in 1790 with spectacular views. Accommodation is in 3 attractive & tastefully furnished en-suite rooms with tea/coffee provided on request. A delicious full English breakfast is served. Tennis court available. Private fishing rights. Set in traditional grounds & adjoining the River Perry with private fishing, there is an elegant garden for guests to relax in. Conveniently located only 6 miles from Shrewsbury.	£19.00	N	N	N
Mr & Mrs Neil Baly **Fitz Manor** **Bomere Heath** **Shrewsbury SY4 3AS** Tel: (0743) 850295 Open: ALL YEAR Map Ref No. 14	Nearest Road: A.5 A 15th century half timbered manor house listed Grade II with a particularly fine panelled interior of great historical interest. Although very old the house is a family home, with a relaxed atmosphere. Full central heating, large garden & farm open to all guests. Heated swimming pool. Private fishing on the River Severn available.	£16.00	Y	Y	Y
J. & B. Grundey **The Sett Country Hotel** **Stanton upon Hine Heath** **Shrewsbury SY4 4LR** Tel: (0939) 250391 Open: ALL YEAR Map Ref No. 15	Nearest Road: A.53 A family run Country Hotel in a beautiful converted barn on a small working farm in the centre of a quiet village. 6 comfortable en-suite rooms, some with hand painted window shutters, all with tea making facilities & hairdryers. Full central heating. Restful lounge with colour T.V. & separate dining rooms. Excellent food cooked on traditional A.G.A. Licenced. Special Ironbrige Breaks.	£22.00	Y	Y	Y
Mrs Janet Jones **Grove Farm** **Preston Brockhurst** **Shrewsbury** **SY4 5QA** Tel: (093928) 223 Open: ALL YEAR Map Ref No. 16	Nearest Road: A.49 A warm and friendly welcome, exccellent home cooking and comfortable rooms await guests in this 17th century farmhouse set in mixed farmland in a small village. Centrally heated and log fires. All bedrooms have tea/coffee facilities. One large double/family room with en-suite shower; one twin, one single with washbasins. Easy access to Shrewsbury, Ironbridge, Chester and Wales.	£15.00	Y	N	N
Roy & Sylvia Anderson **Tankerville Lodge** **Stiperstones** **Minsterley** **Shrewsbury SY5 0NB** Tel: (0743) 791401 Open: ALL YEAR Map Ref No. 17	Nearest Road: A.488 Tankerville Lodge, noted for its caring, friendly atmosphere, nestles peacefully close to the Stiperstones nature reserve & Long Mynd in the beautiful Shropshire hills. There are 4 bedrooms, all with tea/coffee making facilities, a lounge with colour T.V. & a dining room serving good home-cooked food. This is superb walking country & a good base for touring historic Shropshire & the Welsh borderland.	£13.00	Y	Y	Y

Shropshire

			minimum £ per person	children taken	evening meals	animals taken
Mike & Gill Mitchell The White House Hanwood Shrewsbury SY5 8LP Tel: (0743) 860414 Open: ALL YEAR Map Ref No. 18	Nearest Road: A.488 Lovely 16th century black and white half-timbered guest house with nearly 2 acres of gardens and river, 3 miles south-west of mediaeval Shrewsbury. Ironbridge, Mid-Wales and the Long Mynd within half hour drive. 6 guest rooms with T.V., tea/coffee facilities. En-suite available. The dining room offers a fresh, varied menu supplemented by seasonal vegetables and herbs from the garden, and the house hens provide your breakfast eggs!		£19.50	N	Y	N
Mrs Jo Savage Church Farm Wrockwardine Wellington Telford TF6 5DG Tel: (0952) 244917 Open: JAN - DEC Map Ref No. 19	Nearest Road: A.5, M.54 Enjoy a warm welcome in this Georgian, centrally heated farmhouse with oak beams, log fires & spacious gardens with croquet & bowls available. 5 individually furnished bedrooms, some en-suite, all have washbasins, tea trays & colour T.V. Freshly cooked meals are served in the dining room which overlooks the village church. Only 1 mile from A.5 & M.54, giving easy acces to Ironbridge, Shrewbury & the whole of the Mildland area. Dinner by prior arrangement.		£19.00	Y	Y	Y
Mrs G. C. Evans New Farm Muckleton Shawbury Telford TF6 6RJ Tel: (0939) 250358 Open: ALL YEAR Map Ref No. 20	Nearest Road: A.53 New Farm is a 70 acre farm standing in the peace & quiet of the Shropshire/Wales border. Guests have a choice of 4 bedrooms all with modern amenities, T.V. & tea/coffee making facilities, 3 en-suite. A comfortable guests' lounge with colour T.V. & spacious dining room is also avialable. Home cooked meals are available Friday, Saturday & Sunday only. New Farm is ideally located for visiting the historic towns of Shrewsbury, Chester, Ludlow, Bridgnorth & Ironbridge. The potteries are also within driving distance. Meals by arrangement. Close to Hawkstone Park Golf Course.		£15.00	Y	Y	N

All the establishments mentioned in this guide are members of

The Worldwide Bed & Breakfast Association

Somerset

Somerset
(West Country)

Fabulous legends, ancient customs, charming villages, beautiful churches, breathtaking scenery & a glorious cathedral, Somerset has them all, along with a distinctively rich local dialect. The essence of Somerset lies in its history & myth & particularly in the unfolding of the Arthurian tale.

Legend grows from the bringing of the Holy Grail to Glastonbury by Joseph of Arimathea, to King Arthur's castle at Camelot, held by many to be sited at Cadbury, to the image of the dead King's barge moving silently through the mists over the lake to the Isle of Avalon. Archaeological fact lends support to the conjecture that Glastonbury, with its famous Tor, was an island in an ancient lake. Another island story surrounds King Alfred, reputedly sheltering from the Danes on the Isle of Athelney & there burning his cakes.

Historically, Somerset saw the last battle fought on English soil, at Sedgemoor in 1685. The defeat of the Monmouth rebellion resulted in the wrath of James II falling on the West Country in the form of Judge Jeffreys & his "Bloody Assize".

To the west of the county lies part of the Exmoor National Park, with high moorland where deer roam & buzzards soar & a wonderful stretch of cliffs from Minehead to Devon. Dunster is a popular village with its octagonal Yarn market, & its old world cottages, dominated at one end by the castle & at the other by the tower on Conygar Hill.

To the east the woods & moors of the Quantocks are protected as an area of outstanding natural beauty. The Vale of Taunton is famous for its apple orchards & for the golden cider produced from them.

The south of the county is a land of rolling countryside & charming little towns, Chard, Crewkerne, Ilchester & Ilminster amongst others.

To the north the limestone hills of Mendip are honeycombed with spectacular caves & gorges, some with neolithic remains, as at Wookey Hole & Cheddar Gorge.

Wells is nearby, so named because of the multitude of natural springs. Hardly a city, Wells boasts a magnificent cathedral set amongst spacious lawns & trees. The west front is one of the glories of English architecture with its sculptured figures & soaring arches. A spectacular feature is the astronomical clock, the work of 14th century monk Peter Lightfoot. The intricate face tells the hours, minutes, days & phases of the moon. On the hour, four mounted knights charge forth & knock one another from their horses.

Wells Cathedral Choir.

Somerset

Somerset Gazeteer
Areas of Outstanding Natural Beauty
Mendip Hills. Quantock Hills. National Park - Exmoor.

Historic Houses & Castles
Abbot's Fish House - Meare
14th century house.
Barrington Court - Illminster
16th century house & gardens.
Brympton D'Evercy - Nr. Yeovil
Mansion with 17th century front & Tudor west front. Adjacent is 13th century priest's house & church. Formal gardens & vineyard.
Dodington Hall - Nether Stowey
14th & 15th century hall with minstrels' gallery.
Dunster Castle - Dunster
13th century castle with fine 17th century staircase & ceilings.
East Lambrook Manor - South Petherton
15th century house with good panelling.
Gaulden Manor - Tolland
12th century manor. Great Hall having unique plaster ceiling & oak screen. Antique furniture.
Halsway Manor - Crowcombe
14th century house with fine panelling.
Hatch Court - Hatch Beauchamp
Georgian house in the Palladian style with China room.
King John's Hunting Lodge - Axbridge
Early Tudor merchant's house.
Lytes Carry - Somerton
14th & 15th century manor house with a chapel & formal garden.
Montacute House - Yeovil
Elizabethan house with fine examples of Heraldic Glass, tapestries, panelling & furniture. Portrait gallery of Elizabethan & Jacobean paintings.
Tintinhull House - Yeovil
17th century house with beautiful gardens.

Cathedrals & Churches
Axbridge (St. John)
1636 plaster ceiling & panelled roofs.
Bishop's Lydeard (St. Mary)
15th century Notable tower, rood screen & glass.
Bruton (St. Mary)
Fine 2 towered 15th century church. Georgian chancel, tie beam roof, Georgian reredors. Jacobean screen. 15th century embroidery.
Chewton Mendip (St. Mary Magdalene)
12th century with later additions. 12th century doorway, 15th century bench ends, magnificent 16th century tower & 17th century lecturn.
Crewkerne (St. Bartholomew)
Magnificent west front & roofs, 15th & 16th century. South doorway dating from 13th century, wonderful 15th century painted glass & 18th century chandeliers.
East Brent (St. Mary)
Mainly 15th century. Plaster ceiling, painted glass & carved bench ends.
Glastonbury (St. John)
One of the finest examples of perpendicular towers. Tie beam roof, late mediaeval painted glass, mediaeval vestment & early 16th century altar tomb.
High Ham (St. Andrew)
Sumptuous roofs & vaulted rood screen. Carved bench ends. Jacobean lecturn, mediaeval painted glass. Norman font.
Kingsbury Episcopi (St. Martin)
14th-15th century. Good tower with fan vaulting. Late mediaeval painted glass.
Long Sutton (Holy Trinity)
15th century with noble tower & magnificent tie beam roof. 15th century pulpit & rood screen, tower vaulting.
Martock (All Saints)
13th century chancel. Nave with tie beam roof, outstanding of its kind. 17th century paintings of Apostles.
North Cadbury (St. Michael)
Fine chancel. 15th century roofs, parclose & portion of cope, fragments of mediaeval painted glass.
Pilton (St. John)
12th century with arcades. 15th century roofs.
Taunton (St. Mary Magdalene)
Highest towers in the county. Five nave roof, fragments of mediaeval painted glass.
Trull (All Saints)
15th century with many mediaeval art treasures & 15th century glass.

Somerset

Wells Cathedral-Wells
Magnificent west front with carved figures. Splendid tower. Early English arcade of nave & transepts. 60 fine misericords c.1330. Lady chapel with glass & star vault. Chapter House & Bishop's Palace.
Weston Zoyland (St. Mary)
15th century bench ends. 16th century heraldic glass. Jacobean pulpit.

Museums & Galleries

Admiral Blake Museum - Bridgewater
Exhibits relating to Battle of Sedgemoor, archaeology.
Burdon Manor - Washford
14th century manor house with Saxon fireplace & cockpit.
Borough Museum - Hendford Manor Hall, Yeovil
Archaeology, firearms collections & Bailward Costume Collection.
Glastonbury Lake Village Museum - Glastonbury
Late prehistoric antiquities.
Gough's Cave Museum - Cheddar
Upper Paleolithic remains, skeleton, flints, amber & engraved stones.
Wookey Hole Cave Museum - Wookey Hole
Remains from Pliocene period. Relics of Celtic & Roman civilization. Exhibition of handmade paper-making.

Historic Monuments

Cleeve Abbey - Cleeve
Ruined 13th century house, with timber roof & wall paintings.
Farleigh Castle - Farleigh Hungerford
14th century remains - museums in chapel.
Glastonbury Abbey - Glastonbury
12th & 13th century ruins of St. Joseph's chapel & Abbot's kitchen.
Muchelney Abbey - Muchelney
15th century ruins of Benedictine abbey.

Other things to see & do

Black Rock Nature Reserve - Cheddar
Circular walk through plantation woodland, downland grazing.
Cheddar Caves
Show caves at the foot of beautiful Cheddar Gorge.
Cricket St. Thomas Wildlife Park - Nr. Chard
Wildlife park, heavy horse centre, countryside museum, etc.
West Somerset Railway
Minehead to Bishop's Lydeard preserved steam railway.
Wookey Hole Caves - Wookey Hole, Nr. Wells.

Montacute House. Yeovil.

SOMERSET

Map reference

01 Laidler
02 Roe
03 Tinniswood
04 Wheeler
05 Newman-Coburn
06 Swann
06 Smith
07 Bradshaw
08 Collins
09 Tynan
10 Wilkins
11 Vicary
12 Brown
13 Middle
14 Copeland
15 Holloway
16 Clark
17 Mitchem
18 Gothard
19 Slipper
20 Garner-Richards
21 Milward
22 Brewer
23 Attia
24 White
24 Harris
25 Thompson
26 Higgs
27 Frost
28 Durbin
29 Criddle
30 Teague
31 Tilden

Somerset

		minimum £ per person	children taken	evening meals taken	animals taken
Mrs Pam Laidler **Quantock House** Holford Bridgwater TA5 1RY Tel: (0278) 74439 Open: JAN - DEC Map Ref No. 01	Nearest Road: A.39 Quantock House is in the small picturesque village of Holford, historically connected with Wordsworth and Coleridge. Relax in this 400 year old thatched home with cottage garden. The spacious rooms have either en-suite or private bathroom, T.V., & tea/coffee facilities. Sample the home cooking on offer, or enjoy nearby homely hostelrys, Set near hills and the sea, a perfect centre for exploring by car or on foot.	£16.00	Y	Y	Y
Hilary Roe **Swang Farm** Cannington Bridgwater TA5 2NJ Tel: (0278) 67765 Fax 0278 67747 Open: JAN - DEC Map Ref No. 02	Nearest Road: A.39 Swang Farm, mentioned in the Doomsday Book, offers accommodation in 4 charming guest rooms, all with private facilities & modern amenities, including colour T.V. & tea/coffee makers. Residents' lounge & delightful garden for guests' use. Outdoor heated pool. Stabling available during winter. Excellent local pubs & restaurants. Close by are cottages once owned by Coleridge & Wordsworth. Ideal base for touring/ walking in the Quantock Hills & surrounding area.	£20.00 *see PHOTO over*	Y	N	N
Mrs Gillian Tinniswood **Brookland Hotel** 56 North Street Bridgwater TA6 3PN Tel: (0278) 423263 Fax 0278 452988 Open: ALL YEAR Map Ref No. 03	Nearest Road: M.5, A.38 A comfortable, licensed guest house style hotel, with private car park. Comfortable bedrooms, some en-suite, all with washbasins, colour T.V., tea and coffee. Large, attractive T.V. lounge. Friendly service and a relaxed atmosphere. Children welcome, high chairs and cots provided. Evening meals available. Ideal touring base for Somerset, or stopover heading north or south through the West Country.	£15.00	Y	Y	Y
Peter & Margaret Wheeler **The Warren Guest House** 29 Berrow Road Burnham-on-Sea TA8 2EZ Tel: (0278) 786726 Open: ALL YEAR Map Ref No. 04	Nearest Road: M.5, A.38 'The Warren' is an imposing Victorian house offering spacious accommodation with modern amenities including tea/coffee makers & colour T.Vs. The town centre, swimming pool & championship golf course are within easy reach, the beach is 100 yds away. Guests have full use of the comfortably furnished lounge & are encouraged to browse in the attractive garden. Seedlings (in season) are available free to interested amateur gardeners. Ideally situated for touring the West Country, including Bath, Wells & Glastonbury.	£13.50	Y	Y	Y
Roger & Sarah Newman-Coburn **Hawthorne House** Bishopswood Chard TA20 3RS Tel: (0460) 234482 Open: JAN - DEC Map Ref No. 05	Nearest Road: A.303, B.3170 Hawthorne House, a cosy & welcoming 19th century stone house in the scenic Blackdown Hills, is ideally situated for visiting National Trust properties and other attractions in Somerset and Devon. Both guest bedrooms have central heating, washbasins, shaver points, tea/coffee trays. Comfortable lounge with stereo colour T.V. The dining room has panoramic views over the extensive gardens and surrounding hills.	£11.50	N	Y	N

Swang Farm. Cannington.

Somerset

		minimum £ per person	children taken	evening meals	animals taken
Gillian & Robert Swann Broadview 43 East Street Crewkerne TA18 7AG Tel: (0460) 73424 Open: ALL YEAR Map Ref No. 06	Nearest Road: A.30, A.303 Secluded colonial style bungalow offering sun porch, sitting room with comfortable setees & dining hall. A warm, friendly & relaxing atmosphere. Acre feature gardens with many interesting plants & shrubs. Views over Crewkerne & surrounding hills. Carefully furnished ensuite rooms with colour T.V., tea/coffee making facilities, easy chairs & central heating. Substantial home cooked dinner. Dorset/Somerset border. A list of 50 varied places of interset is also provided.	£15.00	Y	Y	Y
Mrs G.Smith Chinnock House Middle Chinnock Crewkerne TA18 7PN Tel: (0935) 881229 Open: JAN - DEC Map Ref No. 06	Nearest Road: A.30, A.303 A beautiful Ham stone Georgian house set in a walled garden with glorious views in a quiet Somerset hamlet. Offering 2 rooms, 1 with private bathroom, 1 en-suite. An ideal centre for visiting Bath, Stonehenge, Wells, Glastonbury, Sherborne, Dorchester & Hardy country. Evening meals by prior arrangement with fresh salmon, home-grown vegetables & raspberries & cream a speciality. Swimming pool & laundry service available.	£20.00	Y	Y	N
Major & Mrs G.H. Bradshaw Dollons House 10 Church Street Dunster TA24 6SH Tel: (0643) 821880 Open: ALL YEAR Map Ref No. 07	Nearest Road: A.396 17th century Dollons House nestles beneath the castle in this delightful mediaeval village in the Exmoor National Park. Dunster is ideal for touring Exmoor & the North Devon Coast. There are 3 en-suite rooms each with its own character & special decor. 100 years ago the local pharmacist had his shop in Dollons & in the back he made marmalade for the Houses of Parliament.	£23.50	N	N	N
Jaqui & Tony Collins Knoll Lodge Church Road East Brent TA9 4HZ Tel: (0278) 760294 Open: JAN - DEC Map Ref No. 08	Nearest Road: M.5 Knoll Lodge is a 19th century listed Somerset house in an acre of orchard, where you are offered comfortable accommodation and quality food in friendly and peaceful rural surroundings. 3 spacious bedrooms - 2 double en-suite; 1 twin with private bathroom. Centrally heated, attractively decorated with antique pine furniture and hand-made American patchwork quilts. Colour T.V.s & tea/coffee facilities. Dinner by arrangement.	£17.50	Y	Y	N
John & Ann Tynan No 3 Restaurant & Hotel 3 Magdalene Street Glastonbury BA6 9EW Tel: (0458) 32129 Open: FEB - DEC Map Ref No. 09	Nearest Road: M.5 A.39 An attractive grade II listed Georgian house adjoining the ruin of the once powerful Abbey. The tomb of King Arthur & Guinevere is claimed to have been discovered here in the 13th century. 6 attractive rooms, each with private facilities, telephone, radio, colour T.V. & tea/coffee makers. The restaurant produces only 'real' food with flair & innovation. Cornish lobster is a speciality. An excellent base for touring Cheddar George, Wookey Hole & Wells Cathedral are all within easy reach.	£35.00	Y	Y	N

Hillards. Curry Rivel.

Somerset

		minimum £ per person	children taken	evening meals	animals taken
J. Wilkins & M. Carter Hillards High Street Curry Rivel Langport TA10 0EY Tel: (0458) 251737 Open: ALL YEAR Map Ref No. 10	Nearest Road: A.378 A.303 A charming 17th century grade II listed house of architectural & historical interest. 6 comfortable bedrooms, 3 with en-suite facilities. Dining room, oak room lounge, T.V. lounge where horse brasses adorn the cat basket hearth. Full central heating. A delightful home with a wealth of oak & elm panelled walls, beamed ceilings & large inglenook fireplaces. An excellent touring base.	£15.00 see PHOTO over	N	N	N
Mrs V. A. Vicary Larcombe Foot Winsford Minehead TA24 7HS Tel: (064385) 306 Open: APR - DEC Map Ref No. 11	Nearest Road: A.396 Larcombe Foot, a comfortable old country house set in the beautiful & tranquil Upper Exe Valley is an ideal base for walking, riding, fishing & touring Exmoor. Guests comfort is paramount. There are 3 bedrooms, 2 with private bathroom & tea/coffee makers in all rooms. A comfortable sitting room with log fire & T.V. plus a pretty garden to relax in. Winsford is considered one of the prettiest villages on the moor.	£15.00	Y	N	Y
Mrs Julia Brown Emmetts Grange Simonsbath Minehead TA24 7LD Tel: (064383) 282 Open: MAR - NOV Map Ref No. 12	Nearest Road: B.3223 This comfortable 19th century farmhouse is peacefully situated on a 1,200 acre farm set in the beautiful Exmoor National Park. 4 bedrooms, 2 en-suite, all with colour T.V. & tea making facilities. The lounge with open fire has a spectacular view across the garden to the moor. Delicious country cooking using local produce. Table licence. North Devon & Somerset coasts nearby. Good local walking, riding & fishing. Stabling provided. Evening meals by prior arrangement only.	£19.00	Y	Y	Y
Mr & Mrs B. H. Middle Church Farm Guest House School Lane Compton Dundon Somerton TA11 6PE Tel: (0458) 72927 Open: JAN-SEPT Map Ref No. 13	Nearest Road: B.3151, A superb thatched cottage over 400 years-old, offering 6 delightful rooms, all with en-suite facilities, colour T.V., tea/coffee making equipment & full central heating. Imaginative home cooking from fresh produce, residents' licence with choice of wines. Nestling below St. Andrew's Church in a lovely village with marvellous views in the heart of the Vale of Avalon. Walking & wildlife on the doorstep. Convenient for coast & countryside, historic houses & towns. Use of pretty garden & guests car park.	£17.50	Y	Y	N
Roy Copeland The Lynch Country House Hotel 4 Behind Berry Somerton TA11 7PD Tel: (0458) 72316 Open: JAN - DEC Map Ref No. 14	Nearest Road: A.303 The Lynch is a charming small hotel, standing in acres of carefully tended, wonderfully mature grounds. Beautifully refurbished & decorated to retain all its Georgian style & elegance, it now offers accommodation in a choice of 5 attractively presented rooms, some with four-posters, others with Victorian bedsteads, all with thoughtful extras including bathrobes & magazines. Each room has en-suite facilities,'phone, radio, T.V.& tea/coffee makers. The elegant dining room overlooks the lawns & lake.	£17.50 see PHOTO over	Y	N	Y

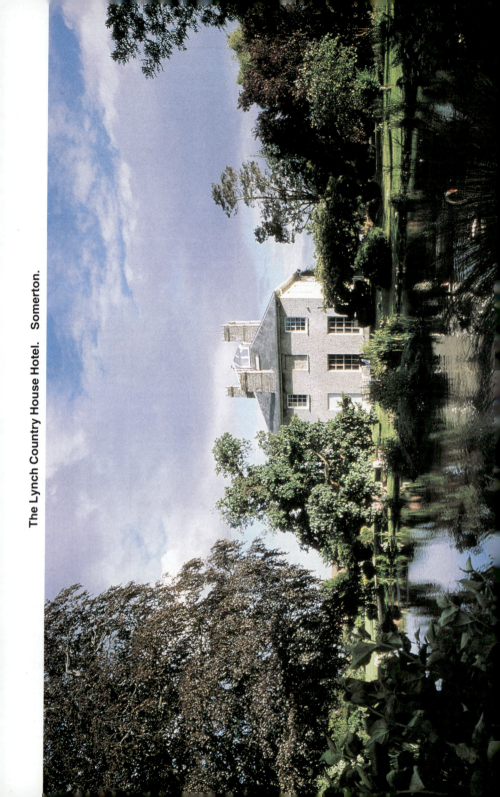

The Lynch Country House Hotel. Somerton.

Somerset

		minimum £ per person	children taken	evening meals	animals taken
Mrs E. Holloway **Manor Farm** **Chiselborough** **Stoke-sub-Hamdon** **TR14 6TQ** Tel: (0935) 881203 Open: APR - OCT Map Ref No. 15	Nearest Road: A.303, A.30 Manor Farm is set in the heart of rural Somerset & stands in 450 acres. A most atractive Victorian Hamstone house offering 4 charming comfortable rooms with modern amenities. A sitting room with colour T.V. for guests as well as a garden & games room. Mrs Holloway welcomes all her guests most warmly. Plenty of good pubs & restaurants within a couple of miles.	£16.00	Y	N	N
Mrs C. Clark **Meryan House Hotel** **Bishops Hull** **Taunton** **TA1 5EG** Tel: (0823) 337445 Open: ALL YEAR Map Ref No. 16	Nearest Road: A.38 Meryan House is a comfortable period residence set in pleasant gardens only 1 1/2 miles from the centre of Taunton. All bedrooms have private bathroom, colour T.V., direct dial telephone & tea/coffee making facilities. There are many places of interest locally including the Quantock, Mendip & Blackdown Hills, Cheddar Gorge, Longleat & Cricket St. Thomas. Ideally located within easy driving distance of Stonehenge, Avebury, Bath, Exeter & Glastonbury.	£25.00	Y	Y	Y
Mrs Claire Mitchem **Whittles Farm** **Beercrocombe** **Taunton** **TA3 6AH** Tel: (0823) 480301 Open: MAR - OCT Map Ref No. 17	Nearest Road: A.358 Guests at Whittles Farm can be sure of a high standard of accommodation & service. A superior 16th century farmhouse set in 200 acres of pastureland, it is luxuriously carpeted & furnished in traditional style. Inglenook fireplaces & log-burners. 3 bedrooms with en-suite facilities, individually furnished, T.V., tea/coffee making. Excellent farmhouse food using own meat, eggs & vegetables & local Cheddar cheese & butter. Table licence. Children over 12.	£19.00	Y	Y	N
Mrs Sally Gothard **Slough Court** **Stoke St. Gregory** **Taunton** **TA3 6JQ** Tel: (0823) 490311 Open: FEB - NOV Map Ref No. 18	Nearest Road: M.5 Delightful 14th century moated manor house situated in the heart of the nationally acclaimed Somerset Levels. The emphasis is on comfort, relaxation, personal service & good food. All rooms are elegantly furnished & have full central heating, yet they retain much of their original character with beamed ceilings, mullioned windows, inglenook fireplaces & an oak-screened hall. Tennis, swimming & croquet are available for the energetic.	£20.00	Y	Y	N
Anne & Bill Slipper **Strawbridges Farm** **Guest House** **Churchstanton** **Taunton TA3 7PD** Tel: (0823) 60591 Open: JAN - DEC Map Ref No. 19	Nearest Road: M.5, A.303 A relaxed, peaceful atmosphere, friendly hosts and high standard of accommodation in a delightful location in the Blackdown Hills. Strawbridges, now a non-working farm, offers 5 charming bedrooms (en-suite available) each with colour T.V. & tea/coffee facilities. Guests have their own comfortable lounge and separate dining room where excellent home cooking using fresh local produce is a speciality. Ideal touring base with ample parking.	£16.00	Y	Y	N

Somerset

		minimum £ per person	children taken	evening meals	animals taken
Mrs Moira Garner-Richards Watercombe House Huish Champflower Wiveliscombe Taunton TA4 2EE Tel: (0984) 23725 Open: EASTER - OCT Map Ref No. 20	Nearest Road: B.3227 Enjoy your stay in this corner of west Somerset at Watercombe House where the River Tone runs through the garden past this modernised former old school house. 3 miles from Wimbleball Lake & a walk away from fly fishing at Clatworthy reservoir. Relaxing holiday for fishermen, walkers & riders. Easy access to Exmoor & the coast. Log fires & imaginative home cooking.	£15.00	Y	Y	N
Joanna Milward Chandlers House Stogumber Taunton TA4 3TA Tel: (0984) 56580 Open: MAR - OCT Map Ref No. 21	Nearest Road: A.358 Chandlers House is a listed period house in the charming conservation village of Stogumber, at the foot of the beautiful Quantock Hills. Convenient for touring Exmoor. Accommodation is in 3 comfortable rooms, 1 en-suite, with radio & tea/coffee makers. The house is beautifully furnished with open fires in all the rooms. The old-fashioned walled garden is completely secluded & quiet. Stogumber gardens open to the public 2nd week in June,	£14.00	Y	N	Y
Mrs Diana Brewer Wood Advent Farm Roadwater Watchet TA23 0RR Tel: (0984) 40920 Open: ALL YEAR Map Ref No. 22	Nearest Road: A.39 Set in the Exmoor National Park, Wood Advent Farm is a 340 acre working sheep farm with beautiful views & breathtaking parks, offering 5 relaxing en-suite bedrooms, with tea/coffee facilities. A chintz lounge with log fire, available at all times, & an inglenook woodburner heats the dining room, where country dishes are West Country.	£16.50	Y	Y	Y
Mrs M. J. Attia Glencot House Glencot Lane Wookey Hole Wells BA5 1BH Tel: (0749) 77160/ 677160 Fax 0749 670210 Open: ALL YEAR Map Ref No. 23	Nearest Road: M.5, A.371 Set in 18 acres of garden & parkland with river frontage, Glencot House is a Grade II listed Victorian mansion, which over the past few years has been restored to its former glory to provide comfortable country house accommodation with friendly service & homely atmosphere. It is elegantly furnished & offers peace & tranquility, yet is only one & a half miles from Wells & a quarter of a mile from Wookey Hole. An ideal base for the tourist who wishes to appreciate the beauty of Somerset.	£25.00	Y	Y	Y
Doug & Carolyn White Box Tree House Westbury-sub-Mendip Wells BA5 1HA Tel: (0749) 870777 Open: ALL YEAR Map Ref No. 24	Nearest Road: A.371 A warm welcome is assured at this delightful, converted 17th century farmhouse located right in the heart of the village. Accommodation is in 3 comfortable en-suite bedrooms with radio & tea/coffee making facilities. A charming T.V. lounge is also available. Full country breakfast is served. The White's also have workshops for stained glass & picture framing with many items for sale in their gallery.	£15.00	Y	N	N

Somerset

			minimum £ per person	children taken	evening meals	animals taken
Lynne Harris The Old Stores Westbury-sub-Mendip Wells BA5 1HA Tel: (0749) 870567 Open: JAN - DEC Map Ref No. 24	Nearest Road: A.371 Charmingly decorated, with many antique features, this 300 year old character cottage offers comfortable twin, double and single rooms with tea and coffee making facilities. Situated near the centre of the village, at the foot of the Mendip Hills, Westbury is ideal for Cheddar Gorge, Wookey Hole and historic Wells. A warm welcome awaits the discerning visitor. Full English breakfasts are served. Ample parking.		£13.00	Y	N	Y
Mrs A.W. Thompson Stoneleigh House Westbury-sub-Mendip Wells BA5 1HF Tel: (0749) 870668 Open: JAN - DEC Map Ref No. 25	Nearest Road: A.371 Stoneleigh House is a delightful 18th century farmhouse on the edge of picturesque village which lies on the southern slopes of the Mendip Hills, between Cheddar with its spectacular Gorge, and Wells with its beautiful Cathedral. The house has a large garden with lovely views and its own Country Life Museum. Excellent accommodation in 2 en-suite rooms with colour T.V., tea and coffee facilities. Children over 10.		£15.00	Y	N	N
Mrs Pat Higgs Home Farm Stoppers Lane Upper Coxley Wells BA5 1QS Tel: (0749) 672434 Open: ALL YEAR (Excl. Xmas & New Year) Map Ref No. 26	Nearest Road: A.39 Home Farm is set in the peace & quiet of the Somerset countryside where guests can enjoy a relaxing holiday. Offering accommodation in a choice of 7 rooms, all with modern amenities & most with lovely views of the Mendip Hills. A colour T.V. lounge & garden are also available. Nearby are Wells, Bath, Cheddar Gorge & Wookey Hole Caves. Plenty of good pubs & restaurants nearby.		£13.50	Y	N	Y
Mr & Mrs C. J. Frost Southway Farm Polsham Wells BA5 1RW Tel: (0749) 73396 Open: MAR-NOV Map Ref No. 27	Nearest Road: A.39 Southway Farm is a Grade II listed Georgian farmhouse, situated half way between Glastonbury & Wells. Accommodation is in 3 comfortable & attractively furnished bedrooms. A delicious full English breakfast is served, although vegetarians are catered for. Guests may relax in the cosy lounge with colour T.V. or in the pretty, tranquil garden. An ideal location for a restful holiday or for touring the glorious West Country.		£14.00	Y	N	N
Ann & Philip Durbin Cutthorne Luckwell Bridge Wheddon Cross TA24 7EW Tel: (064383) 255 Open: FEB - NOV Map Ref No. 28	Nearest Road: B.3224, A.396. An 18th century Yeomans farmhouse totally secluded in the heart of Exmoor National Park. Spacious & comfortable accommodation with log fires & central heating. The 4 bedrooms have lovely views of the countryside. 3 luxury en-suite bathrooms. Four poster bed. Candlelit dinners & delicious home cooking. For extra privacy-beautifully appointed medieval stone cottages on side of farmhouse overlooking pond & cobbled yard. Stabling provided.		£17.50	Y	Y	Y

Somerset

		minimum £ per person	children taken	evening meals	animals taken
Richard & Daphne Criddle Curdon Mill Lower Vellow Williton TA4 4LS Tel: (0984) 56522 Open: ALL YEAR Map Ref No. 29	Nearest Road: A.358 Curdon Mill is a lovely working water mill situated on 200 acres of farmland at the foot of the beautiful Quantock Hills. Offering 6 pretty en-suite bedrooms with T.V. & tea/coffee making facilities. Lounge available for guests' use. Meals are delicious. Real country cuisine using local or home-produced meat & fish with fresh fruit, vegetables & herbs from the garden. A lovely base for touring the region. Heated outdoor pool in spacious relaxing garden, stabling for horses available. Children over 10 only.	£18.50 *see PHOTO over*	N	Y	Y
Mrs Alicia Teague Lower Church Farm Rectory Lane Charlton Musgrove Wincanton BA9 8ES Tel: (0963) 32307 Open: JAN - DEC Map Ref No. 30	Nearest Road: A.303 Lovely countryside surrounds this 18th century farmhouse & its 60 acres of dairy pasture. A pleasant, homely atmosphere prevails in the house with its beams & inglenooks. 3 bedrooms are available to guests with modern amenities & tea/coffee making facilities. There is a lounge with colour T.V. & guests have the use of cottage garden & patio. On the borders of Wiltshire, Dorset, central for touring.	£11.50	Y	N	Y
Mr & Mrs O. Bristow Penscot Farmhouse Hotel Shipham Winscombe BS25 1TW Tel: (0934) 842659 Fax 0934 842576 Open: JAN- NOV Map Ref No. 31	Nearest Road: A.38 This charming 15th century farmhouse set in a quiet village, at the foot of the Mendip Hills, retains much of its original character with oak beams & log fires. The accommodation is very pleasant & comfortable & the food is good. This is excellent walking & riding country. Lake fishing is also available. Close by are Wells, with its great cathedral, Glastonbury with its abbey & Tor, Georgian Bath & Bristol.	£19.50	Y	Y	Y

All the establishments mentioned in this guide are members of

The Worldwide Bed & Breakfast Association

Curdon Mill. Williton.

Suffolk

Suffolk
(East Anglia)

In July, the lower reaches of the River Orwell hold the essence of Suffolk. Broad fields of green and gold with wooded horizons sweep down to the quiet water. Orwell Bridge spans the wide river where yachts and tan-sailed barges share the water with ocean-going container ships out of Ipswich. Downstream the saltmarshes echo to the cry of the Curlew. The small towns and villages of Suffolk are typical of an area with long seafaring traditions. This is the county of men of vision; like Constable and Gainsborough, Admiral Lord Nelson and Benjamin Britten.

The land is green and fertile and highly productive. The hedgerows shelter some of our prettiest wild flowers, & the narrow country lanes are a pure delight. Most memorable is the ever-changing sky, appearing higher and wider here than elsewhere in England. There is a great deal of heathland, probably the best known being Newmarket where horses have been trained and raced for some hundreds of years. Gorse-covered heath meets sandy cliffs on Suffolks Heritage Coast. Here are bird reserves and the remains of the great mediaeval city of Dunwich, sliding into the sea.

West Suffolk was famous for its wool trade in the Middle Ages, & the merchants gave thanks for their good fortune by building magnificent "Wool Churches". Much-photographed Lavenham has the most perfect black & white timbered houses in Britain, built by the merchants of Tudor times. Ipswich was granted the first charter by King John in 1200, but had long been a trading community of seafarers. Its history can be read from the names of the streets - Buttermarket, Friars Street, Cornhill, Dial Lane & Tavern Street. The latter holds the Great White Horse Hotel mentioned by Charles Dickens in Pickwick Papers. Sadly not many ancient buildings remain, but the mediaeval street pattern and the churches make an interesting trail to follow. The Market town of Bury St. Edmunds is charming, with much of its architectural heritage still surviving, from the Norman Cornhill to a fine Queen Anne House. The great Abbey, now in ruins, was the meeting place of the Barons of England for the creation of the Magna Carta, enshrining the principals of individual freedom, parliamentary democracy and the supremacy of the law. Suffolk has some very fine churches, notably at Mildenhall, Lakenheath, Framlingham, Lavenham & Stoke-by-Nayland, & also a large number of wonderful houses & great halls, evidence of the county's prosperity.

Lavenham.

Suffolk

Suffolk Gazeteer

Areas of Outstanding Natural Beauty
Suffolk Coast. Heathlands.
Dedham Vale.

Historic Houses & Castles

Euston Hall - Thetford
18th century house with fine collection of pictures. Gardens & 17th century Parish Church nearby.

Christchurch Mansion - Ipswich
16th century mansion built on site of 12th century Augustinian Priory. Gables & dormers added in 17th century & other alteration & additions made in 17th & 18th centuries.

Gainsborough's House - Sudbury
Birthplace of Gainsborough, well furnished, collection of paintings.

The Guildhall - Hadleigh
15th century.

Glemham Hall - Nr Woodbridge
Elizabethan house of red brick - 18th century alterations. Fine stair, panelled rooms with Queen Anne furniture.

Haughley Park - Nr. Stowmarket
Jacobean manor house.

Heveningham Hall - Nr. Halesworth
Georgian mansion - English Palladian - Interior in Neo-Classical style. Garden by Capability Brown.

Ickworth - Nr. Bury St. Edmunds
Mixed architectural styles - late Regency & 18th century. French furniture, pictures & superb silver. Gardens with orangery.

Kentwell Hall - Long Melford
Elizabethan mansion in red brick, built in E plan, surrounded by moat.

Little Hall - Lavenham
15th century hall house, collection of furniture, pictures, china, etc.

Melford Hall - Nr. Sudbury
16th century - fine pictures, Chinese porcelain, furniture. Garden with gazebo.

Somerleyton Hall - Nr. Lowestoft
Dating from 16th century - additional work in 19th century. Carving by Grinling Gibbons. Tapestries, library, pictures.

Cathedrals & Churches

Bury St. Edmunds (St. Mary)
15th century. Hammer Beam roof in nave, wagon roof in chancel. Boret monument 1467.

Bramfield (St. Andrew)
Early circular tower. Fine screen & vaulting. Renaissance effigy.

Bacton (St. Mary)
15th century timbered roof. East Anglian stone & flintwork.

Dennington (St. Mary)
15th century alabaster monuments & bench ends. Aisle & Parclose screens with lofts & parapets.

Earl Stonhay (St. Mary)
14th century - rebuilt with fine hammer roof & 17th century pulpit with four hour-glasses.

Euston (St. Genevieve)
17th century. Fine panelling, reredos may be Grinling Gibbons.

Framlingham (St. Michael)
15th century nave & west tower, hammer beam roof in false vaulting. Chancel was rebuilt in 16th century for the tombs of the Howard family, monumental art treasures. Thamar organ. 1674.

Fressingfield (St. Peter & St. Paul)
15th century woodwork - very fine.

Lavenham (St. Peter & St. Paul)
15th century. Perpendicular. Fine towers. 14th century chancel screen. 17th century monument in alabaster.

Long Melford (Holy Trinity)
15th century Lady Chapel, splendid brasses. 15th century glass of note. Chantry chapel with fine roof. Like cathedral in proportions.

Stoke-by-Nayland (St. Mary)
16th-17th century library, great tower. Fine nave & arcades. Good brasses & monuments.

Ufford (St. Mary)
Mediaeval font cover - glorious.

Museums & Galleries

Christchurch Mansion - Ipswich
Country house, collection of furniture, pictures, bygones, ceramics of 18th century. Paintings by Gainsborough, Constable & modern artists.

Ipswich Museum - Ipswich
Natural History; prehistory, geology & archaeology to mediaeval period.

Suffolk

Moyse's Hall Musuem - Bury St. Edmunds
12th century dwelling house with local antiquities & natural history.

Abbot's Hall Museum of Rural Life - Stowmarket
Collections describing agriculture, crafts & domestic utensils.

Gershom-Parkington Collection - Bury St. Edmunds
Queen Anne House containing collection of watches & clocks.

Dunwich Musuem - Dunwich
Flora & fauna; local history.

Historic Monuments

The Abbey - Bury St. Edmunds
Only west end now standing.

Framlingham Castle
12th & 13th centuries - Tudor almshouses.

Bungay Castle - Bungay
12th century. Restored 13th century drawbridge & gatehouse.

Burgh Castle Roman Fort - Burgh
Coastal defences - 3rd century.

Herringfleet Priory - Herringfleet
13th century - remains of small Augustinian priory.

Leiston Abbey - Leiston
14th century - remains of cloisters, choir & trancepts.

Orford Castle - Orford
12th century - 18-sided keep - three towers.

The House in the Clouds. Thorpeness.

SUFFOLK
Map reference

02 Dakin
03 Parker
03 Watkins
04 Albrecht
05 Sheppard
06 Hackett-Jones
07 Sharman
08 Debenham
09 Bowden
10 Ridsdale
11 Morse
12 Bagnall

Suffolk

	minimum £ per person	children taken	evening meals	animals taken
Ann & Roy Dakin 'Dunston Guest House 8 Springfield Road Bury St. Edmunds IP3 3AN Tel: (0284) 767981 Open: ALL YEAR Map Ref No. 02 Nearest Road: A.45 A 19th century house, full of character, with a warm, friendly atmosphere. 17 rooms, many with en-suite facilities, all very comfortable, each with colour T.V., tea/coffee & ironing facilities. T.V. lounge, sun lounge & garden for guests' use. A ground floor room is available for handicapped guests. They also have a license. Situated in the centre of East Anglia, it is an ideal base for touring the region, with lovely towns & villages plus coastline.	£18.00	Y	Y	N
Meg Parker The Old Vicarage Higham Colchester CO7 6JY Tel: (020637) 248 Open: JAN - DEC Map Ref No. 03 Nearest Road: A.12 Very comfortable, charming listed Tudor house with beautiful garden overlooking the Rivers Brett and Stour. Deep in Constable country, excellent for visiting the lovely Suffolk villages or the coast. 3 guest bedrooms, en-suite available, all with T.V., tea/coffee facilities. Tennis court & outdoor pool; boating on the river. Children & dogs welcome. Price includes early morning and afternoon tea.	£18.00	Y	N	Y
Mrs P. Watkins The Bauble Higham Colchester CO7 6LA Tel: (0206) 37254 Open: JAN - DEC Map Ref No. 03 Nearest Road: A.12 The Bauble is a delightful house offering accommodation in 3 attractively furnished bedrooms with modern amenities including T.V. & tea/coffee making facilities. A full English breakfast is served. Lounge & garden available for guests' use. Higham lies in the heart of Constable country & is within easy reach of many wool villages with their churches, antiques shops & National Trust Properties. Children over 12 years welcome.	£20.00	Y	N	N
Carole Albrecht Limes Farm House Saxtead Green Framlington IP13 9QH Tel: (0728) 685303 Open: ALL YEAR Map Ref No. 04 Nearest Road: A.12 The Limes is a large listed Grade II farmhouse, dating from 1490, with large garden, 2 meadows, pond, chickens, ducks, dogs & cats. Every comfort is offered to guests & excellent food - vegetarians catered for. Cooked with home grown & local fresh produce. Situated on Saxtead Green, close to historical Framlingham - 25 mins. drive from coast; Aldeburgh Festival.	£16.00	Y	Y	Y
Mrs Jane Sheppard The Old Vicarage Great Thurlow Haverhill CB9 7LE Tel: (044083) 209 Open: JAN - DEC Map Ref No. 05 Nearest Road: A.604 The Old Vicarage is set in the quiet of the Suffolk countryside, with wonderful views. On the edge of Constable country, with Newmarket 10 miles, Cambridge and Saffron Walden 18 miles away. The 2 guest bedrooms have en-suite or private facilities. (No smoking in bedrooms) Evening meals with prior notice or reservations will gladly be made at good nearby Pubs. Children over 7 please. Pets by arrangement.	£18.00	Y	Y	Y

Suffolk

	minimum £ per person	children taken	evening meals	animals taken
Raewyn Hackett-Jones **Pipps Ford** **Norwich Road** **Needham Market** **Ipswich IP6 8LJ** Tel: (044979) 208 Open: ALL YEAR (Excl.Xmas & New Year) Map Ref No. 06	Nearest Road: A.45, A.140 A beautiful Tudor, beamed guest house in a pretty, old fashioned garden by the river Gipping. 6 very attractive bedrooms with private bathrooms & tea/coffee making facilities. A very extensive breakfast menu & delicious 4 course evening meals, served in the delightful conservatory. Licensed. Colour T.V., tennis court & swimming pool. Winner of The Best Bed & Breakfast award for East Anglia. A good central position for touring all of East Anglia.	£22.00 *see PHOTO over*	Y	Y	N
Mrs C. T. Sharman **The Old Rectory** **Monks Eleigh** **Ipswich IP7 7JL** Tel: (0449) 740811 Open: ALL YEAR Map Ref No. 07	Nearest Road: A.1141 Charming listed regency rectory set in 2 acres of mature gardens with croquet lawn & use of all-weather tennis court. 3 comfortable bedrooms with private facilities, each with tea/coffee makers. Visitors have their own drawing room with colour television & log fire. Conveniently located for Constable Country, Cambridge, Norwich & East Coast. Children over 10 years welcome.	£20.00	Y	N	N
Mrs P. A. Debenham **Mulberry Hall** **Burstall** **Ipswich** **IP8 3DP** Tel: (047387) 348 Open: ALL YEAR Map Ref No. 08	Nearest Road: A.12, A.45, A lovely 16th century timber-framed farmhouse, once owned by Cardinal Wolsey, standing in one & a half acres of garden. Accommodation is in a choice of 3 bedrooms with modern amenities, hair dryer & ironing facilities available. The house is comfortably & prettily furnished & guests may use the lounge with log-burning inglenook fireplace. Plenty of games & reading matter plus information on local events. Tennis, badminton & croquet available.	£15.00	Y	Y	N
Mrs J. Bowden **The Old Rectory** **Wetherden** **Stowmarket IP14 3LS** Tel: (0359) 40144 Open: MAR - NOV Map Ref No. 09	Nearest Road: A.45 Situated between Bury St. Edmunds & Stowmarket, this is an attractive square Georgian house set in 13 acres on hill overlooking the village. 3 bedrooms, 2 with own bathroom. Sitting room with log fire & coloured T.V. Large garden with croquet lawn. With over 2,000 books there is plenty to read. Ideally placed for touring East Anglia.	£17.00	N	N	N
Martin & Diana Ridsdale **Cherry Tree Farm** **Mendlesham Green** **Stowmarket** **IP14 5RQ** Tel: (0449) 766376 Open: FEB-DEC Map Ref No. 10	Nearest Road: A.140 Traditional timber-framed farmhouse, standing in three quarters of an acre of garden with orchard & duck ponds in a peaceful Suffolk village. 3 bedrooms, 1 with en-suite facilities. A spacious & comfortable lounge, inglenook fireplaces with log fire. Hearty English breakfast served in the oak-beamed dining room. Home-baked bread, own preserves & honey. Imaginative evening meals, with garden & local produce, good cheeses & fine English wines. Children over 10 yrs. welcome.	£16.50	Y	Y	N

Pipps Ford.   Needham Market.

Suffolk

	minimum £ per person	children taken	evening meals	animals taken
Catherine & David Morse **St. Mary Hall** **Belchamp Walter** **Sudbury** **CO10 7BB** **Tel: (0787) 237202** **Open: ALL YEAR** **Map Ref No. 11**	Nearest Road: A.604 Fine example of mediaeval Suffolk Manor House in lovely 4-acre garden, 2 miles from village of Belchamp Walter (guests advised to obtain directions in advance) On arrival you will be warmly welcomed. Two twin and one single room, not en-suite but with easy access to bathrooms. Book lined library with T.V. Pretty dining room. Large outdoor pool, tennis court, croquet. Catherine, a gourmet cook, will provide dinner with 24 hrs. notice. Children over 12.	£18.00	Y	Y	N
Sue Bagnall **Abbey House** **Monk Soham** **Woodbridge IP13 7EN** **Tel: (0728) 685225** **Open: JAN - NOV** **Map Ref No. 12**	Nearest Road: A.1120 Abbey House is a Victorian Rectory set in 10 acres of peaceful Suffolk countryside. The house is surrounded by secluded gardens, with mature trees & several large ponds. The remainder of the grounds are occupied by Jersey cows. A flock of sheep & an assorted collection of chickens & waterfowl. 3 attractive double bedrooms. Private bathrooms, tea making facilities, imaginative evening meals using home produced meat & vegetables. Outdoor swimming pool	£18.00	N	Y	N

All the establishments mentioned in this guide

are members of

The Worldwide Bed & Breakfast Association

If you have any comments regarding your accommodation

please send them to us

using the form at the back of the guide.

We value your comments

Surrey

Surrey
(South East)

One of the Home Counties, Surrey includes a large area of London, south of the Thames. Communications are good in all directions so it is easy to stay in Surrey & travel either into central London or out to enjoy the lovely countryside which, despite urban development, survives thanks to the 'Green Belt' policy. The county is also very accessible from Gatwick Airport.

The land geographically, is chalk sandwiched in clay, & probably the lack of handy building material was responsible for the area remaining largely uninhabited for centuries. The North Downs were a considerable barrier to cross, but gradually settlements grew along the rivers which were the main routes through. The Romans used the gap created by the River Mole to build Stane Street between London & Chichester, this encouraged the development of small towns. The gap cut by the passage of the River Wey allows the Pilgrims Way to cross the foot of the Downs. Dorking, Reigate & Farnham are small towns along this route, all with attracitve main streets & interesting shops & buildings.

Surrey has very little mention in the Domesday Book, &, although the patronage of the church & of wealthy families established manors which developed over the years, little happened to disturb the rural tranquility of the region. As a county it made little history but rather reflected passing times, although Magna Carta was signed at Egham in 1215.

The heathlands of Surrey were a Royal playground for centuries. The Norman Kings hunted here & horses became part of the landscape & life of the people, as they are today on Epsom Downs.

Nearness to London & Royal patronage began to influence the area, & the buildings of the Tudor period reflect this. Royal palaces were built at Hampton Court & Richmond, & great houses such as Loseley near Guildford often using stone from the monasteries emptied during the Reformation. Huge deer parks were enclosed & stocked. Richmond, described as the "finest village in the British Dominions", is now beset by 20th century traffic but still has a wonderful park with deer, lakes & woodland that was enclosed by Charles I. The terraces & gardens of such buildings as Trumpeters House & Asgill House on the slopes of Richmond overlooking the Thames, have an air of spaciousness & elegance & there are lovely & interesting riverside walks at Richmond.

Polesden Lacey.

Surrey

Surrey Gazetteer

Historic Houses & Castles

Albury Park - Albury, Nr. Guildford
A delightful country mansion designed by Pugin.
Clandon Park - Guildford
A fine house in the Palladian style by Leoni. A good collection of furniture & pictures. The house boasts some fine plasterwork.
Claremont - Esher
A superb Palladian house with interesting interior.
Detillens - Limpsfield
A fine 15th century house with inglenook fireplaces & mediaeval furniture. A large, pleasant garden.
Greathed Manor - Lingfield
An imposing Victorian manor house.
Hatchlands - East Clandon
A National Trust property of the 18th century with a fine Adam interior.
Loseley House - Guildford
A very fine Elizabethan mansion with superb panelling, furniture & paintings.
Polesden Lacy - Dorking
A Regency villa housing the Grevill collection of tapestries, pictures & furnishings. Extensive gardens.

Cathedrals & Churches

Compton (St. Nicholas)
The only surviving 2-storey sanctuary in the country. A fine 17th century pulpit.
Esher (St. George)
A fine altar-piece & marble monument.
Hascombe (St. Peter)
A rich interior with much gilding & painted reredos & roofs.
Lingfield (St. Peter & St. Paul)
15th century. Holding a chained bible.
Ockham (St. Mary & All Saints)
Early church with 13th century east window.
Stoke D'Abernon (St. Mary)
Dating back to Pre-conquest time with additions from the 12th-15th centuries. A fine 13th century painting. Early brasses.

Museums & Galleries

Charterhouse School Museum - Godalming
Peruvian pottery, Greek pottery, archaeology & natural history.
Chertsey Museum - Chertsey
18th-19th century costume & furnishing displayed & local history.
Guildford House - Guildford
The house is 17th century & of architectural interest housing monthly exhibitions.
Guildford Museum - Guildford
A fine needlework collection & plenty on local history.
Old Kiln Agricultural - Tilford
A very interesting collection of old farm implements.
Watermill Museum - Haxted
A restored 17th century mill with working water wheels & machinery.
Weybridge Museum - Weybridge
Good archaeological exhibition plus costume & local history.

The Gardens. Wisley

SURREY
Map reference

01 McCarthy
02 Prideaux
03 Hill
04 Franklin-Adams
05 Allen
06 Carmichael
07 Stocks
07 Shortland
08 Dove
09 Bussandri
10 Pritchard
11 Leeper

Surrey

		minimum £ per person	children taken	evening meals	animals taken
Tommy & Ann McCarthy **Pineleigh** 10 Castle Road (off Waverley Drive) Camberley GU15 2DS Tel: (0276) 64787 Open: ALL YEAR Map Ref No. 01	Nearest Road: M.3 A.325 Pineleigh is a spacious Edwardian house built in 1906, set in half an acre of mature garden in a very quiet area. Accommodation is in 3 comfortable guest rooms, all en-suite with telephone, T.V. & hospitality tray. Attractively furnished in Victorian style with many old prints & pictures. A full English breakfast is served, evening meals by arrangement. Conveninetly located for Heathrow Airport & London.	£25.00	N	Y	N
Mrs D V Prideaux **Mark Ash** Abinger Common Dorking RH5 6JA Tel: (0306) 731326 Open: MAR - NOV Map Ref No. 02	Nearest Road: A.25 A pleasant Victorian house standing in its own delightful garden, located in an area of 'outstanding natural beauty'. Accommodation is in a choice of 2 comfortable rooms, 1 with private facilities. Both have modern amenities, radio & tea/coffee making facilities. A residents' drawing room is also available. Full English or Continental breakfast. Packed lunches can be provided with prior notice. There is also a heated outdoor swimming pool & tennis court. 35 mins. to Gatwick & Heathrow. London under 1 hour's drive.	£20.00	Y	N	N
Mrs Gill Hill **Bulmer Farm** Holmbury St. Mary Dorking RH5 6LG Tel: (0306) 730210 Open: ALL YEAR Map Ref No. 03	Nearest Road: A.25, B.2126 Enjoy a warm welcome at this delightful 17th century farmhouse complete with many beams & an inglenook fireplace. Offering 3 charming rooms all with h &c & tea/coffee making facilities. Adjoining the house around a courtyard are 5 attractive barn conversion en-suite bedrooms for non smokers. Farm produce & homemade preserves are provided. Situated in a picturesque village it is convenient for London airports.	£14.00	N	N	Y
Mrs Carol Franklin-Adams **High Edser** Shere Road Ewhurst GU6 7PQ Tel: (0483) 278214 Open: ALL YEAR Map Ref No. 04	Nearest Road: A.25 A large, handsome Grade II listed home, the earliest part built in the 14th century, situated in an Area of Outstanding Natural Beauty. There are two rooms available; one double and one twin with private facilities. Residents lounge and T.V. Tennis court in grounds and golf nearby. 35 minutes to Gatwick and London Airports. Approximately an hour's drive to London.	£17.50	Y	N	N
Mrs Elizabeth Carmichael **Deerfell** Blackdown Park Fernden Lane Haslemere GU27 3LB Tel: (0428) 653409 Open: ALL YEAR Map Ref No. 06	Nearest Road: A.286 A warm welcome in a spacious & comfortable family home set in downland countryside, with breathtaking views to the hills & valleys of Sussex. Stone built at the turn of the century on a sunny gorse-clad slope, it was the coach house to Blackdown House. Offering 2 comfortable rooms with private facilities. Close by, Haslemere station (4 miles), London three quarters of an hour, Midhurst, Petworth, Goodwood & Chichester. Walking & riding. Children & pets welcome. Gatwick/Heathrow - 1 hour.	£17.00	Y	N	Y

Surrey

		minimum £ per person	children taken	evening meals	animals taken
Mr & Mrs Stocks **The Lawn Guest House** 30 Massetts Road Horley RH6 7DE Tel: (0293) 775751 Open: ALL YEAR Map Ref No. 07	Nearest Road: A.23, M.23 A well appointed Victorian house 4 minutes from Gatwick, 25 miles to London or Brighton. Very useful as a base for travelling, it is close to the rail station & town centre. There are 7 bedrooms 4 with en-suite facilities, very comfortable & well decorated, with colour T.V. A pleasant breakfast room & a garden for guests' use. There is a supplement payable for single use of rooms.	£21.00	Y	N	Y
Mrs Daphne Shortland **Chalet Guest House** 77 Massetts Road Horley RH6 7EB Tel: (0293) 821666 Open: ALL YEAR Map Ref No. 07	Nearest Road: A.23, M.23 A family run guest house offering accommodation with modern facilities in a bright and friendly atmosphere. 7 bedrooms, mostly en-suite, with T.V., tea/coffee trays. Single availability. Garden and ample parking. Local interests include the Six Bells Pub, circa 827. Lovely Sussex countryside adjacent. Gatwick airport 5 minutes. London or the South Coast 30 minutes by train.	£19.00	Y	N	N
Denise & Nigel Dove **Chase Lodge** 10 Park Road Hampton Wick Kingston KT1 4AS Tel: (081) 9431862 Open: ALL YEAR Map Ref No. 08	Nearest Road: M.25, M.4, M.3 Built in 1870 Chase Lodge boarded by Royal Bushey Park offers 5 attractively decorated, comfortably furnished bedrooms, 1 with a four poster; each has tea/coffee making facilities, refrigerator & T.V. Guests may also relax in the colourful patio garden. To the rear a gate leads directly into Hampton Court Palace. An excellent location near to Kew Gardens. Central London only half an hour away. Courtesy car to & from the airport for guests staying 3 nights or more.	£20.00 *see PHOTO over*	Y	Y	Y
Mr & Mrs G. Bussandri **Cranleigh Hotel** 41 West Street Reigate RH2 9BL Tel: (0737) 240600 or 223417 Fax 0737 223734 Open: ALL YEAR Map Ref No. 09	Nearest Road: A.25, M.25 The Cranleigh Hotel has a reputation for comfort, cleanliness & hospitality. Its modern facilities include hairdryers, T.V. & a pleasant bar & lounge etc. Comfortable accommodation in pleasant rooms. Three quarters of an hour from London & a few minutes from Gatwick airport, the hotel stands in lovely gardens which provide flowers & fresh food for the table. Very convenient for travellers to the South West. Ideal for first or last night of travel.	£32.00	Y	Y	N
Mrs Brenda Pritchard **Field House** Babylon Lane Lower Kingswood Tadworth KT20 6XE Tel: (0737) 221745 Open: ALL YEAR Map Ref No. 10	Nearest Road: M.25, A.217 Enjoy your stay in this elegant country home; farmland views from all windows. 2 minutes to A.217 & M.25. Gatwick 15 minutes. Accommodation in 3 attractive rooms each with T.V. & tea/coffee facilities. Double with bathroom, twin with basin & single. Large bathroom close by. A friendly & warm welcome awaits you. Close to Walton Heath & KIngswood golf clubs & allergy clinic.	£22.00	Y	N	N

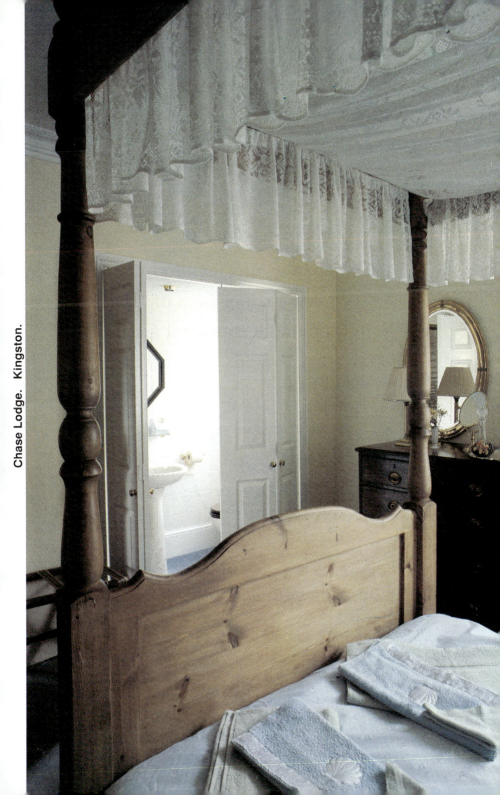
Chase Lodge. Kingston.

Surrey

		minimum £ per person	children taken	evening meals	animals taken
Kevin & Teresa Leeper Knaphill Manor Carthouse Lane Woking GU21 4XT Tel: (0276) 857962 Open: ALL YEAR Map Ref No. 11	Nearest Road: M.25, exit 11 A delightful, large family home dating back to the 1700's, set in 6 acres of grounds with tennis court & croquet lawn. Located in a farming area, the house is quiet & secluded yet Heathrow & Gatwick are only a 35 minute drive. Accommodation is very comfortable with en-suite or private facilities, plus T.V. & tea/coffee makers. A guests' colour T.V. lounge is also available. Early morning arrivals are welcome. London 25 mins. Ascot, Windsor & Oxford are easily reached.	£25.00 *see PHOTO over*	Y	Y	N

All the establishments mentioned in this guide are members of
The Worldwide Bed & Breakfast Association

When booking your accommodation please mention
The Best Bed & Breakfast

Knaphill Manor. Knaphill.

Sussex

Sussex
(South East)

The South Downs of Sussex stretch along the coast, reflecting the expanse of the North Downs of Kent, over the vast stretches of the Weald.

The South Downs extend from dramatic Beachy Head along the coast to Chichester & like the North Downs, they are crossed by an ancient trackway. There is much evidence of prehistoric settlement on the Downs. Mount Caburn, near Lewes, is crowned by an iron age fort, & Cissbury Ring is one of the most important archaeological sites in England. This large earthwork covers 80 acres & must have held a strategic defensive position. Hollingbury Fort carved into the hillside above Brighton, & the Trundle (meaning circle) date from 300-250 B.C., & were constructed on an existing neolithic settlement. The Long Man of Wilmington stands 226 feet high & is believed to be Nordic, possibly representing Woden, the God of War.

Only two towns are located on the Downs but both are of considerable interest. Lewes retains much of its mediaeval past & there is a folk museum in Ann of Cleves' house, which itself is partly 16th century. Arundel has a fascinating mixture of architectural styles, a castle & a superb park with a lake, magnificent beech trees & an unrivalled view of the Arun valley.

The landscape of the inland Weald ranges from bracken-covered heathlands where deer roam, to the deep woodland stretches of the Ashdown Forest, eventually giving way to soft undulating hills & valleys, patterned with hop-fields, meadows, oast houses, windmills & fruit orchards. Originally the whole Weald was dense with forest. Villages like Midhurst & Wadhurst hold the Saxon suffix "hurst" which means wood. As the forests were cleared for agriculture the names of the villages changed & we find Boscham & Stedham whoe suffix "ham" means homestead or farm.

Battle, above Hastings, is the site of the famous Norman victory & 16th century Bodiam Castle, built as defence against the French in later times, has a beautiful setting encircled by a lily-covered moat.

Sussex has an extensive coastline, with cliffs near Eastbourne at Beachy Head, & at Hastings. Further east, the great flat Romney Marshes stretch out to sea, & there is considerable variety in the coastal towns.

Chichester has a magnificent cathedral & a harbour reaching deep into the coastal plain that is rich in archaeological remains. The creeks & mudflats make it an excellent place for birdwatching.

Brighton is the most famous of the Sussex resorts with its Pier, the Promenade above the beaches, the oriental folly of George IV's Royal Pavilion & its Regency architecture. "The Lanes" are a maze of alleys & small squares full of fascinating shops, a thriving antique trade, & many good pubs & eating places. Hastings to the east preserves its "Old Town" where timbered houses nestle beneath the cliffs & the fishing boats are drawn up on the shingle whilst the nets are hung up to dry in curious tall, thin net stores. Winchelsea stands on a hill where it was rebuilt in the 13th century by Edward I when the original town was engulfed by the sea. It is a beautiful town with a fine Norman church, an excellent museum in the Town Hall, & many pretty houses. Across the Romney Marshes on the next hill stands Rye, its profile dominated by its church. It is a fascinating town with timbered houses & cobbled streets.

Sussex

Sussex Gazeteer

Areas of Outstanding Natural Beauty
The Sussex Downs. Chichester Harbour.

Historic Houses & Castles

Arundel Castle - Arundel
18th century rebuilding of ancient castle, fine portraits, 15th century furniture.
Cuckfield Park - Cuckfield
Elizabethan manor house, gatehouse. Very fine panelling & ceilings.
Danny - Hurstpierpoint
16th century - Elizabethan.
Goodwood House - Chichester
18th century - Jacobean house - Fine Sussex flintwork, paintings by Van Dyck, Canaletto & Stubbs, English & French furniture, tapestries & porcelain.
Newtimber Place - Newtimber
Moated house - Etruscan style wall paintings.
Purham - Pulborough
Elizabethan house containing important collection of Elizabethan, Jacobean & Georgian portraits, also fine furniture.
Petworth House - Petworth
17th century - landscaped by Capability Brown - important paintings - 14th century chapel.
St. Mary's - Bramber
15th century timber framed house - rare panelling.
Tanyard - Sharpthorne
Mediaeval tannery - 16th & 17th century additions.
The Thatched Cottage - Lindfield
Close-studded weald house - reputedly Henry VII hunting lodge.
Uppark - Petersfield
17th century - 18th century interior decorations remain unaltered.
Alfriston Clergy House - Nr. Seaford
14th century parish priest's house - pre-reformation.
Battle Abbey - Battle
Founded by William the Conqueror.
Charleston Manor - Westdean
Norman, Tudor & Georgian architectural styles - Romanesque window in the Norman wing.
Bull House - Lewes
15th century half-timbered house - was home of Tom Paine.
Bateman's - Burwash
17th century - watermill - home of Rudyard Kipling.
Bodiam Castle - Nr. Hawkshurst
14th century - noted example of mediaeval moated military architecture.
Great Dixter - Northiam
15th century half-timbered manor house - great hall - Lutyens gardens
Glynde Place - Nr. Lewes
16th century flint & brick - built around courtyard-collection of paintings by Rubens, Hoppner, Kneller, Lely, Zoffany.
Michelham Priory - Upper Dicker, Nr. Hailsham
13th century Augustinian Priory - became Tudor farmhouse - working watermill, ancient stained glass, etc., enclosed by moat.
Royal Pavilion - Brighton
Built for Prince Regent by Nash upon classical villa by Holland. Exotic Building - has superb original works of art lent by H.M. The Queen. Collections of Regency furniture also Art Nouveau & Art Deco in the Art Gallery & Museum.
Sheffield Park - Nr. Uckfield
Beautiful Tudor House - 18th century alterations - splendid staircase.

Cathedrals & Churches

Alfriston (St. Andrew)
14th century - transition from decorated style to perpendicular, Easter sepulchre.
Boxgrove (St. Mary & St. Blaise)
13th century choir with 16th century painted decoration on vaulting. Relic of Benedictine priory. 16th century chantry. Much decoration.
Chichester Cathedral
Norman & earliest Gothic. Large Romanesque relief sculptures in south choir aisle.
Etchingham (St. Mary & St. Nicholas)
14th century. Old glass, brasses, screen, carved stalls.
Hardham (St. Botolph)
11th century - 12th century wall paintings.
Rotherfield (St. Denys)
16th century font cover, 17th century canopied pulpit, glass by Burne-Jones, wall paintings, Georgian Royal Arms.

Sussex

Sompting (St. Mary)
11th century Saxon tower - Rhenish Helm Spire - quite unique.
Worth (St. Nicholas)
10th century - chancel arch is the largest Saxon arch in England. German carved pulpit c.1500 together with altar rails.
Winchelsea (St. Thomas the Apostle)
14th century - choir & aisles only. Canopied sedilia & piscina.

Museums & Galleries
Barbican House Museum - Lewes
Collection relating to pre-historic, Romano-British & ,mediaeval antiquities of the area. Prints & water colours of the area.
Battle Museum-Battle
Remains from archeological sites in area. Diorama of Battle of Hastings.
Bignor Roman Villa Collection - Bignor
4th century mosaics, Samian pottery, hypocaust, etc.
Brighton Museum & Art Gallery - Brighton
Old Master Paintings, watercolours, ceramics, furniture. Surrealist paintings, Art Nouveau & Art Deco applied art, musical instruments & many other exhibits.

Marlipins Museum - Shoreham
12th century building housing collections of ship models, photographs, old maps, geological specimens, etc.
Royal National Lifeboat Institution Museum - Eastbourne
Lifeboats of all types used from earliest times to present.
Tower 73 - Eastbourne
Martello tower restored to display the history of these forts. Exhibition of equipment, uniforms & weapons of the times.
The Toy Museum - Rottingdean, Brighton
Toys & playthings from many countries - children's delight.

Other things to see & do
Bewl Water - Nr. Wadhurst
Boat trips, walks, adventure playground
Chichester Festival Theatre - Chichester
Summer season of plays from May to September.
Goodwood Racecourse

The Royal Pavilion. Brighton.

SUSSEX

Map reference

- 01 Fuente
- 02 Cowpland
- 02 Hawke
- 03 Mitchell
- 04 Hashfield
- 05 Gregory
- 06 Swaine
- 07 Blencowe
- 08 Dridge
- 09 Foden
- 10 Waller
- 11 Setchfield
- 12 Hambleton
- 13 Lloyd
- 13 Tyrie
- 14 Holden
- 14 Pengilley
- 15 Cooper
- 16 Pontifex
- 17 Fowler
- 18 Wilkin
- 18 Forbes
- 19 Cox
- 19 Ticktum
- 21 Gough
- 22 Mulcare
- 23 Field
- 24 Steele
- 25 Brinkhurst
- 25 Hadfield
- 26 Percy
- 27 Taylor
- 28 Williams

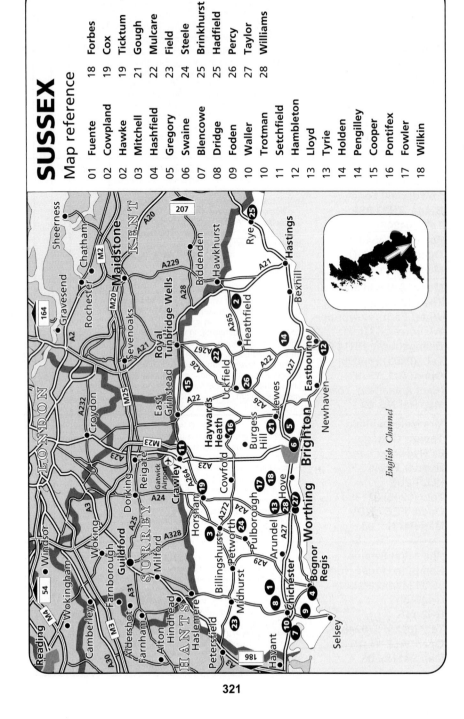

Sussex

	Nearest Road	minimum £ per person	children taken	evening meals	animals taken
Peter & Sarah Fuente **Mill Lane House** Slindon Arundel BN18 0RP Tel: (0243) 65440 Open: JAN - DEC Map Ref No. 01	Nearest Road: A.27, A.29 Magnificent views to the coast. Situated in a beautiful downland village with many miles of footpaths. Superb bird watching locally. All 7 rooms are en-suite & have T.V.s. Within easy reach are Pagham & Chichester Harbour Arundel Castle, Fishbourne Roman Palace, Goodwood, Chichester, cathedral & Festival Theatre. Beaches 6 miles. Excellent pubs within easy walking distance.	£15.00	Y	Y	Y
Mrs J. Cowpland **Powdermills** Powdermill Lane Battle TN33 0SP Tel: (04246) 5511 Fax 04246 4540 Open: ALL YEAR Map Ref No. 02	Nearest Road: A.21 This large, impressive Georgian house is set in 150 acres of woodlands with pleasant walks with three fishing lakes. It was originally part of the Battle Abbey Estate. The house is furnished with antiques. All the bedrooms are stylish & comfortable. A new restaurant, The Orangery, is the latest addition to the hotel. Large Georgian style windows overlook the pool & terrace.	£30.00	Y	Y	Y
Moira & David Mitchell **The Old Wharf** Wharf Farm, Newbridge Wisborough Green Billingshurst RH14 0JG Tel: (0403) 784096 Open: ALL YEAR (Excl.Xmas/New Year) Map Ref No. 03	Nearest Road: A.272 This unique former wharf-side barn has been beautifully restored & converted into a comfortable home with a warm welcome for guests. Located on the canalside in open farmland, it offers high standards in 4 tastefully furnished en-suite bedrooms, each with T.V. & tea/coffee makers & lovely country views. Breakfast choices are a special muesli or traditional farmhouse breakfast. In summer eat outside in the walled courtyard.	£25.00	N	N	N
Mrs Mai Hashfield **Taplow Cottage** 81 Nyewood Lane Bognor Regis PO21 2UE Tel: (0243) 821398 Open: FEB - NOV Map Ref No. 04	Nearest Road: B.2166 A warm welcome is offered in this charming cottage style house, which has 3 most pleasant, cosy bedrooms all with modern amenities including tea/coffee makers & colour T.V. in each room. A comfortable T.V. lounge is also available. It is conveniently situated for visiting the South Downs, the coast, Arundel Castle, Goodwood Racecourse & Portsmouth. Within a few minutes walking distance of the beach, shops & restaurants.	£12.50	Y	N	Y
Phil & Val Swaine **Kempton House Hotel** 33/34 Marine Parade Brighton BN2 1TR Tel: (0273) 570248 Open: ALL YEAR Map Ref No. 06	Nearest Road: A.259 Kempton House is a friendly family run seafront hotel. Offering comfortable accommodation with delightful seaviews, overlooking the beach & palace pier. All rooms are en-suite with colour T.V., radio, hairdryer, private telephone & tea/coffee tray. 4-poster available. Full English breakfast served or breakfast in bed the Continental way. Residents' bar & sea facing patio garden available.	£22.00	Y	Y	Y

Sussex

		minimum £ per person	children taken	evening meals	animals taken
Mrs C. B. Gregory **Braemar Guest House** **Steyning Road** **Rottingdean** **Brighton BN2 7GA** Tel: (0273) 304263 Open: ALL YEAR Map Ref No. 05	Nearest Road: A.259 A charming house, family-run, offering 14 pleasant, comfortable rooms with modern facilities. The proprietors really go out of their way to make their guests' stay a memorable one. From here Rudyard Kipling's house is only 2 minutes' walk. The town is a famous smuggling place with many ancient buildings & a Saxon church. There is a multitude of places to discover in the area.	£14.00	Y	N	Y
Mrs Mary Waller **Hatpins** **Bosham Lane** **Old Bosham** **Chichester PO18 8HG** Tel: (0243) 572644 Open: ALL YEAR Map Ref No. 10	Nearest Road: A.259 Situated in the quiet picturesque harbour village of Old Bosham. 3 miles west of Chichester, this elegant property offers luxurious rooms furnished with antiques, including a half-tester bed & sauna & Victorian brass beds. All rooms are en-suite or have private facilities & T.V. with easy access to a charming courtyard & garden. Ideal for honeymoon couples. A lovely base for a relaxing holiday.	£22.50	N	N	N
Susan & Antony Trotman **White Barn** **Crede Lane** **Bosham** **Chichester** **PO18 8NX** Tel: (0243) 573113 Open: ALL YEAR Map Ref No. 10	Nearest Road: A.259 An outstanding modern, open plan house with heavily timbered interior. Located in the attractive Saxon harbour village of Bosham. Accommodation is in 3 delightful en-suite bedrooms with tea/coffee making facilities & radio. A charming sitting room with colour T.V. & log fire on chilly evenings. Breakfast is served overlooking the pleasant, colourful garden. Meals are memorable using only the freshest ingredients whenever possible. Every care is taken to ensure your comfort.	£23.00	N	Y	N
Mr & Mrs P. J. Blencowe **The Old Rectory** **Cot Lane** **Chidham** **Chichester PO18 8TA** Tel: (0243) 572088 Open: ALL YEAR Map Ref No. 07	Nearest Road: A.259 The Old Rectory is a large, comfortable period house, set in a country lane in the quiet village of Chidham. 3 charming bedrooms all with private facilities, colour T.V., tea making facilities & electric underblankets. There is a delightful lounge with colour T.V. & grand piano & a large garden with swimming pool. Opposite the Saxon church & close to the village pub serving excellent meals. Chichester Harbour is nearby.	£18.00	Y	N	N
Mrs Jeannette Dridge **Chichester Lodge** **Oakwood** **Chichester PO18 9AL** Tel: (0243) 786560 Open: JAN - DEC Map Ref No. 08	Nearest Road: B.1278 A picturesque, Grade II listed 1840's Gothic Lodge set in very quiet country surroundings, yet only 4 minutes drive from the city centre and the Festival Theatre. Two tastefully furnished bedrooms with Four-poster beds, and en-suite bathrooms. Adjoining garden room has tea making facilities and a cosy log burning fire. You are assured of a warm and friendly welcome.	£17.50	N	N	N

Sussex

		minimum £ per person	children taken	evening meals	animals taken
Ron & Pam Foden 'Crouchers Bottom' Birdham Road, Apuldram Chichester PO20 7EH Tel: (0243) 784995 Fax 0243 539797 Open: ALL YEAR Map Ref No. 09	Nearest Road: A.286, A.27 'Crouchers Botttom' is a converted 1920's farmhouse standing in its own grounds. Offering 6 en-suite rooms, colour T.V., clock radio, tea making facilities, hair dryer, etc. A brick-laid patio overlooks a 'sunken' lawn & small pond with waterfowl. Lovely countryside & views of Chichester Cathedral, & Halmaker Mill with the South Downs. The proprietors are keen sailors, providing guests with a unique opportunity to sample a day's sailing. Delicious evening meals available.	£28.50	Y	Y	N
Mrs M. Setchfield Chimneys Ifield Wood Crawley RH11 0LE Tel: (0293) 521312 Open: ALL YEAR Map Ref No. 11	Nearest Road: A.23 A charming Georgian country cottage dating back over 200 years, situated in a peaceful rural area. 2 pleasant & comfortable rooms with modern amenities. Rooms have radio. Tea/coffee facilities are downstairs. A most comfortable & attractive lounge with colour T.V. Guests may use the garden. Very conveniently situated for Gatwick Airport - only 10 mins. away. Brighton, Redhill, Reigate are all easily accessible from here. Free transport to & from Gatwick.	£17.00	Y	N	N
K. & M. Hambleton Southcroft Private Hotel 15 South Cliff Avenue Meads Eastbourne BN20 7AH Tel: (0323) 29071 Open: JAN - NOV Map Ref No. 12	Nearest Road: A.22, A pleasant hotel offering 7 comfortable rooms all with en-suite facilities. Situated in a quiet residential area within easy reach of the beach, shopping centre & theatres. The area offers lovely walks through Friston Forest & the Cuckmere Valley. Plenty for everyone around here. Tea/coffee making facilities in all rooms. Licenced. Friendly atmosphere.	£19.00	N	Y	N
Norma Hawke Little Grandturzel Fontridge Lane Etchingham TN19 7DE Tel: (0435) 882279 Fax 0435 883618 Open: FEB - NOV Map Ref No. 02	Nearest Road: A.265 Little Grandturzel is situated in a beautiful spot right in the heart of 'Kipling Country'. Attractive rooms with modern amenities & tea/coffee making facilities. There are many walks & historic places of interest to visit. An excellent touring base for the many charming villages & towns in Kent & Sussex. Within easy reach of Channel ports & convenient for day trips to London.	£14.00	Y	Y	N
Denis & Jean Lloyd Racehorse Cottage Nepcote Findon BN14 0SN Tel: (0903) 873783 Open: ALL YEAR (Excl. Xmas) Map Ref No. 13	Nearest Road: A.24, A.27 Comfortable cottage in historic & peaceful downland village sheltering under Cissbury Ring. An excellent base for exploring. 4 miles from the South Coast & easily accessible by car, train or bus from Gatwick, Brighton, Arundel, Chichester & London. 2 twin-bedded rooms with downland views, tea/coffee making facilities & a guests' own bathroom. Visitors have full use of house, sun room, garden & T.V. Evening meals with home baking & garden produce by arrangement. Children over 8 years welcome.	£12.00	Y	Y	Y

Sussex

			minimum £ per person	children taken	evening meals	animals taken
Mrs Susan Tyrie Findon Manor Findon Village Findon BN14 0TA Tel: (0903) 872733 Open: ALL YEAR (Excl. Xmas) Map Ref No. 13		Nearest Road: A.24 Set in the picturesque village of Findon, in a delightful garden with splendid trees & colourful shrubs. Findon Manor offers accommodation in 10 en-suite bedrooms with telephone, colour T.V. & tea/coffee making facilities, some with 4-poster bed. Though completely refurbished, the original features remain, amongst elegant & attractive furnishings. Excellent meals are served in the spacious dining room & afterwards guests may relax in the charming lounge or bar.	£42.50	Y	Y	Y
Mrs M. Holden & Family Cleavers Lyng Church Road Herstmonceux Hailsham BN27 1QJ Tel: (0323) 833131 Open: ALL YEAR Map Ref No. 14		Nearest Road: A.271 A delightful 16th century country hotel offering 8 pleasant, comfortable rooms for visitors. Here one finds age-blackened beams, inglenook fire-places & a warm welcome. Situated adjacent to Herstmonceux Castle, it is an ideal base for touring the country as there are many historic sites & houses, museums & galleries plus superb villages within a short drive.	£17.25	Y	Y	Y
Mrs L. Pengilley Blackstock Farm Grove Hill Hellingly Hailsham BN27 4HF Tel: (0323) 844453 Open: APRIL - SEPT Map Ref No. 14		Nearest Road: A.22, A.267 This friendly family warmly welcome guests to their 240 acre working farm. The large rambling Victorian farmhouse is located in lovely country-side yet only 3 miles from Hailsham. Guests have a choice of 2 rooms with T.V. & tea/coffee making facilities. There are a number of excellent local pubs where delicious evening meals can be obtained.	£13.00	N	N	N
Christine & David Cooper Bolebroke Watermill Perry Hill Edenbridge Road Hartfield TN7 4JP Tel: (0892)770425 Open: Mar -Nov Map Ref No. 15		Nearest Road: A.264 Magical Watermill, first recorded in 1086A.D. & Elizabethan Miller's Barn offer 5 en-suite rooms of genuine, unspoilt rustic charm, set amid woodland, water & pasture. The mill is complete with machinery, trap doors & very steep stairs. The barn has low doors & ceilings & includes the enchanting honeymooners hayloft with a four poster bed. Delicious country cooking including Sussex suppers are served in the adjoining house.	£22.50 see PHOTO over	Y	Y	N
Roy & Carol Pontifex Old Cudwells Barn Lewes Road Scaynes Hill Haywards Heath RH17 7NA Tel: (0444) 831406 Open: JAN - DEC Map Ref No. 16		Nearest Road: A.272 Old Cudwells Barn is part of a larger house in an attractive courtyard setting. Roy has renovated this unique barn using original materials in keeping with the period featuring the original character including inglenook fireplaces & beams. Guests can choose from 2 very pretty, comfortable rooms with private facilities. Roy & Carol welcome you as friends. Good food, bonhomie & a warm happy atmosphere awaits you. Convenient for Gatwick Airport & touring.	£19.00	Y	Y	N

Bolebroke Watermill. Hartfield.

Sussex

		minimum £ per person	children taken	evening meals	animals taken
Mrs M. Wilkin Great Wapses Farm Wineham Albourne Henfield BN5 9BJ Tel: (0273) 492544 Open: ALL YEAR Map Ref No. 18	Nearest Road: A.23, B.2115 An attractive Tudor/Georgian farmhouse set in rural & peaceful surroundings with horses, calves, chickens, etc. Offering 3 rooms, all en-suite, 1 with 4-poster bed. T.V. & tea/coffee making facilities. Locally there are plenty of nice pubs & restaurants serving good food. Within easy reach of Brighton, Gatwick, Goodwood & Hickstead. Tennis court available.	£17.00	Y	N	Y
Mrs Sylvia Fowler Frylands Wineham Henfield BN5 9BP Tel: (0403) 710214 Fax 0403 711449 Open ALL YEAR (Excl.Xmas) Map Ref No. 17	Nearest Road: A.272, A.23, Frylands is a timber framed Tudor farmhouse in a quiet setting of farmland, woods & river. 3 lovely bedrooms,1 with private facilities, all with colour T.V., radio & tea/coffee tray with home made biscuits. Traditional breakfast cooked to order with a selection of home made preserves & local honey. Large garden with heated swimming pool. Good pubs & food nearby. 20 mins. Gatwick & Brighton.	£15.00	Y	N	N
Mrs Josie Forbes Little Oreham Farm Woodsmill Henfield BN5 9SB Tel: (0273) 492931 Open: ALL YEAR Map Ref No. 18	Nearest Road: A.23, A.2037 A delightful 300 year-old Sussex farmhouse situated in quiet rural surroundings & set in lovely gardens with roses & dovecote. This charming home retains its original features including oak beams & inglenook fireplaces. 2 comfortable, pleasant bedrooms are available both en-suite & well-equipped with T.V. & tea/coffee makers. Mrs Forbes is an excellent cook & will prepare delicious meals or snacks by arrangement.	£16.00	N	Y	N
Mrs Elizabeth Cox Glebe End Church Street Warnham Horsham RH12 3QW Tel: (0403) 61711 Open: ALL YEAR Map Ref No. 19	Nearest Road: A.24 Glebe End is a fascinating tile, wood & stone, part mediaeval house standing in its own beautifully tended walled garden. Located in a pretty Sussex village in the rolling countryside. The accommodation is in 4 pleasant bedrooms with their own bathrooms, radio, T.V. & tea/coffee making facilities. A colour T.V. lounge with open fireplace & delightful Tudor dining room with log-burning stove. Mrs Cox is an excellent cook & meals are delicious. Tennis & golf nearby. Health centre/gymnasium/sauna next door. 20 mins. from Gatwick.	£18.00	Y	Y	N
K. M. Ticktum Westlands Guest House Brighton Road Monks Gate Horsham RH13 6JD Tel: (0403) 891383 Open: ALL YEAR Map Ref No. 19	Nearest Road: A.281 An attractive large Victorian house in country surroundings with easy access to Gatwick, Brighton & the coast. Offering accommodation in 4 bedrooms, 1 en-suite & 3 large bedrooms with washbasins & colour T.V. Tea/coffee served on request. A comfortable residents' lounge with T.V. is also available. An acre of garden to stroll & relax in. Village pubs & restaurants nearby. A very friendly welcome awaits you.	£17.50	Y	N	N

Sussex

		minimum £ per person	children taken	evening meals	animals taken
Roland & Brenda Gough **Ousedale House** **Offham** **Lewes BN7 3QF** Tel: (0273) 478680 Open: ALL YEAR (Excl. Xmas) Map Ref No. 21	Nearest Road: A.275 Ousedale House is a spacious Victorian country house set on a hillside plateau in three & a half acres of garden & woodland overlooking the River Ouse Valley. There are 3 attractive bedrooms, 2 with private bathroom, radio, T.V. & tea/coffee making facilities. Guest lounge. Delicious country cooking. Centrally located for touring Sussex, with easy access to Gatwick, Newhaven, Brighton & Glyndebourne (hampers provided). Ample parking.	£18.00	Y	Y	N
Gillian & John Mulcare **Huggetts Furnace Farm** **Stonehurst Lane** **Five Ashes** **Mayfield TN20 6LL** Tel: (0825) 830220 / (082585) 220 Open: FEB-DEC Map Ref No. 22	Nearest Road: A.272 A beautiful mediaeval farmhouse, set well off the beaten track amidst unspoilt countryside. Accommodation is in 3 comfortable bedrooms, 2 en-suite, with radio & tea/coffee making facilities. The sitting/dining room for guests has an inglenook fireplace with log fires on chilly evenings & colour T.V. Excellent dinners & breakfasts served using fresh home & local produce. Heated swimming pool. Only half an hour from coast & close to many attractions.	£20.00	Y	Y	N
Mr & Mrs J. R. Field **Mill Farm** **Trotton** **Midhurst GU31 5EL** Tel: (0730) 813080 Open: ALL YEAR Map Ref No. 23	Nearest Road: A.272 A Sussex country house set in 15 acres of pasture & large garden with grass tennis court. Delightful accommodation in 4 pleasant rooms with superb views over the South Downs. Colour T.V.s & teamaking facilities. Log fires in hall & drawing room. Lovely walks & excellent pubs. Chichester, Goodwood & Petworth Houses, Arundel Castle, Heathrow, Gatwick & the coast within easy reach. Ideal as a holiday base.	£12.50	Y	N	Y
Alma Steele **New House Farm** **Broadford Bridge Road** **West Chiltington** **Pulborough RH20 2LA** Tel: (0798) 812215 Open: JAN - NOV Map Ref No. 24	Nearest Road: A.29 A lovely 15th century house with oak beams & inglenook fireplaces. Situated in the village with a 12th century church. 3 delightful rooms, 2 with en-suite facilities. T.V. & tea/coffee makers. A pleasant lounge with T.V. & a lovely garden. Gatwick Airport is easily reached. Parham Gardens, W. Sussex golf course, Amberley Wild Brooks, Arundel Castle, Petworth House. Polo at Cowdray Park. Children over 10 years accepted. Good evening meals available at local inns nearby. Golf nearby.	£18.00	Y	N	N
Sara Brinkhurst **Little Orchard House** **West Street** **Rye** **TN31 7ES** Tel: (0797) 223831 Open: ALL YEAR Map Ref No. 25	Nearest Road: A.259 This charming Georgian townhouse with traditional walled garden, is a delightful surprise at the heart of ancient Rye. Whilst a perfect base for visiting the beautiful castles, gardens and country houses of the region, the house itself has many original features, open fires, antique furnishings and books, to ensure a peaceful, relaxed atmosphere. 3 lovely en-suite bedrooms. Generous country breakfasts feature organic and freerange local produce.	£28.00	N	N	N

Sussex

			minimum £ per person	children taken	evening meals	animals taken
Francis & Jenny Hadfield **Jeake's House** **Mermaid Street** **Rye** **TN31 7ET** Tel: (0797) 222828 Fax 0797 222623 Open: ALL YEAR Map Ref No. 25	Nearest Road: A.259, A.268 Jeakes House is an outstanding 17th century listed building. Retaining original features including oak beams, wood panelling & decorated throughout with antiques. 12 comfortable & well decorated bedrooms overlook the peaceful gardens, with either en-suite or private facilities, T.V. & tea/coffee making facilities. 4-poster available. Guests dine in the galleried former Baptist chapel, where a choice of full English, wholefood vegetarian or Continental breakfast is served. Located in one of Britain's most picturesque mediaeval streets, this makes a delightful & relaxing base for touring.		£19.00 *see PHOTO over*	Y	N	Y
Tessa & Clive Williams **Old Erringham Hall** **Steyning Road** **Shoreham-by-Sea** **BN43 5FD** Tel: (0273) 452755 / 464649 Open: JAN - DEC Map Ref No. 28	Nearest Road: A.27, A.23 Country house hospitality in listed building of great historical interest. First recorded in the Domesday Book of 1086. Peaceful Downland setting with magnificent views ; 5 minutes from beach. Three attractive bedrooms with wash-basins, central heating, T.V., tea/coffee facilities. Four-Poster in oak-panelled room. Visitor access to lounge and gardens. Evening meals by arrangement. Gatwick 30 minutes, Brighton 20 minutes.		£30.00	N	Y	N
Juliet & Alister Percy **Hooke Hall** **250 High Street** **Uckfield TN22 1EN** Tel: (0825) 761578 Fax 0825 768025 Open: ALL YEAR Map Ref No. 26	Nearest Road: A.22, A.26. Hooke Hall is a classic Queen Anne Town House, recently modernised but retaining the old charm of this typically elegant building. All rooms have a wide range of facilities & are decorated individually by Juliet Percy who has her own interior design business. The restaurant is open for dinner on Fridays & Saturdays & other meals, except breakfast, are by arrangement.		£30.00	Y	Y	N
Dorene & John Taylor **Aspen House** **13 Winchester Road** **Worthing** **BN11 4DJ** Tel: (0903) 230584 Open: JAN - DEC Map Ref No. 27	Nearest Road: A.27 Situated in a quiet location, this elegant Edwardian house is ideally sited to discover West Sussex. Goodwood, Arundel, Chichester & Brighton are all a short drive away & Gatwick 40 mins. 2 doubles, 1 twin & 1 single bedroom, all beautifully furnished, have colour T.V., en-suite & tea/coffee making facilities. Traditional full English or Continental breakfast is served in the attractive period dining room.		£18.00	N	N	N

When booking your accommodation please

mention

The Best Bed & Breakfast

Jeake's House. Rye.

Warwickshire

Warwickshire (Heart of England)

Warwickshire contains much that is thought of as traditional rural England, but it is a county of contradictions. Rural tranquillity surrounds industrial towns, working canals run along with meandering rivers, the mediaeval splendour of Warwick Castle vies with the handsome Regency grace of Leamington Spa.

Of course, Warwickshire is Shakespeare's county, with his birthplace, Stratford-upon-Avon standing at the northern edge of the Cotswolds. You can visit any of half a dozen houses with Shakespearian associations, see his tomb in the lovely Parish church or enjoy a performance by the world famous Royal Shakespeare Company in their theatre on the banks of the River Avon.

Warwickshire was created as the Kingdom of Mercia after the departure of the Romans. King Offa of Mercia left us his own particular mark - a coin which bore the imprint of his likeness known as his "pen" & this became our penny. Lady Godiva was the wife of an Earl of Mercia who pleaded with her husband to lessen the taxation burden on his people. He challenged her to ride naked through the streets of Coventry as the price of her request. She did this knowing that her long hair would cover her nakedness, & the people, who loved her, stayed indoors out of respect. Only Peeping Tom found the temptation irresistible.

The 15th, 16th, & 17th centuries were the heyday of fine building in the county, when many gracious homes were built. Exceptional Compton Wynyates has rosy pink bricks, twisted chimney stacks, battlements & moats & presents an unforgettably romantic picture of a perfect Tudor House.

Coventry has long enjoyed the reputation of a thriving city, noted for its weaving of silks and ribbons, learned from the refugee Huguenots. When progress brought industry, watches, bicycles & cars became the mainstay of the city. Coventry suffered grievously from aerial bombardment in the war & innumerable ancient & treasured buildings were lost.

A magnificent new Cathedral stands besides the shell of the old. Mystery plays enacting the life of Christ are performed in the haunting ruin.

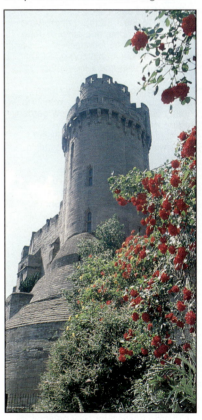

Warwick Castle.

Warwickshire

Warwickshire Gazeteer

Areas of Outstanding Natural Beauty
The Edge Hills

Historic Houses & Castles

Arbury Hall - Nuneaton
18th century Gothic mansion - made famous by George Elliot as Cheverel Manor - paintings, period furnishings, etc.
Compton Wynyates
15th century - famous Tudor house - pink brick, twisted chimneys, battlemented walls. Interior almost untouched - period furnishing.
Coughton Court - Alcester
15th century - Elizabethan half-timbered wings. Holds Jacobite relics.
Harvard House - Stratford-upon-Avon
16th century - home of mother of John Harvard, University founder.
Homington Hall - Shipston-on-Stour
17th century with fine 18th century plasterwork.
Packwood House - Hockley Heath
Tudor timber framed house - with 17th century additions. Famous yew garden.
Ragley Hall - Alcester
17th century Palladian - magnificent house with fine collection of porcelain, paintings, furniture, etc. & a valuable library.
Shakespeare's Birthplace Trust Properties - Stratford-upon-Avon
Anne Hathaway's Cottage - Shottery
The thatched cottage home of Anne Hathaway.
Hall's Croft - Old Town
Tudor house where Shakespeare's daughter Susanna lived.
Mary Arden's House - Wilmcote
Tudor farmhouse with dovecote. Home of Shakespeare's mother.
New Place - Chapel Street
Shakespeare's last home - the foundations of his house are preserved in Elizabethan garden.
Birthplace of Shakespeare - Henley Street
Many rare Shakespeare relics exhibited in this half-timbered house.
Lord Leycester Hospital - Warwick
16th century timber framed group around courtyard - hospital for poor persons in the mediaeval guilds.

Upton House - Edge Hill
Dating from James II reign - contains Brussels tapestries, Sevres porcelain, Chelsea figurines, 18th century furniture & other works of art, including Old Masters.
Warwick Castle - Warwick
Splendid mediaeval castle - site was originally fortified more than a thousand years ago. Present castle 14th century. Armoury.

Cathedrals & Churches

Astley (St. Mary the Virgin)
17th century - has remains of 14th century collegiate church. 15th century painted stalls.
Beaudesert (St. Nicholas)
Norman with fine arches in chancel.
Brailes (St. George)
15th century - decorated nave & aisles - 14th century carved oak chest.
Crompton Wynyates
Church of Restoration period having painted ceiling.
Lapworth (St. Mary)
13th & 14th century - steeple & north aisle connected by passage.
Preston-on-Stour (The Blessed Virgin Mary)
18th century. Gilded ceiling, 17th century glass
Tredington (St. Gregory)
Saxon walls in nave - largely 14th century, 17th century pulpit. Fine spire.
Warwick (St. Mary)
15th century Beauchamp Chapel, vaulted choir, some 17th century Gothic.
Wooten Wawen (St. Peter)
Saxon, with remnants of mediaeval wall painting, 15th century screens & pulpit: small 17th century chained library.

Museums & Galleries

The Royal Shakespeare Theatre Picture Gallery - Stratford-upon-Avon
Original designs & paintings, portraits of famous actors, etc.
Motor Museum - Stratford-upon-Avon
Collection of cars, racing, vintage, exotic, replica of 1930 garage. Fashions, etc. of 1920's era.

WARWICKSHIRE
Map reference

- 01 Waterworth
- 02 Jamouse
- 03 Wilson
- 04 Howard
- 05 Staite
- 06 Lawson
- 07 Lea
- 08 Walliker
- 09 Hutsby
- 10 Mawle
- 11 Evans
- 11 Everitt
- 11 Rush
- 11 Workman
- 11 Castelli
- 11 Short
- 11 Evans
- 11 Childs
- 11 Coulson
- 11 Andrews
- 11 Evans
- 11 Hallworth
- 11 Palmer
- 11 Morton
- 11 Walters
- 11 Tozer
- 11 Mander
- 12 Vernon Miller
- 13 Trought
- 14 Green

8 Clarendon Crescent. Leamington Spa.

Warwickshire

		minimum £ per person	children taken	evening meals	animals taken
Mrs H.P. Waterworth Sandbarn Farm Hampton Lucy CV35 8AU Tel: (0789) 842280 Open: JAN - DEC Map Ref No. 01	Nearest Road: M.40, A.46 Seventeenth century farmhouse in charming village offering luxury bed and breakfast accommodation. Tranquil setting with lovely views, only 3 miles from Stratford-upon-Avon. Warwick and Kenilworth Castles are nearby, also many National Trust houses and parks. Of the 4 guest bedrooms, 3 are en-suite and 1 private. Single availability. Residents lounge and T.V. Children over 5 please.	£20.00	Y	N	N
H.A. Jamouse Ashleigh House Whitley Hill Henley-in-Arden B95 5DL Tel: (0564) 792315 Fax 0564 794133 Open: ALL YEAR Map Ref No. 02	Nearest Road: A.34 A spacious & elegant Edwardian house set in its own lovely grounds with magnificent views towards the Cotswold Hills. Beautifully decorated with many antiques. There are 10 delightful rooms, each with en-suite facilities & T.V. An attractive lounge with colour T.V. & a garden for guests to enjoy. Excellent breakfast. Very convenient for Stratford-upon-Avon only 7 mls., the National Exhibition Centre, Stoneleigh Agricultural Centre & Warwick University.	£39.00	Y	N	N
Mrs Joan Wilson Ferndale Guest House 45 Priory Road Kenilworth CV8 1LL Tel: (0926) 53214 Open: ALL YEAR Map Ref No. 03	Nearest Road: A.46 You are assured of a warm welcome in this family-run spacious Victorian house situated in a quiet tree-lined avenue only 5 mins. walk from town centre. All 8 bedrooms are en-suite & tastefully decorated with colour T.V. & coffee/tea making facilities. A guests' T.V. lounge is available throughout the day. Ideally located for Warwick, Coventry, Leamington Spa, National Exhibition Centre, Stoneleigh Agricultural Centre & Warwick University.	£17.00	Y	N	Y
Carolyn Howard Willowbrook House Lighthorne Road Kineton CV35 0JL Tel: (0926) 640475 Fax 0926 641747 Open: ALL YEAR Map Ref No. 04	Nearest Road: B.4100 M.40 Willowbrook is a peaceful, comfortable house & small farmset in rolling countryside with lovely views. Handy for Stratford-upon-Avon, Warwick & the Cotswolds. 2 twin rooms & 1 double room en-suite, with tea trays. Guests' large sitting room, dining room, log fires, central heating & antiques. Enjoy watching lambs & rare breeds of poultry or sit on the terrace by the garden pool. Friendly attentive service assured. M40 (ex.12) only 3 miles.	£12.00	Y	N	Y
Christine & David Lawson 8 Clarendon Crescent Leamington Spa CV32 5NR Tel: (0926) 429840 Fax 0926 451660 Open: ALL YEAR Map Ref No. 06	Nearest Road: A.452 A grade II listed Regency house overlooking a private dell. Situated in a quiet backwater of Leamington. Elegantly furnished with antiques & offering accommodation in 4 tastefully furnished bedrooms, 3 en-suite. A delicious full English breakfast is served. Located only 5 minutes from the town centre. A convenient base for touring Warwick, Stratford, the Royal Agricultural Centre & the National Exhibition Centre are all within easy driving distance.	£20.00 *see PHOTO over*	Y	N	N

Ambion Court Hotel. Dadlington.

Warwickshire

		minimum £ per person	children taken	evening meals	animals taken
Peter & Dawn Staite Lapworth Lodge Bushwood Lane Lapworth B94 5PJ Tel: (0564) 783038 Fax 0564 783635 Open: ALL YEAR Map Ref No. 05	Nearest Road: A.3400, M.40 This imposing Georgian house, enjoys outstanding views over the glorious Warwickshire countryside. All 7 lovely bedrooms are exceptionally large, with en-suite facilities, co-ordinated decor, colour T.V., tea/coffee makers & central heating. The 4-course breakfast is renowned. This is a guest house for those who prefer superior comforts combined with the warmest of welcomes. Convenient for Stratford, Warwick & the National Exhibition Centre.	£25.00	Y	N	N
Deborah Lea Crandon House Avon Dassett Leamington Spa CV33 0AA Tel: (0295) 770652 Open: ALL YEAR Map Ref No. 07	Nearest Road: B.4100, M.40 Guests receive a specially warm welcome at Crandon House offering a high standard of accommodation & comfort. Set in 20 acres. Beautiful views over unspoilt countryside. Small working farm. Own produce. Excellent food. 3 rooms with private facilities, T.V., tea/coffee tray. Large garden. Full C.H. & log fire. Peaceful & quiet yet within easy reach of Stratford, Warwick, Oxford & the Cotswolds. Located between M.40 junctions 11 & 12 (4 miles).	£16.00	Y	Y	Y
John Walliker Ambion Court Hotel The Green Dadlington Nuneaton CV13 6JB Tel: (0455) 212292 Fax 0455 213141 Open: ALL YEAR Map Ref No. 08	Nearest Road: A.5, M69. A charming, modernised Victorian farmhouse in the village of Dadlington 2 miles north of Hinckley. Each room is comfortably furnished & has en-suite bathroom, hospitality tray, T.V., radio & telephone. The lovely pine room is available for honeymoons etc. There is a guest lounge, a cocktail bar & a restaurant serving traditional country fare. Ambion Court offers exceptional comfort, tranquility & hospitality & is the perfect regional base.	£22.50 see PHOTO over	Y	Y	Y
Sue Hutsby Nolands Farm & Country Restaurant Oxhill CV35 0RJ Tel: (0926) 640309 Open: ALL YEAR Map Ref No. 09	Nearest Road: A.422 Nolands Farm is situated in a tranquil valley surrounded by fields, woods & a lake for fishing. The 9 bedrooms are annexed to the house in converted stables, with some ground floor bedrooms, some with a romantic 4-poster, all are en-suite with central heating, tea/coffee makers & T.V. Dine in the beautiful granary-style restaurant which is licensed & serves the freshest produce & fine cuisine. Everything for the discerning country lover. Clay pigeon shooting, bicycles for hire & riding nearby.	£14.00 see PHOTO over	Y	Y	N
Rebecca Mawle Lower Farm Barn Great Wolford Shipston-on-Stour CV36 5NQ Tel: (0608) 74435 Open: ALL YEAR Map Ref No. 10	Nearest Road: A.44, A.3400 This lovely 100 year-old converted barn stands in the small, peaceful Warwickshire village of Great Wolford. The property retains much of its original form including exposed beams & ancient stone work. Now tastefully modernised, it makes a very comfortable home. The accommodation is in 2 beautifully furnished double rooms with en-suite facilities.	£12.50	Y	N	Y

Nolands Farm & Country Restaurant.   Oxhill.

Warwickshire

			minimum £ per person	children taken	evening meals	animals taken
Richard & Susan Evans **Oxtalls Farm** **Warwick Road** **Stratford-upon-Avon** **CU37 4WR** Tel: (0789) 205277 Open: ALL YEAR Map Ref No. 11	Nearest Road: A.439 This charming thoroughbred stud farm, overlooks the beautiful Welcombe Hills & golf course. It provides excellent accommodation for touring or relaxing in peaceful surroundings. There are 20 tastefully furnished bedrooms many with en-suite facilities, T.V. & tea/coffee makers. For the keen fisherman there is a well stocked trout pond. A guided tour of the farm to see the animals is also available. 1 mile from Stratford town centre.		£13.00	Y	N	N
Margaret Everitt **Eastnor House Hotel** **33 Shipston Road** **Stratford-upon-Avon** **CU37 7LN** Tel: (0789) 268115 Open: ALL YEAR Map Ref No. 11	Nearest Road: A.34 A fine old Victorian town house built in 1896. Restored to provide excellent accommodation with oak panelling, central open staircase, pleasant breakfast room & elegant lounge. The spacious, tastefully furnished bedrooms have colour T.V., welcome tray & include luxury en-suite bathrooms with bath, shower & toilet. Situated only a short stroll from the River Avon, theatres & town centre, ensuring a comfortable restful stay. Private car park.		£22.00	Y	N	Y
Pauline & Jim Rush **Parkfield Guest House** **3 Broad Walk** **Stratford-upon-Avon** **CV37 6HS** Tel: (0789) 293313 Open: ALL YEAR Map Ref No. 11	Nearest Road: A.439, A.34. A delightful Victorian house, in a quiet location in Old Town just 5 minutes' walk to town centre & the Royal Shakespeare Theatre. Ideally situated for touring the Cotswolds, Warwick Castle, etc. 7 spacious & comfortable rooms. 4 en-suite, all with full central heating, colour T.V. & tea/coffee making facilities. Excellent breakfast. Private parking. Lots of tourist information. Guests can be collected from the station.		£14.00	Y	N	Y
Richard & Brenda Workman **Ravenhurst** **2 Broad Walk** **Stratford-upon-Avon** **CV37 6HS** Tel: (0789) 292515 Open: ALL YEAR Map Ref No. 11	Nearest Road: A.439, A4390 A Victorian town house with a warm & friendly atmosphere. Ideally situated on the edge of the old town & only a few minutes walk from the Shakespeare Theatre, town centre & places of historical interest. Enjoy the comfort & quiet of this family run guest house where all bedrooms have colour T.V. & tea/coffee making facilities. The Workman's are Stratfordians, therefore local knowledge a speciality.		£15.00	Y	N	N
Mr & Mrs I. Castelli **Minola Guest House** **25 Evesham Place** **Stratford-upon-Avon** **CV37 6HT** Tel: (0789) 293573 Open: ALL YEAR Map Ref No. 11	Nearest Road: A.439 A comfortable house with a relaxed atmosphere offering good accommodation in 5 rooms, 2 with private shower, all have colour T.V. & tea/coffee makers. Stratford offers a myriad of delights for the visitor including the Royal Shakespeare Theatre. Set by the River Avon, this makes a lovely place for a picnic lunch or early evening meal before the performance. Cots are provided. Italian & French spoken.		£14.00	Y	N	N

Warwickshire

		minimum £ per person	children taken	evening meals	animals taken
Pat & Peter Short **Nando's** **18-20 Evesham Place** **Stratford-upon-Avon** **CV37 6HT** Tel: (0789) 204907 Open: ALL YEAR Map Ref No. 11	Nearest Road: A.34 A.439 Pat & Peter extend the warmest of welcomes to their guests. Nando's is conveniently located only minutes away from the Royal Shakespeare Theatre. Offering 21 rooms, 7 with en-suite facilities, all with T.V. A residents' T.V. lounge is also available. This makes a good base for visiting the many places of interest in the town as well as the surrounding area. Visa accepted.	£12.00	Y	Y	Y
K. A. & R. J. Childs **All Seasons** **51 Grove Road** **Stratford-upon-Avon** **CV37 6PB** Tel: (0789) 293404 Open: ALL YEAR Map Ref No. 11	Nearest Road: A.439 A warm welcome awaits guests to this modernised, spacious Victorian house. Offering a choice of 5 comfortable rooms with modern amenities & tea/coffee making facilities. A residents' colour T.V. lounge is also available throughout the day. Located close to the town centre with good access for rail & coach stations. The Shakespeare Centre & Theatre are also close by. This makes a good base for touring. Children over 12 years.	£16.00	N	N	Y
Mrs M. Evans **Kawartha House** **39 Grove Road** **Stratford-upon-Avon** **CV37 6PB** Tel: (0789) 204469 Open ALL YEAR (Excl.Xmas) Map Ref No. 11	Nearest Road: A.435 Kawartha House is a well appointed town house with a friendly atmosphere overlooking the 'old town' park. It is located just a few minutes walk from the town centre & ideal for visiting the places of historic interest. Private parking is available. With pretty en-suite bedrooms & quality food, these are the ingredients for a memorable stay.	£11.00 *see PHOTO over*	Y	N	Y
Jill & Ernie Coulson **'Hardwick House'** **1 Avenue Road** **Stratford-upon-Avon** **CV37 6UY** Tel: (0789) 204307 Fax 0789 296760 Open ALL YEAR (Excl.Xmas) Map Ref No. 11	Nearest Road: A.439 You will be welcomed to 'Hardwick House', an impressive Victorian home in a quiet area, yet just 5 mins. walk to the town centre & the theatre. Guests have a choice of 14 spacious & comfortable bedrooms, many with private facilities, all with T.V. & tea/coffee making facilities. A residents' lounge is available & there is also parking space. Enjoy its friendly atmosphere & home-cooked breakfasts.	£17.00	Y	N	N
Patricia Ann Andrews **Melita Private Hotel** **37 Shipston Road** **Stratford-upon-Avon** **CV37 7LN** Tel: (0789) 292432 Open: ALL YEAR Map Ref No. 11	Nearest Road: A.3400 An extremely friendly family-run hotel. Offering pleasant service, good food & accommodation in 12 excellent bedrooms, all with private facilities, colour T.V., tea/coffee & direct dial telephones. Comfortable lounge/bar & pretty award winning garden for guests' use. Ample car parking. A pleasant 5 minute walk to Shakespearian properties/theatres, shopping centre & beautiful riverside gardens. Superbly situated for Warwick Castle & the Cotswolds.	£20.00	Y	N	Y

Kawartha House.   Stratford-upon-Avon.

Warwickshire

			minimum £ per person	children taken	evening meals	animals taken
Mrs Liz Vernon Miller **Blackwell Grange Farm** **Blackwell** Shipston-on-Stour Stratford-upon-Avon Tel: (060882) 357 Open: ALL YEAR Map Ref No. 12	Nearest Road: A.34, A.429 Blackwell Grange is a grade II listed farmhouse, part of which dates from 1603. It is situated 2 miles from Shipston-on-Stour & 7 miles from Stratford-upon-Avon, found on the edge of the village with fine views of the Ilmington Hills & surrounding countryside. A peaceful haven with a warm welcome & log fires. 2 en-suite rooms. Ideal for touring the Cotswolds & Shakespeare country. Children over 7 years.		£16.00 *see PHOTO over*	Y	Y	N
Philip Evans **Sequoia House Hotel** 51/53 Shipston Road Stratford-upon-Avon CV37 7LN Tel: (0789) 268852 Fax 0789 414559 Open: ALL YEAR Map Ref No. 11	Nearest Road: A.3400 A beautifully appointed private hotel situated across the River Avon from the Royal Shakespeare Theatre. Offering 25 bedrooms, cocktail bar, cottage annex & garden restaurant. The hotel is comfortably furnished & decorated in a warm & restful style with many extra thoughtful touches. The garden overlooks the town cricket ground & the old tramway. Pleasant walks along the the banks of the River Avon opposite the Theatre & Holy Trinity Church.		£27.50	Y	Y	N
Kevin & Jeanne Hallworth **The Croft Guest House** 49 Shipston Road Stratford-upon-Avon CV37 7LN Tel: (0789) 293719 Open: ALL YEAR Map Ref No. 11	Nearest Road: A.3400 The Croft is a friendly family-run Victorian guest house only 200 yards from the River Avon. 9 pleasant rooms, 3 with private facilities. All with colour T.V. & tea/coffee making facilities. Residents' lounge & garden. 5 minutes from theatre, river boats & town. Ideal base for touring the Cotswolds, Warwick & many local places of interest.		£16.00	Y	Y	Y
Terry & Margarita Palmer **Craig Cleeve House** 67-69 Shipston Road Stratford-upon-Avon Tel: (0789) 296573 Fax 0789 299452 Open ALL YEAR(ExclXmas) Map Ref No. 11	Nearest Road: A.34 A warm welcome & a most hospitable house, offering 15 excellent rooms with comfortable accommodation & modern amenities. All have radio, T.V. & tea/coffee makers, 9 are en-suite. A very good base for visiting this most historic town with its superb theatre & Shakespeare connections. Many museums & galleries in the area & lovely countryside. Cots & highchairs provided. Mr Palmer can collect you from the station.		£19.50	Y	N	Y
Meg & Bob Morton **Grove Farm** Ettington Stratford-upon-Avon CV37 7NX Tel: (0789) 740228 Open: ALL YEAR Map Ref No. 11	Nearest Road: A.422, A.429 A warm & friendly welcome awaits you at this beautiful old farmhouse set on a 500 acre working farm. Superb views. Log fires, antiques a friendly labrador dog & old horses. Private bathrooms. Guests are welcome to ramble through the fields & woods. Peace & tranquility in lovely surroundings very near to Stratford-upon-Avon, Warwick Castle & the Cotswolds. Delicious dinners available nearby.		£14.00	Y	N	N

Blackwell Grange. Shipston-on-Stour.

Warwickshire

		minimum £ per person	children taken	evening meals	animals taken
Mrs Marian J. Walters Church Farm Dorsington Stratford-upon-Avon Tel: (0789) 720471/ (0831) 504194 Open: ALL YEAR Map Ref No. 11	Nearest Road: A.439 There is great farmhouse cooking at this 127 acre mixed farm amid woodlands & stream. The Georgian farmhouse is situated on the edge of this extremely pretty village. All 7 rooms have tea/coffee facilities, 4 en-suite with T.V. in a converted stable block. Gliding, micro lighting, fishing, boating & horse riding locally, Stratford-upon-Avon, Warwick, NEC.	£12.50	Y	N	N
Paul & Dreen Tozer Victoria Spa Lodge Bishopton Lane Stratford-upon-Avon Tel(0789) 267985/204728 Fax 0789 298056 Open: ALL YEAR Map Ref No. 11	Nearest Road: A.3400, A46 Victoria Spa is a very large Victorian house originally opened in 1830 as a health spa. Today Paul & Dreen offer guests comfortable accommodation in 7 rooms, 4 en-suite, each with colour T.V. & tea/coffee makers. Situated only one & a half miles from Stratford Theatre. Your hosts are happy to prepare pre-theatre dinner with prior notice. Ideally placed for visiting Warwick Castle, the Cotswolds or the National Exhibition Centre.	£19.50	Y	Y	N
Mrs Margaret Mander Pear Tree Cottage 7 Church Road Wilmcote Stratford-upon-Avon CV37 9UX Tel: (0789) 205889 Open: ALL YEAR Map Ref No. 11	Nearest Road: A.46, A3400 A delightful half-timbered 16th century house located in the Shakespeare village of Wilmcote. It retains all its original charm & character with oak beams, flagstone floors, inglenook fireplaces, thick stone walls with deep-set windows, decorated with antiques. Offering 5 very comfortable en-suite rooms, all with tea/coffee making facilities & colour T.V. A delicious breakfast is served each morning in the dining room. A comfortable lounge is also provided. A lovely base from which to tour the whole region.	£18.00 *see PHOTO over*	Y	N	Y
Mrs Topsy Trought Brookland Peacock Lane Tysoe Warwick CV35 0SG Tel: (0295) 680202 Open: ALL YEAR Map Ref No. 13	Nearest Road: A.422 Dating from 1634, Brookland is beautifully situated in the pretty village of Tysoe, resting in the Vale of the Red Horse. 3 prettily furnished bedrooms. Comfortable lounge with an open fire & T.V. Topsy provides excellent cuisine, using fresh home-grown produce, served in the 17th century dining room with an inglenook fireplace & wooden beams. Tysoe, a conservation area is well placed for visiting Shakespeare's country, the Cotswolds & the South Midlands. Only 20 mins. from Stratford-upon-Avon.	£13.50	Y	Y	N
Mrs E.J. Green Shrewley House Shrewley Warwick CV35 7AT Tel: (092684) 2549 Open: ALL YEAR Map Ref No. 14	Nearest Road: A.4177, Surrounded by beautiful country, Shrewley House is a Grade II listed 17th Century Georgian Farmhouse home, with converted stables and cottages. An elegant drawing room opens onto lawned gardens. The delightfully furnished bedrooms, some with king-sized Four-poster beds, have en-suite bathrooms and shower, telephones, T.V., hair dryer, tea/coffee facilities, fresh fruit. Dinner by arrangement only;	£29.38	Y	N	Y

Pear Tree Cottage, Wilmcote.

Wiltshire

Wiltshire
(West Country)

Wiltshire is a county of rolling chalk downs, small towns, delightful villages, fine churches & great country houses. The expanse of Salisbury Plain is divided by the beautiful valleys of Nadder, Wylye, Ebble & Avon. In a county of open landscapes, Savernake Forest, with its stately avenues of trees strikes a note of contrast. In the north west the Cotswolds spill over into Wiltshire from neighbouring Gloucestershire.

No other county is so rich in archaeological sites. Long barrows and ancient hill forts stand on the skylines as evidence of the early habitation of the chalk uplands. Many of these prehistoric sites are at once magnificent and mysterious. The massive stone arches and monoliths of Stonehenge were built over a period of 500 years with stones transported over great distances. At Avebury the small village is completely encircled by standing stones and a massive bank and ditch earthwork. Silbury Hill is a huge, enigmatic man-made mound. England's largest chambered tomb is West Kennet Long Barrow and at Bush Barrow, finds have included fine bronze and gold daggers and a stone sceptre-head similar to one found at Mycenae in Greece.

Some of England's greatest historic houses are in Wiltshire. Longleat is an Elizabethan mansion with priceless collections of paintings, books & furniture. The surrounding park was landscaped by Capability Brown and its great fame in recent years has been its Safari Park, particularly the lions which roam freely around the visiting cars. Stourhead has celebrated 18th century landscaped gardens which are exceptional in spring when rhododendrons bloom.

Two delightful villages are Castle Combe, nestling in a Cotswold valley, & Lacock where the twisting streets hold examples of buildings ranging from mediaeval half-timbered, to Tudor & Georgian. 13th century Lacock Abbey, converted to a house in the 16th century, was the home of Fox Talbot, pioneer of photography.

There are many notable churches in Wiltshire. In Bradford-on-Avon, a fascinating old town, is the church of St. Lawrence, a rare example of an almost perfect Saxon church from around 900. Farley has an unusual brick church thought to have been designed by Sir Christopher Wren, & there is stained glass by William Morris in the church at Rodbourne.

Devizes Castle.

Salisbury stands where three rivers join, on a plain of luxuriant watermeadows, where the focal point of the landscape is the soaring spire of the Cathedral; at 404 feet, it is the tallest in England. The 13th century cathedral has a marvellous & rare visual unity. The body of the building was completed in just 38 years, although the spire was added in the next century. Salisbury, or "New Sarum" was founded in 1220 when the Bishop abandoned the original cathedral at Old Sarum, to start the present edifice two miles to the south. At Old Sarum you can see the foundation of the old city including the outline of the first cathedral.

Wiltshire

Wiltshire Gazeteer

Area of Outstanding Natural Beauty
The Costwolds & the North Wessex Downs.

Historic Houses & Castles

Corsham Court - Chippenham
16th & 17th centuries from Elizabethan & Georgian periods. 18th century furniture, British, Flemish & Italian Old Masters. Gardens by Capability Brown.
Great Chalfield Manor - Melksham
15th century manor house - moated.
Church House - Salisbury
15th century house.
Chalcot House - Westbury
17th century small house in Palladian manner.
Lacock Abbey - Nr. Chippenham
13th century abbey. In 1540 converted into house - 18th century alterations. Mediaeval cloisters & brewery.
Longleat House - Warminster
16th century - early Renaissance, alterations in early 1800's. Italian Renaissance decorations. Splendid state rooms, pictures, books, furniture. Victorian kitchens. Game reserve.
Littlecote - Nr. Hungerford
15th century Tudor manor. Panelled rooms, moulded plaster ceilings.
Luckington Court - Luckington
Queen Anne for the most part - fine ancient buildings.
Malmesbury House - Salisbury
Queen Anne house - part 14th century. Rococo plasterwork.
Newhouse - Redlynch
17th century brick Jacobean trinity house - two Georgian wings,
Philips House - Dinton
1816 Classical house.
Sheldon Manor - Chippenham
13th century porch & 15th century chapel in this Plantagenet manor.
Stourhead - Stourton
18th century Palladian house with framed landscape gardens.
Westwood Manor - Bradford-on-Avon
15th century manor house - alterations in 16th & 17th centuries.
Wardour Castle - Tisbury
18th century house in Palladian manner.

Wilton House - Salisbury
17th century - work of Inigo Jones & later of James Wyatt in 1810. Paintings, Kent & Chippendale furniture.
Avebury Manor - Nr Malborough
Elizabethan manor house - beautiful plasterwork, panelling & furniture. Gardens with topiary.
Bowood - Calne
18th century - work of several famous architects. Gardens by Capability Brown - famous beechwoods.
Mompesson House - Salisbury
Queen Anne town house - Georgian plasterwork.

Cathedrals & Churches

Salisbury Cathedral
13th century - decorated tower with stone spire. Part of original stone pulpitum is preserved. Beautiful large decorated cloister. Exterior mostly early English.
Salisbury (St. Thomas of Canterbury)
15th century rebuilding - 12th century font, 14th & 15th century glass, 17th century monuments. 'Doom' painting over chancel & murals in south chapel
Amesbury (St. Mary & St. Melor)
13th century - refashioned 15th & restored in 19th century. Splendid timber roofs, stone vaulting over chapel of north trancept, mediaeval painted glass, 15th century screen, Norman font.
Bishops Cannings (St. Mary the Virgin)
13th-15th centuries. Fine arcading in transept - fine porch doorway - 17th century almsbox, Jacobean Holy table.
Bradford-on-Avon (St. Lawrence)
Best known of all Saxon churches in England.
Cricklade (St. Sampson)
12th -16th century. Tudor central tower vault, 15th century chapel.
Inglesham (St. John the Baptist)
Mediaeval wall paintings, high pews, clear glass, remains of painted screens.
Malmesbury (St. Mary)
Norman - 12th century arcades, refashioning in 14th century with clerestory, 15th century stone pulpitum added.
Fine sculpture.

Wiltshire

Tisbury (St. John the Baptist) 14th-15th centuries. 15th-17th century roofing to nave & aisles. Two storeyed porch & chancel.
Potterne (St. Mary) 13th,14th,15th centuries. Inscribed Norman tub font. Wooden pulpit.

Museums & Galleries

Salisbury & South Wiltshire Museum - Salisbury
Collections showing history of the area in all periods. Models of Stonehenge & Old Sarum - archaeologically important collection.
Devizes Museum - Devizes
Unique archaeological & geological collections, including Sir Richard Colt-Hoare's Stourhead collection of prehistoric material.
Alexander Keiller Museum - Avebury
Collection of items from the Neolithic & Bronze ages & from excavations in district.
Athelstan Museum - Malmesbury
Collection of articles referring to the town - household, coin, etc.
Bedwyn Stone Museum - Great Bedwyn
Open-air museum showing where Stonehenge was carved.
Lydiard Park - Lydiard Tregoze
Parish church of St. Mary & a splendid Georgian mansion standing in park - memorials - also permanent & travelling exhibitions.

Borough of Thamesdown Museum & Art Gallery - Swindon
Natural History & Geology of Wiltshire, Bygones, coins, etc. 20th century British art & ceramic collection.
Great Western Railway Museum - Swindon
Historic locomotives.

Historic Monuments

Stonehenge - Nr. Amesbury
Prehistoric monument - encircling bank & ditch & Augrey holes are Neolithic. Stone circles possibly early Bronze age.
Avebury
Relics of enormous circular gathering place B.C. 2700-1700.
Old Sarum - Nr. Salisbury
Possibly first Iron Age camp, later Roman area, then Norman castle.
Silbury Hill - Nr. Avebury
Mound - conical in shape - probably a memorial c.3000-2000 B.C.
Windmill Hill - Nr. Avebury
Causewayed camp c.3000-2300 B.C.
Bratton Camp & White Horse - Bratton
Hill fort standing above White Horse. West Kennet Long Barrow
Burial place c.4000-2500 B.C.
Ludgershall Castle - Lugershall
Motte & bailey of Norman castle, earthworks, also flint walling from later castle.

Castle Combe.

WILTSHIRE
Map reference

01 Hartland
02 Chapman
02 Roberts
02 Price
03 Denning
04 Cooper
05 Lippiatt
06 Steed
07 Addison
08 Reid
09 Richmond
09 Fletcher
10 Horton
11 Firth
12 Cornelius
13 Eavis
14 Edwards
15 Francis
16 Ross
17 Tucker
17 Arthey
17 Rodwell
17 Bone
17 Hibbs
18 Johnson
19 Gifford-Mead
20 Singer
21 Kirwin
22 Bruges
23 Cronan
24 Cottle

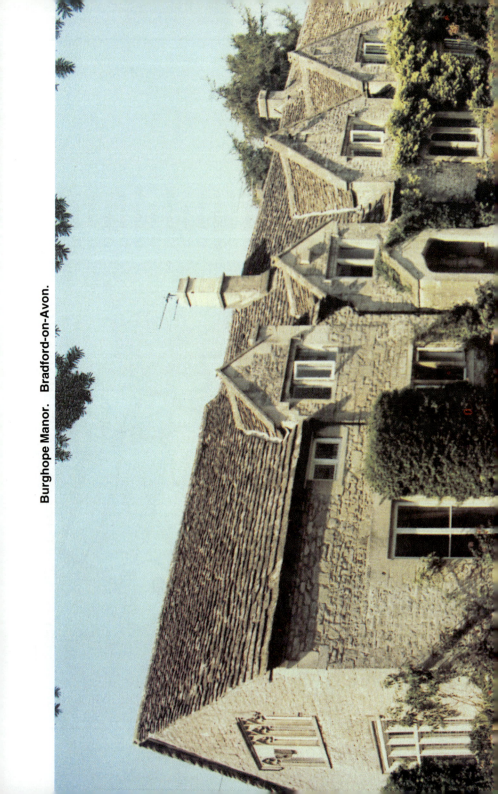

Burghope Manor. Bradford-on-Avon.

Wiltshire

	minimum £ per person	children taken	evening meals	animals taken
Peter & Elizabeth Hartland **Cove House** 2 Cove House Ashton Keynes SN6 6NS Tel: (0285) 861221 Open: JAN - NOV Map Ref No. 01	Nearest Road: A.419 Peter & Elizabeth will welcome you warmly to their historic Cotswold manor house containing many antiques & interesting paintings. The charming old house stands in a large secluded garden & offers 3 spacious bedrooms, 3 with bath/shower en-suite. Dinner 'en famille' is ideal for planning the next day's excursions & guests will enjoy good home cooking, using garden produce when in season. Bath, Oxford, Avebury & the delightful Cotswold villages are within easy reach. Tennis, squash, golf, fishing, riding or wind surfing can be arranged.	£18.00	Y	Y	Y
Carey & Diana Chapman **Priory Steps** Newtown Bradford-on-Avon BA15 1NQ Tel: (02216) 2230 Open: ALL YEAR Map Ref No. 02	Nearest Road: A.363 A warm & friendly welcome awaits you at this delightful mellow stone 17th century former clothiers house. Tastefully renovated & furnished with antiques, Priory Steps offers guests a choice of 5 individually decorated en-suite bedrooms with tea/coffee making facilities & colour T.V. All rooms have super views over the town towards Westbury Hills. A wide choice of delicious breakfasts is available, these are served in the elegant dining room & Diana's delicious evening meals are not to be missed.	£26.00	Y	Y	N
Priscilla & Peter Roberts **Bradford Old Windmill** 4 Masons Lane Bradford-on-Avon BA15 1QN Tel: (0225) 866842 Open: JAN - DEC Map Ref No. 02	Nearest Road: M.4, A.363 This former windmill standing high above the town provides a distinctly different place to stay. The rooms of all shapes & sizes, enjoy wide ranging views over the Avon Valley. Most of the rooms, have distinctive beds & individual bathrooms. The mill is furnished with old pine & finds from around the world. Breakfasts cater for carnivores, omnivores, vegetarians & vegans. The town is 5 mins. walk.	£20.00	Y	Y	N
Mr & Mrs John Price **Widbrook Grange** Trowbridge Road Bradford-onAvonBA151UH Tel: (02216) 4750 or 3173 Open: ALL YEAR Map Ref No. 02	Nearest Road: A.363 Widbrook Grange is a Georgian grade II listed house set in 11 acres & only 8 miles from the fascinating Georgain city of Bath. The house has been lovingly restored by John & Pauline, with elegant rooms offering en-suite facilities & some 4-poster beds in both the house & the courtyard 'cottages'. Peaceful comfort & a warm welcome await you. Restaurant within walking distance.	£25.00	Y	N	N
Elizabeth & John Denning **Burghope Manor** Winsley Bradford-on-AvonBA15 2LA Tel: (0225) 723557 Fax 0225 723113 Open: ALL YEAR Map Ref No. 03	Nearest Road: A.36 This historic 13th century family home is set in beautiful countryside on the edge of the village of Winsley - overlooking the Avon Valley - convenient for the Georgian City of Bath & Bradford-on-Avon. Although steeped in history, Burghope Manor is first & foremost a living family home, which has been carefully modernised so that the wealth of historical features compliment the present day comforts which include central heating & en-suite bathrooms.	£30.00 *see PHOTO over*	Y	N	N

Manor Farm. Alderton.

Wiltshire

	minimum £ per person	children taken	evening meals	animals taken

Mrs Victoria Lippiatt **Manor Farm** Alderton Chippenham SN14 6NL Tel: (0666) 840271 Open: MAR-NOV Map Ref No. 05	Nearest Road: B.4040, M.4, This beautiful 17th century family home in picturesque Alderton, welcomes small numbers of guests to warm hospitality. The bedrooms are large & comfortable, each with private bathroom, colour T.V. The surrounding area is steeped in interest & boasts an excellent variety of places to wine & dine. Guests are most welcome to enjoy the garden & the interest of this working farm. Children over 12 .	£18.50 *see PHOTO over*	Y	N	Y
Caron Cooper **Fosse Farmhouse** Nettleton Shrub Nettleton Chippenham SN14 7NJ Tel: (0249) 782286 Open: ALL YEAR Map Ref No. 04	Nearest Road: B.4039, M.4 This 18th century Farmhouse is situated midway between Bath, Bristol & The Cotswolds. Castle Coombe, one of the prettiest vilages in England lies just across the valley. A warm welcome & delightful en-suite accommodation awaits every guest. The beautiful original interiors were recently featured in the 'American Country Living' magazine. The newly converted stable buildings house a tea room, antique shop & gourmet restaurant.	£30.00 *see PHOTO over*	Y	Y	Y
Gloria Steed **The Cottage** Westbrook Bromham Chippenham SN15 2EE Tel: (0380) 850255 Open: MAR-NOV Map Ref No. 06	Nearest Road: A.3102, M.4 This delightful cottage is reputed to have been a coaching inn & dates back to 1450. There are 3 charming bedrooms all with private shower T.V. & tea/coffee makers, in a beautifully converted barn. Many exposed beams that were ships' timbers. Breakfast is served in the old beamed dining room. There is a lovely garden & paddock for guests' use. This lovely house is an ideal centre for visiting Bath, Bristol, Devizes, Marleborough, Avebury, Stonehenge, Longleat, Castle Combe & Lacock.	£17.50	Y	N	N
Margaret Addison **The Old Rectory** Lacock Chippenham SN15 2JZ Tel: (0249) 730335 Open: JAN - DEC Map Ref No. 07	Nearest Road: A.350, A.4 Situated in the mediaeval village of Lacock, the Old Rectory built in 1866, is a fine example of Victorian gothic architecture with creeper-clad walls & mullioned windows. It stands in 12 acres of its own carefully tended grounds which include a tennis court & croquet lawn. It offers 5 comfortable bedrooms, all with private bath.	£15.00	Y	N	N
Mrs C. Reid **Fairfield House** 44 High Street Corsham SN13 0HF Tel: (0249) 712992 Open: ALL YEAR Map Ref No. 08	Nearest Road: A.4 Fairfield House is a surprisingly spacious 17th century town house, full of interest, in the centre of Corsham's historic & picturesque High Street. Corsham is a small south Cotswold wooltown, with Flemish weavers' cottages, 17th century almshouses, & the magnificent Corsham Court with its art treasures.	£14.00	Y	N	Y

Fosse Farmhouse Country Hotel. Nettleton.

Wiltshire

Listing	Description	minimum £ per person	children taken	evening meals	animals taken
Paul & Sigourney Richmond **Devizes Castle** Devizes SN10 1HL Tel: (0380) 726632 Open: ALL YEAR Map Ref No. 09	The Lord & Lady of the Manor of Willoughby upon the Wolds welcome you to their home. Romantic Devizes castle, situated between Stongehenge & Bath dates back to the 12th century. Offering 3 luxurious rooms with private facilities in the fabulous south tower. Guests have their own magnificent circular drawing room, overlooking the battlement gardens. Modern comfort combines with romantic, circular rooms, spiral staircases, tranquil & secluded setting yet only 2 mins. from Devizes. Avebury, Castle Coombe, Lacock Abbey & Bath easily accessible. Minimum 2 night stay. Advance bookings only.	£55.00 *see PHOTO over*	N	N	N
Mrs Ann Horton **Easton Farmhouse** Bishops Cannings Devizes SN10 2LR Tel: (0380) 860228 Open: ALL YEAR Map Ref No. 10	Nearest Road: A.361 Easton Farmhouse is situated in the pretty village of Bishops Cannings. Accommodation is in 2 rooms with washbasins, which share 1 bathroom. Both have tea/coffee making facilities. Tennis court & garden available for guests' use. Excellent evening meals served in local pub/restaurant. Ideal place for walking along the Kennet & Avon Canal which borders the farm. An excellent base, conveniently located for Bowood, Bath, Salisbury & Stonehenge.	£16.00	Y	N	N
Malcolm & Janet Firth **Eastcott Manor** Easterton Devizes SN10 4PL Tel: (0380) 813313 Open: JAN - DEC Map Ref No. 11	Nearest Road: B.3098 Eastcott is a Grade II listed Elizabethan Manor House set in its own grounds and gardens of 20 acres, in a quiet and tranquil setting on the edge of Salisbury Plain. The interior is furnished with antiques, and the bedooms are fully modernised and comfortable. Ideal centre for Bath, Salisbury, Stonehenge, Longleat, Lacock Abbey etc. Excellent walking and riding on the Ridgeway with fine views.	£18.00	Y	Y	Y
Mrs Ross Eavis **Manor Farm** Corston Malmesbury SN16 0HF Tel: (0666) 822148 Open: ALL YEAR Map Ref No. 13	Nearest Road: A.429 Relax & unwind in a charming 17th century grade 11 listed farmhouse standing in 436 acres. 4 spacious comfortable rooms, some en-suite, all with tea/coffee makers, radio & T.V. on request. Lounge with T.V. & secluded garden available for guests' relaxation. Excellent meals served in the local pub within walking distance. Corston makes a marvellous base for exploring the Cotswolds, Bath & Tetbury.	£14.00	Y	N	N
Mrs Edna Edwards **Stone Hill Farm** Charlton Malmesbury SN16 9DY Tel: (0666) 823310 Open: ALL YEAR Map Ref No. 14	Neares Road B.4040 A warm welcome is yours at Stonehill, a 500 year-old Cotswold stone farmhouse on 200 acres of dairy & sheep farm. In a quiet location, but only 15 mins. from the M.4 (junctions 16 & 17), it is ideally situated for days out in Bath, the Cotswolds, Stratford, Sailisbury & Stonehenge. 3 bedrooms available, 1 with en-suite facilities children arewelcome & enjoy the atmosphere.	£13.00	Y	N	Y

Devizes Castle. Devizes.

Wiltshire

			minimum £ per person	children taken	evening meals	animals taken
Peter & Barbara Fletcher Rathlin Guest House Wick Lane Devizes SN10 5DP Tel: (0380) 721999 Open: ALL YEAR Map Ref No. 09	Nearest Road: A.360 A beautiful detached Edwardian house set in tranquil gardens, with ample car parking space, situated in a quiet residential area only a short walk from the town centre. Tastefully furnished with antiques, the house has great period charm. An elegant staircase leads to individually furnished en-suite bedrooms, all with colour televisions & hospitality tray. Ideal touring base for Bath, Stonehenge, Avebury, Longleat, Salisbury.		£17.00 see PHOTO over	Y	N	N
A. & G. Francis Laurel Cottage Southend Ogbourne St. George Marlborough SN8 1SG Tel: (067284) 288 Open: APRIL - OCT Map Ref No. 15	Nearest Road: A.345 Nestling in a fold of the Marlborough Downs, this 16th century thatched cottage has been fully modernised whilst retaining its unique 'olde worlde' charm. Low beamed ceilings, inglenook fireplace & bread oven are characteristic of these properties. 3 attractive bedrooms, 2 with en-suite facilities. Situated 30-40 miles from Bath, Oxford & Salisbury. Stonehenge & Avebury close by. An ideal base for touring.		£15.00 🚭	Y	N	N
Colin & Susan Ross Chetcombe House Hotel Chetcombe Road Mere BA12 6AZ Tel: (0747) 860219 Open: ALL YEAR Map Ref No. 16	Nearest Road: A.303 Chetcombe is a country house hotel set in an acre of lovely garden in the picturesque little town of Mere. Accommodation is in 5 attractively furnished rooms with private facilities & modern amenities including T.V. & tea/coffee makers. Delicious meals are served. Guests may relax in the comfortable lounge or enjoy the pretty garden. Ideal as a stopover to the West Country, or as a centre to explore Wiltshire.		£23.00	Y	Y	Y
Mary Tucker 1 Riverside Close Laverstock Salisbury SP1 1QW Tel: (0722) 320287 Open: ALL YEAR Map Ref No. 17	Nearest Road: A.30 An executive's home in a quiet area 1 & a half miles from Salisbury Cathedral. A tastefully furnished ground floor suite comprising private shower room, a double & single room with patio door, opening onto a beautiful flower arranger's garden. In addition guests have their own colour T.V. & tea/coffee making facilities. An excellent base for those visiting this historic city. Guests will receive every consideration here.		£17.50 🚭	Y	N	N
Ann & Peter Arthey Byways Guest House 31 Fowlers Road Salisbury SP1 2QP Tel (0722)328364 Fax 0722 322146 Open: ALL YEAR Map Ref No. 17	Nearest Road: A.30, A.36 Attractive family-run Victorian house with cathedral view in a quiet residential area of city centre. Leaving your car in the car park enables you to walk to Salisbury's magnificent cathedral. Comfortable bedrooms are with en-suite bathroom facilities & colour T.V.'s. Traditional English breakfasts together with vegetarian menus are included. The ideal base.		£15.00	Y	Y	Y
Mrs G. Rodwell Farthings 9 Swaynes Close Salisbury SP1 3AE Tel: (0722) 330749 Open: ALL YEAR Map Ref No. 17	Nearest Road: A.30 Farthings is a comfortable old house in a very quiet tree-lined street conveniently close to Salisbury's market square & its many excellent restaurants. There are 4 bedrooms; 2 single, 1 double & 1 twin en-suite each with tea/coffee makers. Residents' lounge with colour T.V. A delicious choice of breakfast is available at Farthings. A "no smoking" establishment.		£14.00 🚭	Y	N	N

Rathlin Guest House   Devizes.

Wiltshire

		minimum £ per person	children taken	evening meals	animals taken
Mrs Jane Cornelius **The Old Vicarage** Burbage Marlborough SN8 3AG Tel: (0672) 810495 Open: FEB - DEC Map Ref No. 17	Nearest Road: A.4, A.346, A large Victorian vicarage on the village green, next to the church, surrounded by thatched cottages. This pleasant country house offers guests 3 large, pretty rooms, decorated & furnished to a very high standard, with en-suite bathrooms. A most attractive lounge where guests can relax, giving out onto 2 acres of mature gardens. Within easy reach is Stonehenge, Avebury & Savernake Forest.	£27.50 see PHOTO over	N	Y	N
Chris & Sandie Bone **Avon Lodge Guest House** 28 Castle Road Salisbury SP1 3RJ Tel: (0722) 331359 Open: ALL YEAR Map Ref No. 17	Nearest Road: A.345 Avon Lodge is a Victorian house conveniently situated on the main Stonehenge road, within a few minutes walk of the city centre with its famous cathedral & many other historical buildings. Accommodation is in 3 attractive rooms with modern amenities including colour T.V. & tea/coffee making facilities. Lounge & garden available for guests' relaxation. Friendly & personal attention is assured in a homely & comfortable atmosphere. An ideal base for touring.	£13.00	Y	N	N
Diana Gifford-Mead **The Mill House** Berwick St. James Salisbury SP3 4TS Tel: (0722) 790331 Open: ALL YEAR Map Ref No. 19	Nearest Road: A.303, A.36 The lovely rooms of Mill House, built in 1785, view the River Till running through beautiful old-fashioned rose gardens & acres of water-meadows, rich with birds & wild flowers. Tea making facilities & T.V. in rooms on request. The old mill, still working, straddles a quarter of a mile of dry fly-fishing. Stonehenge is within walking distance. Numerous stately homes & historic sites. Pubs & eating places are nearby. Diana offers the warmest of welcomes. Children over 5 only.	£18.00	Y	N	N
Ron & Pam Hibbs **Newton Farm Guest House** Southampton Road Whiteparish Salisbury SP5 2QL Tel: (0794) 884416 Open: ALL YEAR Map Ref No. 17	Nearest Road: On A.36 A warm & friendly welcome awaits guests at this delightful family-run 16th century farmhouse, with its original flagstone floors & oak beams. 5 rooms for guests, all charmingly furnished & very comfortable with en-suite facilities & tea/coffee makers. Colour T.V. lounge, outdoor swimming pool & acres of garden. The house was part of the Trafalgar Estate gifted to Lord Nelson. Ideally situated for Broadlands, Salisbury Cathedral & Stonehenge.	£15.00	Y	Y	Y
Jill Johnson **Newcourt Lodge** Nunton Drove Nunton Salisbury SP5 4H2 Tel: (0722) 335877 Open: ALL YEAR Map Ref No. 18	Nearest Road: A.338 An attractive house, with a friendly atmosphere, situated in a quite village 3 miles from Salisbury. Newcourt Lodge incorporates original old bricks & timber features, with a large, mature garden giving extensive views over the rolling Wiltshire countryside. Each bedroom furnished to a high standard. Including T.V., H&C, C.H. & tea/coffee making facilities. Ideal for visiting Salisbury, Stonehenge, New Forest & the West Country. Nearby are attractive country pubs serving evening meals.	£14.50	Y	N	N

The Old Vicarage. Burbage.

Wiltshire

		minimum £ per person	children taken	evening meals	animals taken
Mrs Catherine Kirwin **Old Manor Farm** **Ashton Keynes** **Swindon** **SN6 6QR** **Tel: (0285) 861770** **Open: ALL YEAR** **Map Ref No. 21**	Nearest Road: A.419 A warm, friendly atmosphere is assured at this beautiful 15th century Cotswold manor house, which retains many of its original oak beams & stands in large gardens overlooking the village church. Accommodation is in 4 very pleasant, beamed bedrooms, 2 with en-suite facilities. A comfortable lounge with colour T.V. & wood-burning stove is also available. Breakfast is served in the delightful beamed dining room with inglenook fireplace. The village pubs offer good evening meals.	£14.00	Y	N	Y
Elizabeth Cronan **Welham House** **Bratton Road** **West Ashton** **Trowbridge BA14 6AZ** **Tel: (0225) 755908** **Open: APR-OCT** **Map Ref No. 23**	Nearest Road: A.350 Welham House, built in 1840, is a fine example of Gothic architecture with an impressive stain glass window in the entrance hall & a Jacobean ceiling in the dining room. 3 attractively furnished rooms with en-suite facilities, all have pretty views over the garden. Guests can pass time in the garden putting/playing bowls or relax in the T.V. lounge. An excellent base for visiting Bath, Longleat, Lacock & Avebury.	£14.00	Y	N	N
Mrs Michael Bruges **Brook House** **Semington** **Trowbridge** **BA14 6JR** **Tel: (0380) 870232** **Open: MAR-NOV** **Map Ref No. 22**	Nearest Road: A.350 This Georgian listed house, set in its own grounds, with tennis & croquet lawns, swimming pool & a brook bordering the orchard, where kingfishers can be seen. Offering 2 comfortable twin bedded rooms, with wash basins & tea/coffee facilities. The drawing room & conservatory can be made available for guests' use. Conveniently located for Bath, Longleat, Stourhead & Badminton horse trials.	£17.00	Y	N	Y
Margaret Cottle **Sturford Mead Farm** **Corsley** **Warminster** **BA12 7QU** **Tel: (0373) 832213** **Open: ALL YEAR** **Map Ref No. 24**	Nearest Road: A.362 Sturford Mead is conveniently located between Frome & Warminster opposite Longleat with its Safari Park, lake & grounds. Offering comfortable accommodation in a choice of 4 rooms, 1 with private facilities, all with modern amenities, radio, tea/coffee makers & T.V. on request. There is also a T.V. lounge & garden for guests' use. This is an ideal base for visiting the ancient cities of Wells & Bath. Cheddar Gorge & Wookey Hole are close by.	£16.00	Y	N	N
Colin & Rachel Singer **Springfield** **Crockerton** **Warminster** **BA12 8AU** **Tel: (0985) 213696** **Open: JAN - DEC** **Map Ref No. 20**	Nearest Road: A.350 Situated in the beautiful Wylye Valley, on the edge of the famous Longleat Estate, Springfield is a charming village house dating from the 17th century. Rachel & Colin welcome you to their home with its beams, open fires, fresh flowers, & sunny, south facing rooms, private or en-suite, overlooking the garden & grass tennis court. Marvellous base for touring, walking or just relaxing. Bath, Salisbury, Stonehenge, Wells, Glastonbury easily reached.	£16.00	Y	Y	N

Yorkshire

Yorkshire & Humberside

England's largest county is a region of beautiful landscapes, of hills, peaks, fells, dales & forests with many square miles of National Park. It is a vast area taking in big industrial cities, interesting towns & delightful villages. Yorkshires broad rivers sweep through the countryside & are an angler's paradise. Cascading waterfalls pour down from hillside & moorland.

The North sea coast can be thrilling, with wild seas & cliff-top walks, or just fun, as at the many resorts where the waves break on long beaches & trickle into green rock-pools. Staithes & Robin Hoods Bay are fascinating old fishing villages. Whitby is an attractive port where, below the Abbey, the small town tumbles in red-roofed tiers down to the busy harbour from which Captain Cook sailed.

The Yorkshire Dales form one of the finest landscapes in England. From windswept moors to wide green valleys the scenery is incomparable. James Herriot tells of of the effect that the broad vista of Swaledale had on him. "I was captivated", he wrote, "completely spell-bound....". A network of dry stone walls covers the land; some are as old as the stone-built villages but those which climb the valley sides to the high moors are the product of the 18th century enclosures, when a good wall builder would cover seven meters a day.

Each of the Dales has a distinctive character; from the remote upper reaches of Swaledale & Wensleydale, where the air sings with the sound of wind, sheep, & curlew, over to Airedale & the spectacular limestone gorges of Malham Cove & Gordale Scar, & down to the soft meadows & woods of Wharfedale where the ruins of Bolton Priory stands beside the river.

To the east towards Hull with its mighty River Humber crossed by the worlds largest single-span suspension bridge, lie the Yorkshire Wolds. This is lovely countryside where villages have unusual names like Fridaythorpe & Wetwang. Beverley is a picture-postcard town with a fine 13th century Minster.

The North Yorks National Park, where the moors are ablaze with purple fire of heather in the late summer, is exhilarating country. There is moorland to the east also, on the Pennine chain; famous Ilkley Moor with its stone circle known as the twelve apostles, & the Haworth Moors around the plain Yorkshire village where the Bronte sisters lived; "the distant dreamy, dim blue chain of mountains circling every side", which Emily Bronte describes in Wuthering Heights.

The Yorkshire Pennines industrial heritage is being celebrated in fascinating museums, often based in the original Woolen Mills & warehouses, which also provide workshop space for skilled craftspeople.

Yorkshires Monastic past is revealed in the ruins of its once great Abbeys. Rievaulx, Jervaux & Fountains, retain their tranquil beauty in their pastoral settings. The wealth of the county is displayed in many historic houses with glorious gardens, from stately 18th Century Castle Howard of 'Brideshead Revisited' fame to Tudor Shibden Hall, portrayed in Wuthering Heights.

York is the finest mediaeval city in England. It is encircled by its limestone city walls with four Great Gates. Within the walls are the jumbled roof line, dog-leg streets & sudden courtyards of a mediaeval town. Half timbered buildings with over-sailing upper storeys jostle with Georgian brick houses along the network of narrow streets around The Shambles & King Edward Square.

Yorkshire

Yorkshire Gazeteer

Areas of Outstanding Natural Beauty.
The North Yorkshire Moors & The Yorkshire Dales.

Historic Houses & Castles.

Carlton Towers
17th century, remodelled in later centuries. paintings, silver, furniture, pictures. Carved woodwork, painted decorations, examples of Victorian craftmanship.

Castle Howard - Nr. York
18th century - celebrated architect, Sir John Vanbrugh - paintings, costumes, furniture by Chippendale, Sheraton, Adam. Not to be missed.

East Riddlesden Hall - Keighley
17th century manor house with fishponds & historic barns, one of which is regarded as very fine example of mediaeval tithe barn.

Newby Hall - Ripon
17th century Wren style extended by Robert Adam. Gobelins tapestry, Chippendale furniture, sculpture galleries with Roman rotunda, statuary. Award-winning gardens.

Nostell Priory - Wakefield
18th century, Georgian mansion, Chippendale furniture, paintings.

Burton Constable Hall - Hull
16th century, Elizabethan, remodelled in Georgian period. Stained glass, Hepplewhite furniture, gardens by Capability Brown.

Ripley Castle - Harrogate
14th century, parts dating during 16th & 18th centuries. Priest hole, armour & weapons, beautiful ceilings.

The Treasurer's House - York
17th & 18th centuries, splendid interiors, furniture, pictures.

Harewood House - Leeds
18th century - Robert Adam design, Chippendale furniture, Italian & English paintings. Sevres & Chinese porcelain.

Benningbrough Hall - York
18th century. Highly decorative woodwork, oak staircase, friezes etc. Splendid hall.

Markenfield Hall - Ripon
14th to 16th century - fine Manor house surrounded by moat.

Heath Hall - Wakefield
18th century, palladian. Fine woodwork & plasterwork, rococo ceilings, excellent furniture, paintings & porcelain

Bishops House - Sheffield
16th century. Only complete timber framed yeoman farmhouse surviving. Vernacular architecture. Superb

Skipton Castle - Skipton
One of the most complete & well preserved mediaeval castles in England.

Cathedral & Churches

York Minster
13th century. Greatest Gothic Cathedral north of the Alps. Imposing grandeur - superb Chapter house, contains half of the mediaeval stained glass of England. Outstandingly beautiful.

York (All Saints, North Street)
15th century roofing in parts - 18th century pulpit wonderful mediaeval glass.

Ripon Cathedral
12th century - though in some parts Saxon in origin. Decorated choir stalls - gables buttresses. Church of 672 preserved in crypt, , Caxton Book, ecclesiastic treasures.

Bolton Percy (All Saints)
15th century. Maintains original glass in east window. Jacobean font cover. Georgian pulpit. Interesting monuments.

Rievaulx Abbey
12th century, masterpiece of Early English architecture. One of three great Cistercian Abbeys built in Yorkshire. Impressive ruins.

Campsall (St. Mary Magdalene)
Fine Norman tower - 15th century rood screen, carved & painted stone altar.

Fountains Abbey - Ripon
Ruins of England's greatest mediaeval abbey - surrounded by wonderful landscaped gardens. Enormous tower, vaulted cellar 300 feet long.

Whitby (St. Mary)
12th century tower & doorway, 18th century remodelling - box pews much interior woodwork painted - galleries. High pulpit. Table tombs.

Yorkshire

Whitby Abbey - Whitby (St. Hilda)
7th century superb ruin - venue of Synod of 664. Destroyed by Vikings, restored 1078 - magnificent north trancept.
Halifax (St. John the Baptist)
12th century origins, showing work from each succeeding century - heraldic ceilings. Cromwell glass.
Beverley Minster - Beverley
14th century. Fine Gothic Minster - remarkable mediaeval effigies of musicians playing instruments. Founded as monastery in 700.
Bolton Priory - Nr. Skipton
Nave of Augustinian Priory, now Bolton's Parish Church, amidst ruins of choir & transepts, in beautiful riverside setting.
Selby Abbey - Selby
11th century Benedictine abbey of which the huge church remains. Roof & furnishings are modern after a fire of 1906, but the stonework is intact.

Museums & Galleries

Aldborough Roman Museum - Boroughbridge
Remnants of Roman period of the town - coins, glass, pottery, etc.
Great Ayton
Home of Captain Cook, explorer & seaman. Exhibits of maps, etc.
Art Gallery - City of York
Modern paintings, Old Masters, watercolours, prints, ceramics.
Lotherton Hall - Nr. Leeds
Museum with furniture, paintings, silver, works of art from the Leeds collection & oriental art gallery.
National Railway Museum - York
Devoted to railway engineering & its development.
York Castle Museum
The Kirk Collection of bygones including cobbled streets, shops, costumes, toys, household & farm equipment - fascinating collection.
Cannon Hall Art Gallery - Barnsley
18th century house with fine furniture & glass, etc. Flemish & Dutch paintings. Also houses museum of the 13/18 Royal Hussars.
Mappin Art Gallery - Sheffield
Works from 18th,19th & 20th century.

Graves Art gallery-Sheffield.
British portraiture. European works, & examples of Asian & African art. Loan exhibitions are held there.
Royal Pump Room Museum - Harrogate
Original sulphur well used in the Victorian Spa. Local history costume & pottery.
Bolling Hall - Bradford
A period house with mixture of styles - collections of 17th century oak furniture, domestic utensils, toys & bygones.
Georgian Theatre - Richmond
Oldest theatre in the country - interesting theatrical memorabilia.
Jorvik Viking Centre - York
Recently excavated site in the centre of York showing hundreds of artifacts dating from the Viking period. One of the most important archaeological discoveries this century.
Abbey House Museum - Kirkstall, Leeds
Illustrated past 300 years of Yorkshire life. Shows 3 full streets from 19th century with houses, shops & workplaces.
Piece Hall - Halifax
Remarkable building - constructed around huge quadrangle - now Textile Industrial Museum, Art Gallery & has craft & antique shops.
National Museum of Photography, Film & Television - Bradford
Displays look at art & science of photography, film & T.V. Britain's only IMAX arena.
The Colour Museum - Bradford
Award-winning interactive museum,which allows visitors to explore the world of colour & discover the story of dyeing & textile printing.
Calderdale Industrial Museum - Halifax
Social & industrial Museum of the year 1987
Shibden Hall & Folk Museum of Halifax
Half-timbered house with folk museum, farmland, miniature train & boating lake.
Leeds City Art Gallery & Henry Moore Sculpture Gallery
Yorkshire Sculpture Park - Wakefield
Yorkshire Museum of Farming - Murton
Award-winning museum of farming & the countryside.

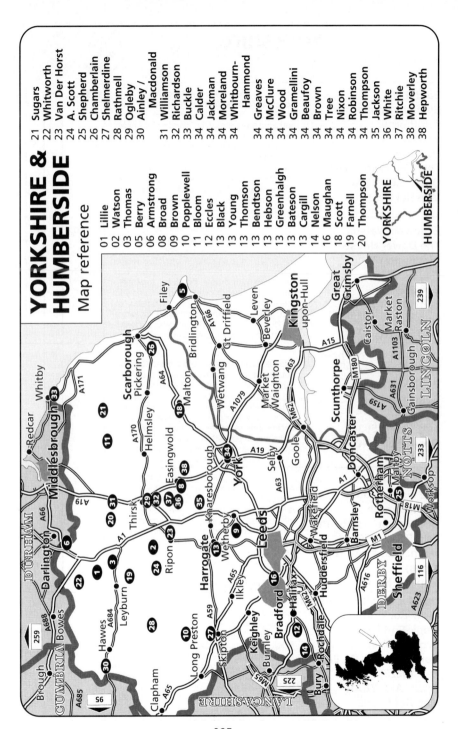

YORKSHIRE & HUMBERSIDE
Map reference

01 Lillie
02 Watson
03 Thomas
05 Berry
06 Armstrong
08 Broad
09 Brown
10 Popplewell
11 Bloom
12 Eccles
13 Black
13 Young
13 Thomson
13 Bendtson
13 Hebson
13 Greenhalgh
13 Bateson
13 Cargill
14 Nelson
16 Maughan
18 Scott
19 Farnell
20 Thompson
21 Sugars
22 Whitworth
23 Van Der Horst
24 A. Scott
25 Shepherd
26 Chamberlain
27 Shelmerdine
28 Rathmell
29 Ogleby
30 Ainley / Macdonald
31 Williamson
32 Richardson
33 Buckle
34 Calder
34 Jackman
34 Moreland
34 Whitbourn-Hammond
34 Greaves
34 McClure
34 Wood
34 Gramellini
34 Beaufoy
34 Brown
34 Tree
34 Nixon
34 Robinson
34 Thompson
35 Jackson
36 White
37 Ritchie
38 Moverley
38 Hepworth

Yorkshire

		minimum £ per person	children taken	evening meals	animals taken
Edith Lillie **Elmfield House** Arrathorne Bedale DL8 1NE Tel: (0677) 50558/50557 Open: ALL YEAR Map Ref No. 01	Nearest Road: A.1 Located in is own grounds in the country. Enjoy a relaxed, friendly atmosphere in spacious surroundings with a high standard of furnishings. Centrally heated with 9 en-suite bedrooms comprising twin bedded, double & family rooms. 2 rooms have been adapted for disabled guests another has a four-poster bed. All rooms have satellite colour T.V.,' phone, radio/alarm & tea/coffee makers. A games room & solarium are also available. Excellent farmhouse cooking. Residential licence.	£18.00	Y	Y	N
Elaine M. Watson **The Dower House** Kirklington Bedale DL8 2LX Tel: (0845) 567271 Open: JAN - NOV Map Ref No. 02	Nearest Road: A.1 The Dower house is a delightful Georgian house set in 2 acres of private gardens, overlooking the green, in a peaceful & attractive village. Offering a choice of 4 most comfortable bedrooms, all with private facilities. A beautiful private sitting room, dining room & laundry for guests' use. Hard tennis court in garden, superb golf nearby. An excellent base for exploring Ripon, York, the Yorkshire Dales & a wealth of historic houses, castles & abbeys.	£22.00	Y	N	N
David & Felicity Thomas **The Old Rectory** Patrick Brompton Bedale DL8 1JN Tel: (0677) 50343 Open: FEB - NOV Map Ref No. 03	Nearest Road: A.684 The Old Rectory is a Grade II listed Georgian house set in a charming village in beautiful North Yorkshire. Tastefully furnished in keeping with it's period. There are 3 spacious bedrooms each with private facilities, some overlooking a walled garden with lawns beyond. Excellent meals are prepared by Felicity & served in the well appointed dining room. Nearby are small market towns, great medieval abbeys, cathedral cities & spa towns.	£17.00	N	Y	Y
Lesley Berry **The Manor House** Flamborough Bridlington YO15 1PD Tel: (0262) 850943 Open: ALL YEAR (Excl. Xmas) Map Ref No. 05	Nearest Road: A.165, A.166 A manor of Flamborough is recorded in the Domesday Book. The current Georgian house is a handsomely proportioned family home offering spacious & comfortable accommodation in well appointed rooms. Historic Flamborough head is designated a Heritage Coast, with many interesting walks & nearby bird reserve. Ideally placed for exploration of North & East Yorkshire. Dinner, by prior arrangement, features local seafood when available.	£23.00	Y	Y	N
David & Heather Armstrong **Clow-Beck House** Monk-End Farm Croft-on-Tees Darlington GD21 8AA1 Tel: (0325) 721205 Open: ALL YEAR Map Ref No. 06	Nearest Road: A.1, A.167 A modern well appointed farmhouse, set in tranquil countryside offering attractive accommodation in 3 bedrooms with modern amenities & tea/coffee making facilities. All rooms are tastefully furnished, one has a tented ceiling & Laura Ashley decor. The elegant dining room features hand-crafted furniture. A charming home with hosts who extend hospitality in true Yorkshire style. Convenient for exploring 'Herriot Country', Durham, York & the East Coast.	£17.50	Y	N	N

Yorkshire

		minimum £ per person	children taken	evening meals	animals taken
Joan & Geoffrey Broad The Old Vicarage Market Place Easingwold YO6 3AL Tel: (0347) 21015 Open: APR-OCT Map Ref No. 08	Nearest Road: A.19 A listed property of immense character, built in the 18th century & thoughtfully brought up to modern standards, yet still retaining many delightful features. Now offering 7 en-suite rooms with T.V. & tea/coffee makers. Standing in extensive lawned gardens, overlooking the market square, with croquet lawn & walled rose garden, it is an ideal touring centre for York, the Dales, the Yorkshire Moors & 'Herriot' countryside.	£17.00	Y	Y	Y
John & Chris Brown High Hedges Whitegate East Keswick LS17 9HB Tel: (0937) 572142 Open: ALL YEAR Map Ref No. 09	Nearest Road: A.1, A.61 A warm welcome awaits all visitors to this comfortable ranch-style bungalow in a charming village convenient for all the Yorkshire beauty spots. Accommodation is in 1 double & 1 single room both with colour T.V. & tea/coffee making facilities. Hairdryers, laundry facilities & afternoon tea are available. Large, private garden. Chris, a Blue Badge tourist guide, plans itineraries & conducts tours on request. No smoking in the house, please.	£18.00	Y	Y	N
Mike & Jill Popplewell Greeenways Guest House Wharfeside Avenue Threshfield Grassington BA23 5BS Tel: (0756) 752598 Open: APR-OCT Map Ref No. 10	Nearest Road: B.6265 Greenways is situated half a mile off the main Skipton to Grassington road & is set overlooking the River Wharfe. The accent is on homely comfort throughout & Jill aims to produce meals prepared from local produce which are satisfying & attractive. Greenways is a good centre to explore from - Bronte Parsonage at Haworth, Fountains Abbey, York, Settle to Carlisle Railway & the lovely Yorkshire Dales are within easy access.	£19.50	Y	Y	Y
Dr. & Mrs M. Bloom Manor House Farm Ingleby Greenhow Great Ayton TS9 6RB Tel: (0642) 722384 Open: ALL YEAR (Exc.Xmas/New Year) Map Ref No. 11	Nearest Road: A.19 A charming old farm in idyllic surroundings at the foot of the Cleveland Hills in the North York Moors National Park. Set in park & woodland, this lovely house with beams & open fires has 3 delightful rooms with modern amenities. A pretty lounge with T.V. for guests & also a garden. Very friendly, personal service. Hosts are proud of their reputation for fine cooking. Wine & dine by candlelight. Horse riding & golf locally, plus stabling if you can bring your own mount.	£19.50	Y	Y	Y
Valerie Eccles Wood End (off Lighthazels Road) Soyland, Sowerby Bridge Halifax HX6 4NP Tel: (0422) 824397 Open: ALL YEAR Map Ref No. 12	Nearest Road: A.58, M.62 A 17th century converted weaver's cottage with beamed ceiling offering comfortable accommodation, excellent cuisine, a friendly, relaxed atmosphere in a peaceful, secluded setting with superb views over the beautiful Ryburn Valley. Located on the edge of a conservation village, it is 7 miles from the M.62 midway between Leeds & Manchester. Ideal for walking or touring with Bronte Country & the Yorkshire Dales within easy reach.	£15.00	Y	Y	Y

Yorkshire

			minimum £ per person	children taken	evening meals	animals taken
Peter Bateson **Acacia Lodge** **21 Ripon Road** **Harrogate** Tel: (0423) 560752 Open: ALL YEAR (Excl. Xmas/New Year) Map Ref No. 13		Nearest Road: A.61 Acacia Lodge offers six luxurious, en-suite rooms in a warm, beautifully furnished Victorian house in a select area with pretty gardens and ample private parking. The breakfasts are 'award winning' and the personal attentions of the owner and his wife - Peter and Dee - contribute to a homely atmosphere. The town centre, with its varied attractions, is two minutes away.	£21.00	Y	N	N
John & Roberta Black **Alexa House & Stable Cottages** **26 Ripon Road** **Harrogate HG1 2JJ** Tel: (0423) 501988 Open: ALL YEAR Map Ref No. 13		Nearest Road: A.61 Built in 1830 for Baron de Ferrier & now a warm & welcoming small hotel. Offering 13 comfortable & charming en-suite bedrooms each with 'phone, colour T.V., clock/radio alarms & tea/coffee makers There is a happy family atmosphere, nurtured by staff who 'belong' & guests who regularly return. The breakfasts are superb. Harrogate's many restaurants are only a stroll away so you may leave your car in Alexa's car park.	£23.00	Y	N	N
Mrs Gill Bendtson **Ashwood House** **7 Spring Grove** **Harrogate HG1 2HS** Tel: (0423) 560081 Open: ALL YEAR (Excl. Xmas & New Year) Map Ref No. 13		Nearest Road: A.61 An elegant 10 bedroomed Edwardian house, situated in a quiet residential cul-de-sac, minutes from the town centre. Charmingly decorated, it offers attractive bedrooms, some with 4-poster beds & en-suite bathrooms. All with tea/coffee making facilities, hair dryers, radio & colour T.V. A high standard of service, a warm welcome & an ample & delicious breakfast is assured.	£20.00	Y	N	N
Mrs E. J. Young **Daryl House** **42 Dragon Parade** **Harrogate HG1 5DA** Tel: (0423) 502775 Open: ALL YEAR (excl. Xmas & New Year) Map Ref No. 13		Nearest Road: A.59 A small, friendly, family-run house offering excellent accommodation in 6 most pleasant rooms with every modern comfort. Tea/coffee makers & T.V. in all rooms. An attractive lounge with colour T.V. & garden for guests' enjoyment. Home-cooked food & personal attention are the hallmarks of Daryl House. Close to the town centre with its conference facilities. A very warm welcome awaits all visitors.	£13.00	Y	Y	N
Mrs Davina Webb **Glenayr** **19 Franklin Mount** **Harrogate HG1 5EJ** Tel: (0423) 504259 Open: ALL YEAR Map Ref No. 13		Nearest Road: A.61, A.59, Set in a peaceful tree-lined avenue, Glenayr is the comfortable Victorian home of Davina Webb who treats each guest as an invited friend. All enjoy a warm welcome & genuine hospitality. Harrogate's elegant town centre, its famous Stray & Valley Gardens, the Georgian Pump Rooms & Victorian Turkish Baths are only a leisurely 5 minute stroll away.	£17.50	Y	Y	N

Yorkshire

		minimum £ per person	children taken	evening meals	animals taken
Peter & Marion Thomson **Knox Mill House** **Knox Mill Lane** **Harrogate HG3 2AE** Tel: (0423) 560650 Open: ALL YEAR (Excl. Xmas & New Year) Map Ref No. 13	Nearest Road: A.61 Built in 1785, this lovely old millhouse stands on the banks of a stream in a quiet rural setting, yet only one & a half miles from the centre of Harrogate. Beautifully renovated, it still retains all its original features: oak beams, inglenook fireplace & stone arches. There are 3 delightful rooms attractively & comfortably furnished, 2 en-suite, each with tea/coffee makers, & views over the stream & fields. A delightful lounge with colour T.V. & garden for guests' enjoyment.	£15.00	Y	N	N
Mr G. W. Cargill **Stoney Lea Guest House** **13 Spring Grove** **Springfield Avenue** **Harrogate HG1 2HS** Tel: (0423) 501524 Open: ALL YEAR(Excl. Xmas/New Year) Map Ref No. 13	Nearest Road: A.61, A.1 An interesting house of mellow stone with part Tudor gabling. Situated in a quiet area, offering 7 excellent rooms, all with en-suite facilities & tea/coffee makers, radio & colour T.V. Only 2 minutes from the centre of the city & the conference centre. It is a perfect base for visiting the historic buildings, Roman baths & superb countryside with its wealth of historic houses. Food excellent value.	£19.00	Y	N	N
Robert & Bryony Hebson **The Ruskin Hotel &** **Gallery Restaurant** **1 Swan Road** **Harrogate HG1 2SS** Tel: (0423) 502045 Open: ALL YEAR Map Ref No. 13	Nearest Road: A.1, A.61 Small Victorian hotel with luxury accommodation, pretty antique-furnished, en-suite bedrooms with T.V., tea/coffee making facilities. Sumptuous bar/lounge, gourmet restaurant themed to a gallery of pre-Raphaelite paintings. Situated in a conservation area of Harrogate. Near the Conference & Exhibition Centre, close to theatres, Valley Gardens, shops. An ideal base for excursions to the dales & stately homes of Yorkshire.	£30.00	Y	Y	Y
Susan Greenhalgh **The Rosedale** **86 Kings Road** **Harrogate** **HG1 5JX** Tel: (0423) 566230 Open: ALL YEAR Map Ref No. 13	Nearest Road: A.1, The Rosedale is a pleasant Victorian villa which has been recently refurbished in keeping with the period. Panelled staircase & open fireplaces create a warm & cosy atmosphere. Accommodation in 8 comfortable bedrooms, 7 en-suite, each with colour T.V. & tea/coffee makers, hairdryer & complimentary toiletries. A guests' lounge & bar are also available. A very comfortable base for touring Yorkshire. Children over 5 years.	£22.50	Y	Y	N
Gail Ainley & **Ann Macdonald** **Brandymires** **Muker Road** **Hawes DL8 3PR** Tel: (0969) 667482 Open: EASTER- OCT Map Ref No. 30	Nearest Road: A.684 A warm welcome awaits you in this comfortable mid-19th century stone house in a tranquil rural setting. Every room has a splendid view over the fells. 4 spacious double bedrooms, 2 with 4-poster beds, full central heating. Good home cooking is an important feature & dinner is available with prior notice except on Thursdays. Brandymires is an ideal centre for exploring the glorious countryside of the Yorkshire Dales & historic towns. No T.V. Ample parking	£15.50	N	Y	Y

Yorkshire

			minimum £ per person	children taken	evening meals	animals taken
Mrs N. W. Nelson 'Springfield' Cragg Road Cragg Vale Hebden Bridge HX7 5SR Tel: (0422) 882029 Open: ALL YEAR Map Ref No. 14	Nearest Road: A.646 A warm Yorkshire welcome awaits visitors at Springfield. Standing in an acre of garden in a picturesque wooded valley in the South Pennines with open views of woods & moorland. Guests may choose from 4 comfortably furnished, centrally heated rooms with adjacent bath/shower, 1 with en-suite facilities. All rooms have modern amenities including T.V., radio & tea/coffee makers. Sauna available. Mrs Nelson's breakfasts have won a "Best Yorkshire Breakfast Award".		£15.00	Y	N	N
Marjorie & Douglas Maughan Lynnwood House 18 Alexandra Road Uppermoor, Pudsey Leeds LS28 8BY Tel: (0532) 571117 Open: ALL YEAR Map Ref No. 16	Nearest Road: A.467 This comfortable centrally heated home has a friendly atmosphere. Only 15 minutes from Leeds/Bradford Airport & the city centre, with rail station & buses nearby. Good shopping & theatre as well as stately homes, castles & the industrial heritage of Northern England. Cricket club, leisure centre & good park within easy reach. Visitors welcome at local golf club. Marjorie is a creative cook & welcomes vegetarians.		£30.00	Y	Y	N
Richard & Stella Scott Red House Wharram-le-Street Malton YO17 9TL Tel: (09446) 455 Open: ALL YEAR Map Ref No. 18	Nearest Road: A.64 Stella & Richard warmly welcome everyone to their elegant 19th century home. Standing in an acre of garden in the heart of the Yorkshire Wolds, it offers 4 very comfortable bedrooms with private facilities, T.V. & tea/coffee makers & guests' lounge with lovely log fires. Good home cooking using their own produce. Special diets catered for. Licenced dining rooms. Nearby are Castle Howard, Sledmere House, Nunnington Hall. York 23 miles. Grass tennis facility.		£22.00	Y	Y	Y
Mrs Olivia Farnell The Old Rectory Thornton Watlass Masham HG4 4AH Tel: (0677) 423456 Open: JAN - DEC Map Ref No. 19	Nearest Road: A.1 Delightful listed Georgian Rectory in peaceful Wensleydale village with cricket on the Green in the very heart of Herriot country. Elegant and welcoming home offering luxury accommodation in 3 double en-suite or private rooms. Beautiful sitting room with colour T.V. In winter, log fires and crumpets for tea! Lovely garden. Excellent inns and restaurants nearby. Central for Dales/Moors, but if wet, York or Harrogate not too far. Children over 14 please.		£20.00	Y	N	N
Peter & Shirley Thompson Porch House 68 High Street Northallerton DL7 8EG Tel: (0609) 779831 Open: ALL YEAR Map Ref No. 20	Nearest Road: A.1, A.19 A charming family house in the centre of this busy & picturesque market town. Built in 1584, the house has many historical connections - Charles I stayed here when in the region. Offering 5 bedrooms with excellent facilities, the present owners have continued the tradition of making improvements yet have retained many of the original features. Dinner by arrangement. Ample parking. York, Durham & Newcastle within 1 hour's drive.		£21.00	Y	Y	Y

Yorkshire

		minimum £ per person	children taken	evening meals	animals taken
Mrs L. Sugars 'Sevenford House' Thorgill Rosedale Abbey Pickering YO18 8SE Tel: (07515) 283 Open: ALL YEAR Map Ref No. 21	Nearest Road: A.170 Originally a vicarage & built from the stones of Rosedale Abbey. 'Sevenford House' stands in 4 acres in the heart of the beautiful Yorkshire Moors National Park. 3 well decorated, comfortable rooms with modern amenities & lovely views. There is a garden for guests' use. This beautiful country house is an excellent base for exploring the region. Riding & golf locally. Ryedale Folk Museum, ruined abbeys, Roman roads, steam railways, the beautiful coastline & pretty fishing towns.	£15.00	Y	N	N
Ian & Angela Whitworth The White House Arkle Town Arkengarthdale Richmond DL11 6RB Tel: (0748) 84203 Open: JAN - NOV Map Ref No. 22	Nearest Road: A.66 18th century former farmhouse, modernised, tastefully decorated and furnished to a high standard. Three rooms offer modern amenities (one en-suite). Cosy visitors' lounge with open fire. Only the best ingredients used in tasty home cooked meals. In the heart of Herriot country, and set above the road with superb uninterrupted views, the ideal centre for exploring the Yorkshire Dales. Children over 10 please.	£14.00	Y	Y	N
Phillip Gill & Anton Van Der Horst Bank Villa Masham Ripon HG4 4DB Tel: (0765) 689605 Open: APR - OCT Map Ref No. 23	Nearest Road: A.6108 A fine Georgian house overlooking the River Ure in large terraced gardens, offering delightful accommodation in 7 comfortable double rooms with modern amenities. It is a super base for visiting the Druids Temple, Jervaulx Abbey, Middleham Castle, Fountains Abbey & the wonderful 'James Herriot Country'. Dutch is spoken. Meals are excellent value. Children under 5 not accommodated.	£16.00	Y	Y	Y
Avril Scott Pasture House Healey Masham Ripon HG4 4LJ Tel: (0765) 689149 Open: ALL YEAR Map Ref No. 24	Nearest Road: A.6108 Pasture House is a large, comfortable house providing guests with pleasant accommodation in the quiet of the lovely Yorkshire Dales. A perfect centre for walkers & horse racing enthusiasts with several courses & Middleham training gallops nearby. 4 comfortable rooms with T.V. & tea/coffee makers, a residents' lounge & large garden are also available. Pony trekking, golf & fishing locally. Children & pets welcome. Facilities for babies.	£11.00	Y	Y	Y
Mr & Mrs M. Shepherd Stonecroft Hotel Main Street Bramley Rotherham S66 0SF Tel: (0709) 540922 Open: ALL YEAR Map Ref No. 25	Nearest Road: M.18 ex. 1 Stonecroft is a grade II listed building with a homely atmosphere. The main building is 300 years old with a profusion of oak beams & open fireplaces. Accommodation is in 9 tastefully furnished rooms, 7 with private bathroom, all with modern amenities including colour T.V., radio & tea/coffee making facilities. Residents' lounge & delightful garden available for guests to relax in. Ideally situated for visiting the many attractions in Yorkshire. & Derbyshire.	£18.00	Y	N	Y

Yorkshire

			minimum £ per person	children taken	evening meals	animals taken
Mrs Sally Chamberlain Church Farmhouse 3 Main Street East Ayton Scarborough YO13 9HL Tel: (0723) 862102 Open: JAN - DEC Map Ref No. 26	Nearest Road: A.170 Listed 18th century farmhouse, now a charming, cosy village hotel retaining many original features. A warm welcome, personal service and good home cooking come naturally here. 3 attractive en-suite rooms plus 1 single with private bathroom; all with radio, T.V., tea/coffee facilities. (No smoking in bedrooms) Children welcome. Large games room. Residential licence. National Park village at entrance to beautiful Forge Valley & North Yorks Moors.		£21.00	Y	Y	Y
Mr & Mrs R.T. Shelmerdine Eshton Grange Gargrave Skipton BD23 3QE Tel: (0756) 749383 Open: ALL YEAR Map Ref No. 27	Nearest Road: A.65 Farmhouse bed & breakfast is found at this attractive, 18th century listed house, situated on a 20 acre working stock farm & Shetland pony stud. Located in the Yorkshire Dales National Park, it is close to many beauty spots with walking, potholing & pony trekking nearby. It offers 4 bedrooms all with private facilities, 2 en-suite, all with T.V. & tea/coffee making facilities. A sitting room with open fire in winter. A lovely walled garden with beautiful views. Evening meals by prior arrangement only.		£18.00	Y	Y	N
Tim & Marie Rathmell Hilltop Country Guest House Starbotton Skipton BD23 5HY Tel: (075676) 321 Open: MAR-NOV Map Ref No. 28	Nearest Road: A.59 Hilltop Country Guest House is a 17th century listed house in 4 acres of beckside gardens overlooking an unspoilt village in the heart of the Yorkshire Dales. Excellent centre for fell & riverside walks or for touring. Spacious & immaculate bedrooms, all en-suite. Fine food & wine served in oak beamed dining room. This delightful house offers the warmth & hospitality of a house party.		£25.00	Y	Y	N
Mrs E. Ogleby St. James House 36 St. James Green Thirsk YO7 1AQ Tel: (0845) 522676/ 524120 Open: APR - OCT Map Ref No. 29	Nearest Road: A.19, A.1 St. James House is a delightful 18th century building standing on the green & only 2 minutes' walk from the market place. Beautifully furnished with antiques throughout. Mrs Ogleby offers 4 lovely rooms with modern amenities & tea/coffee makers, 2 with private facilities. A comfortable lounge with colour T.V. for guests. No smoking in the house. This is James Herriot's town. Children over 10 only.		£16.00	Y	N	N
Mrs Tess Williamson Thornborough House Farm South Kilvington Thirsk YO7 2NP Tel: (0845) 522103 Open: ALL YEAR Map Ref No. 31	Nearest Road: A.19 A warm welcome awaits you at this 200 year old farmhouse, set in lovely countryside. Only one & a half miles north of Thirsk, this working farm is situated in the town made famous by James Herriot. 3 warm & comfortable rooms, 1 en-suite, all with tea/coffee making facilities. Guests have their own sitting/dining room with colour T.V. & open fire. Good home cooking a speciality. Conveniently located for York, Ripon, Pennine Dales & East Coast.		£12.00	Y	Y	Y

Yorkshire

			minimum £ per person	children taken	evening meals	animals taken
Mrs Pat Richardson Eldmire Hill Farm Dalton Thirsk YO7 3JH Tel: (0845) 577252 Open: Open: APR - OCT Map Ref No. 32		Nearest Road: A.1, A.19 A traditional, comfortable farmhouse set in open countryside with magnificent views over the Vale of York, Hambleton Hills & Pennines. Accommodation is in 1 double & 1 twin bedroom each with tea/coffee making facilities. A colour T.V. lounge is also available. Guests may use the large garden with grass tennis court. York, Harrogate, Dales & Moors are only 30 mins. away. Thirsk, where James Herriot wrote his famous books is only 10 mins.	£13.00	Y	N	N
Ian & Rosalie Buckle Dunsley Hall Dunsley Whitby YO21 3TL Tel: (0947) 83437 Open: ALL YEAR Map Ref No. 33		Nearest Road: A.171 Peaceful & elegant Country Hall in 4 acres of secluded grounds, providing a truely relaxed atmosphere. Oak panelled rooms, including superb carved Billiard Room with stained glass window. 5 en-suite bedrooms with full facilities & central heating. Within North York Moors National Park, 3 miles outside Whitby (Captain Cook country) & ideal for Heritage Coast, Castle Howard & York. Offering indoor heated swimming pool, fitness room, tennis, putting or croquet.	£27.00 see PHOTO over	Y	Y	Y
Diana Calder The Dower House 143 Main Street Fulford York YO1 4PP Tel: (0904) 633508 Open: ALL YEAR Map Ref No. 34		Nearest Road: On A.19, A.64 This lovely converted Georgian farmhouse stands on the A.19 in the attractive village of Fulford, just 2 miles south of York city centre. Each of the 4 bedrooms has a private bathroom & tea/coffee making facilities. Whenever weather permits, breakfast is served in the pretty enclosed garden at the rear. A convenient bus service reaches the sights & museums of the fascinating city in 7 minutes.	£25.00	Y	N	Y
Keith Jackman Dairy Wholefood Guest House 3 Scarcroft Road York YO2 1ND Tel: (0904) 639367 Open: ALL YEAR Map Ref No. 34		Nearest Road: A.59, A.64 The Dairy is a tastefully renovated Victorian house within walking distance of the city centre & just 200 yards from the mediaeval city walls. Decorated & furnished in the styles of Habitat, Sanderson's & Laura Ashley, with the emphasis on pine & plants. 5 bedrooms with modern amenities, colour T.V., hot drink facilities & extensive information on York & Yorkshire. There is a lovely enclosed courtyard. Breakfast choices are from English to whole food vegetarian.	£14.00	Y	N	N
Bob & Marilyn Moreland Annjoa House 34 /36 Millfield Road Scarcroft Road York YO2 1NQ Tel: (0904) 653731 Open: ALL YEAR Map Ref No. 34		Nearest Road: A.64 Small family-run licensed hotel, quietly located close to railway station. Offering guests a choice of 12 rooms, 4 en-suite, all with modern amenities, tea/coffee & some with T.V. There's a residents' colour T.V. lounge & a comfortable bar to relax in. Conveniently located for city centre & race course, making this a good base from which to explore the historic city of York with its fine Minster & many interesting museums & ancient Roman & Viking sites.	£12.50	Y	Y	Y

Dunsley Hall. Whitby.

Yorkshire

		minimum £ per person	children taken	evening meals	animals taken
Russell & Cherry Whitbourn-Hammond **Nunmill House** 85 Bishopthorpe Road York YO2 1NX Tel: (0904) 634047 Open: FEB - DEC Map Ref No. 34	Nearest Road: A.64, A.59 A warm friendly welcome awaits you at Nunmill House, a delightful late Victorian house, tastefully restored throughout with Laura Ashley furnishings to enhance the original architectural features. Offering a choice of 9 delightful bedrooms some with ensuite facilities. Ideally situated just outside the mediaeval walls & a 10 minute walk to all the historic attractions of the city. Complimentary tea & coffee are available & diets can be catered for by arrangement.	£15.00	Y	N	N
Liz & Malcolm Greaves **Carlton House Hotel** 134 The Mount York YO2 2AS Tel: (0904) 622265 Open: ALL YEAR(Excl. Xmas/New Year) Map Ref No. 34	Nearest Road: A.1036, A.64 Each & every guest will receive a warm & friendly welcome from proprietors Liz & Malcolm Greaves. This pleasant family run hotel offers guests a choice of 15 rooms, all with colour T.V., radio. & tea/coffee makers. Some have private facilities. The spacious lounges are comfortable & pleasantly furnished. A traditional English breakfast cooked to order. Light refreshments are available at most times throughout the day. Nearby are York race course & the Minster.	£17.50	Y	N	N
Robin & Anne McClure **4 South Parade** York YO2 2BA Tel: (0904) 628229 Open: JAN - DEC Map Ref No. 34	Nearest Road: A.1036, A.64 An elegant Grade II listed Georgian townhouse in private cobbled street. Beautifully decorated and furnished with antiques. Three lovely guest rooms each with its own individual character, en-suite facilities in Edwardian style, original fireplaces with working cast iron hob grates, fresh flowers, bowls of fruit, Teletext remote control T.V., and direct dial telephones. Be pampered with old fashioned hospitality, service and delicious food.	£28.50	N	Y	N
Richard & Wendy Wood **Curzon Lodge & Stable Cottages** 23 Tadcaster Road Dringhouses York YO2 2QG Tel: (0904) 703157 Open: ALL YEAR Map Ref No. 34	Nearest Road: A.64, A.1036 A charming 17th century Grade II listed house & delightful coach house conversion with original oak beams. Formerly a home of the Terry family, the renowned York chocolate makers, guests are now invited to share the unique atmosphere, in 10 imaginatively furnished rooms. All have en-suite, colour T.V., radio & tea/coffee facilities. Some 4-posters & period brass beds. Many antiques, pretty lounge & "farmhouse kitchen" breakfast room. Large enclosed car park. Perfect for historic York.	£22.00	Y	N	N
C. & R Gramellini **Holmwood House Hotel** 114 Holgate Road York YO2 4BB Tel: (0904) 626183 Open: ALL YEAR Map Ref No. 34	Nearest Road: A.59 Holmwood House is an elegant hotel, converted from 2 listed early Victorian town houses, only 10 minutes from the city walls & the railway station. It has recently undergone considerable redecoration & refurbishment to combine traditional elegance with the comfort of every modern facility in 10 attractive en-suite rooms. We aim to offer every guest our personal attention in a warm relaxing atmosphere.	£25.00 *see PHOTO over*	Y	Y	Y

375

Holmwood House Hotel.   York.

Yorkshire

			minimum £ per person	children taken	evening meals	animals taken
Mike & Ann Beaufoy **18 St. Paul's Square** **York YO2 4BD** Tel: (0904) 629884 Open: ALL YEAR(Excl. Xmas/New Year) Map Ref No. 34	Nearest Road: A.59 A delightful Victorian house located in a pleasant Victorian garden square in the centre of York. Skilfully restored & furnished with period antiques, it now offers 4 very comfortable en-suite bedrooms, a guests' colour T.V. lounge & garden. Mike & Ann enjoy sharing their home & knowledge of York with their guests & are happy to give advice on where to go & what to see locally.		£25.00	Y	N	N
Julie & Adrian Brown **Four Seasons Hotel** **7 St. Peters Grove** **Clifton** **York YO3 6AQ** Tel: (0904) 622621 Fax 0904 430565 Open: ALL YEAR Map Ref No. 34	Nearest Road: A.19 An elegant, detached Victorian residence with much character & appeal. Ideally situated in a peaceful cul-de-sac yet only 5 mins walk from York Minster & the cities many famous attractions. Offering pleasant, comfortable accommodation with modern facilities tastefully incorporated into the fine original surroundings. Full English breakfast. Residential licence. A warm & friendly welcome awaits you from Julie & Adrian. Private car park.		£17.00	Y	N	N
Joan Tree **Inglewood Guest House** **7 Clifton Green** **Clifton** **York YO3 6LH** Tel: (0904) 653523 Open: ALL YEAR Map Ref No. 34	Nearest Road: A.19 In this charming Victorian house guests will instantly feel completely at home. The friendliness & warmth of your host will ensure an enjoyable & relaxing stay. Accommodation is in 9 comfortable bedrooms, some with en-suite facilities, all with colour T.V. & modern amenities. The first class breakfast is served in the attractive dining room. An ideal base from which to visit the many attractions of York.		£16.00	Y	N	N
Jennifer Robinson **Grange Lodge** **52 Bootham Crescent** **Bootham** **York YO3 7AH** Tel: (0904) 621137 Open: JAN - DEC Map Ref No. 34	Nearest Road: A.19 The Grange Lodge guest house offers a warm & friendly welcome to every guest. Accommodation is in a choice of 7 comfortable bedrooms, 4 with en-suite facilities, colour T.V. & tea/coffee makers. A residents lounge available throughout the day. Conveniently located for all Yorks attractions. Only a 10 mins. stroll from York Minster.		£12.00	Y	Y	N
Mr Donald Nixon **The Abbingdon** **60 Bootham Cresent** **Bootham** **York YO3 7AH** Tel: (0904) 621761 Open: All YEAR Map Ref No. 34	Nearest Road: A.1237 to A.19 Friendly service & all the comforts expected of a small hotel will be found at The Abbingdon. Beautifully appointed throughout, the house offers a choice of 7 rooms, most with ensuite bathroom facilities. Remote control T.V., hair dryers & courtesy trays. A hearty English or Continental breakfast is served. Residents' lounge. Within easy walking distance of the Minster. If driving take the outer ring road onto the A.1237 onto the A.19.		£15.00	Y	N	N

Yorkshire

			minimum £ per person	children taken	evening meals	animals taken
Mrs Kathleen Jackson Townend Farm Great Ouseburn York YO5 9RG Tel: (0423) 330200 Open: FEB - NOV Map Ref No. 35	Nearest Road: A.1, A.59 A 300 year old farmhouse with open fires in an original inglenook fireplace, situated on an arable farm with livestock. Offering 3 well furnished & comfortable rooms with modern amenities, including tea/coffee making facilities. A lovely secluded garden available for guests to enjoy. Tasty breakfasts served using free-range eggs & freshly baked produce. Good evening meals available locally. Only a short drive from York, Castle Howard & Herriot Country.		£13.00	Y	N	Y
Mrs Yvonne Thompson Brentwood Cottage Main Street Shipton-by-Beningbrough York YO6 1AB Tel: (0904) 470111 Open: ALL YEAR Map Ref No. 34	Nearest Road: A.19 A warm & friendly welcome awaits all guests at Brentwood Cottage. Located 5 miles outside the historic city of York, it offers guests a choice of 4 pleasant bedrooms, all with private facilities, amenities & tea/coffee makers. There is also a residents' lounge & garden available. This makes a good base for touring York & surrounding countryside.		£12.50	Y	N	N
Sue White Brafferton Hall Brafferton, Helperby York YO6 2NZ Tel: (0423) 360352 Open: ALL YEAR Map Ref No. 36	Nearest Road: A.1 Brafferton Hall is a comfortable family home set in a quiet village near the River Swale in the heart of North Yorkshire, yet only 4 miles from the A.1. Ideally placed for exploring York, the National Parks & Herriot country, all within an easy 30 minute drive. Informality accompanied by excellent fare is to be enjoyed at Brafferton Hall.		£20.00	Y	Y	Y
Rachel Ritchie The Old Rectory Thornmanby Easingwold York YO6 3NN Tel: (0845) 401417 Open: ALL YEAR Map Ref No. 37	Nearest Road: A.19 Thormanby is a small village between Easingwood & Thirsk. The Old Rectory built in 1737 retains many of its original features & is furnished with antiques. 3 spacious bedrooms with modern amenities, 1 has a four-poster bed. Charming lounge with colour T.V. & open fire. Large mature garden available. Delightful inns & restaurants nearby. Situated in James Herriot country, convenient for visiting the Dales, Moors, York & historic abbeys & houses.		£13.00	Y	N	Y
Mrs Dorothy Moverley The Hermitage Crayke York YO6 4TB Tel: (0347) 21635 Open: JAN - NOV Map Ref No. 38	Nearest Road: A.19 Set in a large garden on the edge of the picturesque village of Crayke with panoramic views of the Howardian Hills. The Hermitage, an attractive farmhouse, offers accommodation in 3 comfortable & attractively furnished rooms, 1 en-suite. Guests may relax in the pleasant sitting room with colour T.V. & log fires in season. Delicious breakfasts served in the conservatory. A good base for York, the Moors & the Dales; with a warm & friendly host.		£15.00	Y	N	N

Yorkshire

	minimum £ per person	children taken	evening meals	animals taken
Peter & Belle Hepworth Halfway House Crayke York YO6 4TJ Tel: (0347) 22614 Fax 0347 22942 Open: ALL YEAR (Excl. Xmas) Map Ref No. 38 Nearest Road: A.19 Halfway House stands in an acre of mature garden with pleasant views across open farmland to the Dales. Accommodation is in a choice of 2 very comfortable, attractively furnished rooms. The converted granary offers a four-poster bedoom with private facilities, & a games room etc. The twin is located within the house itself & offers en-suite facilities. Each has radio, colour T.V. & tea/coffee makers. Delicious food is served in the oak panelled dining room where evening meals are sometimes provided. Guests may use the hard tennis court.	£28.00	N	N	N

All the establishments mentioned in this guide are members of

The Worldwide Bed & Breakfast Association

If you have any comments regarding your accommodation please send them to us using the form at the back of the guide. We value your comments

Scotland

Scotland

Scotland's culture & traditions, history & literature, languages & accents, its landscape & architecture, even its wildlife set it apart from the rest of Britain. Much of Scotland's history is concerned with the struggle to retain independence from England.

The Romans never conquered the Scottish tribes, but preferred to keep them at bay with Hadrian's Wall, stretching across the Border country from Tynemouth to the Solway Firth.

Time lends glamour to events, but from the massacre of Glencoe to the Highland Clearances, much of Scotland's fate has been a harsh one. Robert the Bruce did rout the English enemy at Bannockburn after scaling the heights of Edinburgh Castle to take the city, but in later years Mary, Queen of Scots was to spend much of her life imprisoned by her sister Elizabeth I of England. Bonnie Prince Charlie (Charles Edward Stuart) led the Jacobite rebellion which ended in defeat at Culloden.

These events are recorded in the folklore & songs of Scotland. The Border & Highland Gatherings & the Common Ridings are more than a chance to wear the Tartan, they are reminders of national pride.

Highland Games are held throughout the country where local & national champions compete in events like tossing the caber & in piping contests. There are sword dances & Highland flings, the speciality of young men & boys wearing the full dress tartan of their clan.

Scotland's landscape is rich in variety from the lush green lowlands to the handsome splendour of the mountainous Highlands, from the rounded hills of the Borders to the far-flung islands of the Hebrides, Orkney & Shetland where the sea is ever-present.

There are glens & beautiful lochs deep in the mountains, a spectacular coastline of high cliffs & white sandy beaches, expanses of purple heather moorland where the sparkling water in the burns runs brown with peat, & huge skies bright with cloud & gorgeous sunsets.

Argyll & The Islands

This area has ocean & sea lochs, forests & mountains, 3000 miles of coastline, about 30 inhabited islands, the warming influence of the Gulf Stream & the tallest tree in Britain (in Strone Gardens, near Loch Fyne).

Sites both historic & prehistoric are to be found in plenty. There is a hilltop fort at Dunadd, near Crinan with curious cup-&-ring carvings, & numerous ancient sites surround Kilmartin, from burial cairns to grave slabs.

Kilchurn Castle is a magnificent ruin in contrast to the opulence of Inveraray. Both are associated with the once-powerful Clan Campbell. There are remains of fortresses built by the Lords of the Isles, the proud chieftains who ruled the west after driving out the Norse invaders in the 12th century.

Oban is a small harbour town accessible by road & rail & the point of departure for many of the islands including Mull.

Tobermory. Isle of Mull.

Scotland

Mull is a peaceful island with rugged seascapes, lovely walks & villages, a miniature railway & the famous Mull Little Theatre. It is a short hop from here to the tiny island of Iona & St. Columba's Abbey, cradle of Christianity in Scotland.

Coll & Tiree have lovely beaches & fields of waving barley. The grain grown here was once supplied to the Lords of the Isles but today most goes to Islay & into the whisky. Tiree has superb windsurfing.

Jura is a wilder island famous for its red deer. The Isles of Colonsay & Oronsay are joined at low water.

Gigha, 'God's Isle', is a fertile area of gardens with rare & semitropical plants. The Island of Staffa has Fingal's Cave.

The Borders, Dumfries & Galloway

The borderland with England is a landscape of subtle colours & contours from the round foothills of the Cheviots, purple with heather, to the dark green valley of the Tweed.

The Lammermuir Hills sweep eastwards to a coastline of small harbours & the spectacular cliffs at St. Abbs Head where colonies of seabirds thrive.

The Border towns, set in fine countryside, have distinctive personalities. Hawick, Galashiels, Selkirk & Melrose all played their parts in the various Border skirmishes of this historically turbulent region & then prospered with a textile industry which survives today. They celebrate their traditions in the Common Riding ceremonies.

The years of destructive border warfare have left towers & castles throughout the country. Roxburgh was once a Royal castle & James II was killed here during a seige. Now there are only the shattered remains of the massive stone walls. Hermitage Castle is set amid wild scenery near Hawick & impressive Floors Castle stands above Kelso.

At Jedburgh the Augustine abbey is remarkably complete, & a visitors centre here tells the story of the four great Border Abbeys; Jedburgh itself, Kelso, Dryburgh & Melrose.

The lovely estate of Abbotsford where Sir Walter Scott lived & worked is near Melrose. A prolific poet & novelist, his most famous works are the Waverley novels written around 1800. His house holds many of his possessions, including a collection of armour. Scott's View is one of the best vantage points in the borderlands with a prospect of the silvery Tweed & the three distinctive summits of the Eildon Hills.

Eildon Hills.

There are many gracious stately homes. Manderston is a classical house of great luxury, & Mellerstain is the work of the Adam family. Traquair was originally a Royal hunting lodge. Its main gates were locked in 1745 after a visit from Bonnie Prince Charlie, never to be opened until a Stuart King takes the throne.

Dumfries & Galloway to the southwest is an area of rolling hills with a fine coastline.

Plants flourish in the mild air here & there are palm trees at Ardwell House & the Logan Botanic Garden.

Scotland

The gardens at Castle Kennedy have rhododendrons, azaleas & magnolias & Threave Gardens near Castle Douglas are the National Trust for Scotland's School of gardening.

The Galloway Forest Park covers a vast area of lochs & hills & has views across to offshore Ailsa Craig. At Caerlaveroch Castle, an early Renaissance building near the coast of Dumfries, there is a national nature reserve.

The first church in Scotland was built by St. Ninian at Whithorn in 400 on a site now occupied by the 13th century priory. The spread of Christianity is marked by early memorial stones like the Latinus stone at Whithorn, & the abbeys of Dundrennan, Crossraguel, Glenluce & Sweetheart, named after its founder who carried her husband's heart in a casket & is buried with it in the abbey.

At Dumfries is the poet Burns' house, his mausoleum & the Burns Heritage Centre overlooking the River Nith.

In Upper Nithsdale the Mennock Pass leads to Wanlockhead & Leadhills, once centres of the lead-mining industry. There is a fascinating museum here & the opportunity of an underground trip.

Lothian & Strathclyde

The Firth of Clyde & Glasgow in the west, & the Firth of Forth with Edinburgh in the east are both areas of rich history, tradition & culture.

Edinburgh is the capital of Scotland & amongst the most visually exciting cities in the world. The New Town is a treasure trove of inspired neo-classical architecture, & below Edinburgh Castle high on the Rock, is the Old Town, a network of courts, closes, wynds & gaunt tenements around the Royal Mile.

The Palace of Holyrood House, home of Mary, Queen of Scots for several years overlooks Holyrood Park & nearby Arthur's Seat, is a popular landmark.

The City's varied Art Galleries include The Royal Scottish Academy, The National Gallery, Portrait Gallery, Gallery of Modern Art & many other civic & private collections.

The Royal Museum of Scotland displays superb historical & scientific material. The Royal Botanic Gardens are world famous.

Cultural life in Edinburgh peaks at Festival time in August. The official Festival, the Fringe, the Book Festival, Jazz Festival & Film Festival bring together artistes of international reputation.

The gentle hills around the city

Inverary Castle.

offer many opportunities for walking. The Pentland Hills are easily reached, with the Lammermuir Hills a little further south. There are fine beaches at Gullane, Yellowcraigs, North Berwick & at Dunbar.

Tantallon Castle, a 14th century stronghold, stands on the rocky Firth of Forth, & 17th century Hopetoun House, on the outskirts of the city is only one of a number of great houses in the area.

North of Edinburgh across the Firth of Forth lies the ancient Kingdom

Scotland

of Fife. Here is St. Andrews, a pleasant town on the seafront, an old university town & Scotland's ecclesiastical capital, but famous primarily for golf.

Glasgow is the industrial & business capital of Scotland. John Betjeman called it the 'finest Victorian city in Britain' & many buildings are remarkable examples of Victorian splendour, notably the City Chambers.

Many buildings are associated with the architect Charles Rennie MacKintosh; the Glasgow School of Art is one of them. Glasgow Cathedral is a perfect example of pre-Reformation Gothic architecture.

Glasgow is Scotland's largest city with the greatest number of parks & fine Botanic Garden. It is home to both the Scottish Opera & the Scottish Ballet, & has a strong & diverse cultural tradition from theatre to jazz. Its museums include the matchless Burrell Collection, & the Kelvingrove Museum & Art Gallery, which houses one of the best civic collections of paintings in Britain, as well as reflecting the city's engineering & shipbuilding heritage.

The coastal waters of the Clyde are world famous for cruising & sailing, with many harbours & marinas. The long coastline offers many opportunities for sea-angling from Largs to Troon & Prestwick, & right around to Luce Bay on the Solway.

There are many places for bird-watching on the Estuary, whilst the Clyde Valley is famous for its garden centres & nurseries.

Paisley has a mediaeval abbey, an observatory & a museum with a fine display of the famous 'Paisley' pattern shawls.

Further south, Ayr is a large seaside resort with sandy beach, safe bathing & a racecourse. In the Ayrshire valleys there is traditional weaving & lace & bonnet making, & Sorn, in the rolling countryside boasts its 'Best Kept Village' award.

Culzean Castle is one of the finest Adam houses in Scotland & stands in spacious grounds on the Ayrshire cliffs.

Robert Burns is Scotland's best loved poet, & 'Burns night is widely celebrated. The region of Strathclyde shares with Dumfries & Galloway the title of 'Burns Country' . The son of a peasant farmer, Burns lived in poverty for much of his life. The simple house where he was born is in the village of Alloway. In the town of Ayr is the Auld Kirk where he was baptised & the footbridge of 'The Brigs of Ayr' is still in use. The Tam O'Shanter Inn is now a Burns museum & retains its thatched roof & simple fittings. The Burns Trail leads on to Mauchline where Possie Nansie's Inn remains. At Tarbolton the National Trust now care for the old house where Burns founded the 'Batchelors Club' debating society.

Perthshire, Loch Lomond & The Trossachs

By a happy accident of geology, the Highland Boundary fault which separates the Highlands from the Lowlands runs through Loch Lomond, close to the Trossachs & on through Perthshire, giving rise to marvellous scenery.

In former times Highlanders & Lowlanders raided & fought here. Great castles like Stirling, Huntingtower & Doune were built to protect the routes between the two different cultures.

Stirling was once the seat of Scotland's monarchs & the great Royal castle is set high on a basalt rock. The Guildhall & the Kirk of the Holy Rude are also interesting buildings in the town, with Cambuskenneth Abbey & the Bannockburn Heritage Centre close by.

Perth 'fair city' on the River Tay,

Scotland

has excellent shops & its own repertory theatre. Close by are the Black Watch Museum at Balhousie Castle, & the Branklyn Gardens, which are superb in May & June.

Scone Palace, to the north of Perth was home to the Stone or Scone of Destiny for nearly 500 years until its removal to Westminster. 40 kings of Scotland were crowned here.

Pitlochry sits amid beautiful Highland scenery with forest & hill walks, two nearby distilleries, the famous Festival theatre, Loch Faskally & the Dam Visitor Centre & Fish Ladder.

In the Pass of Killiecrankie, a short drive away, a simple stone marks the spot where the Highlanders charged barefoot to overwhelm the redcoat soldiers of General MacKay.

Queens View.

Famous Queen's View overlooks Loch Tummel beyond Pitlochry with the graceful peak of Schiehallion completing a perfect picture.

Other lochs are picturesque too; Loch Earn, Loch Katrine & bonnie Loch Lomond itself, & they can be enjoyed from a boat on the water. Ospreys nest at the Loch of the Lowes near Dunkeld.

Mountain trails lead through Ben Lawers & the 'Arrocher Alps' beyond Loch Lomond. The Ochils & the Campsie Fells have grassy slopes for walking. Near Callander are the Bracklinn Falls, the Callander Crags & the Falls of Leny.

Wooded areas include the Queen Elizabeth Forest Park & the Black Wood of Rannoch which is a fragment of an ancient Caledonian forest. There are some very tall old trees around Killiecrankie, & the world's tallest beech hedge - 26 metres high - grows at Meikleour near Blairgowrie.

Creiff & Blairgowrie have excellent golf courses set in magnificent scenery.

The Grampians

This is spacious countryside with glacier-scarred mountains & deep glens cut through by tumbling rivers. The Grampian Highlands make for fine mountaineering & walking.

There is excellent skiing at Glenshee, & a centre at the Lecht for the less experienced, whilst the broad tops of the giant mountains are ideal for cross-country skiing. The chair-lift at Glenshee is worth a visit at any season.

The Dee, The Spey & The Don flow down to the coastal plain from the heights. Some of the world's finest trout & salmon beats are on these rivers.

Speyside is dotted with famous distilleries from Grantown-on-Spey to Aberdeen, & the unique Malt Whisky Trail can be followed.

Royal Deeside & Donside hold a number of notable castles. Balmoral is the present Royal family's holiday home, & Kildrummy is a romantic ruin in a lovely garden. Fyvie Castle has five dramatic towers & stands in peaceful parkland. nearby Haddo House, by contrast, is an elegant Georgian home.

There is a 17th century castle at Braemar, but more famous here is the Royal Highland Gathering. There are wonderful walks in the vicinity - Morrone Hill, Glen Quoich & the Linn O'Dee are just a few.

The city of Aberdeen is famed for its sparkling granite buildings, its uni-

Scotland

versity, its harbour & fish market & for North Sea Oil. It also has long sandy beaches & lovely year-round flower displays, of roses in particular.

Around the coast are fishing towns & villages. Crovie & Pennan sit below impressive cliffs. Buckie is a typical small port along the picturesque coastline of the Moray Firth.

The Auld Kirk at Cullen has fine architectural features & elegant Elgin has beautiful cathedral ruins. Pluscarden Abbey, Spynie Palace & Duffus Castle are all nearby.

Nairn has a long stretch of sandy beach & a golf course with an international reputation. Inland are Cawdor Castle & Culloden Battlefield.

Dunnottar Castle.

The Highlands & Islands

The Northern Highlands are divided from the rest of Scotland by the dramatic valley of the Great Glen. From Fort William to Inverness sea lochs, canals & the depths of Loch Ness form a chain of waterways linking both coasts.

Here are some of the wildest & most beautiful landscapes in Britain. Far Western Knoydart, the Glens of Cannich & Affric, the mysterious lochs, including Loch Morar, deeper than the North Sea, & the marvellous coastline, all are exceptional.

The glens were once the home of crofting communities, & of the clansmen who supported the Jacobite cause. The wild scenery of Glencoe is a favourite with walkers & climbers, but it has a tragic history. Its name means 'the glen of weeping' & refers to the massacre of the MacDonald clan in 1692, when the Royal troops who had been received as guests treacherously attacked their hosts at dawn.

The valleys are empty today largely as a result of the infamous Highland Clearances in the 19th century when the landowners turned the tenant crofters off the land in order to introduce the more profitable Cheviot sheep. The emigration of many Scots to the U.S.A. & the British Colonies resulted from these events.

South of Inverness lie the majestic Cairngorms. The Aviemore centre provides both summer & winter sports facilities here.

To the north of Loch Ness are the remains of the ancient Caledonian forest where red deer & stags are a common sight on the hills. Rarer are sightings of the Peregrine Falcon, the osprey, the Golden Eagle & the Scottish wildcat. Kincraig has excellent wildlife parks.

Inverness is the last large town in the north, & a natural gateway to the Highlands & to Moray, the Black Isle & the north-east.

The east coast is characterised by the Firths of Moray, Cromarty & Dornoch & by its changing scenery from gentle pastureland, wooded hillsides to sweeping coastal cliffs.

On the Black Isle, which is not a true island byt has a causeway & bridge links with the mainland, Fortrose & Rosemarkie in particular have lovely beaches, caves & coastal walks. There is golf on the headland at Rosemarkie & a 13th century cathedral of rosy pink

Scotland

sandstone stands in Fortrose.

Golspie, further north is a pleasant resort with a golf course & the fairytale turrets of Dunrobin Castle nearby.

Helmsdale is at the foot of Strath Kildonan, scene of the Gold Rush of 1868, & it still attracts amateur gold prospectors.

At the western end of the Great Glen & north of Fort William, the landscape is at its most majestic. Nearby Ben Nevis is Britain's highest peak, & hills with dramatic contours - Canisp, Quinag & Cul Mor add grandeur to the skyline of Wester Ross & Sutherland. Countless hill lochs lie in the hollows of this breathtaking landscape. Otters hunt along the tideline & seals swim in the clear waters.

The railway from Fort William to Mallaig is beautiful, & runs a steam-hauled service in summer. A car ferry crosses from Mallaig to Ardvasar on Skye, whilst the more northerly connection to the Isle is at Kyle of Lochalsh.

The matchless Cuillins of Skye work their hill magic on visitors year after year. The island is a charmed landscape of mountain, sea & sky, small towns & crofting communities.

Sailings from Uig go to Harris & North Uist in the Outer Hebrides where the Gaelic culture & language remains strong. Harris is famous for its tweed cloth, & traditional knitters can be seen at work in Lewis & South Uist.

The standing stones of Callanish on Harris form the most elaborate & complete prehistoric site in Britain, & the beaches beneath the wild southern mountains are spectacular.

Returning to the mainland, Applecross is a charming coastal village reached by a fine shoreline drive or by dramatic 'Bealach na Ba' - the Pass of the Cattle - climbing to 2100 feet.

Lochinver is a small village near the Inverpolly Nature Reserve. Canisp & Suilven are nearby, as are some of the most scenic roads in Scotland, notable through Drumbeg & Inverkirkaig.

Plockton, a crofting village is famous for its colourful cottages, gardens & palm trees.

On the north coast the white sands & high rolling waves at Bettyhill are a delight. Puffins float on the winds above the cliffs at Dunnet Head where the lighthouse is open to visitors. Nearby Scrabster ferry port is the departure point for the Orkney Isles.

Orkney is one of the richest historical & archaeological sites in Britain & also a haven for thousands of seabirds.

Neolithic Scara Brae is a Stone Age village that was covered by sand in 2500 B.C. & uncovered by another storm in 1850.

The standing stones at Stenness & the Ring of Brodgar are awesome & there are many burial mounds (Maes Howe is a fine example), & brochs.

Kirkwall & Stromness are fascinating towns with busy harbours. In Kirwall, the Cathedral was built as a memorial to the gentle Earl Magnus who was put to death in the 12th century.

In Orkney & Shetland the Scandinavian influence is strong. The islands were not a part of Scotland until the 15th century when they formed part of the dowry of a Scandinavian princess.

The Norse festival of Up Helly Aa is celebrated annually & with great enthusiasm in Shetland.

Nature abounds in this mosaic of 100 islands with teeming seabird colonies, porpoises, otters & seals. Jarlshof is a remarkable site with extensive remains of Bronze Age, Viking & mediaeval settlements.

Summer nights are magical in these northern parts, where the sun is reluctant to leave the sky.

Scotland

Scotland Gazeteer

Areas of outstanding natural beauty
It would be invidious, not to say almost impossible, to choose any particular area of Scotland as having a more beautiful aspect than another - the entire country is a joy to the traveller. The Rugged Highlands, the great glens, tumbling waters, tranquil lochs - the deep countryside or the wild coastline - simply come & choose your own piece of paradise.

Historic Houses & Castles

Bowhill - Nr. Selkirk
18th-19th century - home of the Duke of Bucceleugh & Queensberry. Has an outstanding collection of pictures by Canaletto, Claude, Gainsborough, Reynolds & Leonardo da Vinci,,Superb silver, porcelain & furniture.16th & 17th century miniatures. -

Traquair House - Innerleithen
A unique & ancient house being the oldest inhabited home in Scotland. It is rich in associations with every form of political history & after Bonnie Prince Charlie passed through its main gates in 1745 no other visitor has been allowed to use them. There are treasures in the house dating from 12th century, & it has an 18th century library & a priest's room with secret stairs.

Linlithgow Palace - Linlithgow
The birthplace of Mary, Queen of Scots.

Sirling Castle - Stirling
Royal Castle.

Drumlanrigg Castle - Nr. Thornhill
17th century castle of pale pink stone - romantic & historic - wonderful art treasures including a magnificent Rembrandt & a huge silver chandelier. Beautiful garden setting.

Braemar Castle - Braemar
17th century castle of great historic interest. Has round central tower with spiral staircase giving it a fairy-tale appearance.

Drum Castle - Nr. Aberdeen
Dating in part from 13th century, it has a great square tower.

Cawdor Castle - Nairn
14th century fortress - like castle - has always been the home of the Thanes of Cawdor - background to Shakespeare's Macbeth.

Dunvegan Castle - Isle of Skye
13th century - has always been the home of the Chiefs of McLeod.

Hopetoun House - South Queensferry
Very fine example of Adam architecture & has a fine collection of pictures & furniture. Splendid landscaped grounds.

Inverary Castle - Argyll
Home of the Dukes of Argyll. 18th century - Headquarters of Clan Campbell.

Burn's Cottage - Alloway
Birthplace of Robert Burns - 1659 - thatched cottage - museum of Burns' relics.

Bachelors' Club - Tarbolton
17th century house - thatched - where Burns & friends formed their club - 1780.

Blair Castle - Blair Atholl
Home of the Duke of Atholl, 13th century Baronial mansion - collection of Jacobite relics, armour, paintings, china & many other items.

Glamis Castle - Angus
17th century remodelling in Chateau style - home of the Earl of Strathmore & Kinghorne. Very attractive castle - lovely grounds by Capability Brown.

Scone Palace - Perth
has always been associated with seat of Government of Scotland from earliest times. The Stone of Destiny was removed from the Palace in 1296 & taken to Westminster Abbey. Present palace rebuilt in early 1800's still incorporating parts of the old. Lovely gardens.

Edinburgh Castle
Fortress standing high over the town - famous for military tattoo.

Culzean Castle & Country Park - Maybole
Fine Adam house & spacious gardens perched on Ayrshire cliff.

Dunrobin Castle - Golspie
Ancient seat of the Earls & Dukes of Sutherland.

Eilean Donan Castle - Wester Ross
13th century castle, Jacobite relics.

Manderston - Duns
Great classical house with only silver staircase in the world. Stables, marble diary, formal gardens.

Scotland

Cathedrals & Churches

Dunfermline Abbey - Dunfermline
Norman remains of beautiful church. Modern east end & tower.
Edinburgh (Church of the Holy Rood)
15th century - was divided into two in 17th century & re-united 1938. Here Mary, Queen of Scots was crowned.
Glasgow (St. Mungo)
12th-15th century cathedral - 19th century interior. Central tower with spire.
Kirkwall (St. Magnus)
12th century cathedral with very fine nave.
Falkirk Old Parish Church - Falkirk
The spotted appearance (faw) of the church (kirk) gave the town its name. The site of the church has veen used since 7th century, with succesive churches built upon it. The present church was much rebuilt in 19th century. Interesting historically.
St Columba's Abbey - Iona

Museums & Galleries

Agnus Folk Museum - Glamis
17th century cottages with stone slab roofs, restored by the National Trust for Scotland & houses a fine folk collection.
Mary, Queen of Scots' House - Jedburgh
Life & times of the Queen along with paintings, etc.
Andrew Carnegie Birthplace - Dunfermline
The cottage where he was born is now part of a museum showing his life's work.
Aberdeen Art Gallery & Museum - Aberdeen
Sculpture, paintings, watercolours, prints & drawings. Applied arts. Maritime museum exhibits.
Provost Skene's House - Aberdeen
17th century house now exhibiting local domestic life, etc.
Highland Folk Museum - Kingussie
Examples of craft work & tools - furnished cottage with mill.
West Highland Museum - Fort William
Natural & local hsitory. Relics of Jacobites & exhibition of the '45 Rising.
Clan Macpherson House - Newtonmore
Relics of the Clan.
Glasgow Art Gallery & Museum - Glasgow
Archaeology, technology, local & natural history. Old Masters, tapestries, porcelain, glass & silver, etc. Sculpture.
Scottish National Gallery - Edinburgh
20th century collection - paintings & sculpture - Arp, Leger, Giacometti, Matisse, Picasso.
Modern Scottish painting.
National Museum of Antiquities in Scotland - Edinburgh
Collection from Stone Age to modern times - Relics of Celtic Church, Stuart relics, Highland weapons, etc.
Gladstone Court - Biggar
Small indoor street of shops, a bank, schoolroom, library, etc.
Burns' Cottage & Museum - Alloway
Relics of Robert Burns - National Poet.
Inverness Museum & Art Gallery - Inverness
Social history, archaeology & cultural life of the Highlands. Display of the Life of the Clans - good Highland silver - crafts, etc.
Kirkintilloch - Nr. Glasgow
Auld Kirk Museum. Local history, including archaeological specimens from the Antonine Wall (Roman). Local industries, exhibitions, etc
Pollock House & Park - Glasgow
18th century house with collection of paintings, etc. The park is the home of the award-winning Burrell Collection
The foregoing are but a few of the many museums & galleries in Scotland - further information is always freely available from the Tourist Information

Historic Monuments

Aberdour Castle - Aberdour
14th century fortification - part still roofed.
Balvenie Castle - Duffton
15th century castle ruins.
Cambuskenneth Abbey - Nr. Stirling
12th century abbey - seat of Bruce's Parliament in 1326. Ruins.
Dryburgh Abbey - Dryburgh
Remains of monastery.
Loch Leven Castle - Port Glasgow
15th century ruined stronghold - once lived in by Mary, Queen of Scots.

Scotland

Newark Castle - Port Glasgow
16th century turreted castle.
Rothesay Castle - Rothesay
13th century moated castle.
Elgin Cathedral - Elgin
13th century cathedral with fine Chapter House - now ruins.
Rosslyn Castle - Rosslyn
14th century castle - ruins.
Tolquhon Castle - Taves
15th century tower - 16th century mansion, now roofless.
Hagga Castle - Glasgow
16th century castle now museum for children.
Jedburgh Abbey
Remarkably well-preserved ruins of Augustinian priory.
Sweetheart Abbey
Cistercian Abbey founded by Lady Dervogilla
Melrose Abbey
Red sandstone ruins of Cistercian Abbey founded by David 1st.

Other things to see & do

Inverewe Gardens - Poolewe
Rare & Sub-tropical plants in remarkable garden sheltered by the mountains of Wester Ross.
Royal Botanic Gardens - Edinburgh
Founded 17th century. Plant houses, rock gardens, arboretum, panoramic view over the city.
Botanic Gardens - Glasgow
40 acres of extensive collection of plants.
Lochwinnoch - Strathclyde
R.S.P.B. Visitor Centre.
New Lanark
18th century industrial village restored & nominated as World Heritage Site.
Scara Brae - Orkney
Stone Age village uncovered in the 19th century.
 Mellerstain House- Gordon
Adam house,fineinterior,paintings, furniture,library.

Castle Stalker

SCOTLAND
Map references

01	Strachan	15	Steven	25	Bewick
02	Jordan	16	Grant	26	Young
04	McKay	17	Scott	28	Shirley
05	Cameron	18	Reid	29	McDonald
06	Wagstaff	18	Hayes	29	Young
07	Taylor	18	Baillie	29	Chisholm
08	MacDonald	18	Fraser	30	Buxton
09	Ptolomey	18	Young	31	Lewis
10	Jeffries	19	Rawson	32	Gray
11	Daniel	20	Paterson	33	MacDonald-Smith
12	Baird	20	Elder	34	Niven
12	Donaldson	21	Pottie	35	Dalziel-Williams
12	Cowan	22	Waugh	36	Irvine
12	Wilson	23	Cairns	37	Smith
12	Thomas	24	Kemp	38	Andrew Haslam
12	Wright			40	Black
12	Cameron				
12	Alexander				
12	Hogg				
12	Deacon				
12	Stuart				
12	Clark				
12	Conway				
12	Welch				
12	Simpson				
12	Celini				
12	Robins				
12	McLellan				
12	Gallo				
12	Hamilton				
12	Telfer				
12	Vidler				
12	Coville				
12	Preston				
13	More Nisbett				
13	Hall				
13	Dewar				
14	MacGeachy				

Scotland
Aberdeenshire

		minimum £ per person	children taken	evening meals	animals taken
Anne & Eddie Strachan **Hazlehurst Lodge** **Ballater Road** **Aboyne AB34 5HY** Tel: (03398) 86921 Open: FEB - DEC Map Ref No. 01	Nearest Road: A.93 Charming former Victorian coachman's lodge to Aboyne Castle & once home to Robert Milne, Queen Victoria's photographer. Set in beautiful wooded garden. Accommodation in 3 cosy bedrooms. Creative cuisine using the best of Scottish produce, imaginatively presented in an intimate restaurant. Ideal centre for Royal Deeside, an area of outstanding natural beauty. Castles, gardens, forests, rivers, lochs, & mountains. Activities include walking, climbing, riding, golf, shooting, fishing.	£18.00	N	N	N
Mrs C Jordan **The Glebe House** **Aboyne** **AB34 5HY** Tel: (03398) 86164 Open: MAY - OCT Map Ref No. 02	Nearest Road: A.93 A lovely 18th century family manse with historic associations set in private gardens on the banks of the River Dee and within walking distance of the village of Aboyne on Royal Deeside. Accommodation is a large twin-bedded room with private bathroom, and guests own sitting room with log fire, T.V., and views of the hills. Good restaurants locally. On the distillery, golf and castle trail.	£18.00	N	N	N

Argyll

Mr & Mrs G.H. McKay **'Allt-na-Craig'** **Tarbert Road** **Ardrishaig** **PA30 8EP** Tel: (0546) 3245 Open: MAR -DEC Map Ref No. 04	Nearest Road: A.83 The McKays warmly welcome all their guests to 'Allt-na-Craig', a lovely old Victorian mansion set in picturesque grounds overlooking Loch Fyne. Accommodation in 7 comfortable en-suite bedrooms with tea/coffee makers. A guests' lounge with open fire & dining room is also available. This is a perfect base for outdoor activities, like hill-walking, fishing, golf, riding & windsurfing or for visiting the islands. Delicious evening meals by arrangement.	£24.00	Y	Y	Y
Mrs Sandra Cameron **Thistle House** **St Catherines** **Cairndow** **PA25 8AZ** Tel: (0499) 2209 Open: APR - OCT Map Ref No. 05	Nearest Road: A.815 Spacious Victorian house superbly situated in large garden looking over Loch Fyne to Inveraray and its famous castle. Five comfortable bedrooms, three en-suite, all with tea and coffee facilities & electric blankets. Full Scottish breakfast. Several good eating places nearby for evening meals. The Cowal peninsula is well located for touring Argyll and Loch Lomond areas. Only one hour from Glasgow Airport. Children over 7 please.	£17.00	Y	N	Y

Brenalder Lodge. Doonfoot.

Scotland
Argyll

		minimum £ per person	children taken	evening meals	animals taken
John & Eleanor Wagstaff Red Bay Cottage Deargphort, Fionnphort Isle of Mull PA66 6BP Tel: (06817) 396 Open: ALL YEAR Map Ref No. 06	A really warm welcome awaits the visitor to this charming modern house offering 3 very comfortable rooms with modern facilities. Situated only 20 metres from the sea & overlooking Iona Sound & the white sandy beaches on the Isle of Iona, this surely must be the ideal base. Mr. Wagstaff offers superb food. Half board rates are excellent.	£14.00	Y	Y	Y

Ayrshire

Brenda & Bert Taylor Brenalder Lodge 39 Dunure Road Doonfoot KA7 4HR Tel: (0292) 43939 Open: ALL YEAR Map Ref No. 07	Nearest Road: A.77 Brenda & Bert Taylor welcome you to Brenalder Lodge. There are panoramic views of the Carrick Hills & overlooking the Firth of Clyde. Easy access to Prestwick airport & the world famous Turnberry & Royal Troon golf courses. The Lodge is an ideal base for touring the Burns country. All rooms have en-suite facilities, colour T.V. & tea/coffee makers. A delicious 4 course Scottish breakfast is served in the new conservatory style dining room. All day access to to the Lodge & ample parking. A 4 course diner is served at 6 P.M. if 24 hrs notice is given.	£21.00 see PHOTO over	Y	Y	Y

Dumbartonshire

S. & G. MacDonald Kirkton House Darleith Road Cardross PA25 8AZ Tel: (0389) 841951 Fax (0389) 841 868 Open: ALLYEAR (Excl.Xmas/ New Year) Map Ref No. 08	Nearest Road: A.814 Loch Lomond, the Trossachs & most Highland routes are easily reached from this 19th century converted farmhouse, which commands superb views from a tranquil rural setting above Cardross village north of the Clyde. It offers well appointed accommodation with an informal & unpretentious ambience. Most bedrooms have en-suite bathroom, each has T.V. & tea/coffee makers. A guest lounge & dining rooms. Good home cooked Table d'hote dinners served by oil lamplight. A warm welcome awaits you.	£19.50	Y	Y	Y

Dumfriesshire

Antony & Brenda Ptolomey Comlongon Castle Clarencefield Dumfries DG1 4NA Tel: (038787) 283 Fax 038787 226 Open: MAR - DEC Map Ref No. 09	Nearest Road: A.75 A magnificent 15th century Border castle set in 50 acres of secluded gardens & woodland. Once the home of a Scottish Earl. Guest rooms have 4 poster or twin beds with private bathrooms. Most evenings guests are taken on a candle lit tour of the castle when the tragic story of the 16th century ghost is explained & afterwards a superb dinner is served. Excellent golf & fishing nearby.	£35.00 see PHOTO over	Y	Y	N

Comlongon Castle. Clarencefield.

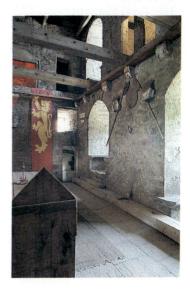

Scotland
Dumfriesshire

			minimum £ per person	children taken	evening meals	animals taken
Mr & Mrs F. D. Jeffries Cavens House Kirkbean-by-Dumfries GD2 8AA Tel: (0387) 88234 Open: ALL YEAR Map Ref No. 10	Nearest Road: A.710 Formerly an old mansion, this charming guest house offers 6 really comfortable rooms with modern facilities, including private bath or shower. Tea making faiclities & colour T.V, in each room. Standing in 11 acres of mature gardens & woodland, it makes a perfect base for those wishing to explore the joys of the Solway Coast with its beautiful scenery & excellent beaches. Sailing, fishing, walking, golfing & riding all local. Excellent cuisine here. Friendly atmosphere & good value.		£20.00 *see PHOTO over*	Y	Y	Y
Alan & Andrea Daniel Hartfell House Hotel Hartfell Crescent Moffat DG10 9AL Tel: (0683) 20153 Open: MAR - NOV Map Ref No. 11	Nearest Road: A.74 Hartfell House is a splendid Victorian manor house located in a rural setting overlooking the hills, yet only a few mins. walk from the town. A listed building known locally for its fine interior woodwork. Offering 9 spacious bedrooms, 5 with en-suite facilities. Standing in landscaped gardens of approximately 2 acres of lawns & trees providing an atmosphere of peaceful relaxation.		£16.00	Y	Y	Y

Edinburgh

Mrs H. Baird 64 Glasgow Road Corstorphine EH12 8LN Tel: (031) 3342610 Open: APR-OCT Map Ref No. 12	Nearest Road: M.8, M9. This is a very pleasant dormi style bungalow with an unusual entrance hall as its main feature. There are 3 comfortable guest bedrooms all with modern amenities including tea/coffee makers. All rooms are tastefully decorated & kept to a high standard. There is a warm, friendly welcome awaiting you here in this atractive home. Only 3 miles from the city centre. Excellent bus service. Children over 10 only.		£13.00	Y	N	N
Mrs H. Donaldson Ivermark 60 Polwarth Terrace Edinburgh EH11 1NJ Tel: (031) 337 1066 Open: ALL YEAR Map Ref No. 12	Nearest Road: A.702, A.70 Ivermark is a Victorian semi-detached village situated in quiet suburbs on a main bus route to the city, only five minutes away. 3 comfortable & well decorated rooms with modern facilities. It is well situated for all the amenities of this lovely capital city. Museums, galleries, Holyrood Palace, the Castle, sports centre & superb countryside. There is a quiet garden for guests. Mrs. Donaldson warmly welcomes all her guests. Parking.		£13.00	Y	N	Y

Cavens House.   Kirkbean-by-Dumfries.

Scotland
Edinburgh

			minimum £ per person	children taken	evening meals	animals taken
Bob & Helen Cowan The Buchan 3 Coates Gardens Edinburgh EH12 5LG Tel: (031) 3371045/8047 Open: ALL YEAR Map Ref No. 12	Nearest Road: A.8 A small, happy family-run hotel, very centrally situated, where the emphasis is on making guests really comfortable. 11 pleasant rooms, all with modern amenities, 2 en-suite each with colour T.V. & tea/coffee makers. A comfortable lounge is also available. Vegetarian & special diets catered for at breakfast. Only minutes away from Princes Street, the Castle & many wonderful antique shops. A warm welcome awaits all visitors.		£17.00	Y	N	Y
Mrs Jenny Wilson Camus House 4 Seaview Terrace Edinburgh EH15 2HD Tel: (031) 6572003 Open: JAN - DEC Map Ref No. 12	Nearest Road: A.1 A Victorian terraced Villa overlooking the Firth of Forth, Camus House enjoys the peace of the seaside along with an excellent bus service to the city centre with its cultural, historical and leisure interests. The three guest rooms are comfortably furnished and have washbasins, colour T.V., radio alarms & tea/coffee facilities. A genuine and friendly welcome is assured.		£13.00	Y	N	Y
Catherine & Ian Thomas "Pearlview" 2 Seaview Terrace Joppa Portobello Edinburgh EH15 2HD Tel: (031) 6698516 Open: ALL YEAR Map Ref No. 12	Nearest Road: A.1 "Pearlview" is a Victorian terraced villa with panoramic views over the Firth of Fourth. Offering guests a choice of 4 attractive bedrooms, 1 with private bathroom. All with modern amenities, including radio, colour T.V. & tea/coffee making facilities. Conveniently located, frequent bus service to the city centre & many sporting facilities nearby. "Pearlview" welcomes all guests with a warm & friendly atmosphere. Free parking.		£13.50	Y	N	N
Mr & Mrs William Wright Salisbury Hotel 45 Salisbury Road Edinburgh EH16 5AA Tel: (031) 6671264 Open: ALL YEAR Map Ref No. 12	Nearest Road: A.7, A.68 Enjoy real Scottish hospitality in the comfort of this Georgian House. The Wright family offer you tastefully decorated comfortable bedrooms, all with private facilities, colour T.V. tea/coffee makers. Their home has been carefully refurbished during their 12 year ownership. Central heating throughout. Secluded garden to the rear. 10 mins. by bus to the city centre, railway station & tourist attractions. Private car park.		£18.00	Y	N	Y
Mrs Jackie Cameron Turret Guest House 8 Kilmaurs Terrace Edinburgh EH16 5DR Tel: (031) 6676704 Open: ALL YEAR Map Ref No. 12	Nearest Road: A.68 A warm Scottish welcome is found at this Victorian mid-terraced villa. Located in a residential area just off the A.68. The house retains many original features including cornices, wooden staircase with minstrel gallery & white marble fireplace in lounge. The 6 bedrooms have been attractively furnished with all the little extra touches that make you feel at home. Full Scottish breakfast including "clootie" dumpling & potato scone is served.		£13.00	Y	N	N

Scotland
Edinburgh

		minimum £ per person	children taken	evening meals	animals taken
Mrs Norah Alexander **Tiree Guest House** 26 Craigmillar Park Edinburgh EH16 5PS Tel: (031) 6677477 Open: ALL YEAR Map Ref No. 12	Nearest Road: A.7 Situated on the south side of Edinburgh about one & a half miles from the city centre. Offering accommodation in 7 rooms, 4 with en-suite facilities. All rooms have colour T.V. & tea/coffee makers. Conveniently located for Edinburgh University, Holyrood Palace & shopping centre. Children are very welcome here & are given reduced rates. Full Scottish breakfast. Dinner is also available & packed lunches can be provided.	£11.00	Y	N	Y
Wilma & Bill Hogg **Kingsley Guest House** 30 Craigmillar Park Newington Edinburgh EH16 5PS Tel: (031) 6678439 Open: ALL YEAR Map Ref No. 12	Nearest Road: A.7 A pleasant Victorian terraced villa offering 6 charming comfortable rooms. All with modern amenities, tea/coffee making facilities & colour T.V., 4 have private shower. Personal attention & a warm welcome await the visitor here. It is most conveniently situated on the south side of the city in the residential university area. A really good base for everyone with an excellent bus service from the door & a private car park.	£13.00	Y	N	N
Alan & Patrea More Nisbett **The Drum** Gilmerton Edinburgh EH17 8RX Tel: (031) 664 7215 Open: ALL YEAR Map Ref No.	Nearest Road: A.7 A.68 If you have never stayed in a stately home, here is your opperuntity. The Drum is Edinburgh's largest private house, a grade 1 listed 15th century castle with extensions by William Adam (1726), yet only 4 miles (15 mins.) from Princes Street & half a mile from the Edinburgh bypass. A family home, with 5 twin & 3 double bedrooms, all with private bathrooms. Furnished with antiques. Sleep in the haunted State Bedroom, in a four poster, & dine in elegant surroundings.	£37.50	Y	Y	N
Annie Deacon 53 Eskside West Musselburgh Edinburgh EH21 6RB Tel: (031) 6652875 Open: ALL YEAR Map Ref No. 12	Nearest Road: A.1 A warm, friendly & helpful hostess awaits you at this very pleasant stone-built terraced house located right on the banks of the River Esk. Charmingly decorated & furnished throughout to a high standard, it offers 2 delightful bedrooms with fresh flowers, radio, T.V., tea/coffee making facilities & a luxurious guests' bathrooms. Annie Deacon is a professional cook & breakfast is excellent, beautifully prepared & served with grace & charm. This makes a really super base. 15 minutes by car from Holyrood Palace & 20 minutes from Edinburgh.	£12.00	Y	Y	N
Jon & Gloria Stuart **Meadows Guest House** 17 Glengyle Terrace Edinburgh EH3 9LN Tel: (031) 2299559 Fax 031 557 0563 Open: ALL YEAR Map Ref No. 12	Nearest Road: A.702 Quietly situated overlooking a park, Meadows is warm, comfortable & spacious with a friendly atmosphere. 7 attractive rooms, all with colour T.V. & tea/coffee making facilities, some with private bathroom. Jon & Gloria will welcome you & help you with where to go, what to do & where to eat. Bookings of 3 nights or more taken in advance. Centrally located within easy reach of the Castle, Princes St., shops, theatres & restaurants.	£17.00	Y	N	Y

Scotland
Edinburgh

		minimum £ per person	children taken	evening meals	animals taken
Sheila & Robert Clark Galloway Guest House 22 Dean Park Crescent Edinburgh EH4 1PH Tel: (031) 332 3672 Open: ALL YEAR Map Ref No. 12	Nearest Road: A.9, A.90 A warm welcome, delightful atmosphere & superb breakfasts combine to make quality the hall mark of this well known Victorian town house. Located half a mile from Princes Street with free street parking. It offers accommodation in 10 comfortable rooms, 6 en-suite, all with colour T.V. & tea/coffee makers. Visitors have the whole of Edinburgh on their doorstep from this central vantage point. 7 nights for the price of 6.	£16.00	Y	N	Y
Mrs Helen Hall 'Woodlands' 55 Barnton Avenue Davidsons Mains Edinburgh EH4 6JJ Tel: (031) 3361685 Open: JAN - NOV Map Ref No. 13	Nearest Road: A.90 A small mansion house set in 2 acres of garden & woodlands, overlooking the Royal Burgesss Golf Course. 3 miles from West End of Princes Street. All bedrooms are equipped with tea/coffee making facilites, hair dryers, electric blankets, radios & colour T.V. Whilst the city itself holds a wealth of interest, the surrounding countryside should not be overlooked. Regional Winner of the Best Bed & Breakfast Award.	£16.00	Y	N	Y
Mrs Moira Conway Crannoch But and Ben 467 Queensferry Road Edinburgh EH4 7ND Tel: (031) 3365688 Open: JAN - DEC Map Ref No. 12	Nearest Road: A.90, A.8 Warm Scottish hospitality at this very pleasant private house. The two ground-floor guest rooms have private facilities and tea/coffee making. Guest lounge has T.V. and evening tea or coffee is served whilst you digest the available informaton on all there is to do in Edinburgh. Private parking on site and excellent bus service to the heart of the city, (just 3 miles to Princes Street.).	£16.00	Y	N	N
Len & Sue Welch Ravensdown Guest House 248 Ferry Road Edinburgh EH5 3AN Tel: (031) 5525438 Open: ALL YEAR Map Ref No. 12	Nearest Road: A.1 Built at the beginning of the 1900's, Ravensdown offers unsurpassed panoramic views of the Edinburgh skyline. Each of the 7 spacious well decorated bedrooms have modern amenities, colour T.V. & tea/coffee making facilities. A warm lounge enables guests to socialise with bar service on the premises. Your friendly hosts are always available to offer assistance with tours, etc. A delicious breakfast gets you off to a good start each morning. Private parking available. Only 3 kilometres from the city centre.	£13.00	Y	N	N
Mr & Mrs D.A. Simpson Greenside Hotel 9 Royal Terrace Edinburgh EH7 5AB Tel: (031) 5570022 Open: JAN - NOV Map Ref No. 12	Nearest Road: A.1 The Greenside, a really delightful hotel, is situated in a Georgian terrace, about 15 minutes' walk from Edinburgh city centre. The hotel has 12 spacious, comfortable rooms, 6 with en-suite facilities., with private facilities & is fully centrally heated. A large lounge with T.V. A hearty breakfast is served between 8 & 9a.m. & coffee is served in the lounge each evening around 9.30p.m. Mr & Mrs Simpson will make you most welcome.	£20.50	Y	N	Y

Scotland
Edinburgh

		minimum £ per person	children taken	evening meals	animals taken
Mrs D. Celini Clarin Guest House 4 East Mayfield Edinburgh EH9 1SD Tel: (031) 667 2433 Open: ALL YEAR Map Ref No. 12	Nearest Road: A.7, A.68 A nicely decorated Victorian terraced town house offering 7 very pleasant comfortable rooms with modern amenities, tea/coffee making facilities & T.V. in each room. This house makes a comfortable & popular base for discovering the joys of the city & countryside.	£11.00	Y	N	Y
Mr & Mrs D. R. Robins Sonas Guest House 3 East Mayfield Edinburgh EH9 1SD Tel: (031) 6672781 Open: ALL YEAR Map Ref No. 12	Nearest Road: A.7, A.68 Guests are assured of a warm welcome & a memorable stay at Sonas (the old Gaelic word for peace & happiness). Built in 1876 & recently refurbished it now provides 7 tastefully decorated bedrooms with en-suite facilities. It retains many of its original features including a lovely sweeping staircase & ornate cornices. A delicious Scottish breakfast is served each morning. Private parking. Excellent bus service.	£17.00	Y	N	Y
Mr & Mrs A. McLellan Allison House Hotel 15-17 Mayfield Gardens Edinburgh EH9 2AX Tel: (031) 6678049 Fax 667 5001 Open: ALL YEAR Map Ref No. 12	Nearest Road: A.7 Elegant Georgian-style listed building in a residential area on A.7 route. 24 comfortable rooms with private facilities, colour T.V., central heating, double glazing & tea/coffee making facilities. After a delicious full Scottish breakfast the frequent bus service will take you to the city centre, rail or bus station in 10 minutes. A warm welcome awaits all guests at the Allison from Archie & Sheila & their staff. Parking.	£17.00	Y	Y	N
Mr & Mrs A. Gallo Rosedene Guest House 4 Queen's Crescent Edinburgh EH9 2AZ Tel: (031) 6675806 Open: MAR - NOV Map Ref No. 12	Nearest Road: A.68, A.7. A fine detached Victorian villa with beautiful garden - situated in a select residential area just off the main road. Queen's Crescent lies between the A.7 /701 & the A.68 main roads into the city from the south & is only one & a half miles from Princes Street. Private parking available. 8 guest bedrooms, 3 with en-suite facilities, each with tea/coffee makers.	£12.50	Y	N	N
John & Gill Hamilton Hamilton House 12 Moston Terrace Newington Edinburgh EH9 2DE Tel: (031) 667 2540 Open: ALL YEAR Map Ref No. 12	Nearest Road: A.7 A comfortable, well-appointed house in a quiet residential area 15 minutes from city centre near to the local bus route. The house is fully centrally heated. All rooms have hot/cold water, tea/coffee facilities & 2 have private facilities. Good home cooking is a speciality & diets catered for (vegetarian etc.). T.V. is availiable. A warm welcome is assured. Unrestricted street parking.	£14.00	Y	Y	N

Scotland
Edinburgh

			minimum £ per person	children taken	evening meals	animals taken
Mrs A.H. Telfer 'Ard-Thor' 10 Mentone Terrace Newington Edinburgh EH9 2DG Tel: (031) 6671647 Open: ALL YEAR Map Ref No. 12	Nearest Road: A.1, A.68, A.7 A charming, 19th century Victorian guest house only 10 minutes from the city centre, castle & Princes Street by good local bus service. The Ard-Thor is quiet & friendly & your comfort is ensured by the personal attention of your host. Guests are offered a choice of 4 rooms, all with T.V., tea/coffee making facilities. Queens Park & Commonwealth Pool are nearby.		£14.00	N	N	N
Alan & Angela Vidler Rowan Guest House 13 Glenorchy Terrace Newington Edinburgh EH9 2DQ Tel: (031) 6672463 Open: ALL YEAR Map Ref No. 12	Nearest Road: A.7, A.68 Quietly located in one of Edinburgh's loveliest areas, Rowan House built in 1880, retains the character of a bygone age with present day comfort. Bedrooms are tastefully furnished, some with private. facilities. Complimentary tea, coffee & biscuits available. Unrestricted parking. City centre only 10 minutes by bus. Breakfast includes traditional porridge & freshly baked scones. You will receive a warm welcome & attentive service.		£15.00	Y	N	N
Mrs Jane Coville Teviotdale House 53 Grange Loan Edinburgh EH9 2ER Tel: (031) 6674376 Open: ALL YEAR Map Ref No. 12	Nearest Road: A.7 Tastefully restored, elegant, Victorian gentleman's town house. Located in a quiet residential conservation area. Lovely original woodwork. All 7 spacious rooms have every modern facility with private or en-suite bath rooms, colour T.V., radio & tea/coffee makers. Some rooms have refrigerator. Breakfast is a banquet. Home baked scones, jams & bread. Guaranteed to delight the most travelled of guests. Parking. 10 mins. to town centre.		£19.00	Y	Y	Y
Mrs M. Dewar Glenesk Delta Place Smeaton Grove Inveresk EH21 7TP Tel: (031) 6653217 Open: MAY - SEPT Map Ref No. 13	Nearest Road: A.1 Quietly situated in the picturesque village of Inveresk, 'Glenesk' is a spacious detached villa. It is convenient for all the scenic beauties, beaches & sporting activities of the east coast, while only 7 miles from the centre of Edinburgh, 1 mile from the busy shopping centre of Musselburgh. All 3 bedrooms have private shower rooms or bathrooms, colour T.V. tea/coffee making facilites. comfortable lounge. Parking space. No signs displayed - conservation area.		£15.00	N	N	N
Mrs Annette Preston Dunedin Guest House 8 Priestfield Road Edinburgh GH16 5HH Tel : (031) 6681949 Open : MAY - SEPT Map Ref No. 13	Nearest Road: A.68 A warm & friendly welcome awaits you from Mrs Preston in this small family run guest house, situated in a quiet residential area on the south side of Edinburgh. There are 3 ground floor rooms, 1 adapted for the disabled with private bathroom, colour T.V. & tea/coffee making facilities. Full Scottish breakfast served. Private parking. Only 10 mins. by bus to the city centre. Dunedin is an ideal location for visiting Edinburgh.		£12.00	Y	N	N

Scotland
Fife

			per person minimum £	children taken	evening meals	animals taken
Mrs Ella MacGeachy 'The Dykes' 69 Pittenweem Road Anstruther KY10 3DT Tel: (0333) 310537 Open: MAR - SEPT Map Ref No. 14	Nearest Road: A.917 A delightful modern bungalow offering 2 comfortable guest rooms, 1 family room, with modern facilities. Situated overlooking the golf course & the sea, this is an ideal base for families & tourists to this lovely region. There are many historic houses & golf courses locally & the walking & riding are excellent. Only 9 miles from St. Andrews.		£13.00	Y	N	N
Mrs Isobel Steven Ardchoille Farmhouse Dunshalt Auchtermuchty KY14 7EY Tel: (0337) 28414 Open: ALL YEAR Map Ref No. 15	Nearest Road: A.91, B.936 This spacious, well appointed, centrally heated farmhouse with superb views of the Lomond Hills offers accommodation in 2 twin bedded & 1 family room with private bathroom, colour T.V. & tea/coffee trays with home-made butter shortbread. Large comfortable lounge. Delicious freshly prepared meals are served with flair & imagination in the attractive dining room. Excellent base for touring, golf (30 courses within 30 miles) St. Andrews, Edinburgh & the Highlands within easy reaach.		£20.00	Y	Y	N
Mrs May Grant Greigston Farm Peat Inn Cupar KY15 5LF Tel: (033484) 284 Open: ALL YEAR Map Ref No. 16	Nearest Road: B.941, B.940 A Scottish Lairds house dating from the 17th-18th century, offering 3 absolutely charming, comfortable guest rooms, 2 with private facilities. Here the welcome is very warm & the cooking is superb. Standing in a sheltered position with lawns, there are marvellous beaches, wildlife reserves, superb golf at Carnoustie & Gleneagles with St. Andrews only 6 miles away. Evening meal by prior arrangement only. This is a working farm.		£13.00	Y	Y	Y
Mrs Patricia Scott Forgan House Newport-on-Tay DD6 8RB Tel: (0382) 542760 Open: ALL YEAR Map Ref No. 17	Nearest Road: A.92 Forgan House, the former manse of the area, is a listed Georgian country house situated in 2 acres of grounds in the tranquil & rural setting of north east Fife. The emphasis is on quality & comfort & the spacious rooms provide panoramic views & private facilities. The surrounding area offers world famous golf courses, outstanding beaches, horse riding, bird watching & much more.		£18.50	Y	Y	N
Mrs Helen Black Milton Farm Milton of Leuchars St. Andrews KY16 0AB Tel: (0334) 839281 Open: ALL YEAR Map Ref No. 40	Nearest Road: A.92, A.919 A warm & friendly welcome awaits you at Milton Farm. A spacious, tastefully modernised & peaceful Victorian farmhouse. Accommodation is in 4 stylish & elegantly furnished bedrooms with very pretty linen. A full English breakfast is served including home made bread, preserves & fresh farm eggs. Packed luches are provided on request. Guest lounge with colour T.V. & delightful garden. Pony trekking & many golf courses nearby. St.Andrews 5 miles.		£15.00	Y	N	N

Scotland
Inverness-shire

		minimum £ per person	children taken	evening meals	animals taken
Peter & Penny Rawson **Feith Mhor Country** **House Station Road** **Beananach** **Carrbridge** **PH23 3AP** Tel: (047984) 621 Open: JAN - DEC Map Ref No. 19	Nearest Road: A.9 A warm friendly atmosphere is found at this charming 19th century house set in an acre of delightful garden, surrounded by peaceful un-spoilt countryside. Tastefully furnished & full of character. Accommodation is in 6 very comfortable en-suite bedrooms with tea/coffee makers & colour T.V.. Excellent views from each room. A pleasant dining room & spacious comfortable lounge are also available. Super home cooking with fresh produce in season. Vegetarian dishes provided with prior notice.	£19.00	Y	Y	Y
Mr & Mrs Hayes **Aberfeldy Lodge** **11 Southside Road** **Inverness IV2 3BG** Tel: (0463) 231120 Open: ALL YEAR Map Ref No. 18	Nearest Road: A.9 A great house, warm & comfortable, offering a high standard of accommodation. Mr & Mrs Hayes will be found most helpful regarding all aspects of travellers' needs. 9 rooms are available, all with private facilities & modern amenities, tea/coffee makers, some with T.V. lounge & garden for guests' use. No single availability. Children over 4.	£18.00	Y	Y	N
David & Katherine Elder **Kinross House** **Woodside Avenue** **Grantown-on-Spey** **PH26 3JR** Tel: (0479) 2042 Open: FEB - NOV Map Ref No. 20	Nearest Road: A.9 Peacefully situated Victorian villa in a delightful country town. Ideal touring centre for Lock Ness Braemar & distilleries. Lovely walks & wildlife nearby. High standard of comfort & delicious home cooking. (David wears his kilt when serving dinner.) 7 attractive bedrooms, some en-suite, all with colour T.V. & tea/coffee makers. Dinner served by your kilted host. Log fire. Table licence. True highland hospitality from your Scottish hosts.	£16.00	Y	Y	N
Jim & Geraldine Reid **The Old Royal Guest** **House** **10 Union Street** **Inverness IV1 1PL** Tel: (0463) 230551 Open: FEB - NOV Map Ref No. 18	Nearest Road: A.9 Personally managed by the resident proprietors Jim & Geraldine. The Old Royal is conveniently situated in the centre of town opposite the railway station. Accommodation is in 14 comfortable guest bedrooms, 5 with en-suite facilities. All have colour T.V. & tea/coffee makers. The Old Royal has "a home from home" atmosphere & provides visitors with a comfortable holiday base from which to tour the locality.	£17.00	Y	N	N
Mrs M.E. Pottie **Easter Dalziel Farmhouse** **Dalcross** **Inverness IV1 2JL** Tel: (0667) 62213/462213 Open: MAR - NOV Map Ref No. 21	Nearest Road: A.96, B.9039 This Scottish farming family offer the visitor a friendly highland welcome on their 200 acre farm, breeding beef cattle & growing barley. 3 charming bedrooms are available in the delightful early Victorian farmhouse. Lounge has log fire & colour T.V. Delicious home cooking & baking served, including a choice of breakfasts. Local attractions are Cawdor Castle, Culloden, Fort George, Loch Ness & nearby Castle Stuart.	£14.00	Y	Y	Y

Scotland
Inverness-shire

			minimum £ per person	children taken	evening meals	animals taken
Andrew & Joyce Paterson Dunstaffnage House Woodside Avenue Grantown-on-Spey PH26 3JR Tel: (0479) 2000 Open: ALL YEAR(Excl. Xmas & New Year) Map Ref No. 20	Nearest Road: A.9 A.95 Dunstaffnage is a spacious, warm & friendly country house of character, set in an acre of garden located next to a pine forest & lake. Conveniently situated within 2 minutes walk of both the town centre & River Spey it offers most attractive & restful accommodation. All rooms have private facilities, tea/coffee makers, colour T.V., etc. Ideal for highland touring. Fishing, golf, walking or birdwatching are available nearby.		£18.50 see PHOTO over	Y	N	Y
Mrs C. Baillie Victoria Guest House 1 Victoria Terrace Inverness IV2 3QA Tel: (0463) 237682 Open: APR - OCT Map Ref No. 18	Nearest Road: A.9 A pleasant Victorian terraced house offering 3 pleasant, comfortable rooms with modern facilities, & private shower. Situated near the site of King Duncan's Castle, it is a good base for touring the region. Clava Stones, a Druid burial ground, is well worth visiting. Cots & highchairs provided for.		£13.00	Y	N	N
Mrs Vera G. Waugh Cabana House Union Road Fort William Inverness PH33 6RB Tel: (0397) 705991 Open: ALL YEAR Map Ref No. 22	Nearest Road: A.82 This elegant Victorian house has been renovated to an exceptional standard. 3 designer-decorated bedrooms, 2 en-suite, all with every modern amenity. T.V. lounge/dining room. Excellent home cooking tastefully presented with true Scottish hospitality. Situated in a prime position close to Fort William town centre with private parking & garden. An ideal holiday base for touring the spectacular Highlands & Islands. Open for winter skiing holidays.		£15.00	N	N	N
Mrs Margaret Cairns Invergloy House Spean Bridge PH34 4DY Tel: (039781) 681 Open: ALL YEAR Map Ref No. 23	Nearest Road: A.82 A really interesting Scottish coach house dating back 110 years, offering 3 charming comfortable twin bedded rooms with modern facilites; 2 bathrooms. Situated 5 miles north of the village of Spean Bridge towards Inverness, it is signposted on the left along a wooded drive. Guests have use of own sitting room, overlooking Loch Lochy in 50 acres of superb woodland of rhododendron & azaleas. Fishing from the private beach & rowing boats, hard tennis court. Children over 12 welcome.Non-smokers only please.		£13.00	Y	Y	N
Mrs Denise L. Fraser Kepplestone House 1 Porterfield Road Inverness IV2 3HW Tel: (0463) 710684 Open: ALL YEAR Map Ref No. 18	Nearest Road: A.9 Kepplestone is a period Victorian semi-detached dwelling house, retaining many of its original features. The 3 guest bedrooms have been tastefully decorated & furnished, each has a wash basin, tea/coffee making facilities, colour T.V. & central heating. Situated in a quiet residential street, only 5 minutes walk from the town centre, Kepplestone is an ideal base for exploring the scenic highlands & Islands.		£14.00	Y	N	N

Dunstaffnage House.   Grantown-on-Spey.

Scotland
Inverness

			minimum £ per person	children taken	evening meals	animals taken
Mr & Mrs J. Young Crownleigh 6 Midmills Road Inverness IV2 3NX Tel: (0463) 220316 Open: ALL YEAR Map Ref No. 18	Nearest Road: A.9 Situated only 5 minutes' walk from the town centre & rail/coach stations, in the old historic part of Inverness. Crownleigh offers comfortable accommodation in 5 bedrooms with tea/coffee making facilities. A full English or Continental breakfast is served. Packed lunches available on request. Guests may relax after a weary day in the cosy lounge with colour T.V. Unlimited parking.		£12.00	Y	N	Y

Isle of Skye

| Mr & Mrs D.D. Kemp
Craiglockhart Guest House
Beaumont Crescent
Portree IV51 9DF
Tel: (0478) 2233
Open: FEB - DEC
Map Ref No. 24 | Nearest Road: A.850, A.87
A house of great architectural interest - a listed building - which has been tastefully modernised, offering 10 comfortable guest rooms with modern facilities. Everyone will love the area as there is much to discover here. Beaches, fishing, swimming, sea trips & riding all locally available. A warm welcome awaits the visitor here. Children over 3 only. | | £15.00 | N | N | N |

All the establishments mentioned in this guide

are members of

The Worldwide Bed & Breakfast Association

Scotland
Lanarkshire

	minimum £ per person	children taken	evening meals	animals taken
Mrs Kate Bewick **Six Fathoms** **6 Polnoon Street** **Eaglesham** **Renfrewshire by Glasgow** **G76 0BH** Tel: (03553) 2321 Open: ALL YEAR Map Ref No. 25	Nearest Road: A.77, M.74, Set in the picturesque Village of Eaglesham, 10 miles from Glasgow. Guests can be sure of a warm, Scottish welcome at this delightful home, with a choice of twin room with sitting room & private facilities & 2 single rooms, 1 spacious, 1 cosy - all rooms with colour T.V. 3 pubs/ restaurants, excellent & varied, within 5 minutes' walk. Convenient for Glasgow & Prestwick International Airports, M.74, Loch Lomond, Burns Country & the Burrell Collection.	£17.50	N	N	N

Lothian

Mrs J. Young **Redheugh Hotel** **Bayswell Park** **Dunbar** **EH42 1AE** Tel: (0368) 62793 Open: ALL YEAR Map Ref No. 26	Nearest Road: A.1 Family run licenced hotel with a quiet cliff top location & panoramic views of the Firth of Forth, yet only 5 minutes walk from town centre & 30 mins. from Edinburgh & 16 golf courses. All bedrooms are en-suite with bath/ shower, central heating, tea/coffee making facilities, 'phones, mini bar & colour T.V. Excellent restaurant where the chef specialises in meals prepared from local fresh produce.	£25.00	N	Y	Y

Perthshire

David & Dee Shirley **Highland House Hotel** **South Church Street** **Callander FK17 8BN** Tel: (0877) 30269 Open: MAR - NOV Map Ref No. 28	Nearest Road: A.84 A delightful Georgian house offering 10 comfortably furnished bedrooms, some with private shower & w.c. en-suite. There is a T.V. lounge & bar with informal atmosphere where guests can relax before dining. The bar has an extensive range of malt whisky. A carefully selected wine list is offered to compliment your meal. A warm welcome & personal attention from your hosts is assured. A real taste of Scotland.	£17.00	Y	Y	Y
Jean & Jimmy Young **The Lodge House** **Crainlarich** **FK20 8RU** Tel: (08383) 276 Open: MAR - NOV Map Ref No. 29	Nearest Road: A.82 Positioned within 1 acre of trees & heather, the Lodge enjoys uninterrupted views of the surrounding mountains, glens & salmon river. 6 extremely well appointed bedrooms, some en-suite & all with tea/coffee making facilities, T.V. lounge (non-smoking) & bar lounge. 'Taste of Scotland' home cooking, quality wines & an extensive range of malt whiskies are served. A relaxing, informal atmosphere is created by your Scottish hosts. Private salmon/trout fishing available.	£17.00	Y	Y	N

Scotland
Perthshire

			minimum £ per person	children taken	evening meals	animals taken
Roger McDonald Allt-Chaorain House Hotel Crainlarich FK20 8RU Tel: (08383) 283 Open: APR - OCT Map Ref No. 29		Nearest Road: A.82 Allt-Chaorain House is a small family hotel situated in an elevated position with commanding views of Ben More & Strathfillian from the south - facing sun lounge. 9 comfortable bedrooms, all with private facilities. 'Taste of Scotland' home cooking & packed lunches available on request. The friendly & relaxing atmosphere will unwind you as you sit by the log fire after walking, fishing or touring central Highlands.	£26.00 *see PHOTO over*	Y	Y	Y
Mr & Mrs S. Chisholm Tigh Na Struith Guest House Crainlarich FK20 8RU Tel: (08383) 235 Open: MAR - NOV Map Ref No. 29		Nearest Road: A.82 Voted the best house in Britain by the Guild of Travel Writers in 1984, this superbly situated guest house comprises 6 luxurious bedrooms, each with unrestricted views of the surrounding hills & glens. A feature remarked upon by many of the guests is the abundance of oil paintings on the walls, & the comforts of T.V. & tea/coffee making facilities in every bedroom. Personally supervised by the owners, Janica & Sandy Chisholm. Tigh na Struith gives visitors a unique opportunity to relax & enjoy rural Scotland at its best. No single occupancy.	£15.00	Y	N	Y
Mrs Patricia Buxton Bheinne Mhor Guest House Perth Road Birnam Dunkeld PH8 0DH Tel: (03502) 779 Open: ALL YEAR Map Ref No. 30		Nearest Road: A.9 A warm welcome awaits you at this comfortable Victorian detached house with turret & private garden, ideally situated for lovely walks in Macbeth's Birnam Woods & alongside the rivers Tay & Braan. Many places of historic interest & beauty nearby including Dunkeld Cathedral, Scottish National Trust's 'The Hermitage' & Loch of Lowes Wildlife Reserve. Boundless opportunities for anglers & golfers. Selection of 4 bedrooms, 2 with en-suite facilities, modern amenities, tea/coffee makers.	£16.50	N	N	N
Robert & Jean Lewis Monachyle Mhor Balquhidder Lochearnhead FK19 8PQ Tel: (08774) 622 Open: JAN - DEC Map Ref No. 31		Nearest Road: A.84 Monachyle Mhor is set in its own 2000 acres overlooking Lochs Voil and Doine, in the beautiful Braes O'Balquhidder, historical home of Rob Roy McGregor. The house is furnished with period furniture and fine pictures. All rooms have the most magnificent outlook; all guest bedrooms are en-suite; the dining room and conservatory restaurant allow you to dine and wine on the very finest of Scottish food. We offer stalking and fishing in season. Children over 10	£18.50	Y	Y	N

When booking your accommodation please

mention

The Best Bed & Breakfast

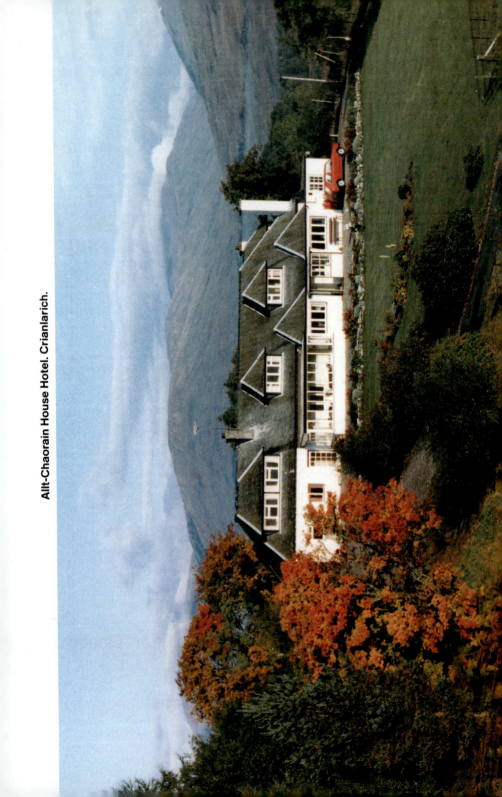
Allt-Chaorain House Hotel. Crianlarich.

Scotland
Perthshire

		minimum £ per person	children taken	evening meals	animals taken
Mr & Mrs MacDonald-Smith Druimuan House Killiecrankie Pitlochry PH16 5LG Tel: (0796) 3214 Fax 0796 2692 Open: APR - OCT Map Ref No. 33	Nearest Road: A.9 An elegant Victorian country house set in secluded grounds with an 18-hole putting green & croquet lawn. 3 beautiful en-suite rooms with wonderful views, colour T.V. & tea/coffee making facilities. A marvellous base for touring with Pitlochry (& its Festival), Blair Castle, golf, fishing, bird-watching & on the doorstep a number of scenic walks in & around the famous Pass of Killiecrankie.	£18.50	Y	N	N
Mr & Mrs I.A. Niven Gloagburn Farm Tibbermore by Perth PH1 1QL Tel: (073884) 228 Open: ALL YEAR Map Ref No. 34	Nearest Road: A.9 Peace & tranquility prevail at Gloagburn Farm, a charming home with outstanding views of open countryside. Accommodation is in 3 attractive rooms. Delicious full English or Continental breakfasts served. An excellent base for golfing - Gleneagles is within easy reach; fishing, touring or visiting the city of Perth with its many attractions.	£15.00	Y	N	N
Morna Dalziel-Williams Dundarroch House Brig O'Turk Trossachs-by-Callander FK17 8HT Tel: (08776) 200 Open: MAR - OCT Map Ref No. 35	Nearest Road: A.821 A.84 Enjoy award winning hospitality in this delightful Victorian country house, set in 14 acres, in the heart of the Trossachs. 3 lovely bedrooms, each with en-suite facilities, colour T.V., refrigerator, radio & tea/coffee maker. Residents' lounge & dining room furnished with paintings & fine antiques have superb views to the river & mountains. Wonderful breakfasts. Delicious dinners served in 'Byre' restaurant with quaint bar set in the grounds of Dundarrock.	£20.00	Y	Y	N

Roxburghshire

Mrs H.H. Irvine 'Froylehurst' Friars Jedburgh TD8 6BN Tel: (0835) 62477 Open: APR - OCT Map Ref No. 36	Nearest Road: A.68 An attractive late Victorian House offering 4 comfortable guest rooms & residents' lounge. H/C, tea/coffee making facilities & colour T.V. in all bedrooms. Situated in a large garden overlooking the town in a quiet residential area. Edinburgh only 1 hour by car. Golf, pony trekking, fishing & sports centre all local.	£13.50	Y	N	N
Mrs Betty Smith Whitehill Farm Nenthorn Kelso TD5 7RZ Tel: (05737) 203 Open: ALL YEAR Map Ref No. 37	Nearest Road: A.6089 A comfortable & peaceful farmhouse with large garden standing on a 455 acre mixed farm, 4 miles from Kelso. 4 attractive bedrooms, 2 single & 2 twin, 1 with en-suite shower room, have superb views over rolling countryside. All have central heating & washbasins. A pleasant sitting room with log fire is available to guests. An ideal base for touring, maps available. Good home cooking. Dinner by arrangement.	£13.50	Y	Y	Y

Scotland
Stirlingshire

	Nearest Road: A.811	minimum £ per person	children taken	evening meals	animals taken
Laird Andrew Haslam Culcreuch Castle Fintry Loch Lomond, Stirling G63 0LW Tel: (036086) 228555 Fax 0532 390093 Open: JAN - DEC Map Ref No. 38	Retreat to 700 years of history at magical Culcreuch, ancestral fortalice and Clan Castle of the Galbraiths, home of the Barons of Culcreuch, now a Country House Hotel where the Laird and his family extend an hospitable welcome. Set in 1600 spectacular acres, yet only 19 miles from central Glasgow, 17 from Stirling. Eight handsome, well-appointed bedrooms with en-suite or private facilities. Elegant period-style decor and antiques, log fires, the romance of dining by candlelight.	£31.00 see PHOTO over	Y	Y	Y

All the establishments mentioned in this guide are members of
The Worldwide Bed & Breakfast Association

When booking your accommodation please mention
The Best Bed & Breakfast

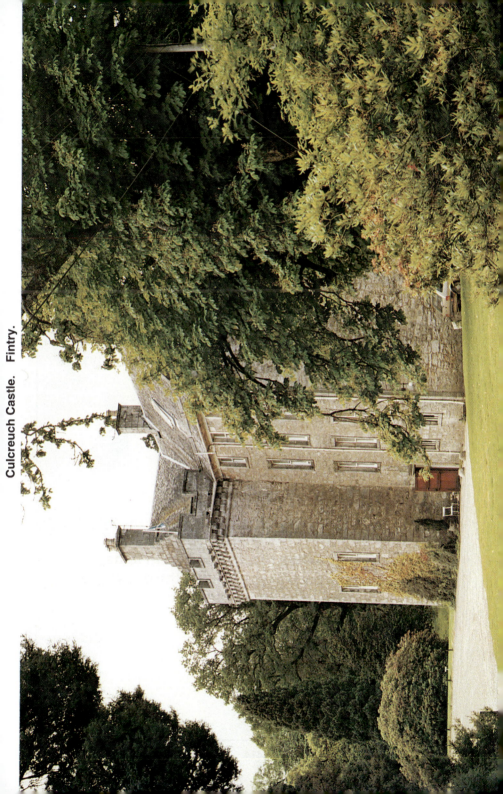

Culcreuch Castle. Fintry.

All the establishments mentioned in this guide are members of the
Worldwide Bed & Breakfast Association.

If you have any comments regarding your accommodation please send them to us using the form at the back of the book.
We value your comments.

Wales

Wales

Wales is a small country with landscapes of intense beauty. In the north are the massive mountains of the Snowdonia National Park, split by chasms & narrow passes, & bounded by quiet vales & moorland. The Lleyn peninsula & the Isle of Anglesey have lovely remote coastlines.

Forests, hills & lakeland form the scenery of Mid Wales, with the great arc of Cardigan Bay in the west.

To the south there is fertile farming land in the Vale of Glamorgan, mountains & high plateaux in the Brecon Beacons, & also the industrial valleys. The coastline forms two peninsulas, around Pembroke & the Gower.

Welsh, the oldest living language of Europe is spoken & used, most obviously in the north, & is enjoying a resurgence in the number of its speakers.

From Taliesin, the 6th century Celtic poet, to Dylan Thomas, Wales has inspired poetry & song. Every August, at the Royal National Eisteddfod, thousands gather to compete as singers, musicians & poets, or to listen & learn. In the small town of Llangollen, there is an International Music Eisteddfod for a week every July

North Wales.

North Wales is chiefly renowned for the 850 miles of the Snowdonia National Park. It is a land of mountains & lakes, rivers & waterfalls & deep glacier valleys. The scenery is justly popular with walkers & pony-trekkers, but the Snowdon Mountain Railway provides easy access to the summit of the highest mountain in the range with views over the "roof of Wales".

Within miles of this wild highland landscape is a coastline of smooth beaches & little fishing villages.

Barmouth has mountain scenery on its doorstep & miles of golden sands & estuary walks. Bangor & Llandudno are popular resort towns.

The Lleyn peninsula reaches west & is an area of great charm. Abersoch is a dinghy & windsurfing centre with safe sandy beaches. In the Middle Ages pilgrims would come to visit Bardsey, the Isle of 20,000 saints, just off Aberdaron, at the tip of the peninsula.

The Isle of Anglesey is linked to the mainland by the handsome Menai Straits Suspension Bridge. Beaumaris has a 13th century castle & many other fine buildings in its historic town centre.

Historically North Wales is a fiercely independent land where powerful local lords resisted first the Romans & later the armies of the English Kings.

The coastline is studded with 13th century castles. Dramatically sited Harlech Castle, famed in fable & song, commands the town, & wide sweep of the coastline.

The great citadel of Edward I at Caernarfon comprises the castle & the encircling town walls. In 1969 it was the scene of the investiture of His Royal Highness Prince Charles as Prince of Wales.

There are elegant stately homes like Plas Newydd in Anglesey & Eriddig House near Wrexham, but it is the variety of domestic architecture that is most charming. The timber-frame buildings of the Border country are seen at their best in historic Ruthin set in the beauti-

The Snowdon Mountain Railway.

Wales

ful Vale of Clwyd. Further west, the stone cottages of Snowdonia are built of large stones & roofed with the distinctive blue & green local slate. The low, snow-white cottages of Anglesey & the Lleyn Peninsula are typical of the "Atlantic Coast" architecture that can be found on all the western coasts of Europe. The houses are constructed of huge boulders with tiny windows & doors.

By contrast there is the marvellous fantasy of Portmeirion village. On a wooded peninsula between Harlech & Porthmadog, Sir Clough Williams Ellis created a perfect Italianate village with pastel coloured buildings, a town hall & luxury hotel.

Mid Wales

Mid Wales is farming country where people are outnumbered three to one by sheep. A flock of ewes, a lone shepherd & a Border Collie are a common sight on these green hills. Country towns like Old Radnor, Knighton & Montgomery with its castle ruin, have a timeless quality. The market towns of Rhyader, Lampeter & Dolgellau have their weekly livestock sales & annual agricultural festivals, the largest of which is the Royal Welsh Show at Builth Wells in July.

This is the background to the craft of weaving practised here for centuries. In the valley of the River Tefi & on an upper tributary of the Wye & the Irfon, there are tiny riverbank mills which produce the colourful Welsh plaid cloth.

Towards the Snowdonia National Park in the North, the land rises to the scale of true mountains. Mighty Cader Idris & the expanses of Plynlimon, once inaccessible to all but the shepherd & the mountaineer, are now popular centres for walking & pony trekking with well-signposted trails.

The line of the border with England is followed by a huge earth work of bank & ditch. This is Offa's Dyke, built by the King of Mercia around 750 A.D. to deter the Welsh from their incessant raids into his kingdom. Later the border was guarded by the castles at Hay-on-Wye, Builth Wells, Welshpool, & Chirk which date from mediaeval times.

North from Rhayader, lies the Dovey estuary & the historic town of Machynlleth. This is where Owain Glyndwr's parliament is thought to have met in 1404, & there is an exhibition about the Welsh leader in the building, believed to have been Parliament House.

Wales lost many fine religious houses during the Dissolution of the Monasteries under Henry VIII. The ruins at Cymer near Dolgellau & at Strata Florida were abbeys of the Cistercian order. However, many remote Parish Churches show evidence of the skills of mediaeval craftsmen with soaring columns & fine rood screens.

The Cambrian Coast (Cardigan Bay) has sand dunes to the north & cliffs to the south with sandy coves & miles of cliff walks.

Llangrannog Headland.

Aberystwyth is the main town of the region with two beaches & a yachting harbour, a Camera Obscura on the cliff top & some fine walks in the area. Water-skiing, windsurfing &

Wales

sailing are popular at Aberdovey, Aberaeron, New Quay, Tywyn & Barmouth & there are delightful little beaches further south at Aberporth, Tresaith or Llangrannog.

South Wales

South Wales is a region of scenic variety. The Pembrokeshire coastline has sheer cliffs, little coves & lovely beaches. Most of the area is National Park with an 80 mile foot path running along its length, passing pretty harbour villages like Solva & Broad Haven.

A great circle of Norman Castles stands guard over South Pembrokeshire, Roch, Haverfordwest, Tenby, Carew, Pembroke & Manorbier.

Tenby.

The northern headland of Saint Brides Bay is the most westerly point in the country & at the centre of a tiny village stands the Cathedral of Saint David, the Patron Saint of Wales. At Bosherton near Saint Govans Head, there is a tiny chapel hidden in a cleft in the massive limestone cliffs.

The Preseli Hills hold the vast prehistoric burial chambers of Pentre Ifan, & the same mountains provided the great blue stones used at faraway Stonehenge.

Laugharne is the village where Dylan Thomas lived & worked in what was a boat-house & is now a museum.

In the valleys, towns like Merthyr Tydfil, Ebbw Vale & Treorchy were in the forefront of the boom years of the Industrial Revolution. Now the heavy industries are fast declining & the ravages of the indiscriminate mining & belching smoke of the blast furnaces are disappearing. The famous Male Voice Choirs & the love of rugby football survives.

The Vale of Glamorgan is a rural area with pretty villages. Beyond here the land rises steeply to the high wild moorlands & hill farms of the Brecon Beacons National Park & the Black Mountains, lovely areas for walking & pony trekking.

The Wye Valley leads down to Chepstow & here set amidst the beautiful woodlands is the ruin of the Great Abbey of Tintern, founded in 1131 by the Cistercian Order.

Swansea has a strong sea-faring tradition maintained by its new Marine Quarter - marina, waterfront village, restaurants, art gallery & theatre.

Cardiff, the capital of Wales, is a pleasant city with acres of parkland, the lovely River Taff, & a great castle, as well as a new civic centre, two theatres & the ultra-modern St. David's Concert Hall. It is the home of the Welsh National Opera & here also is the National Stadium where the singing of the rugby crowd on a Saturday afternoon is a treat.

Pony Trekking

Wales

Wales Gazeteer

Areas of Outstanding Natural Beauty
The Pembrokeshire Coast. The Brecon Beacons. Snowdonia. Gower.'

Historic Houses & Castles

Cardiff Castle - Cardiff
Built on a Roman site in the 11th century.
Caerphilly Castle - Caerphilly
13th century fortress.
Chirk Castle - Nr. Wrexham
14th century Border Castle. Lovely gardens.
Coity Castle - Coity
Mediaeval stronghold - three storied round tower.
Gwydir Castle - Nr. Lanrwst
Royal residence in past days - wonderful Tudor furnishings. Gardens with peacocks.
Penrhyn Castle - Bangor
Neo-Norman architecture 19th century - large grounds with museum & exhibitions. Victorian garden.
Picton Castle - Haverfordwest
12th century - lived in by the same family continuously. Fine gardens.
Caernarfon Castle - Caernarfon
13th century - castle of great importance to Edward I.
Conway Castle - Conwy
13th century - one of Edward I's chain of castles.
Powis Castle - Welshpool
14th century - reconstruction work in 17th century. Murals, furnishings, tapestries & paintings, terraced gardens.
Pembroke Castle - Pembroke
12th century Norman castle with huge keep & immense walls. Birthplace of Henry VII.
Plas Newydd - Isle of Anglesey
18th century Gothic style house, home of the Marquis of Anglesey. Stands on the edge of the Menai Strait looking across to the Snowdonia Range. Famous for the Rex Whistler murals.
The Tudor Merchant's House - Tenby
Built in 15th century.
Tretower Court & Castle - Crickhowell
Mediaeval - finest example in Wales.

Cathedrals & Churches

St. Asaph Cathedral
13th century - 19th century restoration. Smallest of Cathedrals in England & Wales.
Holywell (St. Winifred)
15th century well chapel & chamber - fine example.
St. Davids (St. David)
12th century Cathedral - splendid tower - oak roof to nave.
Gwent (St. Woolos)
Norman Cathedral - Gothic additions - 19th century restoration.
Abergavenny (St. Mary)
14th century church of 12th cventury Benedictine priory.
Llanengan (St. Engan)
Mediaeval church - very large with original roof & stalls 16th century tower.
Esyronen
17th century chapel, much original interior remaining.
Llangdegley (St. Tegla)
18th century Quaker meeting house - thatched roof - simple structure divided into schoolroom & meeting room.
Llandaff Cathedral (St. Peter & St. Paul)
Founded in 6th century - present building began in 12th century. Great damage suffered in bombing during war, now restored with Epstein's famous figure of Christ.

Museums & Galleries

National Museum of Wales - Cardiff (also Turner House)
Geology, archaeology, zoology, botany, industry, & art exhibitions.
Welsh Folk Museum - St. Fagans Castle - Cardiff
13th century walls curtaining a 16th century house - now a most interesting & comprehensive folk museum.
County Museum - Carmarthen
Roman jewellery, gold, etc. Romano-British & Stone Age relics.
National Library of Wales - Aberystwyth
Records of Wales & Celtic areas. Great historical interest.
University College of Wales Gallery - Aberystwyth
Travelling exhibitions of painting & sculpture.

Wales

Newport Museum & Art Gallery - Newport
Specialist collection of English watercolours - natural history, Roman remains, etc.
Legionary Museum - Caerleon
Roman relics found on the site of legionary fortress at Risca.
Nelson Museum - Monmouth
Interesting relics of Admiral Lord Nelson & Lady Hamilton.
Bangor Art Gallery - Bangor
Exhibitions of contemporary paintings & sculpture.
Bangor Museum of Welsh Antiquities - Bangor
History of North Wales is shown. Splendid exhibits of furniture, clothing, domestic objects, etc.
Also Roman antiquities.
Narrow Gauge Railway Museum - Tywyn
Rolling stock & exhibitions of narrow gauge railways of U.K.

Museum of Childhood - Menai Bridge
Charming museum of dolls & toys & children's things.
Brecknock Museum - Brecon
Natural history, archaeology, agriculture, local history, etc.
Glynn Vivian Art Gallery & Museum - Swansea
Ceramics, old & contemporary, British paintings & drawings, sculpture, loan exhibitions.
Stone Museum - Margam
Carved stones & crosses from pre-historic times.
Plas Mawr - Conwy
A beautiful Elizabethan town mansion house in its original condition. Now holds the Royal Cambrain Academy of Art.

Historic Monuments

Rhuddlan Castle - Rhuddlan
13th century castle - interesting diamond plan.
Valle Crucis Abbey - Llangollen
13th century Cistercian Abbey Church.

Cader Idris.

WALES
Map references

01	Webb	34	Bayles	42	Cole
02	Sumner	35	Pinnock	43	Hammond
03	Gallagher	36	Clayton	44	N. Jones
05	B. Jones	36	Murray	45	Usborne
06	Spencer	37	Newton Davies	46	Roberts
07	Parry	37	Roberts	47	Hood
08	Roberts	38	Hirst	48	Knott
09	Vaughton	39	Hughes	49	Bright
10	Heard	40	Rigby	50	Richards
11	Barlow	40	Cotton	51	Marriott
12	Moore	41	Barker	52	Emberton
13	McHugh			53	G.Jones
15	Fielder			54	Gilder
16	Milliner			55	Park
16	Shumack				
17	Hurley				
18	Renwick				
19	Wearing				
20	Weatherill				
21	Price				
22	Stubbs				
23	Hunter				
24	Watkins				
25	Harris				
26	Bradley				
27	Hayman- Joyce				
27	Armitage				
28	Wilde Reynolds				
29	Fullard				
30	Thompson				
31	Cutler				
31	Howard				
31	Muskus				
31	Fakhri				
31	Ratcliffe				
31	Valadini				
32	Michael				
33	Stephens				

Wales
Clwyd

		minimum £ per person	children taken	evening meals	animals taken

Mrs Gwyneth Webb Plas Newydd Farm Llanddulas Abergele LL22 8HH Tel: (0492) 516038 Open: APR - OCT Map Ref No. 01	Nearest Road: A.55 A lovely 400 year-old Welsh farmhouse retaining its original character including lots of oak beams. Accommodation is in 3 pleasant bedrooms with modern amenities. An ideal base for touring as Snowdonia, Conway & Anglesey are within easy reach, also conveniently placed for the local beaches & outdoor activities.	£12.50	Y	N	N
Cedric B. Sumner & Frances Williams-Lee Buck Farm Hanmer SY14 7LX Tel: (094874) 339 Open: ALL YEAR Map Ref No. 02	Nearest Road: On A.525 between Wrexham/Whitchurch. Warm hospitality in an unspoilt, half timbered 16th century farmhouse. A 1 acre woodland lovely with changing drifts of wildflowers from Spring to mid-Summer. A wild garden alive with butterflies. Ideal for touring North Wales, Cheshire, Shropshire & Staffordshire. Excellent wholefood country cooking using fresh local produce, organic when possible. Wholemeal breads, granola, vegetable soups (no M.S.G.) Vegetarian, vegan, meat meals. Special diets on request. Library, music.	£15.00	Y	Y	N
A. Gallagher & B. Jones Bwlch-y-Rhiw Farmhouse Bwlchrhiw Llansilin SY6 7PT Tel: (0691) 70261 Open: MAR-NOV Map Ref No. 03	Nearest Road: A.5, B.4580 A fine 18th century farmhouse perched above the Welsh/English border with superb views. Offering spacious en-suite guest rooms with colour T.V., radio & tea/coffee makers. A hearty breakfast is served in the oak beamed dining room. A large, elegant & comfortable lounge is also available. Patio & garden for guests use. An ideal area for walking, pony trekking, bird watching & private fishing. Within easy reach are Shewsbury, Chester, Llangollen & various National Trust properties.	£16.00	Y	N	N
Beryl J. Jones Bryn Awel Farm Brynawel Bontuchel Ruthin LL15 2DE Tel: (08242) 2481 Open: ALL YEAR Map Ref No. 05	Nearest Road: A.5105, A.5 This 35 acre working farm is situated in the beautiful hamlet of Bontuchel, where you can relax in perfect peace & tranquility & enjoy a wealth of wonderful walks, wild flowers & wild life. Beryl has many cooking awards to her credit & can oblige most requests for special diets. Tea making facilities in all rooms. Heating throughout. A warm welcome & good food is top priority at this farmhouse.	£13.00	Y	Y	N
Mrs E.A. Parry Llainwen Ucha Pentre Celyn Ruthin LL15 2HL Tel: (097888) 253 Open: ALL YEAR Map Ref No. 07	Nearest Road: A.525 A working farm set in 130 acres overlooking the beautiful Vale of Clwyd. Offering 2 pleasantly decorated rooms with modern amenities, accommodating up to 5 persons. All rooms are centrally heated. Good home cooking made with fresh local produce. Offa's Dyke, fishing & pony riding nearby. Conveniently situated for visiting Chester, Llangollen, Snowdonia & the Coast. A home from home atmosphere with a warm & friendly welcome is assured.	£11.00	Y	Y	N

Wales
Clwyd

			minimum £ per person	children taken	evening meals	animals taken
Mrs Jen Spencer Eyarth Station Llanfair D.C. Ruthin LL15 2EE Tel: (08242) 3643 Open: ALL YEAR Map Ref No. 06	Nearest Road: A.525 A warm & friendly reception awaits the visitor to Eyarth Station. A super converted former railway station located in the beautiful countryside of the Vale of Clwyd. A choice of 6 bedrooms, all with private shower. There is a comfortable colour T.V. lounge & guests are welcome to use the garden, sun patio & outdoor heated pool. Conveniently located for the many historic towns in the region including Conwy, Caernarfon & Ruthin Castles with mediaeval banquet 2 minutes drive. Chester is also within driving distance. Winner of Best Bed & Breakfast Award.		£17.00 *see PHOTO over*	Y	Y	Y
Anwen Roberts Bach-y-Graig Farm Bach-y-Graig Tremeirchion St. Asaph LL17 0UH Tel: (0745) 730627 Open: ALL YEAR Map Ref No. 08	Nearest Road: A.55, A.541 Stay in the Vale of Clwyd in the oldest brick built house in Wales having a datestone of 1567, recently modernised yet still retaining its former charm. The comfort of guests is a priority here. 3 en-suite bedrooms with T.V., radio alarm & tea/coffee making facilities. Central heating, log fire, colour T.V. in lounge. Walk a medieval woodland trail on this 200 acre dairy farm.		£15.00	Y	N	N

Dyfed

Mrs C.M. Vaughton Awel-Y-Grug Boncath SA37 0JP Tel: (0239) 841260 Open: ALL YEAR Map Ref No. 09	Nearest Road: B.4332 Awel-Y-Grug is a small family-run guest house where guests are welcome to a relaxed homely atmosphere. Good & plentiful home-cooked food is served using home grown fruit & vegetables when available & vegetarian meals are a speciality. Licenced. 4 bedrooms, 2 with en-suite facilities. Dining room, T.V. lounge with log fires, games room & a large & pleasant garden. Children welcome. Laundry facilities & cots & highchairs available. Credit cards accepted.		£14.00	Y	Y	Y
Peter Heard Tregynon Country Farmhouse Hotel Gwaun Valley Fishguard SA65 9TU Tel: (0239) 820531 Fax 0239 820531 Open: ALL YEAR Map Ref No. 10	Nearest Road: B.4313, This is a traditional beamed, award winning 16th century family-run farmhouse, standing in acres of grounds by ancient oak woodlands, overlooking the glorious Gwaun Valley in the Pembrokeshire Coast National Park. It is unique & of great natural beauty & still quite unspoiled. Offering 8 rooms, all en-suite & on the ground floor. Traditional & special diets, wholefood & vegetarian specialities, using fresh local produce when possible. A good range of wine is also available. Own trout ponds, 200ft waterfall & Iron Age fort, abundant wildlife.		£19.90	Y	Y	N

Eyarth Station. Llanfair D.C.

Wales
Dyfed

			minimum £ per person	children taken	evening meals	animals taken
Mrs P. Barlow Rosehill Farm Slebech Haverfordwest SA62 4AY Tel: (0437) 751204 Fax 0437 751204 Open: ALL YEAR Map Ref No. 11	Nearest Road: A.40 Large Georgian farmhouse within the Pembrokeshire National Park. Formerly the home farm for the Slebech Estate. Beautifully situated in the centre of its own land with extensive views over surrounding countryside & woodland. Fully modernised to a very high standard whilst retaining its character & comfortably furnished with antiques. Cleddau Estuary & Picton Castle 2 minutes drive. Coast 2 mins. Fishguard & Pembroke ferries 35 minutes.		£15.00	Y	N	Y
Mr & Mrs M. J. Moore Hotel Plas Glyn-y-Mel Lower Fishguard SA65 9LY Tel: (0348) 872296 Open: MAR - NOV Map Ref No. 12	Nearest Road: A.40, A487. Plas Glyn-y-Mel is an imposing Grade 11 listed Georgian country house. Splendidly located in the shelter of the Gwaun Valley, it nestles in 20 acres of mature, wooded grounds offering beautiful views across the garden meadows to the River Gwaun. Recently refurbished, it now offers elegant accommodation in a choice of 4 individually designed & furnished bedrooms each with en-suite facilities & tea/coffee makers. Chef-proprietor Mike provides excellent cuisine & extensive wine list.		£34.00 *see PHOTO over*	Y	Y	Y
Mrs Jill McHugh The Old Vicarage Manorbier SA70 7TN Tel: (0834) 871452 Open: ALL YEAR Map Ref No. 13	Nearest Road: A.4139 Overlooking the coastal villages of Manorbier with its 11th century castle. The Old Vicarage is set in its own mature grounds of 2 & a half acres & offers the perfect stepping off point for exploring the magnificent scenery of Pembrokeshire. There are 2 spacious bedrooms with views across Barafundle Bay. The renowned Pembrokeshire coastal path passes through the village. A non-smoking establishment. Beaches a 5 mins. walk.		£15.00	Y	N	N
L.E. & J.M. Fielder Old Stable Cottage Carew Tenby SA70 8SL Tel: (0646) 651889 Open: APR - OCT Map Ref No. 15	Nearest Road: A.477 At one time a carthouse and stables for Carew Castle, Old Stable Cottage, (Grade II listed), with its Inglenook fireplace and original bread oven, is full of charm. The stable is now a games room and a spiral staircase leads to the 3 well-appointed, en-suite bedrooms. Delicious food is prepared in the farmhouse kitchen with Aga cooker. A conservatory overlooks the walled garden and barbeque area. Children over 5 .		£22.50	Y	Y	N
P.G. & M.J. Gilder Llangwm House Whitland SA34 0RB Tel: (0994) 240621 Open: ALL YEAR Map Ref No. 54	Nearest Road: A.40 Llangwm House is a large, fully modernised farmhouse set in 11 acres of grass & woodland with panoramic views over the surrounding country. It is ideally situated for the Pembrokeshire Coast with its beautiful beaches, walks & abundant wildlife. All bedrooms are tastefully furnished & decorated with comfort in mind. Superb cuisine prepared by Margaret using fresh local produce. Local activities include riding, golf, course fishing, etc.		£13.00	Y	Y	Y

Hotel Plas Glyn-y-Mel. Lower Fishguard.

Wales
Glamorgan

		minimum £ per person	children taken	evening meals	animals taken
Mr & Mrs C.H. Milliner Clayton Hotel 65 Stacey Road Roath Cardiff CF2 1DS Tel: (0222) 492345 Open:ALLYEAR(excl.Xmas) Map Ref No. 16	Nearest Road: A.48 Clayton Hotel is a long established family-run hotel. Accommodation is in 10 guest bedrooms, 4 with private showers & tea/coffee makers. A colour T.V. lounge & licenced bar are also available. This makes a convenient base from which to visit Cardiff's many local attractions. Special diets can be catered for with prior notice.	£15.00	Y	Y	N
Mr & Mrs G. J. Shumack Princes Guest House 10 Princes Street Roath Cardiff CF2 3PR Tel: (0222) 491732 Open: ALL YEAR Map Ref No. 16	Nearest Road: A.48, M.4 A long established family-run guest house with a homely atmosphere. Offering 7 rooms with modern amenities including colour T.V. & tea/coffee makers; some are with private showers. Residents' lounge available throughout the day. Special diets can be catered for by arrangement. 'Princes' makes a convenient base from which to visit Cardiff & the surrounding area with its many attractions.	£13.00	Y	Y	N
Michael & Kathleen Hurley Tregenna Hotel Park Terrace Merthyr Tydfil CF47 8RF Tel: (0685) 723627/82055 1 800 926 3193(USA TollFree) Open: ALL YEAR Map Ref No. 17	Nearest Road: A.470 Family-run hotel with high degree of comfort & class. 23 bedrooms with bathroom, 7 of which are designated for tourists & family use at special rates (50% reduction for children sharing). Telephone, tea/coffee service tray, colour T.V. in all rooms. Lunch, afternoon tea & dinner served 7 days a week. Brecon Beacons National Park 8 minutes drive. 45 minutes Cardiff/Wales Airport. Two & a quater hours London Heathrow Airport.	£17.50	Y	Y	Y
Paul & Monica Renwick Sant-Y-Nyll House St. Brides-Super-Ely CF5 6EZ Tel: (0446) 760209 Open: ALL YEAR Map Ref No. 18	Nearest Road: M.4 You can be assured of a friendly welcome to Sant-Y-Nyll, a charming Georgian country residence in its own extensive grounds with spectacular views over the Vale of Glamorgan. 6 guests rooms with modern facilities, T.V., tea/coffee making, comfortable, warm & relaxing. Licenced. Children welcome. Cardiff just 7 miles. St. Fagans Welsh Folk Museum 2 miles. Paul & Monica look forward to meeting you.	£15.00	Y	N	Y
Heather & Bruce Wearing Parkway Hotel 253 Gower Road Sketty Swansea SA29JL Tel(0792) 201632/201839 OpenALLYEAR(Excl.Xmas) Map Ref No. 19	Nearest Road: A.4118 A small mansion-style house in its own grounds offering 15 pleasant, comfortable en-suite rooms with tea making facilities. This is an ideal base for touring the lovely Gower Peninsula & Swansea Bay. The city centre is easily accessible & is full of interest, as are the many historic sites which are found in this region. Personal service & warm welcome await all visitors in a friendly & relaxed atmosphere.	£23.00	N	Y	Y

Wales
Gwent

			minimum £ per person	children taken	evening meals	animals taken
Mr & Mrs Bruce Weatherill Llanwenarth House Govilon Abergavenny NP7 9SF Tel: (0873) 830289 Open: MAR - JAN Map Ref No. 20	Nearest Road: A.465 A truly delightful 16th century manor house, standing in its own beautiful grounds & surrounded by the tranquil scenic hills of the Brecon Beacons National Park. Elegantly furnished, tastefully decorated & with superb views, this house is a real pleasure to visit. Dinner prepared by Amanda, a Cordon Bleu cook, is a delight. It is served by candlelight in the lovely dining room. Accommodation is in 5 rooms all with en-suite facilities. Fishing, golf, climbing, walking & shooting nearby. Children over 10 yrs. please. 1992 Garden Festival at Ebbw Vale.		£30.50	Y	Y	Y
Mrs Dinah Price 'Great House' Isca Road Old Village Caerleon NP6 1QG Tel: (0633) 420216/312 Open: ALL YEAR Map Ref No. 21	Nearest Road: A.48, M.4 'Great House' is an attractive 17th century home located on the banks of the River Usk. Retaining much of its original character, including beams & inglenook fireplaces, this delightful home offers very pretty accommodation in 4 rooms with T.V. & tea/coffee making facilites. An attractive T.V. lounge & pretty garden are also available for guests' use. Within easy reach are riding, golf, fishing & forest trails. Roman amphitheatre, museums & the ancient village of Caerleon. Ideal as a stop over.		£18.00	Y	N	N
Mrs Julia Hunter Spring Farm Brockweir Chepstow NP6 7NU Tel: (0291) 689439 Open: ALL YEAR (excl. Xmas & New Year) Map Ref No. 23	Nearest Road: A.466 Spring Farm is located in an area of outstanding beauty with breathtaking views across the Wye Valley. This lovely old stone farmhouse stands in an idyllic, peaceful setting, nestled into the hillside overlooking the River Wye. Beautifully furnished, with 3 lovely bedrooms, 2 with en-suite bathrooms. In addition to the traditional English breakfast a 4-course dinner is available. Close to Tintern Abbey & many Welsh border castles Riding, fishing, pony trekking, golf		£23.00	N	Y	N
Mrs Beryl Watkins The Glebe Croes-Y-Ceiliog Cwmbran NP44 2DE Tel: (063349) 251 Open: ALL YEAR Map Ref No. 24	Nearest Road: A.4042, M.4. A friendly & helpful host awaits you at Glebe Farm. A spacious, modern farmhouse overlooking a lovely corner of rural Wales where the family have farmed for generations. Offering 4 attractive & comfortable rooms with modern amenities. A substantial breakfast is served in the morning & in the evening good pub fare can be found a pleasant walk away. Ideal for a relaxing break. Convenient for the M.4./M.5		£15.00	Y	N	N
Mr & Mrs B.L. Harris The Wenallt Abergavenny Gilwern NP7 0HP Tel: (0873) 830694 Open: ALL YEAR Map Ref No. 25	Nearest Road: A.465 A 16th century Welsh longhouse set in 50 acres of farmland in the Brecon Beacons National Park commanding magnificent views over the Usk Valley. Retaining all its old charm with oak beams, inglenook fireplace, yet offering a high standard of accommodation with en-suite bedrooms, good food & a warm welcome. An ideal base from which to see Wales & the surrounding areas. Licenced.		£14.50	Y	Y	Y

Wales
Gwent

		minimum £ per person	children taken	evening meals	animals taken

Dereck & Vickie Stubbs **Parva Farmhouse Hotel** **& Restaurant** Tintern Parva, Tintern Chepstow NP6 6SQ Tel: (0291) 689411 Open: ALL YEAR Map Ref No. 22	Nearest Road: A.466, M.4, A delightful 17th century stone farmhouse situated 50 yards from the River Wye. The quaint bedrooms with their designer fabrics are gorgeous, some offering breathtaking views over the River Wye & woodland. The beamed lounge with log fires, leather chesterfields & 'Honesty Bar' is a tranquil haven in which to unwind. Mouth-watering dishes served in the intimate candlelit, Inglenook Restaurant, reflects the owner's love of cooking.	£21.00	Y	Y	Y
			see PHOTO over		
Mrs C.T. Park **Brick House Country** **Guest House** Redwick Newport NP6 3DX Tel: (0633) 880230 Open: ALL YEAR Map Ref No. 55	Nearest Road: M.4 Brick House Farm is a listed Grade II Georgian farmhouse dating from about 1765, but with up-to-date conveniences. All double bedrooms have en-suite bathroom. A pleasant T.V. lounge, dinning room & bar. Full central heating. There is a delightful garden where guests may take cream teas, weather permitting. Brick House is ideally placed for touring South Wales & the Wye Valley, or as a stopping-off point just over the Severn Bridge.	£19.00	Y	Y	N
Ann Bradley **Pentwyn Farm** Little Mill Pontypool NP4 0HQ Tel: (049528) 249 Open: MAR - OCT Map Ref No. 26	Nearest Road: A.472 Pentwyn, where good food and hospitality are of prime importance, is a 120 acre farm situated on the edge of the Brecon Beacons National Park. The 16th century pink-washed Welsh longhouse has the comforts of the 20th century without loss of traditional character. Large garden with swimming pool. 4 pretty bedrooms (2 en-suite), with tea making facilities. Lounge with open fire and piano. Restaurant licence. Rough shooting available.	£13.00	Y	Y	N
Mrs D Hayman-Joyce **Ty Isha** Mamhilad Pontypool NP4 0JE Tel: (049528) 573 Open: JAN - DEC Map Ref No. 27	Nearest Road: A.4042 An attractive Welsh farmhouse set amongst the peaceful green fields of Gwent with views of the Black Mountains. Comfortable accommodation is offered in 2 rooms, twin or family, with wash-basins, shaver points, tea trays and adjoining bathroom with shower. Cots and high chairs available. Breakfast, traditional or continental, is served in the spacious farmhouse kitchen. Evening meals on request only.	£14.00	Y	N	Y
Mrs S. D. Armitage **Ty'r-Ywen Farm** Lasgarn Lane Mamhilad via Trevethin Pontypool NP4 8TT Tel: (049528) 200 Open: ALL YEAR Map Ref No. 27	Nearest Road: A.472, M.4 A remote & secluded 16th century Welsh longhouse high on the Gwent Ridgeway in the Brecon Beacons National Park with 30 mile views down the Usk Valley. Spacious bedrooms including 1 twin & 2 four poster rooms. One delightful four-poster room with jacuzzi. All have colour T.V.'s, radio & luxury en-suite bathrooms. An ideal centre for walking. Dinner available with advance notice only. 'Phone for directions.	£16.00	N	Y	Y

Parva Farmhouse and Restaurant. Tintern.

Wales
Gwynedd

			minimum £ per person	children taken	evening meals	animals taken
Mr & Mrs R. Fullard Melin Meloch Llanfor Bala LL23 7DP Tel: (0678) 520101 Open: FEB-DEC Map Ref No. 29	Nearest Road: A.494 Close to the River Dee, just outside Bala, stands this interesting old water mill & Miller's house. Set in 3 acres of lovely landscaped watergardens with trout stream, fish from which may be served at the table for dinner. Offering accommodation in 3 pretty rooms all with en-suite facilities. Relax in the hospitable atmosphere of very comfortable spacious lounges filled with interesting by-gones.		£14.00	Y	Y	Y
Barbara Wilde Reynolds Dewis Cyfarfod Llandderfel Bala LL23 7DR Tel: (06783) 243 Open: ALL YEAR Map Ref No. 28	Nearest Road: A.494 A charming 300 year-old stone-built house standing in 7 acres of beautiful grounds overlooking the River Dee in a magnificent wooded valley. Traditionally & most comfortably furnished with antiques, old prints & original paintings. Log fires, oak beams, lots of good books, maps & guides create a wonderful, friendly atmosphere. Offering 5 comfortable bedrooms, most with en-suite facilities, radio, T.V., hairdryers & tea/coffee makers. The food is excellent & special diets can be catered for with advance notice. Plenty to do nearby: fishing, swimming, sailing & windsurfing. Children over 9 only.		£19.00	Y	Y	Y
Paula Thompson Llwyndu Farmhouse Llwyndu Llanaber Barmouth LL42 1RR Tel: (0341) 280144 Open: FEB-NOV Map Ref No. 30	Nearest Road: A.496 Enjoy a relaxed, friendly stay in this 17th century farmhouse & converted granary. Wonderfully situated over Cardigan Bay. All 7 bedrooms have great charm & are en-suite some with T.V. Savour imaginative dishes, including vegetarian, in a superb atmosphere of oak beams & inglenooks. Dinner by candlelight Licenced. Log fires in Winter. Children very welcome. Beaches nearby. Peacefully secluded yet convenient for Barmouth.		£18.00	Y	Y	Y
Modwena and Ian Cutler Penmachno Hall Penmachno Betws Y Coed LL24 0PU Tel: (06903) 207 Open: JAN - DEC Map Ref No. 31	Nearest Road: A.5 Discover the secret Snowdonia at Penmachno. Formerly the rectory & now set in the secluded & peaceful Glascwn Valley, but only 5 miles from the bustle of Betws-y-Coed. Ideally located for walking, bird watching, pony trekking & canoeing. The motto here is; good food, good wine, good company. The aim is to create an informal house party atmosphere while providing the best in home cooking. Visa accepted.		£22.00	Y	Y	N
Ann Howard Tan Dinas Guest Hosue Coed Cynhelier Road Betws-Y-Coed LL24 0BL Tel: (0690) 710635 Open: ALL YEAR Map Ref No. 31	Nearest Road: A.5 A warm welcome awaits you at this lovley Victorian country home, situated in 3 acres of woodland gardens, offering peace & seclusion, & only 500 yards from village centre. Guests may choose from 7 spacious, centrally heated rooms, with lovely views. All rooms have h&c & tea/coffee making facilities. 3 rooms en-suite. Log fires in winter. Forest walks from house. Golf & fishing nearby. Ideal touring centre. Ample parking. Non-smokers only. Evening meals available. Licenced.Video library.		£15.00	Y	Y	N

431

Wales
Gwynedd

			per person minimum £	children taken	evening meals	animals taken
M. & R.E. Fakhri **Bryn Bella Guest House** Llanrwst Road Betws-Y-Coed LL24 0HD Tel: (0690) 710627 Open: ALL YEAR Map Ref No. 31		Nearest Road: A.5, A.470 Nestling in a quiet wooded hillside in the Snowdonia National Park, Bryn Bella is a small Victorian guest house overlooking the picturesque village of Betws-Y-Coed, standing at the junction between the Conwy, Llugwy & Lledr Rivers & their valleys. 6 comfortably furnished rooms with washbasins, tea/coffee making facilities & colour T.V. Some rooms have shower/w.c. en-suite. Betws-Y-Coed is an ideal base for touring, climbing, riding, fishing, golf & many other outdoor activities.	£13.00	Y	N	N
Jim Ratcliffe **Ty Gwyn Hotel** Betws-Y-Coed LL24 0SG Tel: (0690) 710383/ 710787 Open: ALL YEAR Map Ref No. 31		Nearest Road: A.5 Open fire, beamed ceilings & antique furniture all help to recall the days when this small friendly family hotel was a coaching inn. Each pretty bedroom (some with 4-poster beds) has its own tasteful colour scheme & interesting"bric a brac"to add a homely touch. Ty Gwyn offers food which is a tribute to the local area & is ideal for exploring the Snowdonia range, coastal towns & Lleyn Peninsula.	£17.00	Y	Y	Y
Raymond & Barbara Valadini **Henlly (Old Court) Hotel** Old Church Road Betws-Y-Coed LL24 0AL Tel: (0690) 710534 Open: ALL YEAR Map Ref No. 31		Nearest Road: A.5 A non-smoking, informal hotel, peacefully situated on the banks of the River Conwy, away from traffic, 5 minutes walk from town centre. Tastefully converted Court House & Police Station full of charm & character. 10 individual bedrooms, all with private facilities, 8 en-suite, tea/coffee making facilities, colour T.V. Riverside Lounge, fire side Cocktail Bar. Superb cuisine, personally run by resident proprietors.	£21.50	Y	Y	N
Barrie & Hazel Michael **Tan-y-Foel Country House** Capel Garmon Betws-y-Coed LL26 0RE Tel: (0690) 710507 Open: MAR - JAN Map Ref No. 32		Nearest Road: A.470 Located in a uniquely peaceful valley high above the busy village of Betws-y-Coed, the views from Tan-y-Foel are outstanding. Peace, tranquility & hospitality are made perfect by the exceptionally fine food & the relaxed informality of the Michaels who are generous hosts with an infectious sense of humour. Facilities include heated swimming pool, antique billiard table, private fishing.	£35.50 *see PHOTO over*	N	Y	Y
Richard Bayles **The White House** Llanfaglan Caernarfon LL54 5RA Tel: (0286) 673003 Open: JAN - DEC Map Ref No. 34		Nearest Road: A.487 The White House is a large detached house in its own grounds, overlooking Foryd Bay with the Snowdonia mountains behind. There are 5 tastefully decorated bedrooms all with bath or shower, tea/coffee making facilities & colour T.V. Guests are welcome to use the residents' lounge, outdoor pool & gardens. Ideally situated for birdwatching, walking, windsurfing, golf & visiting the historic Welsh castles.	£16.00	Y	N	Y

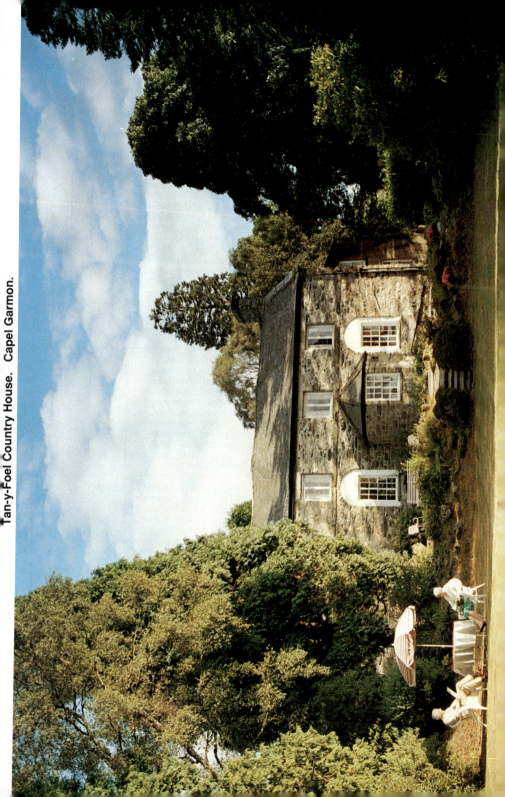

Tan-y-Foel Country House. Capel Garmon.

Wales
Gwynedd

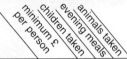

			per person minimum £	children taken	evening meals	animals taken
Maureen & Clive Muskus Ty'n-Y-Celyn House Llanrwst Road Betws-Y-Coed LL24 0HD Tel: (0690) 710202 Fax 0690 710800 Open: MAR - DEC Map Ref No. 31	Nearest Road: A.470 A high standard of comfort & friendly, helpful hosts await you at Ty'n-Y-Celyn. This large Victorian home located in a lovely position above the picturesque village of Betws-Y-Coed has panoramic views of the Llugney Valley, mountains & Conway river. Accommodation is in a choice of 8 very comfortable en-suite bedrooms with T.V. & tea/coffee makers, most also have wonderful views. A residents' T.V. lounge & garden are also available. This is an ideal centre for touring, walking, fishing & golf.		£17.00 see PHOTO over	Y	N	Y
Mr & Mrs J. Pinnock Cae Cyd Groeslon Caernarfon LL54 7DP Tel: (0286) 880253 Open: APR - OCT Map Ref No. 35	Nearest Road: A.487 For a peaceful bed and breakfast stay in Cae Cyd, a small Welsh stone cottage with character, set in 3 acres of garden, on the edge of Snowdonia National Park. Delight in the views of Caernarfon Bay and Anglesey, walk in the fields, watch the sunsets over the sea. Accommodation is in two guest bedrooms, a double and a twin-bedded room.		£14.00	N	N	Y
Pat Clayton Trefaes Guest House Y Maes Criccieth LL52 0AE Tel: (0766) 523204 Fax 0766 523013 OpenALL YEAR(Excl. Xmas) Map Ref No. 36	Nearest Road: A.497 An elegant Edwardian house on the edge of Criccieth Green, with views of the sea and Castle. The three comfortable bedrooms have en-suite facilities, T.V., tea/coffee tray, central heating. Quiet lounge for reading, writing, cards. Delicious breakfasts. Guests may relax in the garden with a Welsh tea. Evening meals are fish and vegetarian cuisine only. Parking in grounds. Excellent base for historic sites, sea and walking holidays. Children over 5 please.		£15.00	Y	Y	N
Mrs Rita Murray Min-Y-Gaer Hotel Porthmadog Road Criccieth LL52 0HP Tel: (0766) 522151 Open: MAR- OCT Map Ref No. 36	Nearest Road: A.497 A pleasantly licenced house, in a quiet residential area, offering very good accommodation in 10 comfortable rooms, of which most have a bathroom en-suite, all have a colour T.V. & tea/coffee making facilities. The hotel enjoys commanding views of Criccieth Castle & the scenic Cardigan Bay coastline & is only 2 minutes walk from the safe, sandy beach. Car parking on the premises. An ideal base for touring Snowdonia.		£14.50	Y	Y	Y
Gillian & Eric Newton Davies Noddfa Hotel Lower Road Harlech LL46 2UB Tel: (0766) 780043 Open: ALL YEAR Map Ref No. 37	Nearest Road: A.496 A Victorian country house situated within the National Park with superb views of Snowdon, Tremadog Bay & Harlech Castle. 5 comfortable rooms (3 en-suite, T.V.). Extensive menu, licenced. Gillian & Eric will be delighted to explain the Medieval weaponry displayed in the bar, the history of Harlech Castle & give archery lessons in the hotel grounds. Very close to the Castle, beach, indoor swimming pool & theatre.		£15.00	Y	Y	N

Ty'n-Y-Celyn House.   Betws-Y-Coed.

Llwydiarth Fawr Farm. Anglesey.

Wales
Gwynedd

		minimum £ per person	children taken	evening meals	animals taken
Mr & Mrs G. H. Roberts Castle Cottage Hotel Pen Llech Harlech LL46 2YL Tel: (0766) 780479 Open: ALL YEAR Map Ref No. 37	Nearest Road: A.496, A.470 Castle Cottage is a comfortable family-run hotel & restaurant. This delightful house, dating back at least 200 years, has many exposed beams offers 6 rooms of great character which are comfortable & have modern amenities. The restaurant is know for its good food. Only 200 yards from Harlech Castle. The beach & nature reserve are within 5 miles. An ideal base for touring this lovely region. Golf arrangements at Royal St. Davids. Garden for guests' use.	£19.00	Y	Y	Y
Tony & Gina Hirst Hafod Country House Cemaes Bay Isle of Anglesey LL67 0DS Tel: (0407) 710500 Open: ALL YEAR Map Ref No. 38	Nearest Road: A.5025 A spacious Edwardian house standing in an acre of garden. Set in peaceful surroundings with superb sea & mountain views. Only a 10 mins. walk to the village with its picturesque harbour & sandy beach. Accommodation is in 3 comfortable bedrooms, 2 en-suite, with beverage facilities. A large, elegant lounge with colour T.V. & dining room are also available. Garden with tennis & croquet. Renowned for excellent food. Licenced. Nearby is golf, bird sanctuary, lake & sea fishing.	£14.50	Y	Y	N
Mrs Margaret Hughes Llwydiarth Fawr Farm Llanerchymedd Isle of Anglesey LL71 8DF Tel: (0248) 470321/ 470540 Open: JAN - DEC Map Ref No. 39	Nearest Road: A.5 Secluded Georgian mansion set in 800 acres of woodland & farmland with lovely open views. Ideal touring base for the island's coastline, Snowdonia & North Wales Coast. 4 delightfully furnished bedrooms with en-suite facilities & T.V. Full central heating, log fires Enjoy a taste of Wales with delicious country cooking using farm & local produce. Personal attention & a warm Welsh welcome to guests who will enjoy the scenic walks & private fishing. Convenient for Holyhead to Ireland crossings.	£17.50 see PHOTO over	Y	Y	N
Eileen & Peter Rigby White Lodge Hotel 9 Neville Crescent Central Promenade Llandudno LL30 1AT Tel: (0492) 877713 Open: APR - OCT Map Ref No. 40	Nearest Road: A.5, A.55 Situated on the promenade of this beautiful Victorian holiday resort; all bedrooms are en-suite & have tea/coffee making facilities & colour T.V.'s. There is a small bar & pleasant lounge facing the sea for guests' use. 'White Lodge' offers an ideal touring centre for those day trips to Conway Castle, Caernarfon Castle, Chester or the mountains & valleys of Snowdonia.	£19.50	Y	Y	Y
Eric & Brenda Cotton Rose-Tor Hotel 120/4 Mostyn Street Llandudno LL30 2SW Tel: (0492) 870433 Open: ALL YEAR Map Ref No. 40	Nearest Road: A.55 Rose-Tor is situated in an ideal position for shops, theatres, pier, promenade, ski slope & all the attractions of Llandudno & the Great Orne. It is decorated throughout with great flair & creates a calm, relaxing atmosphere. All bedrooms are en-suite with central heating, colour T.V., direct dial telephone, clock/radio, tea/coffee makers & hairdryers. The restaurant offers a full carvery & bar meals are available in the cosy licenced bar.	£17.50	Y	Y	Y

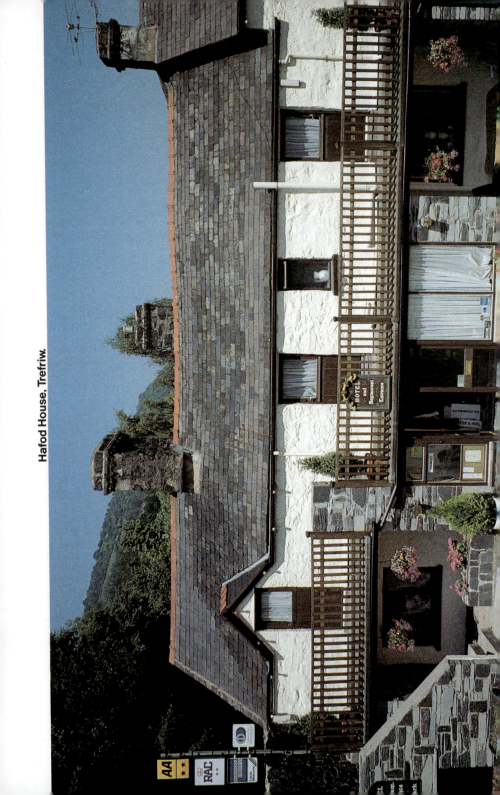

Hafod House, Trefriw.

Wales
Gwynedd

		minimum £ per person	children taken	evening meals	animals taken
Brian Stephens **Cae'r Berllan** **Betws Road** **Llanrwst** **LL26 0PP** **Tel: (0492) 640027** **Open: JAN - DEC** **Map Ref No. 33**	Nearest Road: A.5, B.470 Tranquility reigns in this magnificent 16th century Country House with Massive oak beams and family antiques, set in beautiful private gardens in the Conwy Valley. Ideal base for Snowdonia and North Wales. Luxurious beamed bedrooms, private facilities, T.V. etc. Wonderful views from every window. Renowned for high standards of international cuisine served in the relaxed atmosphere of the inglenook dining room. The warmest of welcomes awaits you.	£20.00	Y	Y	Y
Norman Terence Barker **Hafod House Hotel** **Trefriw** **LL27 0RQ** **Tel: (0492) 640029** **Fax 641351** **Open: ALL YEAR** **Map Ref No. 41**	Nearest Road: A.5 A most attractive 17th century traditional Welsh stone farmhouse in a peaceful setting on the edge of Trefriw in the beautiful Conway Valley, inside Snowdonia National Park. All 8 guest rooms are very well appointed, 2 having luxury status with designer decor, 4-poster beds & whirlpool baths. Your host is your chef serving first class dishes. Children over 11 years welcome. Centrally located for touring all North Wales.	£25.00 *see PHOTO over*	N	Y	N

All the establishments mentioned in this guide are members of
The Worldwide Bed & Breakfast Association

Wales
Powys

			minimum £ per person	children taken	evening meals	animals taken
Brian & Mary Cole **'Dolycoed'** **Talyllyn** **Brecon LD3 7SY** Tel: (0874) 84666 Open: ALL YEAR Map Ref No. 42		Nearest Road: A.40 Dolycoed, built at the turn of the century, retains many of its interesting original features. Standing in a sheltered position in Brecon Beacons National Park, it offers a warm, friendly, homely welcome to all. 2 comfortable guest bedrooms with radio & tea/coffee makers & a guests' lounge with colour T.V. Many outdoor activities nearby, pony trekking, riding, fishing, watersports & walking.	£13.00	Y	N	Y
Mrs C.M. Hammond **Querida** **43 Garth Road** **Builth Wells** **LD2 3AR** Tel: (0982) 553642 Open: ALL YEAR Map Ref No. 43		Nearest Road: A.483 A pleasant stone-built guest house within easy reach of the town centre. Accommodation is in 3 rooms with modern amenities. 1 double & 1 twin room with tea/coffee making facilities. A guests lounge with colour T.V. is also available. Golf, fishing & 2 sports halls are nearby. There are excellent walks along the River Wye. The Brecon Beacons, Black Mountains & the Elan Valley are easily reached.	£11.00	Y	N	Y
Nancy N. Jones **Ty-Isaf Farm** **Erwood** **Builth Wells LD2 3SZ** Tel: (0982) 560607 Open: ALL YEAR Map Ref No. 44		Nearest Road: A.470 Ty-Isaf Farm situated in the attractive village of Erwood, offers accommodation in 3 comfortably furnished rooms with modern amenities & tea/coffee making facilities. Plentiful English or Continental breakfasts are served. Special diets, packed lunches provided by arrangement. Guests may relax in the cosy lounge with T.V. throughout the day. An ideal base for touring.	£11.00	Y	Y	Y
Mr & Mrs J.H. Usborne **Glan-Nant** **Brecon Road** **Crickhowell** **NP8 1DL** Tel: (0873) 810631 Open: APR - OCT Map Ref No. 45		Nearest Road: A.40 A substantial country family house, part Georgian, part Regency, with an attractive verandah, standing in peaceful grounds with superb views over the mountains & countryside. 3 attractive rooms with modern facilities, 1 with bath en-suite. Tea/coffee makers provided. Situated in a marvellous area for touring & walking. Pony trekking & fishing locally. Excellent pub opposite for evening meals. Children over 8.	£13.00	Y	N	N
Peter & Olwen Roberts **York House** **Hardwicke Road** **Cusop** **Hay-on-Wye HR3 5QX** Tel: (0497) 820705 Open: JAN - DEC Map Ref No. 46		Nearest Road: A.438 Peter and Olwen Roberts welcome you to their traditional Victorian Guest House quietly situated in beautiful gardens on the edge of Hay. Sunny mountain views are enjoyed by the well-appointed rooms, mostly en-suite. Ideal for a relaxing holiday browsing the world famous bookshops, exploring the National Park and Kilvert country, or just enjoying the freshly prepared home cooking. Private parking. Children over 8 please.	£16.50	Y	Y	Y

Wales
Powys

			minimum £ per person	children taken	evening meals	animals taken
Mrs C.H. Hood Pilleth Court Whitton Knighton LD7 1NP Tel: (05476) 272 Open: ALL YEAR (Excl. Xmas & New Year) Map Ref No. 47	Nearest Road: A.488 An Elizabethan house with all the character & atmosphere retained. 3 delightful guest rooms, 1 en-suite, with radio & tea/coffee making facilities. Set in 600 acres it is surrounded by marvellous unspoilt countryside. The site of the Battle of Pilleth & a 12th century church are close by. A wonderful base for walking or touring. Evening meals cooked with 'flair' are available by arrangement. Children over 9 welcome.		£14.00	Y	Y	N
Leslie & Sylvia Knott The Ffaldau Country House & Restaurant Llandegley Llandrindod Wells LD1 5UD Tel: (059787) 421 Open: ALL YEAR Map Ref No. 48	Nearest Road: A.44 Nestling in the lee of the Radnor Hills, this charming Welsh stone 'cruck' built long-house, c.1500, set in 1 & a half acres of garden, enjoys uninterrupted views of beautiful countryside. Pretty bedrooms are furnished with extra little touches. Guests may enjoy our library of approximately 400 books. Oak beamed dining room with log fire, excellent country produce cooked to Cordon Bleu standards. A la carte menu, good wine list. Excellent centre for outdoor pursuits. Children over 10 welcome.		£16.50	Y	Y	N
Gaynor & Robert Bright Little Brompton Farm Montgomery SY15 6HY Tel: (0686) 668371 Open: ALL YEAR Map Ref No. 49	Nearest Road: B.4385, A.489 Little Brompton Farm is a 17th century farmhouse standing on a 100 acre mixed working farm, including geese & peacocks. Retaining much of its original character with oak beams & inglenook fireplace. Furnished with period pieces & antiques. Offering 3 comfortable bedrooms, 2 en-suite, all with modern amenities & tea/coffee making facilities. Good home-cooked food is served. A good base for touring & walking. Offa's Dyke runs through the farm.		£13.50	Y	Y	Y
Mrs Ceinwen Richards The Drewin Farm Churchstoke Montgomery SY15 6TW Tel: (0588) 620285 Open: APR - NOV Map Ref No. 50	Nearest Road: A.489 A warm Welsh welcome awaits you at Drewin, a delightful 17th century farmhouse retaining much of its original character with many oak beams & inglenook fireplace. It has panoramic views overlooking beautiful unspoilt countryside. 2 pleasant bedrooms with tea/coffee making facilities, T.V. if required. Good home cooking is a feature with vegetarian dishes available. Games room with snooker table for guests' use. Offa's Dyke footpath runs through this 104 acre mixed farm.		£13.50	Y	Y	Y
Graham & Sue Jones Lower Trelydan Farm Guilsfield Welshpool SY21 9PH Tel: (0938) 553105 Open: ALL YEAR Map Ref No. 53	Nearest Road: A.483 Graham and Sue offer you warm country hospitality, good farmhouse cooking and comfortable accommodation in their beautiful, 16th century half-timbered farmhouse set in picturesque surroundings in rural Wales. All en-suite rooms, warm and tastefully furnished. Evening meals served in the oak beamed dining room. Local activities include riding, golf, canal trips, clay pigeon shooting, enjoyable walks and Powis Castle.		£13.00	Y	Y	N

Wales
Powys

		minimum £ per person	children taken	evening meals	animals taken
Paul & Maureen Marriott A Country Manor Dysserth Hall Powis Castle Welshpool SY21 8RQ Tel: (0938) 552153 Open: MAR-NOV Map Ref No. 51	Nearest Road: A.483 Dysserth is a delightful Georgian house standing in the beautiful countryside of mid-Wales on the Powys Estate. The accommodation is very comfortable, with antique furnishings. The 4 bedrooms are individually decorated, 1 with antique mahogany bed, all have delightful views of the valley & garden. An excellent 4-course dinner is available. Paul & Maureen are most helpful hosts & arrange visits to private country house gardens, forestry & shooting parties. Ideally located for exploring Wales, Shropshire & within walking distance of Powys Castle. Children over 10 yrs. Dinner by arrangement.	£14.00	Y	Y	N
Mrs Freda Emberton Tywllwyn Farm Welshpool SY21 9BW Tel: (0938) 553175/ 553054· Open: JAN - DEC Map Ref No. 52	Nearest Road: A.490 A friendly, informal family atmosphere exists at Tynllwyn Farm. This delightful 100 year-old farmhouse stands on a hillside surrounded by 150 acres of its own dairy farmland. Accommodation is in 6 rooms with modern amenities & T.V. Colour T.V. lounge for guests' use. Good farmhouse food is served using local or own produce where possible. There is also a full bar licence, so guests can enjoy a relaxing drink. This is a lovely base from which to explore the area. Guests are also welcome to wander around the farm. Only 1 mile from Welshpool.	£12.50	Y	Y	Y

All the establishments mentioned in this guide are members of
The Worldwide Bed & Breakfast Association

Towns & Counties Index

Town	County	Country
Abergavenny	Gwent	Wales
Abergele	Clwyd	Wales
Abingdon	Oxfordshire	England
Aboyne	Aberdeenshire	Scotland
Allendale	Northumberland	England
Alnwick	Northumberland	England
Ambleside	Cumbria	England
Andover	Hampshire	England
Anstruther	Fifeshire	Scotland
Ardrishaig	Argyll	Scotland
Arundel	Sussex	England
Ascot	Berkshire	England
Ashbourne	Derbyshire	England
Ashford	Kent	England
Ashton Keynes	Wiltshire	England
Attleborough	Norfolk	England
Auchtermuchty	Fifeshire	Scotland
Axminster	Devon	England
Aylesbury	Buckinghamshire	England
Bala	Gwynedd	Wales
Bampton	Oxfordshire	England
Banbury	Oxfordshire	England
Barmouth	Gwynedd	Wales
Barnstable	Devon	England
Bath	Avon	England
Battle	Sussex	England
Betws Y Coed	Gwynedd	Wales
Bideford	Devon	England
Billericay	Essex	England
Billingshurst	Sussex	England
Bishop Auckland	Durham	England
Bishops Norton	Gloucestershire	England
Bishops Stortford	Hertfordshire	England
Blackpool	Lancashire	England
Bodmin	Cornwall	England
Bognor Regis	Sussex	England
Boncath	Dyfed	Wales
Boscastle	Cornwall	England
Botley	Oxfordshire	England
Bournemouth	Dorset	England
Bourton-on-t-Water	Gloucestershire	England
Bovingdon	Hertfordshire	England
Bowland Bridge	Cumbria	England
Bradford-on-Avon	Wiltshire	England
Brampton	Cumbria	England
Braunton	Devon	England
Brecon	Powys	Wales
Bridgnorth	Shropshire	England
Bridgwater	Somerset	England
Bridlington	Yorkshire	England
Bridport	Dorset	England
Brighton	Sussex	England
Bristol	Avon	England
Broadway	Worcestershire	England
Broadwell	Gloucestershire	England
Bromsgrove	Worcestershire	England
Bude	Cornwall	England
Builth Wells	Powys	Wales
Burnham-on-Sea	Somerset	England
Burnhope	Durham	England
Bury St. Edmunds	Suffolk	England
Buttermere Valley	Cumbria	England
Buxton	Derbyshire	England
Caerleon	Gwent	Wales
Cairndow	Argyll	Scotland
Callander	Perthshire	Scotland
Callington	Cornwall	England
Camberley	Surrey	England
Cambridge	Cambridgeshire	England
Canterbury	Kent	England
Cardiff	Glamorgan	Wales
Cardross	Dumbartonshire	Scotland
Carlisle	Cumbria	England
Carnforth	Lancashire	England
Carrbridge	Inverness-shire	Scotland
Castle Hedingham	Essex	England
Chagford	Devon	England
Chard	Somerset	England
Chelmsford	Essex	England
Cheltenham	Gloucestershire	England
Chepstow	Gwent	Wales
Chesham	Buckinghamshire	England
Chichester	Sussex	England
Chippenham	Wiltshire	England
Chipping Campden	Gloucestershire	England
Chipping Norton	Oxfordshire	England
Church Stretton	Shropshire	England
Cockermouth	Cumbria	England
Colchester	Essex	England
Colchester	Suffolk	England
Colyton	Devon	England
Combe Martin	Devon	England
Corbridge	Northumberland	England
Corbridge	Northumberland	England
Corsham	Wiltshire	England
Corstorphine	Edinburgh	Scotland
Crainlarich	Perthshire	Scotland
Cranbrook	Kent	England
Craven Arms	Shropshire	England
Crawley	Sussex	England
Crediton	Devon	England
Crewe	Cheshire	England
Crewkerne	Somerset	England
Criccieth	Gwynedd	Wales

Towns & Counties Index

Town	County	Country	Town	County	Country
Crickhowell	Powys	Wales	Haslemere	Surrey	England
Cupar	Fifeshire	Scotland	Havant	Hampshire	England
Cwmbran	Gwent	Wales	Haverfordwest	Dyfed	Wales
Darlington	Yorkshire	England	Haverhill	Suffolk	England
Dartford	Kent	England	Hawes	Yorkshire	England
Devizes	Wiltshire	England	Hawkhurst	Kent	England
Diss	Norfolk	England	Hawkshead	Cumbria	England
Doonfoot	Ayrshire	Scotland	Hay-on-Wye H	Powys	Wales
Dorchester	Dorset	England	Haywards Heath	Sussex	England
Dorking	Surrey	England	Headcorn	Kent	England
Dover	Kent	England	Hebden Bridge	Yorkshire	England
Droitwich	Worcestershire	England	Helston	Cornwall	England
Droxford	Hampshire	England	Henfield	Sussex	England
Dumfries	Dumfriesshire	Scotland	Henley-in-Arden	Warwickshire	England
Dunbar	Lothian	Scotland	Henley-on-Thames	Oxfordshire	England
Dunkeld	Perthshire	Scotland	Hereford	Herefordshire	England
Dunster	Somerset	England	Hexham	Northumberland	England
Dursley	Gloucestershire	England	High Wycombe	Buckinghamshire	England
Easingwold	Yorkshire	England	Holmesfield	Derbyshire	England
East Brent	Somerset	England	Holt	Norfolk	England
East Keswick	Yorkshire	England	Honiton	Devon	England
Eastbourne	Sussex	England	Horley	Surrey	England
Edinburgh	Edinburgh	Scotland	Horsham	Sussex	England
Ely	Cambridgeshire	England	Hunstanton	Norfolk	England
Etchingham	Sussex	England	Huntingdon	Cambridgeshire	England
Evershot	Dorset	England	Hyde	Cheshire	England
Ewhurst	Surrey	England	Hythe	Kent	England
Exeter	Devon	England	Ilfracombe	Devon	England
Fakenham	Norfolk	England	Inveresk	Edinburgh	Scotland
Falmouth	Cornwall	England	Inverness	Inverness-shire	Scotland
Faversham	Kent	England	Ipswich	Suffolk	England
Findon	Sussex	England	Isle of Anglesey	Gwynedd	Wales
Fishguard	Dyfed	Wales	Isle of Mull	Argyll	Scotland
Fordingbridge	Hampshire	England	Isle of Wight	Hampshire	England
Framlington	Suffolk	England	Jedburgh	Roxburghshire	Scotland
Frinton	Essex	England	Kelso	Roxburghshire	Scotland
Gilwern	Gwent	Wales	Kendal	Cumbria	England
Glastonbury	Somerset	England	Kenilworth	Warwickshire	England
Goudhurst	Kent	England	Keswick	Cumbria	England
Grantham	Lincolnshire	England	Kettering	Northamptonshire	England
Grantown-on-Spey	Inverness-shire	Scotland	Kidlington	Oxfordshire	England
Grasmere	Cumbria	England	Kineton	Warwickshire	England
Grassington	Yorkshire	England	King's Lynn	Norfolk	England
Great Ayton	Yorkshire	England	Kingham	Oxfordshire	England
Great Yarmouth	Norfolk	England	Kingsbridge	Devon	England
Hailsham	Sussex	England	Kingston	Surrey	England
Halifax	Yorkshire	England	Kirkbean	Dumfriesshire	Scotland
Hampton Lucy	Warwickshire	England	Kirkby Lonsdale	Cumbria	England
Hanmer	Clwyd	Wales	Knighton	Powys	Wales
Harlech	Gwynedd	Wales	Langport	Somerset	England
Harrogate	Yorkshire	England	Lapworth	Warwickshire	England
Hartfield	Sussex	England	Launceston	Cornwall	England

Towns & Counties Index

Town	County	Country	Town	County	Country
Leamington Spa	Warwickshire	England	Newbury	Berkshire	England
Leeds	Yorkshire	England	Newcastle-upon-Tyne	Tyne & Weir	England
Leek	Staffordshire	England	Newent	Gloucestershire	England
Leominster	Herefordshire	England	Newnham-on-Severn	Gloucestershire	England
Lewes	Sussex	England	Newport	Gwent	Wales
Lincoln	Lincolnshire	England	Newport-on-Tay	Fifeshire	Scotland
Liverpool	Merseyside	England	Newquay	Cornwall	England
Llandrindod Wells	Powys	Wales	Newton Abbot	Devon	England
Llandudno	Gwynedd	Wales	Northallerton	Yorkshire	England
Llanrwst	Gwynedd	Wales	Northwich	Cheshire	England
Llansilin	Clwyd	Wales	Norton	Gloucestershire	England
Loch Lomond	Stirlingshire	Scotland	Norwich	Norfolk	England
Lochearnhead	Perthshire	Scotland	Nuneaton	Warwickshire	England
Loddon	Norfolk	England	Okehampton	Devon	England
Long Hanborough	Oxfordshire	England	Ongar	Essex	England
Looe	Cornwall	England	Oswestry	Shropshire	England
Lostwithiel	Cornwall	England	Oundle	Northamptonshire	England
Louth	Lincolnshire	England	Oxford	Oxfordshire	England
Lower Fishguard	Dyfed	Wales	Oxhill	Warwickshire	England
Lydney	Gloucestershire	England	Painswick	Gloucestershire	England
Lyme Regis	Dorset	England	Par	Cornwall	England
Lymington	Hampshire	England	Penrith	Cumbria	England
Lynton	Devon	England	Penshurst	Kent	England
Malmesbury	Wiltshire	England	Penzance	Cornwall	England
Malton	Yorkshire	England	Perranporth	Cornwall	England
Malvern	Worcestershire	England	Perth	Perthshire	Scotland
Manningtree	Essex	England	Peterborough	Northamptonshire	England
Manorbier	Dyfed	Wales	Petersfield	Hampshire	England
Mansfield	Nottinghamshire	England	Pickering	Yorkshire	England
Margate	Kent	England	Pitlochry	Perthshire	scotland
Market Drayton	Shropshire	England	Polperro	Cornwall	England
Marlborough	Wiltshire	England	Polruan-By Fowey	Cornwall	England
Masham	Yorkshire	England	Pontypool	Gwent	Wales
Matlock	Derbyshire	England	Portree	Isle of Skye	Scotland
Mayfield	Sussex	England	Pulborough	Sussex	England
Mere	Wiltshire	England	Reading	Berkshire	England
Merthyr Tydfil	Glamorgan	Wales	Redmile	Nottinghamshire	England
Mevagissey	Cornwall	England	Redruth	Cornwall	England
Midhurst	Sussex	England	Reigate	Surrey	England
Minchinhampton	Gloucestershire	England	Renfrewshire by Glasgow	Lanarkshire	Scotland
Minehead	Somerset	England	Retford	Nottinghamshire	England
Moffat	Dumfriesshire	Scotland	Richmond	Yorkshire	England
Montgomery	Powys	Wales	Ringwood	Hampshire	England
Morchard Bishop	Devon	England	Ripon	Yorkshire	England
Moreton-in-Marsh	Gloucestershire	England	Ropley	Hampshire	England
Moretonhampsted	Devon	England	Ross-on-Wye	Herefordshire	England
Morpeth N	Northumberland	England	Rotherham	Yorkshire	England
Mortehoe	Devon	England	Roxton	Bedfordshire	England
Much Wenlock	Shropshire	England	Royston	Cambridgeshire	England
Mundford	Norfolk	England	Ruthin	Clwyd	Wales
Nailsworth	Gloucestershire	England	Rye	Sussex	England
Newark	Nottinghamshire	England	Saffron Walden	Essex	England

Towns & Counties Index

Town	County	Country	Town	County	Country
Salcombe	Devon	England	Thirsk	Yorkshire	England
Salisbury	Wiltshire	England	Tibbermore by Perth	Perthshire	Scotland
Scarborough	Yorkshire	England	Tintagel	Cornwall	England
Sedbergh	Cumbria	England	Tiverton	Devon	England
Sevenoaks	Kent	England	Tonbridge	Kent	England
Sheffield	Derbyshire	England	Torquay	Devon	England
Sherborne	Dorset	England	Totnes	Devon	England
Shipston-on-Stour	Warwickshire	England	Trefriw	Gwynedd	Wales
Shoreham-by-Sea	Sussex	England	Trossachs-by-Callander	Perthshire	Scotland
Shrewsbury	Shropshire	England	Trowbridge	Wiltshire	England
Sidmouth	Devon	England	Truro	Cornwall	England
Skipton	Yorkshire	England	Tunbridge Wells	Kent	England
Sleaford	Lincolnshire	England	Uckfield	Sussex	England
Smarden	Kent	England	Uffington	Oxfordshire	England
Somerton	Somerset	England	Uppingham	Leicestershire	England
South Brent	Devon	England	Uttoxeter	Staffordshire	England
Spean Bridge	Inverness-shire	Scotland	Wadebridge	Cornwall	England
Spennymoor	Durham	England	Wargrave	Berkshire	England
St. Andrews	Fifeshire	Scotland	Warminster	Wiltshire	England
St. Asaph	Clwyd	Wales	Warwick	Warwickshire	England
St. Briavels	Gloucestershire	England	Watchet	Somerset	England
St. Brides-Super-Ely	Glamorgan	Wales	Wells	Somerset	England
St. Clears	Dyfed	Wales	Welshpool	Powys	Wales
St. Ives	Cornwall	England	Weymouth	Dorset	England
Stoke-on-Trent	Staffordshire	England	Wheddon Cross	Somerset	England
Stoke-sub-Hamdon	Somerset	England	Whitby	Yorkshire	England
Stone	Staffordshire	England	Whitland	Dyfed	Wales
Stow-on-the-Wold	Gloucestershire	England	Wigmore	Herefordshire	England
Stowmarket	Suffolk	England	Wigton	Cumbria	England
Stratford-upon-Avon	Warwickshire	England	Williton	Somerset	England
Stroud	Gloucestershire	England	Wimborne	Dorset	England
Sturminster Newt	Dorset	England	Wincanton	Somerset	England
Sudbury	Suffolk	England	Winchcombe	Gloucestershire	England
Swansea	Glamorgan	Wales	Winchester	Hampshire	England
Swindon	Wiltshire	England	Windermere	Cumbria	England
Tadworth	Surrey	England	Winscombe	Somerset	England
Taunton	Somerset	England	Witney	Oxfordshire	England
Tavistock	Devon	England	Woking	Surrey	England
Teignmouth	Devon	England	Wolverhampton	Staffordshire	England
Telford	Shropshire	England	Woodbridge	Suffolk	England
Tenbury Wells	Worcestershire	England	Woolacombe	Devon	England
Tenby	Dyfed	Wales	Worcester	Worcestershire	England
Tenterden	Kent	England	Worksop	Nottinghamshire	England
Tetbury	Gloucestershire	England	Worthing	Sussex	England
Tewkesbury	Gloucestershire	England	Yelverton	Devon	England
Thame	Oxfordshire	England	Yeovil	Dorset	England
Thetford	Norfolk	England	York	Yorkshire	England

Recommendations / Complaints

Proprietors _____

House Name _____

Address _____

_____

_____

_____

**General infomation about your
stay, the house & hosts etc.**

_____

_____

_____

_____

_____

_____

_____

Your Name _____

Address _____

_____

Reply to:
W.W.B.B.A.
P.O. Box 2070
London W12 8QW